D1474285

The Anatomy of a Compiler

COMPUTER SCIENCE SERIES

Computers: A Systems Approach, Ned Chapin
Computer Architecture, Caxton C. Foster
Advanced Programming, Harry Katzan, Jr.
APL Programming and Computer Techniques, Harry Katzan, Jr.
APL User's Guide, Harry Katzan, Jr.
Computer Data Security, Harry Katzan, Jr.
Computer Organization and the System/370, Harry Katzan, Jr.
Operating Systems: A Pragmatic Approach, Harry Katzan, Jr.
The Anatomy of a Compiler, Second Edition, John A. N. Lee
Computer Semantics, John A. N. Lee
Numerical Analysis for Computers, John A. N. Lee
The Psychology of Computer Programming, Gerald M. Weinberg

The Anatomy of a Compiler

second edition

John A. N. Lee
Virginia Polytechnic Institute

COMPUTER SCIENCE SERIES

VNR **Van Nostrand Reinhold Company**
New York Cincinnati Toronto London Melbourne

VAN NOSTRAND REINHOLD COMPANY Regional Offices:
New York Cincinnati Chicago Millbrae Dallas

VAN NOSTRAND REINHOLD COMPANY International Offices:
London Toronto Melbourne

Library of Congress Catalog Card Number: 74-10766
ISBN: 0-442-24733-8

Manufactured in the United States of America

Published by VAN NOSTRAND REINHOLD COMPANY
450 West 33rd Street, New York, N.Y. 10001

Published simultaneously in Canada by
Van Nostrand Reinhold Ltd.

15 14 13 12 11 10 9 8 7 6 5 4 3 2 1

Library of Congress Cataloging in Publication Data

Lee, John A N
The anatomy of a compiler.

(Computer science series)
1. Compiling (Electronic computers) I. Title.
QA76.6.L37 1974 001.6'425 74-10766
ISBN 0-442-24733-8

Preface

Since the publication of the first edition in 1968, there has been a tremendous awakening to the need for applying the scientific method to all aspects of the computer field. The subject of compiler design has not been neglected, and thus we find ourselves today far better prepared to develop and implement more reliable and efficient systems. At the same time, our knowledge of computer languages has been expanded considerably, and we can attempt to implement more sophisticated languages than in the 1960s. We have gone so far as to prove the validity of a compiler and the correctness of an interpreter.

This new edition of *The Anatomy of a Compiler* has been expanded to take into account much of our experience in compiler implementation over the past few years and the extensions in language usage which have resulted from this experience. The author has made an effort, however, not to get so deeply embroiled in the theoretical aspects of compiler design as to obscure the practical aspects of the task. To this end, the text still remains a "How to" book, and it is the author's hope that even more implementations will result from its use.

The first edition was distinctly a one-language text, namely, FORTRAN. This new text is multilingual and, in many instances, invents vignettes of language to exemplify certain points. As with the previous edition, it has not been the author's intention to remain within the bounds of any particular language but to show, instead, how extensions can be achieved at relatively little cost.

To those who used the previous edition and who took the time to write to the author about their experiences and experiments, many thanks for your encouragement.

Contents

1 Introduction

To the novice, kneeling at the footstool of the all-powerful programming instructor, the computer is sufficiently complex that he cannot begin to understand the even greater complexities of the compiler. Even yet, the experienced programmer, having written his program in some high-level language, goes to bed each night, satisfied that both the computer and the compiler performed their tasks with an exactitude that could not be expected of the programmer himself. He does not stop to wonder at the products of many man-years of effort that have culminated in his ability to do his own work devoid of the frustrations of bits, bytes and binits. Yet let him take care, for even if one electron fails to find its right path home, he will curse every man-minute that was consumed in the production of the machine and its software, in an attempt to prove himself free of any blame.

Confronted with another machine of our age, the automobile, his personality undergoes a radical change. Having been exposed to the operation of an internal combustion engine, he is sensitive to every rattle. At the first sign of trouble, he confronts the garage mechanic with a barrage of constructive suggestions as to the probable cause of the trouble, knowing full well that given the time, tools, and parts, he could fix it himself.

In the same manner, this text will allow the programmer to move from the stage of merely being the "driver" to a state of understanding where he can be a diagnostician, a fiddler, or even an implementer. To this end, let us therefore review some of the concepts in computer language translation.

TRANSLATORS

The mention of computer translation to the noncomputer person often leads to the thought of natural language translation, whereas in fact *most* of the work performed within a computer is a form of translation. That is, if we will accept the definition[1]: translate, v.t., ... to transform; to render into another language; to explain by using other words; . . . . then the transformation of data by an algorismic process can be considered a translational process. However, the American National Standard Vocabulary for Information Processing[2] (ANSVIP) has provided a more restrictive definition of the term: "Translate: to transform statements from one language to another without significantly changing the meaning." In this sense, the process of translation is restricted to a particular set of algorismic processes, not including the general process of transformation of data or "explaining in other words" which we took to include the meaning of "explaining by deriving some result." As a noun, *translator* is the generic term for computer programs that accept as input a nonnatural computer language and output some other nonnatural computer language. Only when modified by certain adjectives, may the term "translator" refer to any more specific system. Thus we shall encounter such terms as "syntax-oriented translator" and "natural language translator."

In one sense, a cryptographer may be considered a translator; however, the difference between creating a cipher from a message given the key (algorithm) and decoding a cipher to a message lacking the key is extremely great. As an example of the latter, consider the task undertaken by Legrand, the leading character in Edgar Allan Poe's *The Gold Bug,* who discovers the following cipher:

53◆◆†305))6*;4826)4◆.)4◆);806*;48†8¶60))
85;1◆(;:◆*8†83(88)5*†;46(;88*96*?;8)*◆(;485);
5*†2:*◆(;4956*2(5*-4)8¶8*;4069285);)6†8)
4◆◆;1(◆9;48081;8:8◆1;48†85;4)485†528806*81(
◆9;48;(88;4(◆?34;48)4◆;161;:188;◆?;

1. From the *Webster Modern Reference Dictionary of the English Language* (Chicago: Consolidated Book Publishers, 1964).

2. American National Standards Institute document X3.12-1970 (New York, 1970).

Having decided by other logical reasoning that the author of the cipher was concealing a message originally written in English, and recognizing that there were no word delimiters, Legrand made a count of the frequency of occurrence of the individual characters:

Character	*Number of Occurrences*
8	33
;	26
4	19
◆	16
)	16
*	13
5	12
6	11
†	8
1	8
0	6
9	5
2	5
:	4
3	4
?	3
¶	2
-	1
.	1

Now the frequency of occurrence of letters in the English language is (from most frequently used on the left to least frequently used on the right):

eaoidhnrstuycfgvlmwbkpqjxz

Observing that the accretion *ee* occurs often and that a common three character group is *the,* Legrand comes to the conclusion that 8 represents *e* , ; represents *t,* and 4 stands for *h.* After much further rumination based on the possible character combinations in the English language (such as the fact that the accretion *qq* never occurs), the following partial key is developed:

Character in Cipher	*Character in Message*
5	*a*
†	*d*
8	*e*
3	*g*
4	*h*
6	*i*
*	*n*
◆	*o*
(	*r*
;	*t*

Legrand then inserts the other characters in the cipher after further inspection and produces an unpunctuated version of the message. Only by close examination of the actual script and a knowledge of the neighborhood, does he determine the actual message:

> A good glass in the Bishop's hostel in the Devil's seat—twenty-one degrees and thirteen minutes—northeast and by north—main branch seventh limb east side—shoot through the left eye of the death's head—a bee line from the tree through the shot fifty feet out.

While Sherlock Holmes was no less adept at cryptography[3] than Legrand, he was an expert at deduction to the point that the amalgamation of data lead him to some remarkable conclusions. Only in the sense of *translation* given to Webster can this deductive process be considered to be translation, since it is an interpretation of data leading toward a target, that is, an explanation using different words.

Such deductive processes are outside the scope of this text, though deductive processes will be employed in deriving the tools to accomplish translational processes.

COMPUTER LANGUAGES

Since the construction of the EDSAC computer at Cambridge University—the first computer which contained the Von Neumann concept of a stored memory—the problem of communication between man and machine has been ever present. Even Von Neumann and Goldstein gave priority attention to this problem, as demonstrated by

3. See *The Adventure of the Dancing Men* by Sir Arthur Conan Doyle.

the meticulous detail contained in the "first program." The language of that program was more closely allied to the operations to be performed by the computer than the mathematical operations being described. Whilst the concept of program writing, instead of wiring a plug board, may have seemed, at the time, to be the ultimate tool of machine direction, the stilted language of the machine was not even close to being even in the style of the languages developed thereafter. Basically, the machine language of a computer has been designed by a computer hardware specialist with an eye to easier implementation of the control circuitry of the machine rather than the efficient communication between the human and the machine. (For a detailed discussion, see D. E. Knuth, "Von Neumann's First Computer Program," *Computing Surveys*, vol. 2, no. 4, Dec. 1970.)

"In the beginning" the knowledge necessary to learn and understand machine language was not inconsequential, and thus the field of programming was not directly open to all potential users of the machinery. Accordingly, only those persons who could spare the time, who were forced by the necessity of their employment, or who were already involved in this infant technology gained the knowledge sufficient to program a computer.

However, as computers were moved from the university laboratory to the commercial world, the problems of user/machine communication became more acute. The grandiose statements of the computer replacing n accountants was becoming a little tarnished as the "owners" of a machine were forced to hire n programmers to convert the problems into programs. Further, the persons with problems were finding that the task of describing the problem to be solved to a programmer (who was not necessarily conversant with the field of the problem) and the formalization of what were human judgments, was far more trouble than actually solving the problem by hand! Thus the initial impetus to the development of problem-solving languages was for the benefit of the noncomputer expert in the main, though there may have been some sense of "Let's get this guy off my back" on the part of the programmers (now turned language implementers).

A historical overview of this development of computer languages may be found in Sammet.[4]

Continued language development by manufacturers in the competitive arena has meant not only the evolution of more meaningful

4. Jean E. Sammet, *Programming Languages: History and Fundamentals* (Englewood Cliffs, N.J.: Prentice Hall, 1969).

communication systems, but also a diversity of languages that are machine- or, at least, manufacturer-dependent.

To complicate this situation, specialized languages that are slanted toward particular problems in certain disciplines have also developed. Thus the language useful to the civil engineer will be of little use and perhaps even meaningless to a physicist.

The so-called algorithmic or procedure-oriented languages, such as ALGOL, FORTRAN, and PL/I, were intended to provide a mode of communication akin to normal (as opposed to natural) mathematical nomenclature. However, the restrictions imposed by these languages have confined their use to problems that are well defined in scalar algebra. This has, in some instances, led to the development of brilliant techniques to circumvent these shortcomings; however, the effort expended or required to create the algorisms, by those who are merely trying to solve a problem, has tended to create the illusion in some minds that the mystic art of programming is still a land of forbidden territories to the nonprogrammer.

Conversely, at least one language has taken the tack that the fundamental data element in the system is the *n*-dimensional array, and that vectors and scalars are special cases of these entities. APL[5] is such a system. However, in the opinion of the author, Iverson (the originator of APL) has taken one step back—away from the regularly accepted notations of mathematics—thus adding to the illegibility of the language from the point of view of the novice. From a computer scientist's point of view, APL is far more capable of expressing complex algorithms in a concise fashion, devoid of many of the purely programming attributes which clothe a FORTRAN or ALGOL program. Whereas a program written in one of those two languages requires the programmer to define complex looping systems and subprograms, and to make explicit definitions (declarations) of the attributes of the data elements, APL takes these all in stride, doing its own housekeeping and leaving the programmer to worry over his problem rather than its representation in a computer language.

Once the notation of APL is understood, the user finds the language to be extremely easy to handle. Further, APL functions can be written and placed in a library, so that a nonprogrammer can use a language which is geared more closely to his interests than even APL

5. S. Pakin, *APL/360 Reference Manual* (Chicago: Science Research Associates, Inc., 1968).

itself. Thus, in an elementary fashion, APL is also a language-implementing system.

One of the foremost difficulties we have experienced in the use of the first two generations of computers has been the fact that the computer could accept only a linearized input medium. Only in the third generation are we being supplied with input devices capable of accepting a two-dimensional communication. The development of page-reading devices, providing communication with the computer in humanly readable form, will eventually make it possible to present a problem definition in terms of the algorithm printed in a standard text or technical journal—with the addition, for data, of a sketch of the known information. In one instance[6] such a two-dimensional input system has been successful. Using a modified flexowriter as an input device, a page of standard text, complete with integrand and summation signs, was introduced in the computer and a linearized algebraic program was produced. Such a system is sure to be implemented with a cathode ray tube and light pen as input devices.

Besides the desire to manipulate numerical values, the need to manipulate algebraic and symbolic data is of significance. Since much of the work in the design of a new engineering product consists of the manipulation of algebraic expressions, with the subsequent substitution of numeric values for the algebraic symbols, it is reasonable to request that the computer undertake the menial and well-defined tasks of manipulation. Thus the development of algebraic manipulation languages is of considerable importance. To such an end primitive systems such as FORMAC[7] and ALPAK[8] have been developed.

Whilst both systems are excellent examples of the road to be pursued, the present restrictions lead the author to believe that by the time both systems have been developed to a satisfactory level, other systems will have been produced that will preclude their general acceptance. For example, the logical decision-making facilities of both systems discourage the writing of extensive production programs and encourage their use for one-off problems. Further, in a time-sharing remote-access environment with cathode ray tube displays, an algebraic manipulator could fall back on the real-time user to define the

6. M. Klerer, "Two Dimensional Programming," in *Proc. AFIPS 1965 Fall Joint Computer Conf.* (Montvale, N.J.: AFIPS Press, 1965).
7. E. Bond et al., "On FORMAC Implementation," *IBM Systems Journal*, vol. 5, no. 2 (1966).
8. W. S. Brown, "The ALPAK System," *Bell System Technical Journal*, vol. 42, no. 5 (1963).

tasks to be undertaken, thereby eliminating the necessity to prewrite a program.

Symbol manipulating languages have enjoyed more popularity than either FORMAC, or ALPAC, but are not in general commercial use. Both COMIT and SNOBOL have had significant effects on the science of computation, but their uses have generally been restricted to universities, colleges and computer-research institutions. In fact, it is interesting to note that the majority of production work in symbol manipulation is being performed in PL/I rather than one of the languages specifically designed for that purpose.

Similarly, the manipulation of list structures (including all the structures that can be represented as compound lists, such as trees) has lead to the development of specialized (and elegant) languages which are little used outside of research establishments. Such a language is LISP.

For a comparison of the features of computer languages, the reader is referred to Higman.[9]

LANGUAGE FEATURES

The machine language of a computer is defined by the features which are built into the machine by its designers. Although there has been a growing influence of the software community on the types of instructions which should be available at this level, very few new features have been added since EDSAC. Although it has been shown[10] that a single instruction performing the actions "replace subtract and branch on minus" is sufficient to duplicate the behavior of a Turing machine and hence is sufficient to develop any computable number, the designers of computers have been a little more generous. But only a little. If the programming languages available were to be restricted to those in which the statements had a direct relationship to the available instructions of the computer, we should only be in possession of some high-powered assembly languages. In some respects this might be advantageous.[11]

However, the programmer's success in mapping complex ideas into a small set of instructions has led to the existence of languages whose

9. Bryan Higman, *A Comparative Study of Programming Languages* (New York: American Elsevier Publishing Co., 1967).

10. A. M. Turing, "On Computable Numbers, with an Application to the Entscheidungs Problem," *Proc. London Math. Soc.*, Ser. 2, 42 (1936–37): 230.

11. C. J. Shaw, "Assemble or Compile?", *Datamation*, vol. 12, no. 9 (Sept. 1966): 59.

features bear little relation to the instructions of the machine on which the language is implemented. Thus whilst the "replace subtract and branch on minus" instruction can be shown to be sufficient to solve all problems, there is no generally accepted minimum set of instructions which must be provided in the machine language of a computer.

One of the smaller computers available (the PDP-8) contains an instruction set composed of only eight instructions, which would seem to be extremely limited. However, careful examination of the **OPR** (operate) and **IOT** (I/O transfer) instructions will reveal that each is composed of several microinstructions, which essentially expand the instruction set to approximately twenty[12] instructions.

Rather than attempt to show that the minimum set of instructions that *must* be provided with a computer should include certain instructions or even certain classes of instructions, such as arithmetic, logical, or control, let us rather consider the set we would implement if the machine could only handle (say) eight instructions.

Although it might be claimed that communication could be conducted through the neon lights in the console, let us insist that there be one instruction dedicated to input/output. We shall not specify the means of data transfer between the memory and the communication devices. Then irrespective of the organization of the registers of the machine, whether index registers are available or some form of indirect addressing is provided, we shall assume that some form of arithmetic operations are required if for no other reason that to provide indexing through an arithmetic table to execute (simulate) arithmetic operations. Such a system was available in the IBM 1620 computer and is being built into some smaller machines currently being developed. It will suffice to have an instruction to increment (by one) the accumulator.

If operations are to be defined over the accumulator, it will be necessary to provide instructions which will load the accumulator and store the contents. The PDP-8 not only solves this problem very neatly, but also another problem—clearing the accumulator to zeros; the PDP-8 is provided with the instruction *deposit and clear the accumulator*. On the basis that the instruction most likely to follow a *deposit* is the *load,* this instruction not only sets the accumulator to zeros, but also effectively turns the normal *add* instruction into a

12. Depending on whether you count instructions which are composed of more than one microinstruction such as **CIA** (complement and increment accumulator) but discounting the extended arithmetic instructions.

load. However, if the only style of *add* is to be the *increment* instruction, then a proper *load* instruction will be necessary.

The manipulation of the bits of a word can be accomplished by the combination of shifts of the accumulator and the ability to zero out one bit of the accumulator. If the leftmost (high-order) bit of the accumulator is considered to be the sign bit, then the ability to alter this bit may be useful in other situations. However, the combination of one-digit shifts and a zero out of the sign bit will produce "end-off" shifting. With the further ability to shift either left or right, a bit or byte of the accumulator may be selected. However, the same result may be obtained by the masking of the accumulator with a word in memory through the use of a logical *and* operation. Combined with a *complement* instruction, most arithmetic operations may be emulated.

Most practical programs could not exist without some form of decision making and transfer of control instructions. Indeed, most machines possess both a *jump* or *branch* instruction which permits the transfer of control to a "distant" instruction, and at least one instruction which performs a *skip* of an instruction when a certain condition is met. However, these may be combined into a single instruction of the form *branch* to the prescribed address *when* the contents of the accumulator satisfy *condition X*.

On the basis of these concepts let us propose that the minimum "practical" set of instructions might be the following:

Input/Output transfer
Add to the accumulator
Deposit and clear the accumulator
Shift the accumulator
Clear the sign of the accumulator
AND the accumulator and the prescribed word in memory
Complement the accumulator
Jump when the accumulator is negative

Based on the unproven claim that these instructions are sufficient to represent any desired algorithm, it would be logical for this set to become the minimum set of *statements* in a higher level language. That is, instead of using mnemonics such as **CMP** for complement, a "basic" higher-level language could be a more humanized form of the regular assembly language for the set of machine language instructions above. However, such a language would not substantially improve the means of communication between the human and the machine. To provide a language which is easier to understand does not necessarily also provide a language in which it is easier to express an idea. The concept of a "higher-level language" is not to provide a more humanized means of communicating with a machine but rather to provide a more readily understood means of communicating an idea or concept, through the description of an algorithm. For example, is it easier to describe the algorithm to invert a matrix by the eight instructions above (perhaps in their assembly language equivalent forms), or by the BASIC statement **INV(A)**, where **A** is the name of the matrix to be inverted and **INV** is an abbreviation for "invert"?

Having concluded that a "higher-level language" is not for the purpose of expressing, in a more humanized form, machine language, we must choose the purposes of such a language. Since such a language is not required to be a direct relation of machine language, then two purposes can be fulfilled: the phrases of the language can be chosen to be related to the problem to be solved rather than the method of solution, and the phrases may express processes which are complex compositions of machine-language instructions.

However, apart from APL, higher-level languages have been developed to contain many features other than just those to manipulate the data. Certain features—which the programmer is required to specify—must be carried through from the machine language implementation of a language. Features have also been added to the higher-level languages which further facilitate the usage of the machine by the novice programmer. Thus, besides data manipulation statements and general transfer of control, general purpose higher-level languages may contain a selection of the following features:

1. Formatted input/output;

2. Data structures and related operations;

3. Specifications of variable and data types, and the means to check the types of the results of calculations and potential assignments.

4. Block structures and rules for the scope of variables; and

5. Subprogram, procedure, and function definitions together with the means of invoking such entities and the definitions of the means of sharing data between the calling routine and the invoked routine.

Additional features may be added to problem-oriented languages, but in general the features listed above form the basis for the construction of program in most languages.

On the assumption that a language is composed of instances of these features, it would appear that the problem of designing a computer language is solved. However, the manner of combining these features and the methods of syntactically representing statements cannot be as easily categorized or systematized as the features themselves. Given a need to express an algorithm as a program for a computer, it is expected that the programmer would survey the available languages and only resort to developing a new language when the dire necessity arises. This is not always true however. The availability of a language for a specific purpose does not necessarily preclude the development of other languages for the same purpose. The dislike by the programmer of the method of expression of terms in the language may be sufficient to cause him to develop his own version. For example, symbol manipulation had been provided with a language in the form of IPL-V before SNOBOL or COMIT was provided. In the author's opinion, the peculiar notation of IPL-V was responsible for its demise and replacement by the other languages.

Although a great deal has been deduced by linguists relating to the properties of languages, such as the conditions which define an ambiguous language or a context free language, few computer language designers pay any attention to such "trivia." Computer languages are, in general, developed by trial and error, the proof of the validity of the language being defined by its implementation.

PROBLEM-ORIENTED LANGUAGES

The algebraic, algorithmic, or procedure-oriented languages such as ALGOL, FORTRAN, or PL/I are designed to further the communication of mathematical problems to the computer, and therefore may be considered to the special forms of problem-oriented languages. However, by general usage, problem-oriented languages refer to those languages that are restricted to the description of more specialized problems. For example, COGO[13] is a language for civil engineers and surveyors, and uses phrases containing keywords that are indigenous to the standard vocabulary of the prospective user. On the slightly lower level, a system known as MAGIC[14] enables the user to describe computations in terms of matrix operations by using such key words as **ADD**, **INVERT**, or **SOLVE**.

13. D. Roos and C. L. Miller, "The Internal Structure of GOGO," *Report No. R64-5*, (Dept. of Civil Eng., Massachusetts Institute of Technology, February, 1964).
14. J. A. N. Lee, "MAGIC—A Matrix Algebra General Interpretive Coding," Report No. 43 Queen's University Computing Centre, 1964.

Although most problem-oriented languages are interpretively translated and executed, this is more because of convenience than special design. However, it must be anticipated that such languages will be of importance in commercial time-sharing, remote-access systems, where a console may be placed in a small office where business is confined to a single type of product. Whereas in the past only large institutions and corporations could afford computers as the "jack-of-all trades," the sharing of a central computer by many small companies will lead to the desire for the availability of more specialized languages at the console.

The major advantage of these problem-oriented languages lies in the fact that very few new notions are included above those learned by the prospective user in his own apprenticeship, and thus little time is lost in the programming course that elucidates the intricacies of the particular language. Using COGO, the author has found that a group of sophomore students taking a course in surveying (and their instructor), none of whom had previous computer experience, could write competent programs after only one hour of instruction. In fact, most of these same students wrote a COGO program the same evening, which solved a surveying problem that was originally intended as a term project. Within 24 hours, the instructor revised his estimate of the work load in the course and was able to assign problems that required much more thought than those given previously, without the fear of an overload of tedious calculation.

Since the early development of specialized languages for the solution of specific problems in engineering, there has also grown up a series of software systems[15] which encompass these languages and which provide "computer-aided design" or "design automation." These types of systems are stepping stones in a total process of attempting to integrate programs which solve specific problems into a system which given a problem in engineering can deliver a design for the product. For example, the design of a bridge structure involves a number of elements, including foundation design, based on a knowledge of the subsurface properties of the bridge site, superstructure design based on the expected traffic loadings, and approach design based on the surrounding terrain and other features of the roadway system of which the bridge is to be a part. Based on the weight of the superstructure, the foundations can be designed, and based on the flexibilities of the foundations, the superstructure can

15. For example, see: R. C. Hurst, and A. B. Rosenstein, "Integrated Computer Aided Design Systems," in *Proc. AFIPS 1970 Fall Joint Computer Conf.*, vol. 37 (Montvale, N.J.: AFIPS Press, 1970), pp. 297–314.

be designed. Such a design is not a "straight-line" process, but rather is an iterative system. Surrounding the technical aspects of such a design, the financial and economic considerations are of importance. What materials are readily available in the vicinity and at what cost? What is the cost of land and what will be the effect of the placement of a road on the surrounding communities? Design systems which include routines which take into consideration many of these components of a design are the successors to the simple problem-oriented language and require greater sophistication on the part of both the program designer and the user.

However, from the point of view of the language designer or language implementer, once the algorithms of solution have been defined (presumably by the engineer user), no new computational problems are introduced.

TECHNIQUES OF PROGRAM DEVELOPMENT

Machine Language Coding

A programmer writing in the basic language of the computer can stay close enough to the elemental operating procedures of the computer to take advantage of some specialized techniques, but he has to contend with several major disadvantages. Among these we may list:

1. All operation codes and operand addresses must be written in some numeric code.

2. All addresses in this code must be absolutely defined. Thus the programmer must either possess extrasensory perception—enabling him to choose the address of a piece of data or instruction not yet defined—or be prepared to backtrack over the coding and fill in holes that were left when he attempted to make the forward references.

Even the availability of relative addressing (addressing relative to the address of the instruction currently being executed) does not solve this problem completely. In fact, relative addressing encourages a programmer to indulge in techniques which may lead to disaster later, as indicated in (3) below, when new coding must be introduced between the referencing instruction and its reference.

3. Any changes in coding or data assignment (such as the insertion of an instruction) will necessitate the reassignment of many existing data and instructions, and the consequent modifications of all references in the original program.

4. Though the actual data to be processed may be in (say) decimal mode, the programmer must (for most computers) convert this data to binary mode for manipulation.

5. An inherent fear of the necessity to rearrange the addressing structure of the program often leads the programmer to leave sufficient space around certain portions of the program and data to permit insertions. This leads in turn to an inefficient use of the available memory. This disadvantage is not inherent to machine language coding, but rather to most machine language programmers.

6. Since the mere writing of the code does not solve the original problem, the programmer is faced also with the task of transferring (and translating) the coding into a machine-readable form (holes in cards, magnetic influences on tape or switch settings on a machine console), proofreading the transformation, and loading the code into the memory of the computer. Further, if the host system requires the code to be prepared in such a form that it is either relocatable, reentrant or re-entrable, then the problems facing the machine language coder are increased by many orders of magnitude.

7. Portions of previously written programs, which may have a use in the present coding effort, cannot be included without being recoded to conform with the present address assignments.

Symbolic Language Coding

Because of the format of machine language and the consequent tediousness of transforming a problem definition into that language, *symbolic languages* have been developed to overcome many of the inconveniences. In this mode of man-to-machine communication, the programmer uses mnemonic, easily remembered codes for operation codes, instead of bit patterns or octal codes, and can choose symbolic names to represent data items and the labels attached to instructions. Further, references to constants in decimal notation (say) are automatically converted to the internal representation system of the machine.

By definition the process of *assembly* is "to prepare a machine language program from a symbolic language program by substituting absolute operation codes for symbolic operation codes and absolute or relocatable addresses for symbolic addresses."

Thus an *assembler* is a machine-language program that translates symbolic code into machine language and also provides the facilities to relieve the programmer of many housekeeping chores. For example, since symbolic language is a sequence of statements with a one to one correspondence with machine language instructions, it is a simple task for the assembler—given a starting address for the first instruction—to keep track of the relationship between symbolic instruction labels and actual machine addresses. Thus symbolic references to instructions can be correctly related to the referenced instruction.

To ease the task of coding, a symbolic language not only has statements that are in a one to one correspondence with machine codes, but also *declaratives,* which enable the programmer to declare constants and data areas and to append symbolic names thereto, and *control statements,* which will direct actions within the assembler itself.

An assembly system may also contain the ability to incorporate sets of standard instructions by including a single statement in the symbolic code. In certain systems, all references produce linkages to such standard routines. For example, some computers have no built-in floating point hardware, whereas most scientific computations are performed in the floating point mode. Thus such a system, which enables the programmer to write a code akin to a machine language, but which in fact creates linkages between the data and the specialized routines that simulate floating point hardware, is an immense boon.

Further, whilst the availability of prewritten routines aids the programmer, the provision of "skeleton" programs for inclusion in-line expands the capabilities of the system even more. The instructions necessary to link from the "main" program to a pre-written routine which performs both the transfer of control and the interchange of data elements are costly of both time and space. On the other hand the writing of the same code over and over again is costly of human time. Thus a skeleton code in which symbolic names or values are to be filled in can provide benefits to both the programmer and the system. Additionally, if the programmer is given the ability to define the skeleton code, his own programming abilities can be used to their utmost. In such a programming system, known as a *macroexpansion* system, the programmer can define skeleton code sequences and later develop a code sequence by reference to the sequence name and giving the arguments which are to be filled in. Following the development of the symbolic code by a macroexpansion system, a "normal" assembler completes the task of code generation. For example, the definition

```
GET  MACRO  A, D1, D2, S1, S2, T
     LDA    S2
     SUB    =1
     MUL    D1
     ADD    S1
     SUB    =1
     RVSG
     ADD    A
     ST     T
     LDA    -T
```

might be the skeleton sequence of instructions for loading into the accumulator the value currently assigned to the element of array A of dimensions D1, D2 with subscripts S1, S2. The parameter T is used as a temporary location and will contain the address of the element after execution of the code sequence.

In the symbolic code sequence, the instruction

```
GET X, =3, =5, I, J, TEMP
```

will produce the sequence

```
LDA   J
SUB   =1
MUL   =3
ADD   I
SUB   =1
RSVG
ADD   X
ST    TEMP
LDA   -TEMP
```

Note that in this definition, the parameter D2 is not used but is present in the parameter list simply so as not to confuse the user!

Higher-Level Languages

The advantages of developing programs in higher-level languages are, in general, complementary to the disadvantages of using either machine language or an assembly language. In the main, higher-level languages have the advantage that the user need not be familiar with the intricacies of the machine on which the program is to be run. Programmers who were brought up on a diet of FORTRAN or ALGOL are not familiar with such "buzz" words as register, page, relocatable code, dynamic storage and so on. And in fact, higher-level languages were designed to protect the higher-level language user from such notions and concepts.

The author's personal experience in teaching programming at all levels is that the highest hurdle for a beginning programmer to clear is the notion that programming is 90% developing instructions to the machine on procedural aspects of problem solution and only 10% developing the instructions to manipulate the data. In fact, it may be clear that APL is showing such marked successes because of the absence of looping and control instructions which are automatically taken care of for (hidden from) the user.

The disadvantages of using higher-level languages for the development of programs are mainly due to the restricted domain of those languages. Clever programmers, usually with a knowledge of the machine being used and an understanding of the compiling processes, can "fool" the machine into performing tasks for which a particular language was not intended. But such tricks are not for the normal user. The idea that some language should be all things to all people at all times lead us to the development of PL/I, a language which, though useful in some instances, is one of the minor failures of computer science in the 1960s. To develop a programming language as the conglomerate of features of other languages would seem to solve a problem of generality but the resulting language is then a hodgepodge of differing philosophies. It may be we have gone as far as is feasible in the style of programming language of FORTRAN or ALGOL and a fresh start is needed if we are to achieve the goal of language generality.

PROGRAM TRANSLATION AND EXECUTION

Since the only language acceptable to a computer is its own (private and unique) machine language, the mere existence of higher-level languages does not solve the problem of both problem solution expression *and* evaluation of the solution of the problem. A problem solution (or algorithm) expressed in a higher-level language must be first transformed (translated) into the machine language of the computer on which the solution is to be performed. Once this process has been performed, then the solution can be achieved. This separation of phases of problem expression, translation, and execution are well expressed by the accompanying cartoon (Figure 1.1), which is the brain child of Arthur Kahn of Westinghouse Corp.

In this cartoon, the original message (set of instructions) is expressed in a code not immediately understood by the spy (the com-

FIGURE 1.1 The two-pass nature of compilers—I. (From A. B. Kahn, "An Appreciation of Computer Appreciation," in *Proc. 22nd Nat. ACM Conf.*, Aug. 1967. Reproduced with permission of ACM and A. B. Kahn, Westinghouse Electric Corp., Baltimore, Md.)

puter). Thus the first phase of the processing is to translate the code into the readily understood language. Once this has been accomplished, the second phase of carrying out those instructions can be performed, that is, the phase of execution. This two-step process is shown more formally in Figure 1.2.

Obviously the phase of execution is one which needs no assistance from the programmer (except to make corrections and so on), but rather is under the full control of the computer itself. We shall concern ourselves only with the translation phase of this process of problem solution.

The Generalized Process of Translation

The steps which compose the process of translation of the statements of a higher-level computer programming language into machine language are shown in Figure 1.3.

In this figure, the processor portions of the translation system are shown as rectangular blocks whilst the data groups over which they operate and which they develop are indicated by the elliptical elements. This diagram is extremely formalized—the individual processors are not readily recognizable in most translatory systems. Nor

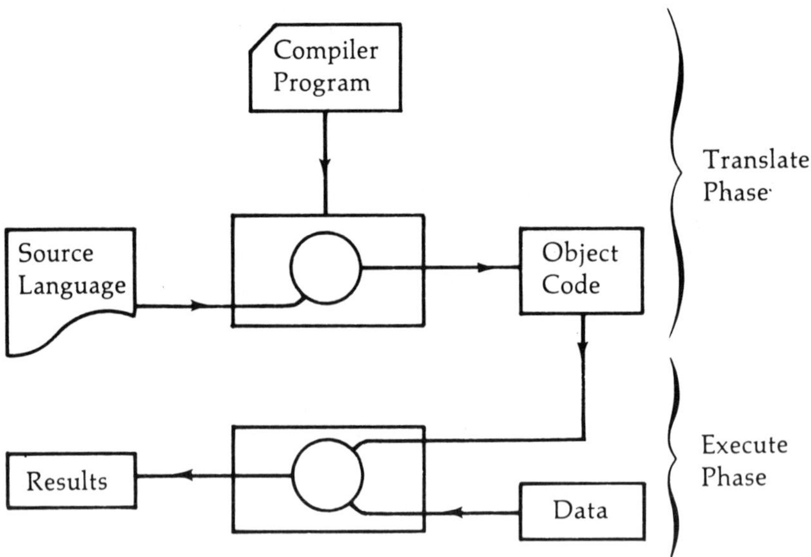

FIGURE 1.2 The two-pass nature of compilers—II.

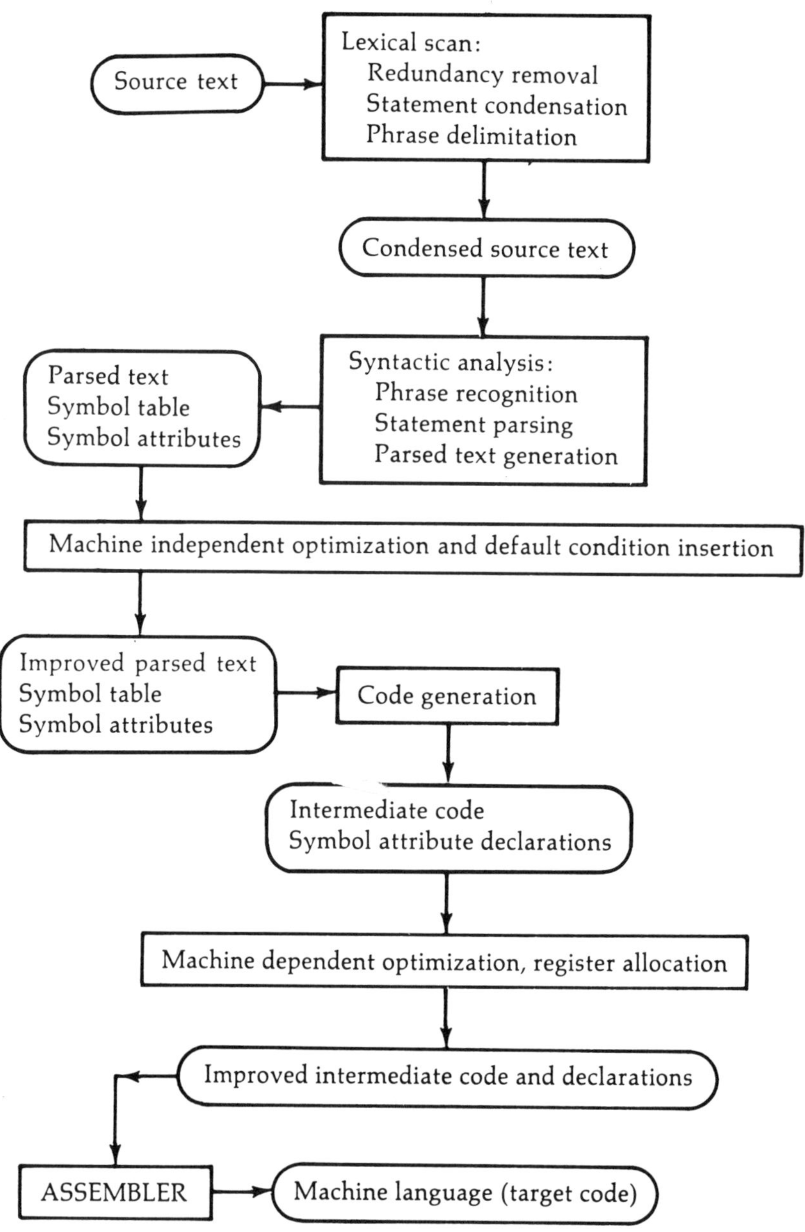

FIGURE 1.3 The translation process in detail.

is it necessary, as may be inferred from this diagram, that each phase of translation be completed before the next be entered. Such departures from this diagram and other organizations of the components processors will be discussed in detail later. For the moment, let us briefly describe the functions of each component processor.

The lexical analyzer used in the lexical scan performs the task of preparing the source text (the user's program in machine-readable form) for the syntactic analyzer phase and at the same time attempts to condense the text so as to improve the efficiency of later examinations of the text. For example, in FORTRAN, the inclusion of blanks in the statements is tolerated by the language so as to provide a more readable text for the programmer. In fact, except in Hollerith constants (that is, literal strings), blanks may be inserted randomly. However, such niceties can considerably slow down the statement-scanning routines which must examine each and every character of the statement. Hence, one of the assigned tasks of a FORTRAN lexical scan will be to eliminate nonsignificant blanks, and condense the statements to their "raw" symbolic content. Further, to assist the syntactic analyzer, the delimitation of the statements into words or phrases can be accomplished, for some languages. For example, in BASIC, the design of the language (to ease implementation) is such that the first three characters following the line number are a unique characterization of the type of statement that follows. Thus if the lexical analyzer will separate these characters into (say) one word, the recognition of the type of statement by the syntactic analyzer can be enhanced. This type of operation over the text can also be applied to FORTRAN programs, as will be shown later.

Further, in BASIC, it is possible to recognize variables and language constants by simple lexical rules (as opposed to syntactic rules). Any string which starts (has the leftmost character) with an alphabetic character is a candidate for recognition as a variable. The right delimiter of such a string is a nonalphanumeric character, except in the case of **FOR** statements, where special character sequences are of importance. However, it is possible in a lexical scan to recognize about 90% of all instances of variables and constants, and to collect the characters which compose those language elements into (say) words or other well defined units. By this means, punctuation in **READ** and **PRINT** statements can be eliminated, language elements now being delimited by logical boundaries in the representation of the text. For example, if the text is represented by a linked list, it is possible to reduce substantially the length of the list (and hence the amount of scanning necessary) by a lexical scan of the type described above, without disturbing the semantic content of the statement. A sample of the possible result of a lexical scan over a BASIC **PRINT** statement is shown in Figure 1.4.

Original statement:

After input:

After lexical scanning and reorganization:

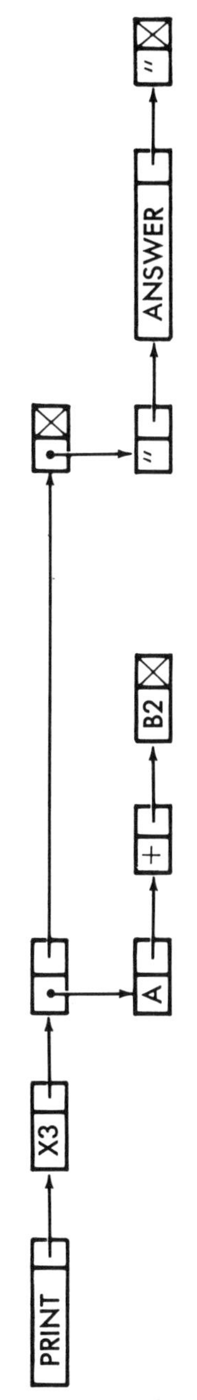

FIGURE 1.4 Lexical scan.

The syntactic analyzer of a translatory process completes the task of analyzing the input text by converting the text into a completely specified (parsed) text, in which the grammatical components of the language are appropriately connected with the elements of the text. Syntactic analyzers may appear in one of two possible forms—a generalized analyzer which uses a set of syntactic specifications to direct the analysis of a text, or a specialized analyzer specifically designed for the analysis of text related to one specific language. Whilst the lexical analyzer has "worked over" the text on the basis of readily recognizable characters in the text, such as punctuation, the syntactic analyzer must determine the structure of the text based on the grammar of the language. For example, in the English language it is straightforward in a lexical scan to determine and coalesce words, which are separated by spaces and to extract from the text, phrases which are separated by conjunctions. However, to determine the structure of the sentence requires a knowledge of the grammar of English. For example, it would not be possible for a lexical analyzer to recognize whether the word "read" was being used in the past or present tense from the information available to it. Only a knowledge of grammatical rules would lead to that determination.

Whilst "pure" syntactic analysis of a text develops only a parsed version of the text, the syntactic analyzer in a translatory process as we shall consider here also acts as a "collection agency" by building a table of recognized elements (variables and constants) and the attributes assigned (or implied) over those elements by the language. This collection will be known as the "symbol table."

The form in which a syntactic analyzer provides the parsed text to the next process is by no means fixed. It is necessary that the output from this analyzer be in the form of a structure so as to convey the nested nature of the language to the succeeding processes. Syntactically parsed texts are typically displayed as trees (Chapter 2) though a phrase marked form or a canonical form may be more appropriate for machine representation. We shall not concern ourselves with such representation systems here.

Once the text has been scanned by the syntactic analyzer and the parsed text developed, a machine-independent optimization process may be used over the text to improve the anticipated code to be generated in a later phase. Machine-independent optimization can be distinguished from the later stage of machine-dependent optimization not only by the fact that the domains of the two optimization processes are different, but also by mechanisms of optimization. In the case of machine-dependent optimization, it is the general intent to eliminate instructions which are either repetitious or redundant. For example, the translation of a multiple assignment in PL/I may result in a series of successive store and load pairs of which many of the loads can be eliminated (barring certain side effects which must be taken into account by the optimizer). For example, the statement

A = B = C = D = E

where all variables have identical attributes and are of scalar (simple) mode, might have been compiled into the assembly language sequence

```
LDA  E
ST   D
LDA  D
ST   C
LDA  C
ST   B
LDA  B
ST   A
```

due to some quirk of the syntactic analysis system. Obviously, under the conditions stated above, this sequence could be reduced to

```
LDA  E
ST   D
ST   C
ST   B
ST   A
```

In this type of optimization it is not possible to directly relate instructions and be assured that certain optimizing changes will not affect the result. On the other hand, in a language such as FORTRAN, it is known that each statement is not subject to division or changes in control during its execution. Thus any changes made within a single statement do not affect any other statement than that one. For example, the recognition of "common subphrases" which has been the subject of several papers in the literature, is a process which provides optimization at the machine independent level. The FORTRAN statement

```
X = A * B + A * B + A * B
```

may be reduced to the two sequential (mandatory condition) statements

```
Z = A * B
X = Z + Z + Z
```

which will develop the same result in X.

On the other hand optimization of the type where one specified operation is replaced by another, known to be faster on a particular machine is specifically machine dependent optimization. For example, on a certain machine, the author found that the subroutine to perform the operation A^B took longer to develop a result than successive multiplications, when B was an integer less than 15. Thus a compiler written for that machine took this knowledge into account and transformed the FORTRAN phrase A**B into A*A*A*···*A in those circumstances. On the other hand, optimization of an expression to eliminate sign reversals and thus minimize the number of operators in the expression, as discussed in chapter 10, is not machine dependent.

At the stage of machine-independent optimization of the statements of a language, the implied elements of the language may be inserted. For example, in the FOR statement of BASIC, the absence of a STEP clause implies that the step size (or more accurately, value) be one. Thus at this stage, the FOR statements in the parsed text would be examined and this default condition applied where necessary. Further, still in BASIC, arrays whose size was not declared in a DIM statement would be presumed to have a dimension of 10 elements (or 10 × 10 if a table), and an appropriate entry would be made in the symbol table. Further, since the attributes of the elements of the text have been collected into the symbol table, the declaratives of the program may be eliminated from the text.

Additional improvements may be made to the text by eliminating the keywords which assisted the syntactic analyzer in recognizing the type of statement. However, since the grammatical type of each element of the text is associated with each element then additional identifiers are not necessary, and can be omitted. Thus, although the syntactic analyzer developed a canonical form of the BASIC FOR statement

FOR I = J TO K STEP L

of the form:

(*for-st*(FOR, *index*(I), =, *initial*(J), TO, *limit*(K), STEP, *increment*(L)))

this can now be condensed to the form

(*for-st*(*index*(I), *initial*(J), *limit*(K), *increment*(L)))

The process of code generation (or in fact, what code is appropriate to a certain facet of a language) is the basis for much of this text. Suffice to state at this point that code generation is the process of generating from the parsed, economized, optimized text, code relative to the target language of the machine on which the program is to be run. This code too, may be optimized later and then assembled into absolute machine language.

LANGUAGE PROCESSORS AND TRANSLATORS

In the previous section we discussed the generalized techniques of language text translation based on the concept of a two-phase system of problem solution—translation and execution. However, it is not required that these two phases be totally complete over a whole program; it is possible that each phase be operated over a single statement at a time. The "all-at-a-time" and "one-at-a-time" concepts of translation and execution essentially distinguish a compiler system from an interpretative system. However, one more difference is worth noting. It is general practice not to save the result of translating a single statement in an interpretive system. Thus, in a loop, the same statement may be translated several times rather than just once, as would be expected in a compiler system.

The American National Standard Vocabulary for Information Processing (ANSVIP) provides the following definitions of terms related to translation of computer languages:

> *Compile:* to prepare a machine language program from a computer program written in another programming language by making use of the overall logic structure of the program, or by generating more than one machine instruction for each symbolic statement, or both, as well as performing the function of an assembler.

This definition is very specific in its insistence that the output of a compiler be a machine language program (presuming that *machine instruction* is meant as a machine *language* instruction) rather than simply translating a higher level language into some other target language. It is assumed that "overall logic structure" is meant to include relationships between declaratives (such as the DECL statement in PL/I) and the references to the variables in the "executable" statements of the program, rather than the logical relationships between statements such as may be expressed by a flow chart of the program. However, on two points, we agree: there exists a one-to-many relationship between a statement in the language of the program being compiled and the target language, and compilation does not encompass the process of execution of the machine language result.

The ANSVIP does not include a definition of the verb *interpret* but rather defines the noun *interpreter:*

Interpreter: a computer program that translates and executes each source language statement before translating and executing the next one.

This definition is very weak but will serve our purpose since it does not specifically eliminate certain features that should be permitted to be part of an interpreter. For example, it is not fundamentally necessary to require that an interpreter actually generate machine language code relative to a higher level language statement, though it could. That is, there is no reason why an interpreter cannot simply examine (scan) a statement and on the basis of some analysis initiate the execution of some prewritten routine or sequence of routines which will accomplish the aim of the higher-level language statement. Alternatively, the interpreter might translate the statements (one by one) into some other well-formatted higher-level language which is then interpreted by another system. In fact, the definition given above does not restrict the domain of interpreters to higher-level computer languages. An interpreter could accept as source text an assembly language program or even the machine language program of some other machine! This may lead to the modelling of another machine which is generally given the term *simulation* rather than interpretation.

An interpreter does not have distinct translate and execution phases, the two being interleaved continually. That is, as soon as one phrase of the source language has been translated to an executable code, the code is executed without waiting for the translation of the complete source document. Further, since the interpreter must be resident in the computer memory during execution, and hence memory space is at a premium, the executable code is not saved. This then implies two other features:

1. If looping is to be permitted in the problem description, the source language must also be retained in memory.

2. Even though a phrase may have been translated once, any attempted reexecution of that phrase will require a retranslation.

As a consequence, the execution speed of a program operating under the control of an interpreter is slow, and only relatively small programs can be executed. However, on the credit side, there is a definite affinity between the object code and the source language at all times, so that diagnostics during the execution phase can be stated in terms of the original code written by the programmer rather than in terms of the object code with which he may not be familiar.

Many interpretive systems have been stopgaps in providing systems for newer machines intended to replace existing computers; they are intended to save an overwhelming burden of reprogramming at the instant of the changeover. For example, when the author was Director of Computing at Queen's University at Kingston, Ontario, in 1961, the Computing Center converted from a Bendix G-15D to an IBM 1620. During the period in which the Bendix had been resident, many programs had been written in a language known as INTERCOM 500, itself an interpreter. Such a language was not immediately available on the IBM 1620 and thus, to ease the burden of reprogramming, a similar compatible language interpreter, QUICK,[16] was developed. With the use of this system, many already operating programs were operational immediately, and no manpower was lost among the users as a result of the changeover—though, of course, manpower was utilized in the development of the system.

However, such a system substantially slowed down the potential speed of the computer and subsequently an assembly system was written, EASY,[17] which performed a simple translation from the INTERCOM language to the machine language of the IBM 1620. At this point most of the speed advantage of the newer machine had been achieved and already debugged programs from the G-15D were operational on the 1620. However, new programs were being written in the languages available for the 1620.

With the advent of System/360, interpreters were important again, taking their place in the panorama of programs to enable programs that were written in the machine language of older machines to operate on this new machine. However, this is not unexpected since such interpreters, known in this peculiar instance as *simulators,* were available on prior machines. What is different here is that the interpreter for System/360 was partially implemented by the provision of auxiliary computer hardware, and consequently has been given the name of *emulator*.

The eminent computer text author, D. D. McCracken, tells the story of a certain corporation which, in the infancy of the computer business, possessed a machine known as the CPC, for which it had many programs written, including one for payroll calculations. The CPC was a pre-Von Neumann machine, which had no stored program and which interpreted instructions punched into a sequence of

16. J. A. N. Lee, "Queen's University Interpretive Coder, Kingston," Report No. 28, Queen's University Computing Centre, 1962.

17. J. A. N. Lee, "Exchange Assembly System," Report No. 30, Queen's University Computing Centre, 1962.

cards to activate the execution of the program. Looping was achieved by the operator who took the instruction cards from the output stacker and returned them to the input hopper.

Eventually, the CPC was replaced by an IBM 650, a far superior machine, but with an incompatible machine language. Thus to save reprogramming, a CPC simulator was written and existing programs were operated under this program's control. When the 650 was replaced by the IBM 704, it was only natural to write a 650 simulator for the 704 so that the 650 machine language programs could continue to operate without being reprogrammed. Of course, one of the programs to be run under the 650 simulator was the CPC simulator, under which the payroll program was still running.

The IBM 704 was eventually replaced by an IBM 7090 with a 704 simulator, and that machine by the STRETCH. . . .

While compiler-developed machine language programs do not suffer from many of the disadvantages listed above with respect to interpreters, the major disadvantage of using a compiler is the eventual separation between source code and target code. This is particularly disadvantageous at the time of program debugging. Although the compiler can recognize and report on syntactic errors in a program, errors realized at execution time (either by the machine or by the programmer) are not easily related to the source code. In fact, even though the type of error may be known, such as "bounds error" in referencing an array, it may not be easy to determine either which statement (in the source code) was being executed at the time of the error or which array is being referenced! Many attempts have been made by compiler implementers to give the programmer sufficient information so as to be able to "work back" from the reported error to the source code. However, such facilities require (often) more knowledge than was expected at the time the language was designed. That is, it is the avowed intent of programming languages to provide a means of man–machine communication which does not require the programmer to have an in-depth knowledge of the workings of the computer!

Many factors must be considered by a language implementer before the decision is made to compile or interpret, to develop optimized code or not, to load-and-go or to expect completely separate translate and execute phases. The environment within which the system is to operate may help determine the type of system to be developed. For example, if it is expected that the system will be used primarily for education, then an interpretive system may be advantageous, provided that error reports are directly related to the source code. Or, in a mixed education and research environment, where many programs will be run but few will ever become production programs run repeatedly, a load-and-go system may suit the needs best. That is, the code developed by a compiler is stored directly in the memory of the computer instead of being output on some intermediate storage medium, control is transferred to first executable statement in the compiled program after compilation is complete, the developed code not being saved for subsequent executions. In the same type of situation, where the number of compiles is high, a highly efficient (or fast) compiler is necessary, and thus the optimization phases may be omitted on the basis that the overall cost of compilation overwhelms the cost of execution. Conversely, in a shop where compiled programs are to be developed into production systems, and one compile may result in many thousands of runs, then a methodical compiler which develops highly optimized machine code is of importance.

The answer to the question of whether to compile or to interpret, all other economic questions being equal, and assuming that the source code is susceptible to either interpretation or compilation, may depend on other factors which are less easy to express in quantitative terms. With regard to storage, it can be realized that the amount of storage required by a compiler is not substantially different from that required to perform the same tasks within the interpreter, and in fact the interpreter will contain additional features to perform the execution phase of the problem solution. On the other hand, while it is obvious that there need be no significant differences between the user data storage requirements of an interpretive system over that of a compiler system, nor between the storage requirements for the symbol tables of the two systems, a judicious design of the interpretative symbol table can substantially reduce the combined storage requirements of the symbol table and the user data storage. Conversely, the interpreter must be self-sufficient and except in comparatively large computer systems with fast access ancillary storage facilities, the interpreter must also have, readily available in memory, all anticipated library routines. On the other hand, the compiler can take advantage of the hiatus between compilation and execution to load into memory only those which are needed by this particular program.

Often it has been shown empirically that the amount of storage required by the compiled code of a source text is not substantially different (but is always less) from that for the source text itself.

Based on these premises we may deduce two interesting relationships. *For the same program* (source text):

$$\begin{aligned}
IM_{\text{interpreter}} &> CM_{\text{compiler}} \\
IM_{\text{user data}} &= EM_{\text{user data}} \\
IM_{\text{symbol table}} &= CM_{\text{symbol table}} \\
IM_{\text{source text}} &= EM_{\text{target code}} \\
IM_{\text{library}} &\gg EM_{\text{library}}
\end{aligned}$$

where *IM* stands for *I*nterpretative *M*emory, *CM* stands for *C*ompile time *M*emory and *EM* stands for *E*xecute time *M*emory. If ΣIM is the sum of all necessary parts of the memory or the interpreter, ΣCM is the sum of memory used at compile time, and ΣEM is the memory used at execute time, then it is obvious that

$$\Sigma IM > \Sigma CM$$
$$\text{and } \Sigma IM \gg \Sigma EM$$

Other features relevant to the problem of whether to interpret or to compile are listed in the following table.

	INTERPRETERS	*COMPILERS*
1.	Available storage must contain at the same time the interpreter, the source text, the symbol table, *all* library routines, and the data. Hence the size of program (as measured by the number of statements in the program and the number of data elements defined) is restricted compared to that available for use with a compiler system.	The available storage at compile time must contain the compiler, the symbol table and *one* statement from the source text. At execute time, the available storage must contain the compiled code, the required library routines and the data.
2.	There is always a direct relationship between the source text and the code being executed, hence there is a good relationship between detected errors and the source text, which promotes easy debugging.	The relationship between the source text and the code being executed is remote. Hence the burden of error/source relations is placed on the programmer and his knowledge of the machine and its compiler.
3.	Syntactic errors detected by the interpreter can be corrected during a run (at the request of the interpreter)	Syntactic errors can be corrected at the instant of recognition, but the loss of the source text at execution time requires that

	and do not require the whole run to be restarted. Execution errors can be reported to the programmer and source text changes made under the same controls.	corrections be made in the source text and recompilation of the whole text be performed.
4.	Because of 2 and 3 above, and recognizing that condition 1 may not be too restrictive in this mode, an interpreter may be well suited to a conversational time sharing mode of programming.	Compared to the interpreter, a compiler system is better suited to batch environments.
5.	Due to the successive recompilations of the statements in the source text and the need to reference all data through the symbol table, an interpretive system is expensive to use.	A compiler system makes best use of the available resources of the computer system.

The question of whether a program written in a certain language can be compiled or can be interpreted is not directly related to the question of to interpret or to compile, except as related to available storage. Obviously, if the average size program (determined by some undefined means) cannot be interpreted due to a lack of available storage, there is a possibility that it may be compiled, and thus the question is answered. However, there would seem to exist languages which are not susceptible to compilation and which must be interpreted. It would seem that any language that can be compiled can be interpreted (storage requirements aside). There are some languages which contain elements which cannot be compiled but which must be interpreted, thus raising the possibility of "hybrid" translator systems. In fact, FORTRAN is one of the latter languages. Due to the inclusion in the language of variable **FORMAT** which is specified by the user at execution time, a portion of the compiler is left in the generated program to interpret the corresponding **READ** or **WRITE** statement. Similarly, it would appear that languages (such as PL/I or APL) which permit dynamic storage allocation must be interpreted to some extent. The conditions which force interpretation rather than compilation should be the subject of further study by the reader.

A FUNCTIONAL LOOK AT COMPILATION VERSUS INTERPRETATION

In general, a translationary process between a source text and some target text may be expressed by the mapping function T:

$$\textit{source} \xrightarrow{\;T\;} \textit{target}$$

In accordance with the description of a translator given in the previous section, the mapping function can be considered as being composed of the subfunctions of lexical analysis, syntactic analysis, first optimization, code generation, second optimization, and assembly. That is,

$$T = t_{\text{assembly}} \circ t_{\text{2nd optimize}} \circ t_{\text{generate}} \circ t_{\text{1st optimize}} \circ t_{\text{syntactic}} \circ t_{\text{lexical}}$$

in which the normal left to right ordering of functional composition is followed. That is, if the source text is S, then the first subfunction applied to the text is t_{lexical}, the result of that application being subject to the function $t_{\text{syntactic}}$. Now each of these subfunctions may be composed of other mapping functions. For example, t_{lexical} is composed of functions which perform the operations of condensation, redundancy removal and phrase delimitation. This is,

$$t_{\text{lexical}} = t_{\text{redundancy}} \circ t_{\text{condensation}} \circ t_{\text{delimitation}}$$

Each of these mapping functions is applicable to the whole text of the program being translated (as compared with a function which is applicable only to one statement or group of statements), thus each mapping produces a new version of the original text, modified as appropriate to that mapping function:

$$\begin{matrix}\textit{original}\\ \textit{text}\end{matrix} \xrightarrow{t_{\text{delimitation}}} \begin{matrix}\textit{marked}\\ \textit{text}\end{matrix} \xrightarrow{t_{\text{condensation}}} \begin{matrix}\textit{condensed}\\ \textit{text}\end{matrix} \xrightarrow{t_{\text{redundancy}}} \begin{matrix}\textit{lexically scanned}\\ \textit{text}\end{matrix}$$

However, even though these mapping functions are applicable to the whole text, there is no necessity to apply them to a whole text simultaneously. As will be needed later in the description of an interpreter, these same functions can be applied to a single statement at a time.

On the other hand, certain mapping functions are applicable to only a certain portion of a text, such as a statement or a block of statements. For example, t_{generate} can be considered to be composed of a sequence of generator routines which are applicable to the whole text but which in fact affect only selected portions of that text. That is, in a BASIC translator, the generators may be related to each type of statement:

$$t_{\text{generate}} = t_{\text{let}} \circ t_{\text{if}} \circ t_{\text{on}} \circ t_{\text{goto}} \circ t_{\text{for}} \circ t_{\text{next}} \circ t_{\text{print}} \circ t_{\text{read}} \circ t_{\text{gosub}} \circ t_{\text{return}} \circ t_{\text{end}}$$

where the actual order of application of these generator functions is immaterial. That is, if t_{let} generates code for *all* **LET** statements in the text but only for **LET** statements, then since there is no logical relationship between executable statements which necessarily prescribes the order of code generation, it is immaterial whether t_{let} operates over the text before or after t_{end}.

Conversely, a partial ordering of the mapping function applications may be required if certain generator functions do not actually generate intermediate code but instead produce an equivalent source code. For example, the BASIC generator t_{on} (for **ON** statements) may convert the source code statement

```
ON I + 2 GO TO 19, 53, 32
```

into the sequence

```
   TEMP = I + 2
IF TEMP = 1 THEN 19
IF TEMP = 2 THEN 53
IF TEMP = 3 THEN 32
```

where **TEMP** is a "system defined" variable which is local to this statement. In this case, it will be necessary to prescribe that the **IF** generator (t_{if}) be applied to the text following (though not necessarily directly following) the application of the **ON** generator (t_{on}). Similarly, since many BASIC statements contain arithmetic expressions, a special expression generator (say t_{exp}) may be applied to the text primarily to generate code for all embedded expressions in all types of statements. By this means only one copy of the expression generator will be required, but the ordering of mapping function applications is further restricted.

The process of executing a program can be symbolized by the mapping function E:

$$\begin{pmatrix} \textit{Program} \\ + \\ \textit{Data} \\ + \\ \textit{Starting Address} \end{pmatrix} \xrightarrow{\quad E \quad} \textit{results}$$

This mapping function can be considered to be composed of a sequence of n "machine instruction cycles," that is

$$E = e^n = e \circ e \circ e \circ \cdots \circ e$$

where the circle denotes composition, where n is the number of instructions executed (as compared with the number of instructions generated by T) and the mapping function e represents a single instruction cycle. Looking more closely at a machine instruction cycle, it may be seen that each cycle e is composed of at least two subcycles —fetch(f) and execute (x) cycles. Thus

$$e = x \circ f$$

While we may think of the mapping function e as operating over the whole text (program) M and the data set D, in fact, there exists a pointer (p) (originally set to the address of the first instruction to be executed) which selects from the text one particular instruction. Thus e operates over a composite object and develops a succeeding composite object which contains a modified data set (D) which in turn contains the results. That is, whilst we may write

$$\begin{pmatrix} M \\ D_i \\ p_i \end{pmatrix} \xrightarrow{\quad e \quad} \begin{pmatrix} M \\ D_{i+1} \\ p_{i+1} \end{pmatrix}$$

in fact, p is a mapping or selector function over M which develops the actual argument for e. While the function f (fetch cycle of a machine instruction cycle) is total, the execute cycle (x) is composite, though its components are applicable to (or more precisely, are affected by) only certain instructions within M. That is,

$$x = x_{\text{lda}} \circ x_{\text{st}} \circ x_{\text{add}} \circ x_{\text{mul}} \circ \cdots$$

where **LDA, ST, ADD, MUL,** . . . are related to the individual instructions of the machine.

In terms of these formalisms, the two phase process of compilation and execution can be expressed by the composition

$$E \circ C(S) = e^n \circ C(S)$$

where E is the process of executing the compiled code and C is the compiler. It is assumed that S, the source text, also contains the data set, which may be passed intact and unsullied to the execute phase. It is further assumed that C generates an object which contains the "address" of the first instruction to be executed by E. In a language such as FORTRAN, where subprograms may contain **ENTRY** points or where the text contains subprograms definitions such that the physically first subprogram is not the main program, it is obvious that it is part of the task of the compiler C to provide a pointer to the first instruction to be executed.

Let us assume that our model compiler C, operating over a particular text S which contains m statements, is composed of m subfunctions c such that

$$C = c^m = c \circ c \circ \cdots \circ c \circ c$$

where each c contains the components of a lexical scan, a syntactic analyzer, optimizers, code generator and assembler relative to each statement in S. Thus the total process of compilation and execution is represented by the composition

$$e^n \circ c^m$$

With respect to an interpretive system, there are no distinct homogenous compile and execute phases, though the components of an interpreter are identical to those of a compile/execute system. A "cycle" of an interpreter is equal to a compile cycle c followed by a number of execute cycles. If the compile cycle c applied to statement k of the text S develops r_k instructions (in either a compile/execute system or an interpreter), then an "interpret" cycle i_k is composed of one compile cycle and r_k execute cycles,

$$i_k = e^{r_k} \circ c$$

which is applicable to S_k, the kth statement in the text S. Let us now modify (conceptually) the text S by unwinding any contained loops and selecting branches of S appropriate to any logical decision statements (**IF**, **ON** etc), to develop a linear text U which contains j statements. That is, U contains j instances of statements S_k from S. This "unwound" form of S represents the same program as S and thus the interpretation of the entire program is composed of j interpretive cycles;

$$I = (i_k)^j = (e^{r_k} \circ c)^j$$

If "timing" or "elapsed time" is measured in terms of the total numbers of compile and execute cycles, we may obtain some measure of the relative efficiencies of the two types of systems. The execute time of a compiler/execute system is a function of n, the number of instructions generated by C. For an interpretive system, the execute time (accumulated over the j interpretive cycles) is

$$\sum_{k=1}^{j} r_k$$

It can be expected that there would be no significant difference between the two counts since the logic of the program is not different whether it be expressed in machine language or in the original higher level language. The only differences that might have an effect on this time would be the result of optimization processes which are performed over the program such that the interactions of the statements are taken into account. However, this type of optimization can be broken into two types; machine dependent and machine independent. Where the user is willing to give up an *exact* copy of his original program, and will permit an interpreter to develop an equivalent program in which some redundancies have been removed and in which some common subphrases have been collected together, then the compiler has no advantage over the interpreter. However, in machine-dependent optimization, the interaction of generated code between two statements cannot be recognized by an interpreter, and thus the compiler has a slight advantage. However, this difference is not to be expected to be significant.

Looking now at the comparative timing of the translation phases of compile/execute and interpretive systems, it will be seen that there is a significant advantage to be gained by using a compile/execute system. That is, in the latter system, the translation time is a function of the number of statements m in S, whereas in the interpretive system, this time is a function of j, the number of statements in the "unwound" version of S. Since j is expected to be far greater than m, then the power of the compile/execute system is obvious.

This advantageous position cannot be improved by more efficient coding of the functions c since that which may be improved for the interpreter is equally applicable to the components of the compile/execute system. Or, interpretive translations may be speeded up by omitting certain optimization phases which would be included in a compile/execute system, thus producing "quick and dirty" code. Invariably, however, that which is gained by such a process is lost during the execution phase.

BOOTSTRAPPING AND COMPILER GENERATION

Whenever a new computer is placed on the production line, its usability is not only dependent on the ingenuity of its electronic designers but also on the competence of the software development group. However, such a group, at its inception, is itself devoid of languages except the one built into the machine, that is, machine language. The group's first task then must be to produce an assembly system capable of producing machine code for the minimum set of instructions, that is, the set of instructions necessary to implement the minimum assembler. This recursive definitive of the minimum set of instructions is necessary for the next phase of development, for once the assembler has been written and debugged in machine language, it may be recoded in the assembly language itself. Thus after the initial writing, debugging and rewriting, the assembler may be reassembled from the assembler code.

Bootstrapping is a process of translation using language **A** as input to a program, written also in language **A**, to produce another translator that will accept language **A+** as input. At the level of the assembler, bootstrapping is a common procedure for developing higher level assemblers. For example, in the primitive assembler there may be no facility for the declaration of data blocks, such blocks being declared by the repetitive definition of single words or the redefinition of the object-time-memory allocation register so as to leave an area of memory for storing the array. Similarly, the primitive system may not allow the occurrence of arithmetic operations within the symbolic operands, while this added feature in later versions will help ease program data referencing. Thus, as the implementation of an assembly system progresses, more convenience-features may be added. During such a development, it may be difficult to judge when one version is suitable for general release to the users and work on further embellishments should be halted. These are managerial decisions, each of which can substantially affect the subsequent success of the total computer system.

Though much rarer, there is a growing tendency on the part of both manufacturers and educational institutions to write the compiler for a procedure-oriented language in that language itself. There is at least one FORTRAN/FORTRAN and one ALGOL/ALGOL, while it is rumored that a high level PL/I is written in a lower level PL/I. One of the reasons for this emergence of the bootstrapped compiler is the need to teach compiler writing without the added complication of getting involved in the intricacies of machine code. In fact, most of the problems that appear in this text can be programmed in an algebraic language that also has the facility for the testing of alphabetic data, or any FORTRAN that allows Hollerith constants in assignment statements and **IF** statements.

At this level of sophistication it should be possible for a programmer, given the knowledge that the particular compiler available in the local computer shop is written in its own source language, to implement those features of the language which he feels to be omissions and to recompile the compiler. However, the haphazard intrusion of new features without regard for their interaction could lead to havoc in short order. As will be seen in later chapters, the avoidance of ambiguity in a language is of paramount importance in the design of the language itself; added features must not create a situation wherein a standard feature becomes unusable.

If algebraic compilers can be regarded as one end of the spectrum of problem-oriented languages, then the compiler-compiler must be the other extreme. As opposed to the technique of bootstrapping, which has no real, distinct source language and which by definition is restricted to a single target language, a compiler-compiler is a translator that accepts a language descriptor as input, and outputs a compiler capable of translating the language described in the descriptor. In this manner a single descriptor language would be capable, along with a compiler-compiler, of producing compilers for many different user languages. By this simple definition, any assembler might be considered to be a compiler-compiler, but since this is not the prime purpose of an assembler and since no special features to implement compiler writing are built into an assembler, we shall exclude assemblers from the class of compiler-compilers. Similarly, any system that is not specifically designed to compile compilers will be excluded from the set.

Fundamentally, systems which result in the production of a compiler for a particular language can be classified into one of two groups—those systems which, with the addition of specifications of syntax and semantics, themselves become the compiler, and those systems which, based on the specifications of syntax and semantics, generate a compiler. These two types of systems are parallel in conception with interpreters and compilers respectively. That type of system which itself becomes the translator, known as a syntax directed translator, has its parallel in the interpreter since no intermediate code is generated, while the compiler-compiler style of system, also known as TWS (translator writing system), follows the compiler philosophy of construction. A detailed and in-depth treatment of syntax directed translator systems is to be found in Ingerman,[18] while a description of a particular TWS (known as XPL) is provided by McKeeman et al.[19]

THE PASSES QUANDARY

In the implementation of a translatory process, one of the first decisions to be made is the number of passes to be included in the system.

18. P. Z. Ingerman, *A Syntax Directed Translator* (New York: Academic Press, 1966).

19. W. M. McKeeman, J. J. Horning, and D. B. Wortman, *A Compiler Generator* (Englewood Cliffs, N.J.: Prentice-Hall, Inc., 1970).

In a large computer system with high-speed, secondary level storage devices, the time to reload the main memory may not be significant, and therefore the overhead time in translating in phases with intermediate output to an auxiliary memory for input to a later phase can be accomplished at little cost. However, in a primitive computer system with slow auxiliary memory, or in one relying on intermediate card output and the input of phases from a card reader, the overhead time may be great enough to warrant minimizing the number of passes through the computer. Further, the availability of immediately accessible memory may decree that since the whole compiler or assembly system cannot reside in memory at one time, a multipass translation system is necessary.

If one defines the number of passes in a translatory process as the number of distinct programs that must be introduced into the computer to complete the conversion from source language to machine language, then it is evident that very few compilers are truly a single pass system. In fact, most compilers are four-pass systems, as shown in Figure 1.5. One of the principal advantages of such a four-pass process is that it utilizes the utility routines in the assembler to allocate memory space, thus reducing the size of the basic compiler. Of secondary importance is the ability to obtain a copy of the intermediate assembly code. While this may be of considerable importance to some programming specialists, it is generally incomprehensible to the nonspecialist (who form 90% of the users of a computer), and only wastes machine time in its production. However, in a corporation where the task is to produce operating software in the shortest possible time, the duplication of effort in writing memory allocation routines for both the compiler and assembler is obviously not economical.

Thus if the features of the assembler are combined into the compiler, the number of passes can be reduced to two without loss of machine time or efficiency of the object code, although with the expenditure of memory to accommodate the extra code.

As is common in many physical processes, where it is possible to streamline the process and where the accomplishment of streamlining by a factor of two is comparatively straightforward, further improvement may take an inordinate amount of energy. Similarly reducing the number of passes from two to one in a compiler can cause innumerable headaches. A pseudo one-pass system can be accomplished by maintaining all processor phases in memory simultaneously and by storing intermediate results in the same memory, instead of using auxiliary storage devices. However, this is merely a degenerate

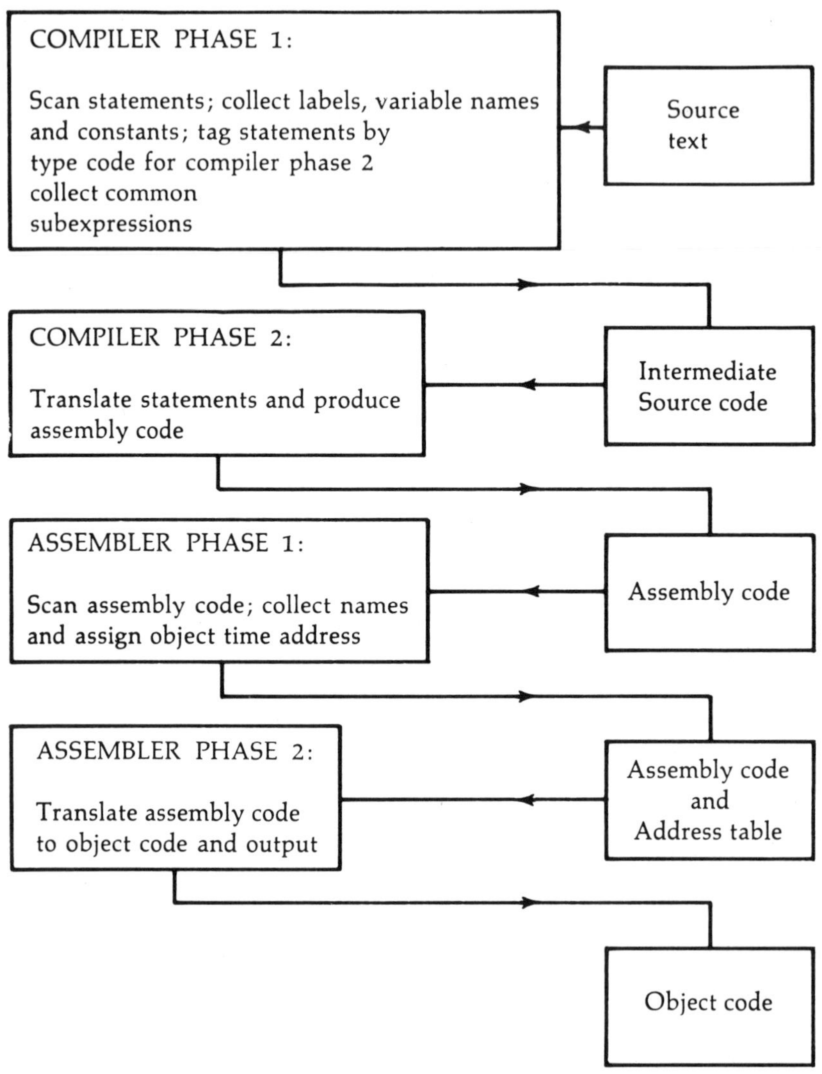

FIGURE 1.5 A typical four-pass compiler organization.

multipass system, since it is not *required* that each phase exist in memory simultaneously. A true one-pass system is one in which the omission of any one routine would not enable the whole scope of the language to be translated.

In general, the desire to implement a one-pass system will entail the adoption of one of the following solutions:

1. The entire source program is stored in memory together with all phases of the compiler so that only one input and output operation is

required. In this manner, the translator may scan each statement many times as if the processor were a multipass system.

2. Stringent restrictions to the source language to include only those statements capable of being sustained in a one-pass system are applied.

3. Relaxations in the target language efficiency are allowed, and some of the features existent in the program loader are utilized to overcome problems in backtracking.

The first of the alternatives presents no new ideas and merely decrees that, given sufficient memory, almost anything and everything can be accomplished. The second alternative detracts from the objective of implementing a translator for a proper language and does not allow for language extension. Thus we are left with the third alternative. However, it would be illogical to accept this as the best solution, having eliminated the other two, since it has not been established that only one alternative is best or that these are in fact the only three solutions. The acceptance or rejection of alternative (3) must be predicated on the answer to the question: "How much efficiency do I lose?" Also in any particular computer shop, the time lost in execution of the object code must be balanced against that gained during compilation. For example, in an educational institution where the greatest proportion of jobs are run for students in computer-programming courses, the time expended in compilation far exceeds that for execution, so that any decrease in compilation time is significant. On the other hand, in a production shop where a single program (debugged and compiled) may be run many times, the execution time is of considerable importance.

The major problems of compiling in a single pass are concerned with the compilation of forward references from one portion of the source program to yet undefined statements. In particular, a FORTRAN GO TO statement containing a statement identifier of a statement not yet encountered cannot be compiled as a simple unconditional jump or branch. This may be overcome by compiling an indirect branch referencing a memory word into which the address of the statement identified will be stored by the loader, or by outputting a branch instruction with a null address, which is to be overlaid by the actual address during the loading of the object program. The latter technique (known herein as backtracking) conserves object-time-memory space, but wastes both overhead time in the loader and temporary storage, which maintains a list of the addresses of the instructions to be overlaid. The former technique wastes only one object-time-storage location (per forward referenced identifier) and introduces extra machine cycles in chaining through the indirect addressing. These problems will be discussed in greater detail in Chapter 5.

In earlier generation computers, using drums as main memory with a $1 + 1$ addressing system[20] in which each instruction contained the address of the next instruction to be executed, a forward reference could be coded directly and a notation left in a table designating the address at which the referenced statement was to start. The choice of the starting address of the referenced statement would be made on the basis of the time taken to interpret the branching instruction and the angular position of the drum at the time the next instruction was to be accessed. After the first forward reference to a particular statement identifier had been encountered, every other reference would be coded as if the identifier had been defined.

In a one-pass system, the interactive features of certain statements can cause insoluble problems if the ordering of statements is not specified. For example, the interaction of the FORTRAN statements **DIMENSION**, **EQUIVALENCE** and **COMMON** (as will be discussed in Chapter 4) can be overcome by requiring that the statements occur in the order:

```
COMMON
DIMENSION
EQUIVALENCE
```

and precede any executable statement in any subprogram.

Whilst one group is striving to minimize the number of passes in a compiler, it is quite feasible that another group will elect to increase the number of passes so that a compiler can be implemented on a minimum-memory machine. For example, the users of a computer with minuscule memory have as much right to an algebraic compiler as the users of a larger machine. The means by which this right is attained may engender an entirely different philosophy from that for the implementation on a large machine, and—provided that the need justifies the computer time expended—the almost impossible can be brought about. Thus the building-block compiler was born.

As a starting premise, it has been found from experience that the amount of memory needed to store the source language in internal mode is greater than that required to accommodate the object code. Thus if a portion of the available memory is reserved for the storage of the source program, and the remainder is used for the compiler and work areas, it should be possible to convert the source code to object

20. For example, the Bendix G-15D and IBM 650.

code in situ. This was found to be possible in the IBM 1401, but the memory remaining after the reservation of the input zone (which incidentally had to be large enough to contain certain object-time routines such as input/output and library functions) permitted only very small portions of the compiler to be resident at any one time. However, by placing all work areas in COMMON with respect to each phase of the compiler, a 61 pass system was developed to afford the opportunity of FORTRAN programming to 1401 users. A complete description of each phase is given in Appendix A.

The question "how many passes" may well be significant in the development of a time-sharing operation. In a computer system with a single central processing unit, the overhead time of moving data in and out of the main memory and searching for a specific compiler, assembler or utility system must be kept to a minimum, or else the setup times will accrue to the extent that the amount of actual production work is reduced to the point where time sharing is no longer economical. In a system with multiple processors and overlapped input/output, the location and transfer of shorter programs can be achieved with little loss of main processor time. Thus in a small time-sharing environment, a resident one-pass system may be more profitable (but restrictive on the size of program to be executed and the diversity of languages available), while in a multiprocessing situation, a building-block compiler with the ability to select the appropriate generator will be more suitable. Similarly, to gain a spectrum of languages at the console, a syntax-oriented translator resident in memory with shuffling descriptors could offer sufficient advantages to outweigh the disadvantages of the loss of memory and slower compilation and execution times.

SUMMARY

The preceding review is certain to have omitted some of the concepts of some of the members of the computer fraternity, and to have propounded some definitions that will not satisfy all readers. However, neither can the following chapters be construed as representing all the techniques of any single system, each particular algorithm having a place in most systems. It is left to the reader therefore to construct his own translator for the purpose he desires, and not to be constrained by the artificial barriers of the semantic definitions of the terms compiler, assembler, etc.

The remainder of this text will describe the various routines and the algorithms that are used in compilers and assemblers to translate from the source language to the object code. Throughout, the object language shall be referred to as a symbolic code, though a one-to-one translation of this would result in machine language. The computer considered to be the ultimate receiver of the object code is purely imaginary, as is the symbolic code. However, it is assumed that the machine has index registers, a single accumulator, indirect addressing, and specific commands for the manipulation of characters or bytes. Both binary and decimal internal number representations will be considered.

2

The Syntactic Definition of Language—Generative Grammars

LANGUAGE AND GRAMMAR

The concept of language in everyday communications is generally related to one or another particular version of natural language. For example, we talk of students "studying the French language" or more colloquially, "studying French." In this context, we envisage a formalism which enables one to express concepts or ideas in the chosen language. Such language studies generally can be divided into two parts—the study of vocabulary and the study of grammar. Thus while it cannot be expected that a student of a foreign language has a knowledge of the whole language (as expressed by sentences) it is expected that by the use of a vocabulary and a knowledge of the grammar, utterances may be formulated which are "in" the language. In fact, the purpose of studying more than simply the vocabulary of a language is to be able to separate the *grammatical* instances of sequences of elements of the vocabulary from the *ungrammatical* sequences. Thus we may define a grammar as a device which generates all the grammatical sequences of a language and none of the ungrammatical ones.

The concept of "grammatical" cannot be directly related to other terms in the semantic sense of language. That is, "grammatical" cannot be equated with "meaningful" or "significant." On the other hand, grammaticalness can be associated with structure and can be used to show "meaningful" structure within an instance of the language. As will be shown later, grammar can be used to show the essential hierarchical structure of algebraic expressions, though this "structured" grammar is not unique in specifying grammatical algebraic expressions.

If we were given a grammar for the English language, that is a grammar which would be capable of developing not only all, but also only the grammatical instances of the English language, it would be possible to construct sentences (instances of the language) which are meaningless or nonsensical. For example, the grammar might specify that a valid instance of the language may be formed by the sequence of parts of speech:

adjective noun verb pronoun noun

From such a sequence we may construct such sentences as

clever children play the piano
large books fill the shelf
beautiful pictures cover the wall

or even such sentences as may be created by permuting some of the words used above:

large children fill the piano
large pictures cover the piano
beautiful children play the shelf

and so on. These sentences are grammatically correct, though the meaning of some may be in question.

The use of grammars to develop humorous or grandiose phrases has become part of the "one-upmanship" of our society. In particular, witness Philip Broughton's "Systematic Buzz Phrase Projector."[1] Obviously, these phrases are grammatical instances of the English language, but their precise meaning may be in question.

Another form of this use of grammars is exemplified by the "Mad Lib" publications. The instructions for the creation of a Mad Lib are based on a knowledge of parts of speech and a set of stories in which certain key words are scientifically (?) left out. The following description (p. 50) is taken from the instructions in *Mad Libs Six.* [2]

1. Reprinted with permission from the September 1968 *Reader's Digest.* Copyright 1968 by the Reader's Digest Assn., Inc.
2. Reprinted From *Mad Libs Six* (New York: Price/Stern/Sloan Publishers, Inc., 1970) by permission of the publisher.

By their very form of definition, that is, the skeleton story and the indication of substitutionable parts of speech, a generated Mad Lib is a grammatical instance of the English language. However, the semantics of such word sequences may be questionable. Such humorous forms of grammatical English phrases also appear in much of our vaudeville humor or the joke section of either *Boy's Life* or *Playboy*. Many of these forms are based on the *pun;* the use of words in such a way as to suggest a different meaning, or the use of words having close phonetic sounds. Plays on the words of well-known proverbs also fall into the same category.

Classically, the misuse of words is associated with Mrs. Malaprop, a character in *The Rivals* (1775) by Sheridan. As a result of her lack of education and the environment of her later life (as landlady to a

How to Win at Wordmanship

After years of hacking through etymological thickets at the U.S. Public Health Service, a 63-year-old official named Philip Broughton hit upon a sure-fire method for converting frustration into fulfillment (jargonwise). Euphemistically called the Systematic Buzz Phrase Projector, Broughton's system employs a lexicon of 30 carefully chosen "buzzwords":

Column 1	Column 2	Column 3
0. integrated	0. management	0. options
1. total	1. organizational	1. flexibility
2. systematized	2. monitored	2. capability
3. parallel	3. reciprocal	3. mobility
4. functional	4. digital	4. programming
5. responsive	5. logistical	5. concept
6. optional	6. transitional	6. time-phase
7. synchronized	7. incremental	7. projection
8. compatible	8. third-generation	8. hardware
9. balanced	9. policy	9. contingency

The procedure is simple. Think of any three-digit number, then select the corresponding buzzword from each column. For instance, number 257 produces "systematized logistical projection," a phrase that can be dropped into virtually any report with that ring of decisive, knowledgeable authority. "No one will have the remotest idea of what you're talking about," says Broughton. "But the important thing is that they're not about to admit it."

group of well-to-do young gentlemen), Mrs. Malaprop used overheard, rich-sounding words in sentences instead of ones which were intended. These substitutions were always phonetically close to the intended word and thus little meaning was lost, though the word was ludicrously wrong in the context. Such generated word sequences, like Mad Libs, are grammatically correct, but semantically meaningless.

Following is some secret, inside data regarding parts of speech which you will need for Mad Libs:

A NOUN *is the name of a person, place or thing.*
Swinger
Clothes-closet
Belly-button
Box

An ADJECTIVE *is a word that describes something or somebody.*
Inexpensive
Horse-faced
Over-cooked
Groovy

A PLACE *is a Place.*
Brooklyn, Spain, Cleveland
The Powder Room
The Plaza Hotel

EXCLAMATIONS
Pasta-fa-zool!
Crazy!
Up, the Irish!
Bah!

NONSENSE SOUNDS
Oooooook
Merg
Wallaballa-hoogalala
Cheeeeeeeee

An ADVERB *is an Adjective with "ly" added.*
Disgustingly, sloppily

(Before)

"__________ (EXCLAMATION)", he said, __________ (ADVERB), as he jumped into his convertible __________ (NOUN) and drove off with his __________ (ADJECTIVE) wife.

(After)

"*Crazy* (EXCLAMATION)", he said, *nastily* (ADVERB), as he jumped into his convertible *mousetrap* (NOUN) and drove off with his *impossible* (ADJECTIVE) wife.

THE MODES OF DEFINITION

In the process of learning a new computer (or nonnatural) language, the format of a statement or phrase is often presented in terms of a natural language description that defines the permitted components and required features. For example, the definition of a DO statement in FORTRAN may take the form:

$$\text{DO } n\ i = m_1, m_2, m_3$$

where n is a statement identifier, i is a simple integer variable, and m_1, m_2 and m_3 are simple integer variables or constants. In this manner, the syntactic prescription for the writing of a legal DO statement may be described depending on the user's knowledge of several other prescriptions. For example, in this case it is assumed that the reader is familiar with the formalisms that describe statement identifiers, integer variables, and integer constants. However, such a description must be adjoined by a semantic description to permit the reader to formulate a statement that will be compiled to a set of object code, which in turn will execute the desired operations.

In particular, a semantic description must indicate that the statement identifier contained in the DO statement refers to a statement not previously defined in the subprogram, and that the assigned values of the variables or constants replacing m_1, m_2 and m_3 must relate to each other in a specific manner. That is,

$$\mathrm{V}(m_2) > \mathrm{V}(m_1) > 0 \qquad \text{and} \qquad \mathrm{V}(m_3) > 0$$

where $\mathrm{V}(x)$ is the value at execution time of the variable or constant that replaces the pseudovariable x.

While such a description is readable and gives sufficient information for the correct formulation of a statement, the exceptions and alternatives must be given in appended descriptions or in a set of alternate prescriptions.

Only in recent times has there been developed means for the formal semantic specification of elements of computer programs or the elemental phrases of a programming language. However, these means are still far beyond the scope of regular programmers, being purely of academic interest in most cases. Only in one case, the formal specification of PL/I[3] has there been any attempt to use such formalisms in the development of practical systems. In this case, the

3. P. Lucas, and K. Walk, "On the Formal Description of PL/I," in *Annual Review in Automatic Programming*, vol. 6, Pt. 3 (Oxford: Pergamon Press, 1969).

formal definition of PL/I, composed of both syntactic and semantic prescriptions, was used by IBM as a control and reference vehicle for the development of PL/I compilers for the IBM/360 line of computers. In such a controlled environment it is reasonable to expect that the compiler development team could be expected to be familiar with the formalisms. However, in general this is not true. In fact, such formalisms are still regarded by many as being merely another level of programming in which no common language has yet been accepted. Cries of "too mathematical" or "too complex" will stall the formal definition of languages for some time yet, until perhaps the current crop of computer science students can effectively control the industry.

Syntactic definition, contrariwise, has been successfully developed in a complete, efficient and concise form. In fact, the success of the manner of definition can be judged from the diversity of language descriptors that have been developed from a single original proposition. The formal definition of syntax is more compact and less ambiguous than a similar definition in conventional text material. However, this does not imply that, by definition, a formal definition cannot produce an unambiguous result. Whilst an English language description with many *if . . . then*, *or*, and *and* connectives can be ambiguous in that the reader is left bewildered as to what procedure to follow to formulate a valid statement, the formal definition may clear up this dilemma. For example, consider the definition of *pun* from Webster's Seventh New Collegiate Dictionary:

> *pun:* the humorous use of a word in such a way as to suggest different meanings or applications or of words having the same or nearly the same sound but different meanings.

In this definition the multiple use of *or* can lead to the division of the sentence into a number of different phrases only one of which is to be assumed to be the one intended by the lexicographer. If such ambiguous definitions are developed at such a high (linguistic) level as Webster's dictionary, how then can we expect perfection of the definers of programming languages? Let us suggest here that a more formal approach has the potential attribute of clarity and provided that the rules of conjunctive formation of strings are defined then the ambiguities associated with multiple *ors* may be eliminated. However, it is possible that two definitions may allow the formulation of the same sequence of characters. In the same manner, formal definitions of the syntax of a natural language may allow the construction of the same sentence from differing specifications. For example, those

English words that perform double duty as both verb and noun, such as *rose*, *bow* and *list*, or exist as both an adjective and verb, such as *live*, can cause the evolution of an ambiguous creation. However, although ambiguity of definition can be eliminated, the elimination of ambiguity in determining the origin of an object is difficult. For example, taken out of context, the written word *read* can have multiple meanings, and the impingement of the same word on the ear can engender thoughts of a color or a plant. Thus to say that the origin of the word was from the definition of a verb, noun, or adjective is impossible. Similarly, FORTRAN has sequences of digits which, when taken out of context, can either represent an unsigned integer or a statement number.

Whilst semantic and pragmatic ambiguities are of considerable interest, they are without the scope of this text. Only syntactic ambiguity will be of concern, and then only with respect to its avoidance.

LANGUAGE DESCRIPTORS

The language in which a language may be defined is termed a *metalanguage* and must be uniquely distinguishable from the language being described. Thus attempts to define a language in terms of itself can lead to paradoxes due to the indistinguishability of the metalanguage and the language. For example, we may say in the metalanguage of English that a sentence has certain qualities, such as *it is grammatically correct* or *that sentence is true*. Consider then the sentence: *This statement is false.* If, not being given the information as to whether this sentence is written in the language or metalanguage, one assumes that the word *this* refers to the statement itself, then the sentence is paradoxical. However, the same utterance on the part of a scholar pointing to some other statement is clearly valid. Thus the metalanguage for ALGOL, for instance, must be clearly distinguishable from ALGOL. By these requirements, the symbolism of a metalanguage must not include the symbols used in ALGOL.

A language is defined by a grammar which is a system over the operations of concatentation and substitution and which is composed of four parts—the alphabet to be used, the parts of speech, the fundamental construction (such as "sentence,") and the set of rules to construct instances of the language.

Thus for the language BASIC, the alphabet is the set of characters available on a model 33 Teletype; the parts of speech (more concisely called *components* of the language) are such elements as constant, variable, statement, function reference, and so on; the fundamental construction (or *initial component*) is a program; and the set of rules include the rules to form each of the components from the alphabet or other components

In general, the four parts of a grammar are not separated but instead compose the rules of construction. That is, components may be identified in constructs as being the name given to a string composed of other components and/or elements of the alphabet. For example, we may recognize that the name *verb* is a component of the English grammar since there exists a construct of the form

verb = lift, run, walk, climb, talk, sing, ...

Similarly, the alphabet can be recognized as being the set of characters which exist in the grammar but which are not components. The initial component is not so easy to recognize, though it has certain properties which aid its recognition. For example, the initial component (such as *program* in BASIC) can never be an element of the construction of any other component.

The use of the English language to describe a metalanguage is already causing us some confusion, since it is impossible in English to distinguish between the component and strings formed from the alphabet. That is, the word *verb* occurs both in the English language and in meta-English. Hence, restricting ourselves to computer languages let us describe a formal metalanguage such that these ambiguities of representation are obviated. The metalanguage which is used herein is a variant of the language known as BNF, which may be variously taken to be the acronym for Backus normal form or Backus Naur form. The original metalanguage was developed for the description of ALGOL[4] and has been used extensively since then to describe syntactically other languages.

Mathematically, a grammar can be considered to be the definition of sets in terms of elements of other sets. For example, a member of the alphabet of BASIC is a member of the set named (say) *character*, that is

character = {A, B, C, D, E, . . . , X, Y, Z, 0, 1, . . . 8, 9, +, *,/, −, . . .}

and further the class of objects named *variable* is composed of objects which are instances of the roman alphabet (*roman* = {A, B, C, . . . , X, Y, Z}) or the set of single instances of roman letters concatenated

4. C. Backus, "The Syntax and Semantics of the Proposed Algebraic Language," UNESCO Conf. on Info. Proc., Paris, 1959.

with single instances of the set of digits. That is,

$$variable = roman \cup (roman \times digit)$$

where $digit = \{0, 1, 2, \ldots, 8, 9\}$ and the operation $\times$ signifies the cross product of the two sets.

Although this style of language would satisfy our needs, and, incidently, has a basis in mathematics which could be useful in determining the properties of such sets, the BNF system defines not the classes (or sets) but rather a set of rules by which the substitution of elements is more clearly defined. The alphabet of the metalanguage BNF (as extended) is chosen so as to be distinct from the languages to be described, and to explicitly distinguish between the character set of the language being described and the component names for elements of the language. The following table illustrates the symbolism of BNF and compares the notation with set notation.

Symbol	*BNF meaning*	*Set notational meaning or equivalent*
$<x>$	the component named x	The class of objects named x
$::=$	. . . is to be replaced by . . .	. . . is composed of the set of strings. . . .
$\mid$	or (the exclusive or)	(when the separator between two class names) set union $\cup$, (when the separator between two elements of the alphabet) the set separator ","
$\frown$	[5]the operation of concatentation	the cross product of two sets
$\{z\}_i^j$	if z^k represents k concatenated occurences of z, then $\{z\}_i^j = z^i \mid z^{i+1} \mid \ldots \mid z^j$	the set $\{z^i, z^{j+1}, \ldots, z^j\}$

Further, for the sake of clarity, another convention of typesetting will be adopted. Those characters which are to form part of the language being described will be set in sans serif type, such as A, B, C . . . , whilst the names of objects (enclosed in corner braces $< >$) will be set in italics. Thus an object appearing outside the corner braces in

5. Represented on the printed page by juxtaposition.

sans serif type is explicity a language character. The corner braces used to parenthesize a component name will not become confused with the *less than* or *greater than* symbols.

The format of a metalanguage construct will be (in the *meta*-metalanguage of English) as follows:

> The object named on the left may be formed from the objects named or specified on the right.

This definition specifically avoids any reference to concatenation on the right-hand side of the construct, since not all constructs contain the operation of concatenation, and where desired, the alternation operator is specified. In fact, concatenation is implied by the juxtaposition of names or objects in the construct. Thus the metalanguage construct

A<*x*>;

is intended to symbolize the linear concatenation of the object A, the object named *x* and a semicolon. If <*x*> had previously been defined as any single digit, then a legal construct of A<*x*>; would be

A1; or A9;
but not A*x*; or even AX;

since neither *x* nor X is a legal replacement of <*x*>.

To signify alternatives in the construct, the *or* symbol is used. Thus a decimal digit might be defined by the metalanguage statement:

<*decimal digit*> ::= 0|1|2|3|4|5|6|7|8|9

which is taken to mean:

> The object named "decimal digit" may be formed from any one of the characters 0, 1, 2, 3, 4, 5, 6, 7, 8 or 9.

Note that while the names used in corner braces are generally chosen in this text to be indicative of the semantic nature of the resulting accretion, in fact, they are merely a collection of marks that are distinguishable one from another. Thus the above definition might well have been written:

<*dd*> ::= 0|1|2|3|4|5|6|7|8|9

Two definitions cause problems in the metalanguage, and thus will be explained in the meta-metalanguage:

<*null*> ::=
<*blank*> ::= b

The first definition above declares that the object named *null* is to be formed from a nonexistent character. That is, the item is absent from the language being described. This gives us the opportunity to state in the metalanguage such statements as:

> . . . the third index may be omitted.

In particular, consider the statement from a FORTRAN text:

> Negative constants are prefixed with a − sign; positive constants may have a + sign, but do not require it.

If an unsigned constant has been predefined and given the name *<constant>*, then a signed constant may be defined by the construct:

<signed constant> ::= *<sign><constant>*

where a *<sign>* has been defined by the construct

<sign> ::= *<null>*|+|−

which indicates that a *<sign>* may be chosen from either of the symbols + or −, or may be omitted.

The definition of *<blank>* is necessary when it is desired to make the metalanguage both readable and unambiguous. For example, take the above definition of *<sign>*. Although this definition appears in print as a number of characters followed by a white space to the right-hand edge of the page, it is in fact typeset using a special set of slugs that leave no mark on the paper. This lack of marks leaves one in a quandary as to whether the blank belongs to the set of italicized characters or the sans serif set. So, in the definition, we are uncertain as to whether a *<sign>* is defined as the *<null>* object or a + sign or a − sign and a large number of blanks. To overcome this ambiguity, we shall specify that printed blanks are not part of the metalanguage and will be ignored, except when such a blank is a mandatory part of the language being described. When a blank is to be included in the accretion, the mark **b** or the name *<blank>* will be used. Thus in the language being described, the object produced will be " ", while in the metalanguage the mark denoting the same mark will be **b**, which is given the name *<blank>*. For a similar distinction between the object, the symbol for the object, and the name of the object, see the conversation between Alice and the White Knight in Lewis Carroll's *Alice through the Looking Glass*.

Based on this definitional scheme, let us now translate the sample Mad Lib into a formal grammar. Due to its length, let us first divide the sentence into several clauses:

<sentence> ::= *<phrase 1><phrase 2>* and *<phrase 3>*
<phrase 1> ::= "*<exclamation>*", he said *<adverb>*
<phrase 2> ::= as he jumped into his convertible *<noun>*
<phrase 3> ::= drove off with his *<adjective>* wife.

Then, based on the samples given for the Mad Lib, the following descriptions of the parts of speech can be developed:

<noun> ::= swinger|clothes-closet|belly-button|box
<adverb> ::= disgustingly|sloppily
<adjective> ::= inexpensive|horse-faced|over-cooked|groovy
<exclamation> ::= pasta-fa-zool!|crazy!|Up, the Irish!|Bah!

Similarly the grammar to describe the language of the Systematic Buzz Phrase Projector can be developed:

<buzz phrase> ::= *<column 1><column 2><column 3>*
<column 1> ::= integrated|total|systematized|parallel| . . .
<column 2> ::= management|organizational|monitored| . . .
<column 3> ::= options|flexibility|capability| . . .

RECURSION AND REPETITION

The definition of some portions of a language give so many options that the specific definition of the statement by the concatenation of only those items listed in the construct becomes unwieldy, if not impossible. For example, many statements in computer languages contain a list of unspecified length, each item of which is a variable, the items being separated by commas. To define such a list as

<list extender> ::= ,*<variable>*|*<null>*
<list> ::= *<variable><list extender><list extender>*
<list extender>

not only prescribes a limit to the number of items in the list, but also fails to be concise. A technique of recursive definition solves this problem both concisely and without recourse to special symbolism. Thus the above two definitions may be consolidated to:

<list> ::= *<variable>*|*<list>*,*<variable>*

Such a construct would seem to be redundant, for it contains two alternatives, only one of which can be used since, at the outset of using the construct, a *<list>* does not exist. However, if the first of these alternatives is regarded as a starter and the other as an expander, then one can use the *<list>* chosen from the starter to form another longer *<list>* by using the expander. As an alternative, we introduce a set of symbols indicating the repetitive concatenation of a given set of objects. The symbolism for repetition is $\{z\}_i^j$ where the subscript and superscript define the limits on the number of repetitions to be performed. The subscript i of the braces indicates the mandatory number of components to be concatenated while the superscript j specifies the maximum permitted number of components. In general

$$\{z\}_i^j = z \frown \{z\}_{i-1}^{j-1} \text{ for } j \geqq i \geqq 1$$

and

$$\{z\}_1^k = z|zz|zzz| \ldots |zz \ldots z$$

where $zz \ldots z$ represents k occurrences of the component z, and

$$\{z\}_0^0 = <null>$$

Where z is a set of alternatives such as A|B|C, then the repetition group is equivalent to a group containing a uniquely named component and another production rule with that uniquely named component on the left hand side and the set of alternatives on the right. For example, $\{A|B|C\}_i^j$ is equivalent to $\{<name>\}_i^j$ and the rule

$$<name> ::= A|B|C$$

Without restriction we shall permit any form of syntactic specification within the repetition braces, including other repetition groups. Examples of the use of repetitive braces include:

$\{A\}_1^3$	can be expanded to	A,AA, or AAA
$\{AB\}_1^2$		AB or ABAB
$\{A\}_1^\infty$		A,AA,AAA, . . . or a string of As of any length.
$\{AA\|A\}_1^3$		A,AA,AAA,AAAA,AAAAA, or AAAAAA[a]
$\{A\|B\}_1^2$		A,B,AB,BA,AA or BB
$X\{A\}_1^3Y$		XAY,XAAY or XAAAY
$X\{A\}_0^2$		X,XA or XAA
$\{A\|B\|C\|D\}_1^1$		A,B,C or D

[a]This is an ambiguous syntactic statement (see page 65) since there are two distinct means of generating the string AA.

With this mode of specification, a <*list*> may be defined as:

$$<list> ::= <variable>\{,<variable>\}_0^\infty$$

This type of definition has the advantage that the size of an accretion may be defined explicitly, if so desired, while a conciseness that is not possible without the use of a recursive definition is maintained. As an adjunct to recursion, but without adding a complete new metalanguage definition, Ledley[6] has suggested the use of a qualified ::=. He has used the notation of a superscripted ::=, in which the superscript defines the maximum number of times that the construct may recur to formulate the object. Thus

$$\langle \mathit{list} \rangle \overset{9}{::=} \langle \mathit{variable} \rangle | \langle \mathit{list} \rangle , \langle \mathit{variable} \rangle$$

may construct an accretion in which the object named *<variable>* occurs no more than nine times, but at least once.

Both the notations of repetitive braces and restricted recursion contain the disadvantage of not being linear definitions and therefore are not immediately suitable as input to a syntax-oriented translator.

The indices of repetitive braces can be variables or expressions, provided the value of the variables is defined within the construct. For example, although a statement number[7] (in FORTRAN) can be defined as:

$$\langle \mathit{statement\ number} \rangle ::= \{\langle \mathit{digit} \rangle\}_1^5$$

where $\langle \mathit{digit} \rangle ::= \mathsf{0|1|2|3|4|5|6|7|8|9}$

this definition is only applicable to the statement number that occurs within the body of a statement. Thus if we distinguish between a statement number and a statement identifier (in this discussion) by stating that a statement number occurs only in a statement body whereas a statement identifier precedes the statement body, then a FORTRAN statement may be defined as being in the form:

$$\langle \mathit{FORTRAN\ statement} \rangle ::= \langle \mathit{statement\ identifier} \rangle \mathsf{b} \langle \mathit{statement\ body} \rangle$$

To conform with the standard 80 column card format of input to a card oriented FORTRAN compiler system, we require that the *<statement identifier>* be composed of exactly five characters. Further for certain compiler implementations it is required that the numeric portion of the identifier be right justified in the field of five characters. In this highly restricted case, the following definition will

6. R. S. Ledley, *FORTRAN IV Programming* (New York: McGraw-Hill Book Company, 1965).

7. This particular definition will permit the construction of statement numbers which are composed of all zeros which is not permitted in the language, whereas leading zeros preceding at least one nonzero digit is in the language. The definition of a nonzero statement number is left as an exercise for the reader.

suffice:

$$<\textit{statement identifier}> \ := \ \{<\textit{blank}\}_{5-n}^{5-n} \ \{<\textit{digit}>\}_{0}^{n\leq 5}$$

whereas, if the number may occur anywhere in the five-column field:

$$<\textit{statement identifier}> \ := \\ \{<\textit{blank}>\}_{5-m-n}^{5-m-n} \{<\textit{digit}>\}_{0}^{n\leq 5} \{<\textit{blank}>\}_{0}^{m\leq 5-n}$$

In rules of production where variables are utilized to transfer repetition index values from one group to another, as in the above examples, the domain of these variables is the rule itself, and their "life span" is the duration of a single use of that rule. For example, consider the case where two instances of a given component occur in the same production, and that the component is described in terms of repetition groups which depend on variable indices:

$$<\textit{this}> \ ::= \ \cdots \ <\textit{that}> \ \cdots \ <\textit{that}>$$
$$<\textit{that}> \ ::= \ \{<\textit{blip}>\}_{f_1(n)}^{f_2(n)} \ \cdots \ \{<\textit{blap}>\}_1{}^{n} \cdots$$

Then by definition of the domain of the variable n given above the replacement of the first (leftmost) occurrence of the component <*that*> in the definition of <*this*> does not preset or influence the choice of the value of n in the replacement of the second occurrence of <*that*> in the same definition.

REDUCING SETS

A type of description that is difficult to convert into the metalanguage is of the form:

> A *widget* may be formed by the concatenation of one to six different digits.

Now since a *widget* is constructed from digits, the choice of characters is restricted to one each of the set:

0,1,2,3,4,5,6,7,8,9

That is, once a character has been used, it is no longer available as a component of a *widget*. To permit such a choice, let us define a *reducing set*, symbolized by square brackets, in which it is understood that once an element has been used, the set is reduced by that element. That is, in terms of set notation,

if $\mathbf{N} = \{0,1,2,3,4,5,6,7,8,9\}$
and $a \in \mathbf{N}$
then $\mathbf{R} = \mathbf{N} - \{a\}$

where N is the original set, a the chosen element and R the reduced set. However, the reduced set becomes the set from which the next choice may be made. Thus the choice of characters to construct a *widget* may be described by the following algorithm:

if

$$N = \{0,1,2,3,4,5,6,7,8,9\}$$

then

(choice 1) $a \in N$ and $R1 = N - \{a\}$
(choice 2) $b \in R1$ and $R2 = R1 - \{b\}$
(choice 3) $c \in R2$ and $R3 = R2 - \{c\}$
(choice 4) $d \in R3$ and $R4 = R3 - \{d\}$

and so forth.

Using this notation, one sees that a *widget* may be defined by the construct:

$$\langle \mathit{widget} \rangle ::= \{[0|1|2|3|4|5|6|7|8|9]\}_1^6$$

In use, this metadefinition operates as follows:

Step	*Choice*	*Widget*	*Remaining Set*
0			0,1,2,3,4,5,6,7,8,9
1	3	3	0,1,2,4,5,6,7,8,9
2	7	37	0,1,2,4,5,6,8,9
3	0	370	1,2,4,5,6,8,9
4	1	3701	2,4,5,6,8,9
5	9	37019	2,4,5,6,8

As in the case of repetition groups the domain of a reducing group is the rule in which it is embedded. That is, each new application of the embedding rule commences with the full set of components in the reducing set. For example, consider the description below of a nonzero number (that is, a digit string containing at least one nonzero digit) and a nonzero number stream:

$\langle \mathit{nonzero\ number} \rangle ::=$
$$\{[\{\langle \mathit{digit} \rangle\}_0^\infty | \langle \mathit{nonzero\ digit} \rangle | \{\langle \mathit{digit} \rangle\}_0^\infty]\}_3^3$$
$\langle \mathit{nonzero\ number\ stream} \rangle ::=$
$$\langle \mathit{nonzero\ number} \rangle \{,\langle \mathit{nonzero\ number} \rangle\}_0^\infty$$
$\langle \mathit{nonzero\ digit} \rangle ::= 1|2|3|4|5|6|7|8|9$
$\langle \mathit{digit} \rangle ::= \langle \mathit{nonzero\ digit} \rangle | 0$

In the generation of a string which conforms to the specification nonzero number stream, it is obvious that the definition of nonzero number will have to be referenced many times. Each new reference will commence with the total set of alternatives in the reducing set which defines a nonzero number. One further limitation on reducing sets concerns the values of the indices of the surrounding repetition group. Obviously, there must exist some relationship between the number of alternatives within a reducing set and the indices of repetition. For our purposes here we shall prescribe that neither index may exceed the number of alternatives in the reducing set, so that at each iteration of the generation of the string from the components of the reducing set, there exists at least one element in the set from which to make a choice. It could be argued that if the set is reduced to an empty set that any further choices result in the selection of the null object. That is,

$$\{[\mathsf{A}|\mathsf{B}|\mathsf{C}]\}_n^n$$

is equal to

$$\{[\mathsf{A}|\mathsf{B}|\mathsf{C}]\}_3^3$$

for all values of n greater than 3.

This metalanguage feature will permit, for example, the definition of PL/I **DECLARE** statements, wherein the attributes of a name may occur in any order, but may not be repeated. In particular, consider the case where in defining the file attributes, the programmer is permitted to define a file option and/or a key option in any order, neither of which elements are mandatory. The file attribute may be defined as:

$$<\textit{file attribute}> := \{[<\textit{file option}>|<\textit{key option}>]\}_0^2$$

CONTEXT DEPENDENCY

In the use of syntax constructs, the progression from the initial metavariable to the actual string of characters may be visualized as the progressive substitution of metavariables by their components (which may contain further metavariables) until all metaelements have been replaced by elements of the character set of the language. This may be further visualized as the progression through certain branches of a tree structure wherein each branch is independent of all other branches. However, this tree-like structure with no interdependence of branches only exists for *context free* languages. If the left-hand side of a construct contains more than one metavariable, then the production of the right-hand side is dependent on the occurrence of more than one metavariable, and the language is said to be *context sensitive.* In such languages, constructs of the type:

<*a*><*b*><*c*> ::= <*a*> π <*c*>

indicate that in the context of <*a*> and <*c*> (which may be empty strings) the component <*b*> is to be replaced by the string π, where π may be any combination of characters and components. Although the majority of elements of computer languages are susceptible to description by a context-free grammar, certain features may require the use of a context-sensitive grammar, thus developing a totally context-sensitive grammar for that language. For example, one apparently simple feature of the BASIC language is not susceptible to context-free definition and thus the whole language becomes context-sensitive. In BASIC, the punctuation of a PRINT statement may be omitted between a literal string (which is delimited by quotes) and any other print element. In particular, the format specification inferred by a comma is assumed to be operative in the absence of punctuation. For example, the two partial statements

"EXAMPLE",X and "EXAMPLE"X

are equivalent in PRINT statements of the BASIC language. Thus in a description of BASIC, the following rules of production of the elements of a PRINT statement are included:

<*print st*> ::= PRINT <*print-string*>{<*punct*>}$_0^1$
<*punct*> ::= ,|;
<*message*> ::= "{<*char*>}$_1^n$"
<*char*> ::= <*letter*>|<*digit*>|<*special char*>
<*print string*> ::= <*message*>|<*expression*>|{<*print string*>}$_1^n$

The following four context-sensitive productions specify the permitted forms of punctuation in a print string:

<*message*><*expression*> ::=
<*message*>{<*punct*>}$_0^1$<*expression*>
<*expression*><*message*> ::=
<*expression*>{<*punct*>}$_0^1$<*message*>
<*message*><*message*> ::= <*message*>{<*punct*>}$_0^1$<*message*>
<*expression*><*expression*> ::=
<*expression*><*punct*><*expression*>

For a discussion and formal definition of context-sensitive languages, see Ginsburg.[8]

8. S. Ginsburg, *The Mathematical Theory of Context Free Languages* (New York: McGraw-Hill Book Co., 1966).

SUMMARY

The syntax of a language more complex than those briefly described in previous sections is composed of a nontrivial set of production rules. In turn, these rules define the character set of the language (the so-called "alphabet"), the set of component names (in BNF, the names enclosed in corner braces) and the name of the initial component from which, by the use of the productions rules, sentences in the language may be generated. Although we have been informal in our presentation of the rules for the creation of a grammar for a language, certain formal properties of context-free grammars[9] are of importance:

1. There may exist only one initial component of a grammar and all possible instances of the language (that is, the sentences) must be generable from that component by the application of the production rules.

2. Every component shall occur on the left hand side of at least one production rule.

3. There may be only one sequence of the application of production rules to generate any string of characters in the language, that is, the grammar must be unambiguous

4. The set of rules must be so arranged and organized that from every component, a string of only characters of the language can be generated.

There is no known algorithmic technique to test for the existence of ambiguities in a grammar. However, examples of ambiguous grammars may help to indicate common sources of ambiguity. For example, consider the grammar:

<integer> ::= *<digit>*|*<integer><integer>*
<digit> ::= 0|1|2|3|4|5|6|7|8|9

Using this syntax, there are at least two possible generation sequences to generate any string composed of three or more digits. For example consider the string 123:

Sequence 1.

<integer> → *<integer><integer>* → *<integer><digit>* →
*<integer>*3 → *<integer><integer>*3 →
*<integer><digit>*3 → *<integer>*23 →
*<digit>*23 → 123

9. N. Chomsky, "Formal Properties of Grammars," in *Handbook of Mathematical Psychology*, vol. 2 (New York: Wiley, 1963).

Sequence 2.

<integer> → *<integer><integer>* → *<digit><integer>* →
1*<integer>* → 1*<integer><integer>* →
1*<digit><integer>* → 12*<integer>* →
12*<digit>* → 123

The differences between these two generation sequences can be seen best by examination of the generation trees (syntactic trees) corresponding to these sequences. In these trees, the replacement of a component by the use of a production rule is represented by a single level tree structure with the component being replaced at the top and its replacement(s) below, branch lines connecting the component and its replacement(s). Thus sequence 1 is represented by the tree shown in Figure 2.1. That for sequence 2 is shown in Figure 2.2. Obviously these two trees are not equivalent and thus we may state that this grammar appears to be ambiguous. However, apparent ambiguity can result from a failure to be consistent in the order in which components partially expanded string are replaced. In fact, any rule which contains in its right hand part more than one component is a potential source of apparent ambiguity. Thus we shall insist that the order of replacement of components in a string be strictly left-to-right or right-to-left. That is, the leftmost (rightmost) component in a string is the candidate for replacement at each generation stage. Such a strict sequence of generation is known as *canonic* generation.

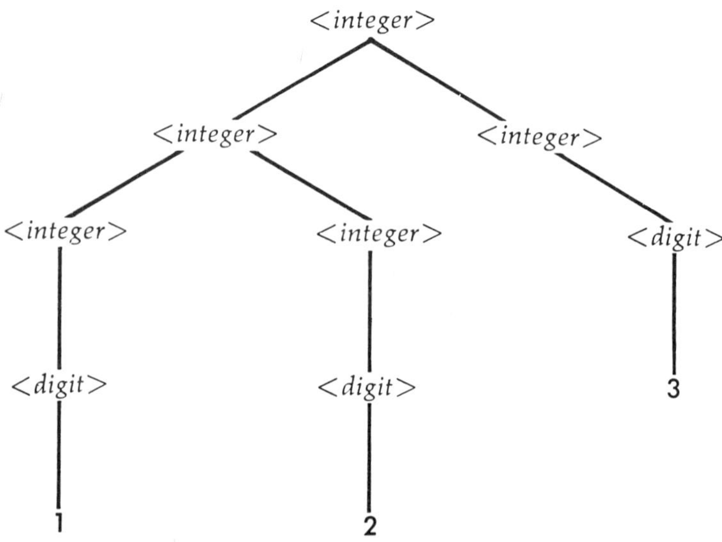

FIGURE 2.1 Generation sequence 1.

Returning to the definition of a digit string above, it may be seen that a canonic generation would not alleviate the ambiguousness of the grammar. However, a simple change to the grammar below would solve this problem.

<integer> ::= *<digit>*|*<integer><digit>*
<digit> ::= 0|1|2|3|4|5|6|7|8|9

From this grammar, it would appear that there are at least two distinct manners of generating the string 123 depending on the order of application of the productions rules. That is, left or right canonic generation:

Sequence 3—left canonic generation.

<integer> → *<integer><digit>* →
<integer><digit><digit> →
<digit><digit><digit> →
1*<digit><digit>* → 12*<digit>* → 123

Sequence 4—right canonic generation.

<integer> → *<integer><digit>* → *<integer>*3 →
*<integer><digit>*3 → *<integer>*23 →
*<digit>*23 → 123

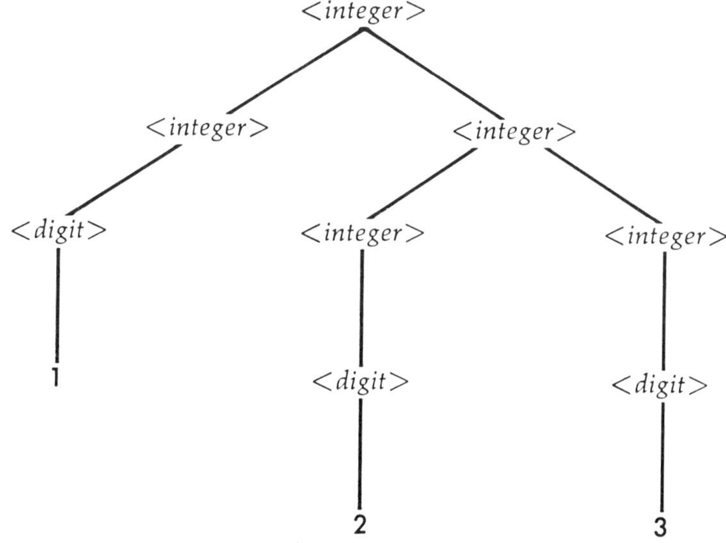

FIGURE 2.2 Generation sequence 2.

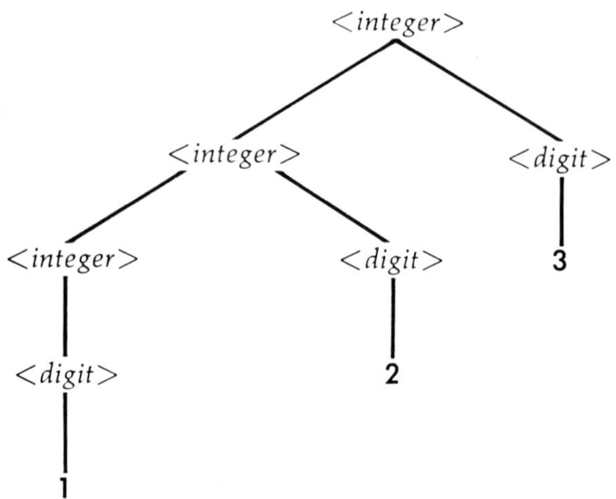

FIGURE 2.3 Generation sequences 3 and 4.

Whilst it would appear that these two generation sequences are distinct, their generation trees are, in fact, identical as is shown in Figure 2.3.

In general, an ambiguous grammar will be formed when two grammars are combined which define languages which have at least one element in common. For example, consider the grammar

$$\langle \mathit{this} \rangle ::= \{\mathsf{A}\}_1^3$$

which generates the language with the sentences A,AA and AAA. Then if this were to be combined with the grammar

$$\langle \mathit{that} \rangle ::= \mathsf{AA}$$

there would be two canonic generation sequences to develop the string AA. Thus the grammar

$$\langle \mathit{this\text{-}or\text{-}that} \rangle ::= \langle \mathit{this} \rangle | \langle \mathit{that} \rangle$$

is ambiguous.

In this chapter we have described a metalanguage that will enable us to define nonnatural languages, such as those used in both computing and logic. However, we have only discussed the definitions with respect to the formulation of a statement of the object language and not with regard to the determination of the name of a string of characters with which we are presented. That is, we have been given the key to the creation of a cipher, but have not checked to see whether it is the same key that will allow us to decipher the message.

Problems

2.1 Write definitions that will permit the construction of odd and even integers.

2.2 In a FORTRAN program, the format of the input data is described by the following statement:

FORMAT(F16.3,17,416,3X,6HOUTPUT)

Assuming that the **READ** statement referring to this **FORMAT** contains the names of six variables of the appropriate mode, write a set of constructs that will describe the valid forms of preparing the input data documents.

2.3 Write a construct that will describe a nonzero integer number.

2.4 Find the algorithms that enable the prediction of the next letter in each of the following sequences, and then describe these algorithms in terms of the metalanguage such that infinite sequences can be generated from cyclic Roman alphabets (i.e., **A** follows **Z** after each pass through the alphabet):

(a) ABABAB . . .
(b) ATBATAATBAT . . .
(c) DEFGEFGHFGHI . . .

2.5 Consider the following (verbal) description of the set of number representations for a new programming language:

Subset 1. A positional notation in which each numeric value is represented by a string of digits, optionally preceded by a sign character, and suffixed by the radix of representation.

Example: +3126(8)

Subset 2. A positional notation in which each numeric value is represented by a string of characters, optionally preceded by a sign character, and suffixed by the radix of representation, the position of the radix point being specific by a special character at that position.

Example: −110.1(2)

Subset 3. A representation system in which each number, as represented by a significand (optionally preceded by a sign character), a signed exrad, and a radix, equals the value represented by the significand in the specified radix notation times a power, where the power is equal to the value represented by the radix raised to the value represented by the exrad with the sign of the sign character.

Example: −32.0111+4(5)

Based on these specifications, develop a set of syntactic specifications for these representations of numeric values, with the root component <*standard number*>. What effect would fixed-field length have on your specifications?

2.6 Beg, borrow (but hopefully do not steal) a text or manual on APL. Note that APL has a very peculiar hierarchial ordering of arithmetic operators. Restricting the set of operators to +, −, × and ÷ in their monadic or diadic forms as appropriate, develop a syntax for APL expressions. If the replacement symbol is regarded as an operator, where would it occur in your hierarchy?

3
Syntactic Analysis

The purpose of expressing either a natural or nonnatural language in a specific form is not primarily centered around our innate desire to conform, but rather on the need to communicate. However, the success of communication is measured by the amount of information that is gleaned by the receiver. Thus, although a phrase may be grammatically correct (such as *convict an indulgent mandrake* or *a nice derangement of epitaphs*), the listener or reader may gain little information, and therefore, for the sake of conversation, reply in like manner.

The use of grammatically correct sentences is therefore merely a prelude to the deconcatenation of the statement by the receiver. A grammar or formalism that allows the generation of a statement which is not deconcatenable or is deconcatenable in more than one way is useless. In natural language syntactic ambiguity is not always disastrous since the meaning of a certain word may be derived from the context or (as in a malapropism) from the knowledge of a similar word that would make the phrase meaningful. Similarly, permissible errors that allow a phrase to be formed without the loss of meaning are nondisastrous. As an example, read any cablegram couched in terms that minimize the number of words (and hence the cost of the message) while maintaining the meaning of the message. Ambiguity resulting from the inability to deconcatenate a phrase due to a lack in the definition of the scope of an adjective in a natural language is similarly important, though many such ambiguities are resolved by a knowledge of normal (as opposed to standard) usage.

THE PROBLEM

The problem of associating a given string of symbols with the grammar for a language, such that an answer to the question "Does this string belong to the language?" may be determined is the topic of this chapter. However, it is intended (having determined the existence of the string in the language) that the syntactic tree for that string should be created. In fact, in terms of syntactic trees, the process of association can be thought of as the determination of the syntactic tree which was used to generate the string.

Cheatham[1] has likened the problem of tree generation to the game of dominoes, wherein the dominoes contain the left- and right-hand sides of each syntactic production. The problem is to fit the dominoes together in such a manner that there exists a complete tree between the root symbol and the string in question. Such a structure is shown in Figure 3.1.

Another means for validating the existence of a string in a language is to generate all possible strings of that language and then to investigate the existence of the string in question in the generated set. Obviously, in some languages this is impossible since the language is infinite. However, given a string of a prescribed length (that is, number of distinct characters in the string) it is possible to generate all sequences of that length, provided that the null element is rejected from the grammar. That is, if each and every production in a given grammar either maintains or increases the length of the generated string upon application, then it is possible to discard many alternative generation sequences when the generated string is too long. In this sense, a string may consist of both characters in the language as well as components. Such strings are known as *sentential forms* of the language.

For example given the grammar

(1) <*s*> ::= <*e*>
(2) <*e*> ::= <*e*> + <*t*>|<*t*>
(3) <*t*> ::= A <*t*>|A

1. T. E. Cheatham, *The Theory and Construction of Compilers*, 2nd ed. (Wakefield, Mass.: Computer Associates, 1967).

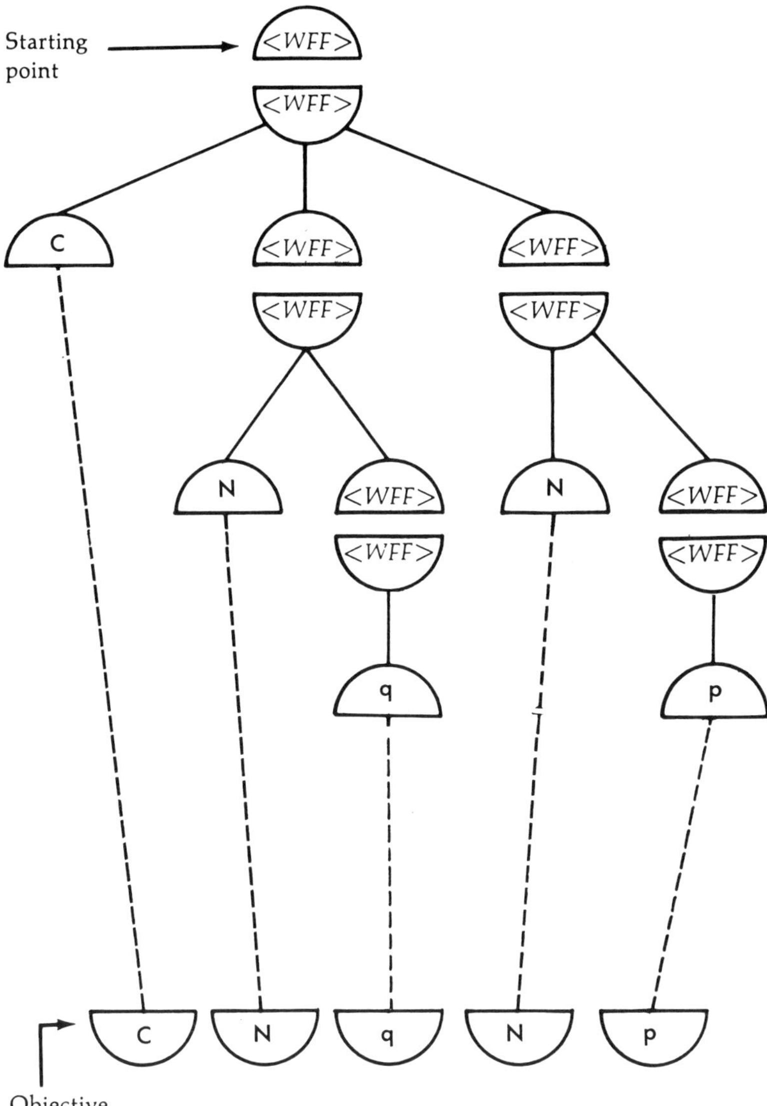

FIGURE 3.1 Syntactic tree as a dominoes game. Given a starting point and an objective as semicircles, the game is finished when all semicircles match with another containing the same character or component name.

we may see that the initial symbol (root symbol) is <*s*> and that the character set of the language is {A,+}. The set of component names is {<*s*>, <*e*>, <*t*>}. Given that <*s*> is the root symbol, then <*s*> is a sentential form of the language and the replacement of any component in a sentential form by the use of one of the productions also develops a sentential form. Hence the sequence of sentential forms

$$<s> \rightarrow <e> \rightarrow <e> + <t> \rightarrow <t> + <t> \rightarrow \mathsf{A}<t> + <t> \rightarrow \mathsf{AA} + <t> \rightarrow \mathsf{AA} + \mathsf{A}$$

may be developed, showing that each form is *in* the language. However, usually we shall be concerned only with those sentential forms which are composed totally of characters of the language, that is sentential forms which contain no components which are candidates for replacement through the use of any production. In the language defined by the grammar above, the *proof* that a string exists is the existence of a sequence of steps (using one production rule at each step) which leads from the root symbol to the desired string.

Such a definition of the proof of the existence of a string in a language is consistent with the definition of *proof* as related to formal systems:

> A *proof* . . . is a sequence $A_1, A_2, \ldots A_n$ of well-formed formulas such that, for each i, either A_i is an axiom (of the system) or A_i is a direct consequence of some preceding well-formed formula by virtue of one of the rules of inference.[2]

In terms of syntactic forms, the existence proof may be defined as follows:

> An *existence proof* over a string of characters ϕ_n in the language is a sequence $\phi_1, \phi_2, \ldots, \phi_n$ of sentential forms of the language such that, for each $i>1$, ϕ_i is a sentential form which is the result of applying one of the production rules of the grammar to ϕ_{i-1} and where ϕ_1 is the root symbol of the language.

The means for determining this sequence is the task of a syntactic analyzer and the sequence of productions which generate the sentential forms is known as the *parse* of the string. For example, in the sequence of sentential forms which relate the root symbol <*s*> to the string AA+A above the parse is the sequence of rules applied. Thus if the rules were numbered *i.j* where *i* is the rule number and *j*

2. E. Mendelson, *Introduction to Mathematical Logic* (New York: Van Nostrand Reinhold, 1964), p. 29.

the alternative used, then this sequence of sentential forms is equivalent to the parse

1.1, 2.1, 2.2, 3.1, 3.2, 3.2

Whilst we will develop the parse of a string, at least by implication, the most important derivative of a syntactic analysis of a string from the point of view of a compiler is the relationships between component names and the string. For example, it is comparatively easy to see in FORTRAN that the component name <*variable*> can be related to strings of characters in statements. Once this relationship has been established, then the generator of the compiler can (say) create addresses in target language instructions. But more of this operation later.

The task of analysis of a string initially must be to determine the existence of the string in the language. One way to do this is by developing all strings of the same length as the string in question from the root component. Consider the grammar

$$<WFF> := \mathbf{p}|\mathbf{q}|\mathbf{r}|\mathbf{s}|\mathbf{N}<WFF>|\{\mathbf{C}|\mathbf{A}|\mathbf{K}|\mathbf{E}\}_1^1<WFF><WFF>$$

Now obviously, since the definition of this language includes a recursive production, then the language is an infinite language and hence it will not be feasible to generate all possible strings in the language to test against any string which is believed to exist in the language. However, it is possible to generate all strings of a certain length and then to check the existence of some string in this generated set. For example consider the string

CNqNp

This string is composed of 5 characters (symbols in the language) and from an examination of the possible substitutions that can be made it can be seen that there are approximately 2500 five-character strings that may be generated from this grammar! Thus even for strings with comparatively few (5, even) characters, the number of alternatives to be considered is very large. Obviously as the number of characters in the string increases, the number of elements in the set of *n*-character strings will increase geometrically. Hence even with a language as simple as BASIC, the number of alternatives will be outside the range of feasibility for comparison in this manner.

The judicious use of a prior lexical analysis of a string can substantially reduce the number of elements in such a set of strings. In our diagram which represented the gross flowchart of a translator shown in Figure 1.3, the syntactic analyzer is preceded by a lexical analyzer which performs three specific tasks—redundancy removal, statement condensation, and phrase delimitation. These tasks could be performed by the syntactic analyzer and the machine independent optimizer together but this tends to be analogous to "using a pile driver to break a walnut." These tasks can be performed without reference to those portions of the syntactic specifications which relate the spatial orderings of the symbols in the language. In fact, the essential difference between a pure lexical analyzer and a syntactic analyzer is that the former, using a direct dictionary look-up procedure, can identify certain elements of the language without reference to spatial relationships. For example, in a simple language where the alphabet used to construct (say) single character variables is distinct from the alphabet used to compose key words, it does not require a syntactic analyzer to develop symbol to component name associations. However, a pure lexical analyzer, disregarding spatial relationships would be incapable of recognizing that a multicharacter string represented a variable even though the characters of the variable were distinct from those of all other language elements. In this case a spatial relationship (derived from the generative operation of concatentation) is required to identify the character string to component name (variable) association.

Rarely, however, does there exist a *pure* lexical analyzer, since juxtaposition is very easily recognizable. Thus, allowing this, simple extended lexical analysis can be used in unambiguous cases to identify certain language elements in a text. For example, a pure lexical analyzer would not be capable of recognizing statements in a text since the characters which compose a statement are related spatially. However, that lexical analyzer would be capable of recognizing statement delimiters provided that the delimiters were distinct. The simple specification that "everything that lies between two statement delimiters is a statement" is truly a syntactic specification since it implies spatial relationships, but recognizing that this specification only encompasses juxtaposition of characters, it is simple for a lexical analyzer to be extended to recognize statements. In the same manner, if the delimiters of (say) variables are distinct in all cases, then lexical analysis can be extended to identify variables. This same reasoning can be applied to phrases.

As will be seen in the discussion of syntactic analyzers which follows, the cost of syntactic analysis can sky rocket if it is necessary for the analyzer to perform very many character comparisons. For example, if the syntactic analyzer has to identify a member of the roman alphabet by comparison of the character with every known member of the alphabet until a match is found, then the average number of comparisons necessary is possibly 13. Possibly, because the ordering of the alphabet might be changed so as to improve the chances of identifying the character with the minimum number of comparisons. For example, in Chapter 1 we noted that the frequency of usage of characters in the English language is (partially)

$$eaoidhnrstuy \ldots z$$

Now in the usual alphabetical ordering, comparison with y would be the 25th operation, whereas y is the 12th most frequently used character in the language. Thus by comparing the characters in the order of the frequency of usage we can improve the algorithm for recognition. In a machine we can improve on this even further by a knowledge of the lexical properties of character representations; that is the coding of the character. In an ASCII[3] machine we could determine that a character was contained in the (upper case) alphabet by testing its containment in the range $1000001 \leqq \alpha \leqq 1011010$ (7 bit ASCII). This is impossible to specify syntactically using BNF.

Subsequent to lexical processing, a text can be analyzed syntactically far more rapidly if occurrences of components for which there exist many alternative forms have been recognized lexically. Thus occurrences of (say) variables have been replaced in the text by a pair (V, α) where V is a tag indicating variable and α is the variable name. The syntactic analyzer then only has to examine the first element of the pair to determine its place in the remaining syntactic structure.

The processes of lexical analysis are discussed in further detail in the next chapter and in part again in the section of this chapter entitled "Ad Hoc Analyzers."

Where there is a direct relationship between characters of the language and components in the language, it is possible to scan the string and to generate another sentential form which is easier to analyze in the manner described above. For example, in the grammar above, there is an unambiguous relationship between the characters **p**, **q**, **r** and **s** and the component name *<WFF>*. Thus a simple scan of the string (any string) can reduce all characters of this set to the component *<WFF>*, and since this is the only possible manner in which these characters could have been generated then the reduced form is a potential sentential form to be considered. In the case above, the string

3. American Standard Code for Information Interchange.

CNqNp is reduced to **CN**<*WFF*>**N**<*WFF*>

and the number of strings generated from the root symbol <*WFF*> which contain none of the characters **p**, **q**, **r** or **s** is reduced to approximately 50. At this point it might be possible to examine all restricted 5 character/component strings.

However, such "bull at the gate" techniques, while guaranteeing success (given sufficient time) are all too often impractical for use in a compiler system. Thus we must look to ways in which the number of alternatives to be considered is substantially reduced and there is at least some element of deductive reasoning in the algorithm for analysis, rather than blind guesswork.

Syntactic analyzers can be broadly classified into two methods—the predictive methods which, starting from the root symbol, attempt to predict the means by which the string was generated and the reductive methods, which attempt to reduce the string to the root symbol. These methods are loosely termed the *top-down* and *bottom-up* methods respectively. The direction implied by these terms is related to the syntactic trees which may be generated wherein the root symbol is at the top of the page and the string at the bottom. It may then be seen that a predictive (top-down) method starts at the top of the (yet unconstructed) tree and builds down towards the string, whereas the bottom-up (reductive) method starts at the string and attempts to develop a tree which converges onto the root symbol.

PREDICTIVE ANALYSIS

Let us firstly consider the method of predictive analysis, and for an example consider the grammar for a <*WFF*> described above and the string, considered previously, **CNqNp**. Initially the "work area" for the analysis will consist of the root symbol and the string as shown below:

<*WFF*>

CNqNp

Assuming that the string was developed by a left canonic generation, then we should assume that it is possible to analyze by considering a left-to-right matching of predictions with the string. That is, in the example here, the first sequence of predictions should encompass the leftmost symbol in the string—that is, **C**.

Taking the alternatives of the grammar in order, it may be seen that it will take six false starts before it is possible to create a link between the root symbol and the leftmost character, **C**. That is, the first prediction is that the leftmost character is **p**, which is obviously not true. The next prediction would be **q** and then **r** and next **s**. Having failed all these tests, the next alternative is the sentential form **N**<*WFF*>. However, this does not satisfy the condition that the leftmost character be **C** and thus this alternative is similarly rejected. Finally, the string **C** <*WFF*><*WFF*> is predicted and a match is made. However, this match implies that the remainder of the string is composed of <*WFF*><*WFF*>. This is not certain and must be verified. At this point the work space has the form

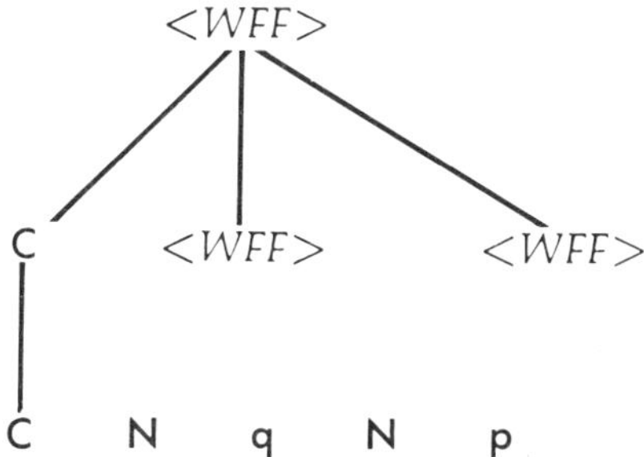

The remainder of the tree (the part not linked between the root symbol and the string) may now be regarded as a new problem, the character **N** now being the leftmost. After testing **N** against all the one character <*WFF*>s a match is made in the fifth alternative and one more link is forged so that the work space now contains

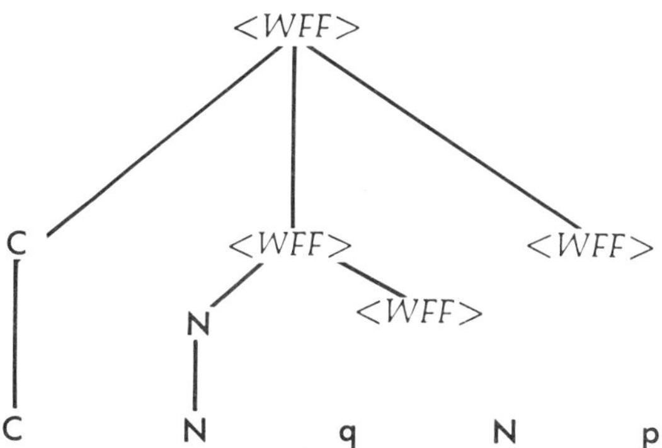

Systematically taking the leftmost unlinked component in the tree, so as to conform to the left canonic generation which has been assumed, the next character in the string can be shown to map onto the leftmost <*WFF*> prediction, after only one mismatch of the character **q** with the character **p**. The tree structure then takes the form

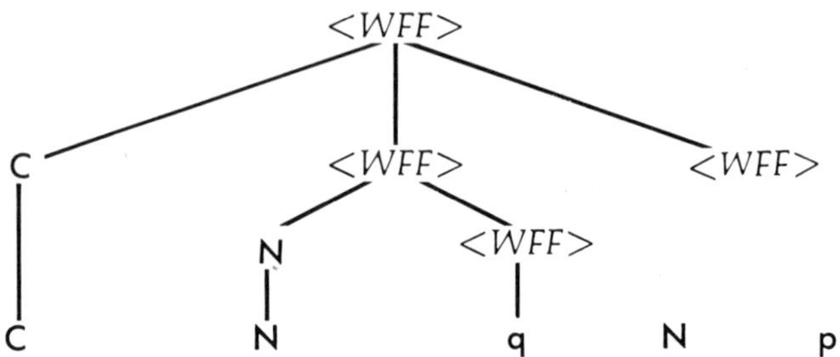

Finally after two more successful predictions, the total tree is formed there being no characters of the string which are not leaves of the tree and no components which do not map onto the string. At this final point the work area contains

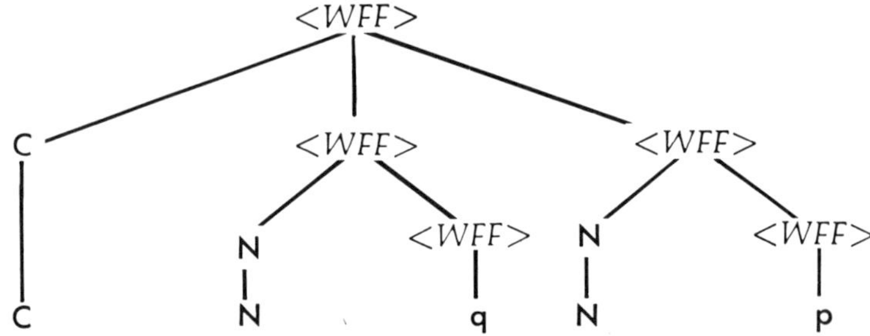

This particular example of an analysis by top-down predictive methodology is comparatively simple since the language is simple and each type of component is readily recognizable. However, there exist grammars which generate strings whose components are not immediately recognizable as belonging to one and only one higher level (in the tree sense) component. In such cases predictions may turn out to be false some considerable time (and hence number of other seemingly successful predictions) later. In such cases it is necessary to back up (or *backtrack*) to the last successful match in order to attempt some other alternative. The structure of the syntactic specifications determine whether backtracking is likely to be necessary or not. For example, in the description of <*WFF*> above, no backtracking is necessary since: (1) The leftmost character in an alternative is always unique, and (2) The alternatives are contained on a single level and thus are immediately available for comparison with the character in the string under investigation. However, a simple change in the syntax would develop a set of productions that would induce backtracking.

<*WFF*> ::= <*name*>|<*expression*>
<*name*> ::= <*p-or-q*>|<*r-or-s*>
<*expression*> ::= <*unary exp*>|<*binary exp*>
<*p-or-q*> ::= **p**|**q**
<*r-or-s*> ::= **r**|**s**
<*unary exp*> ::= **N**<*WFF*>
<*binary exp*> ::= <*binary opr*><*WFF*><*WFF*>
<*binary opr*> ::= **C**|**A**|**K**|**E**

It should be obvious that the language developed by this syntactic set of productions is identical with that developed from the previous definition based on the root symbol <*WFF*>. Such a pair of grammars are said to be *weakly equivalent* since they have the same language. However, they are not *structurally* equivalent since the syntactic trees do not have the same basic form.

Let us consider the string **CNqNp** again as a candidate for the language developed by the grammar above. Taking the same procedures as before the work space is laid out as:

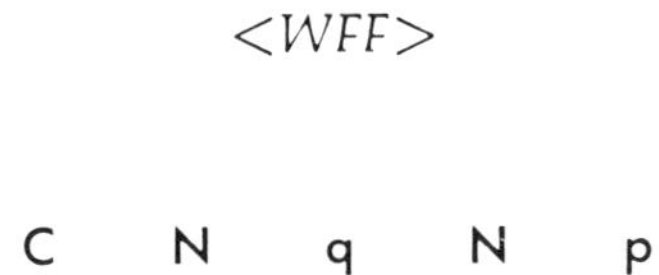

and the first prediction (leftmost, as usual) would be

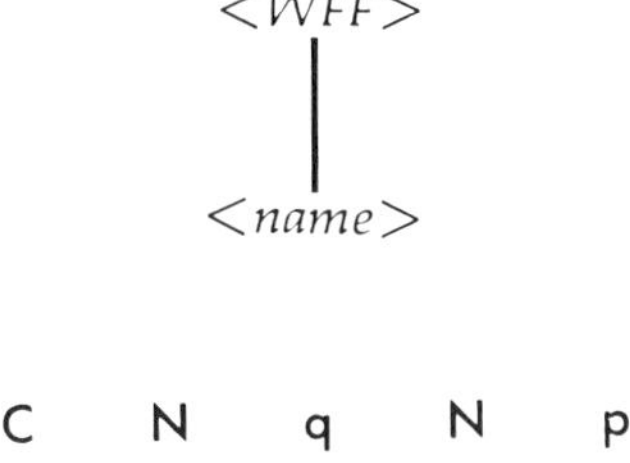

Now obviously, no comparison can be made between the prediction and the string as yet since no character has been predicted; hence at least one more prediction is necessary.

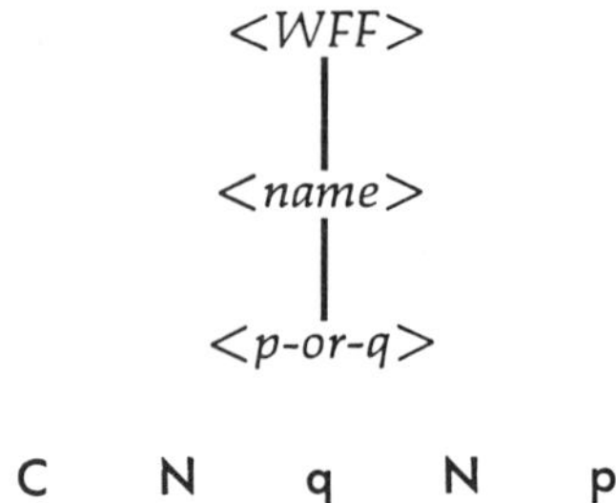

Still no character has been developed that can be compared with the string and thus the predictive process must continue.

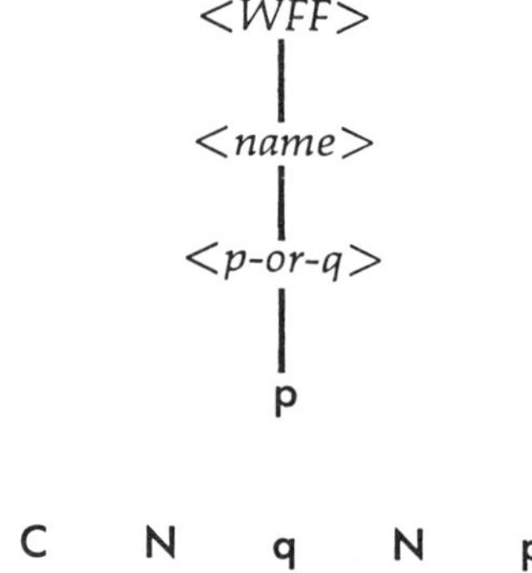

At this point a character has been developed and thus a comparison can be made. Obviously, no match is made in this comparison and thus the first step is to "ask" if there is an alternative to the character currently predicted. Thus we *backtrack* to the component which developed the character (*<p-or-q>*) and search for an alternative. Obviously in this case, there is an alternative (the character **q**) and thus the work space is updated to the form

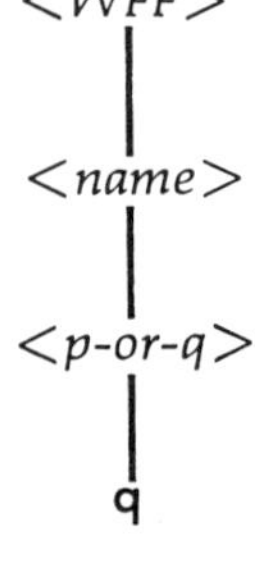

C N q N p

Failing to match again, it is necessary to backtrack again. Going back to the level of the component *<p-or-q>* we find that we have exhausted all alternatives and thus we must backtrack at least one more level. In fact, we shall backtrack to *<name>*, predict *<r-or-s>*, predict **r**, fail to match, predict **s**, fail to match and then backtrack to *<name>* again. At this point all alternatives for the component *<name>* have been exhausted, and thus the backtracking must return to the next level, that is, the root symbol *<WFF>*. In the first prediction based on this component, the first alternative *<name>* was chosen, thus the second alternative should be utilized this time. Further since this is the first time that the component *<expression>* has been used in the current predictive cycle, then the first alternative is the next sequential prediction. Thus the work space contains the following predictions

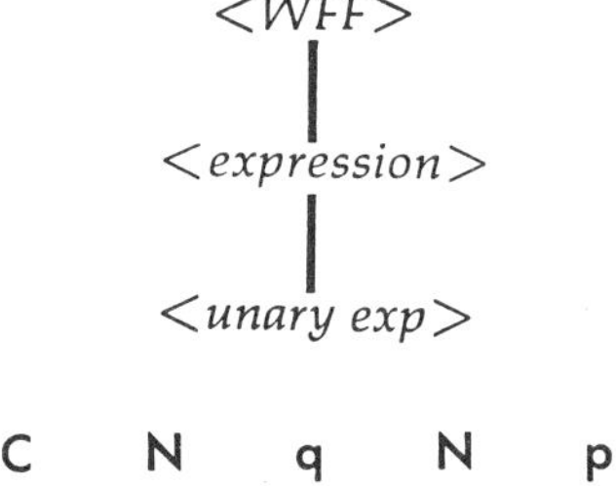

Continuing to make predictions, the first generable character (and the leftmost generable) from *<unary exp>* is **N** which obviously does not match with the string's leftmost character. Thus an alternative is sought. There exists no alternative at the *<unary exp>* level and thus we must backtrack to *<expression>* again. Since the first alternative has been used already, the second alternative is now a candidate for prediction. Finally, in the first prediction from the component *<binary opr>* a match is attained.

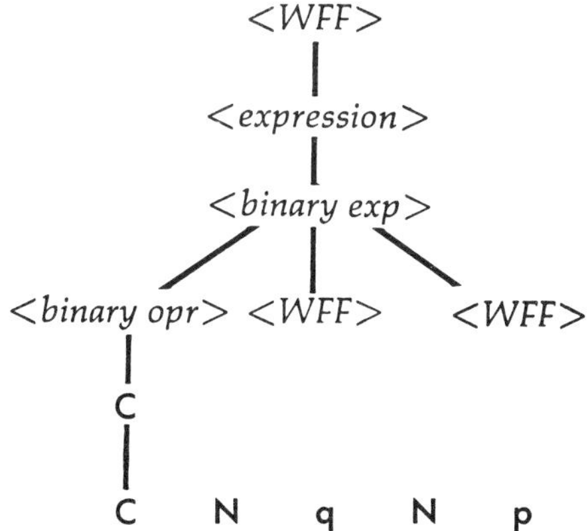

The process is then repeated with backtracking until all the other characters in the string are predicted by this means and the string is recognized to be an element of the language defined by the grammar.

In the example here, backtracking was recognized to be necessary since no match could be found for the very first (leftmost) character in the string in question. However, this is not always the case. There can exist situations where apparent success in matching is attained until (say) the *n*-th character is compared with some prediction. In this case, it may be necessary to wipe out all the previous predictions which matched since the component which generated them is being removed in the process of backtracking.

For example, consider a segment of the syntactic description of FORTRAN, where a statement is defined:

<statement> ::= *<assignment st>*|*<Do statement>*|· · ·

where

<assignment st> ::= *<variable>* = *<expression>*

and

<Do statement> ::= DO*<statement number><variable>* = *<initial>*, · · ·

Now, without expanding these productions further, we may see that the string DO1I = 1 can satisfy both sets of descriptions up to a point. That is, if we followed the algorithm for prediction developed above, the syntactic tree would be developed to the following form before any noticeable irregularities would be identified:

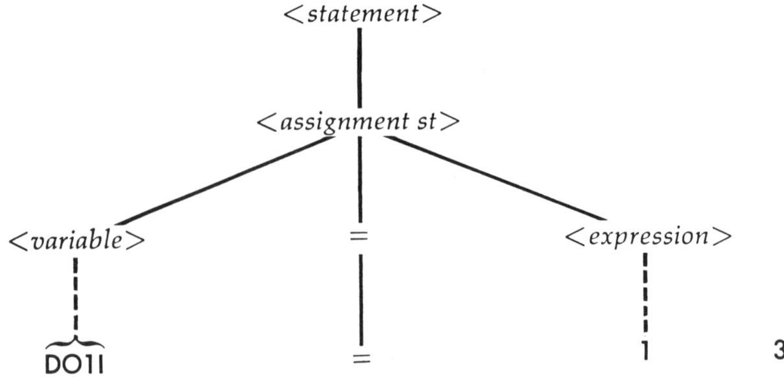

At this point, it would be noticed that the whole string has not been encompassed by the predictions and further there are no predictions under the component *<assignment st>* which could develop the character "," as the next sequential character. Thus backtracking must take place removing all previously connected branches of the tree to the point where an alternative production can be inserted.

Fundamentally, backtracking may be defined as the process of removing predictions following the mismatch of a prediction with the string in question and when there exist no alternatives at the matching level to be considered.

This process of top-down predictive analysis is the basis for the algorithm developed by Cheatham and Sattley.[4] The algorithm is based on two tables whose contents describe the syntactic productions which comprise the description of the language against which strings are to be tested. The syntactic productions are firstly reorganized so that the relationships between the elements of the productions are redefined. That is, the relationships between an element and its successor element or the element and its alternatives are developed. To simplify the process of construction, let us assume that we have primarily modified the grammar to an equivalent grammar in which the productions contain at the most one alternation operator and each alternative contains no more than two elements. That is, the most complex production is of the form

<left-hand side> ::= <alt-1><alt-2>|<alt-3><alt-4>

Having accomplished this, a successor/alternate tree may be formed from the syntax. This special type of tree shows succession by horizontal lines emanating from a node while replacement (the relationship between the left-hand side and the leftmost element of the right-hand side) is indicated by a vertical line. Alternatives are linked through the first element of each string of components, and are indicated in the diagram by a curvilinear line between the two first elements. Thus the general form of diagram generated from the general production is as shown below:

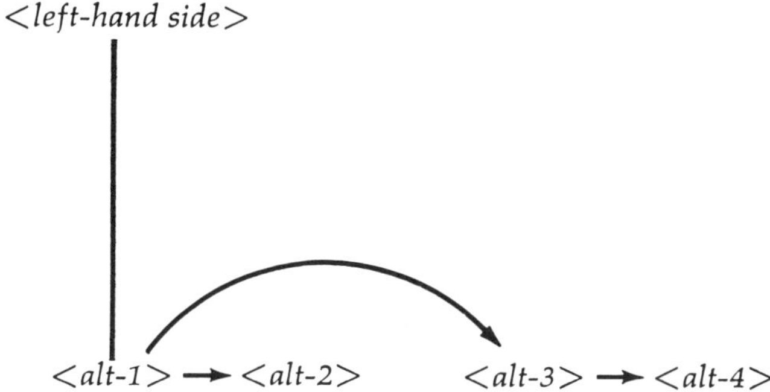

4. T. E. Cheatham, and K. Sattley, "Syntax Directed Compiling," *Proc. AFIPS 1964 Eastern Joint Computer Conference* (Montvale, N.J.: AFIPS Press, 1964), pp. 31–57.

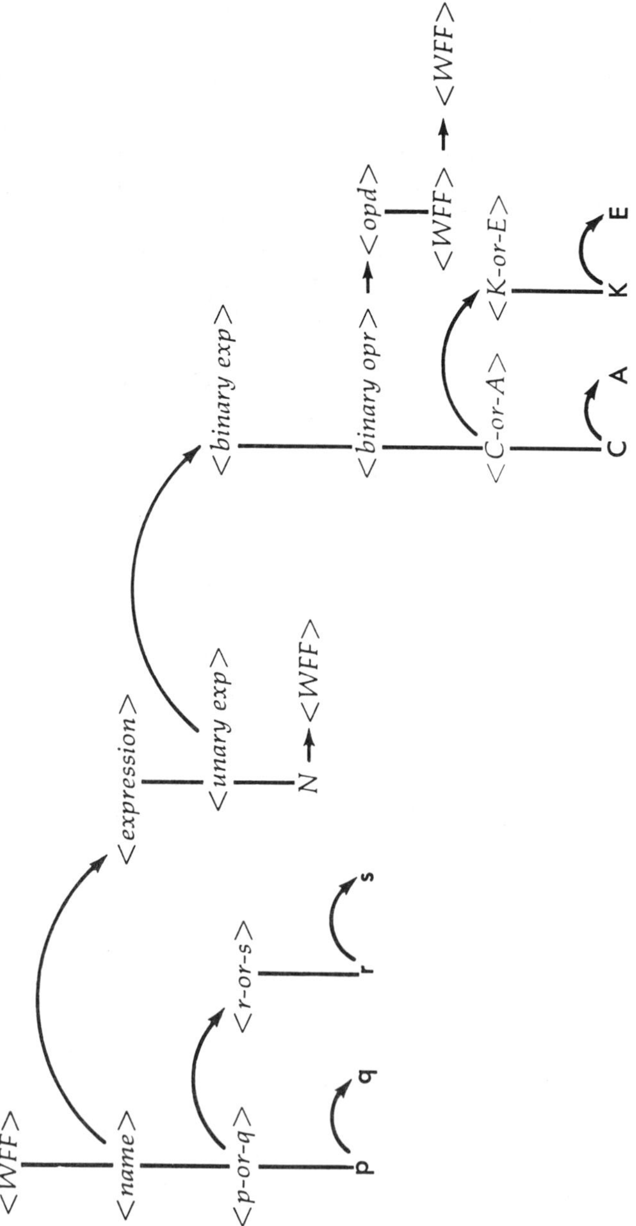
<WFF>
<name>
<p-or-q>
p
q
<r-or-s>
r
s
<expression>
<unary exp>
N → <WFF>
<binary exp>
<binary opr> → <opd>
<WFF> → <WFF>
<C-or-A>
<K-or-E>
C
A
K
E

FIGURE 3.2

On this basis the grammar based on the root symbol $<WFF>$ on page 81 will be converted into the graph shown in Figure 3.2.

The two tables which are the basis of the Cheatham/Sattley algorithm are now derived from these graphs. Leaving aside the productions which are recursive (that is, contain on their right-hand side the component on the left-hand side) the procedure for establishing the tables is as follows.

Establish the syntax type table by reserving a line for each element of the language, that is, the set of characters and the set of component names. This table should be indexed for reference purposes. In this description we shall use lower case roman numerals for these indices. Under the heading of "Terminal?" fill in for each element of the language the answer to the question "Is this element a character (terminal) in the language?" One more column is required, though its contents cannot be determined at this point. This column will contain a pointer to the second table (in the form of the line index of the table) which describes the structure of the component named in the type table. Obviously, characters have no structure and thus their entry in this column of the type table is null.

Let us consider the simple language

$$
\begin{aligned}
<s> &::= <x><y> \\
<x> &::= \mathsf{a}|\mathsf{b} \\
<y> &::= \mathsf{c}|\mathsf{d}
\end{aligned}
$$

The set of characters in the language is $\{\mathsf{a,b,c,d}\}$ whilst the set of component names is $\{<s>, <x>, <y>\}$. With this knowledge, the type table will take the form:

Index	*Name or character*	*Terminal?*	*Pointer to structure table*
i	$<s>$	no	
ii	$<x>$	no	
iii	$<y>$	no	
iv	a	yes	–
v	b	yes	–
vi	c	yes	–
vii	d	yes	–

Now to the construction of the syntax structure table. Take each production as generated in the modified form from the original syntax and develop the successor/alternate tree for that production. In the case of the simple grammar above, these trees are as follows.

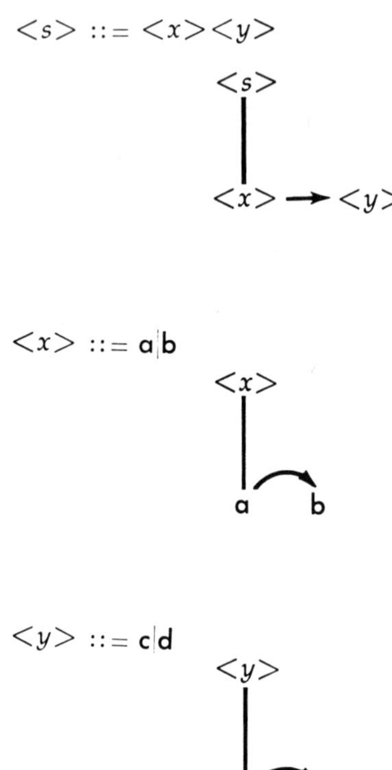

Considering the productions in turn, and only those which do not contain recursive specifications:

1. Assign a line in the structure table for each component or character in each alternative of the production.

That is, in the simple grammar above, for the first production:

Index	*Type*	*Ending?*	*Successor*	*Alternate*	(*Element*)
1					<*x*>
2					<*y*>
3					
4					

In this table, the last column headed "element" is included here merely to show the correspondence between the production and the table. In implementation, this column is not necessary. Similarly the index column may not be explicitly present if the table is represented in a regular array.

2. Set the structure table pointer in the line of the type table which corresponds to the component on the left hand side of the production (that is at the head of the successor/alternate tree) to the line in the structure table corresponding to the first element in the first (leftmost) alternative.

In the example, this will set a pointer in line i of the type table to line 1 of the structure table.

3. In the lines of the structure table corresponding to the elements assigned in (1) above, set the type pointers (column headed "type") to the corresponding type table entry.

Thus, the structure table is updated to the form:

Index	*Type*	*Ending?*	*Successor*	*Alternate*	(*Element*)
1	ii				<x>
2	iii				<y>
3					

4. In each line of the structure which corresponds to a component which is the first element in the alternative, set the "ending?" to NO and the "successor" to the line number (in the structure table) of its successor as indicated by the successor/alternate tree. Where there is no successor leave the entry under "successor" blank.

Action under this heading will affect only line 1 of the structure table for the presently considered production. Thus line 1 becomes

Index	*Type*	*Ending?*	*Successor*	*Alternate*	(*Element*)
1	ii	NO	2		<x>

5. In each line of the structure table which corresponds to an element which is the last element of an alternative, set the "Ending?" to YES and the "successor" to OK.

It may seem to be illogical to set the successor of the last element of an alternative to OK. However, except in one very special case (that is, the production which contains the root symbol on the left hand side) it is not known whether there may or may not be some successor in the string which is developed by some other production. Further, recursive productions may develop strings in which a successor may be either OK or invalid. Failing to have a definite solution to this question of succession, the OK symbol is inserted, so as indicate "possibly."

Under this step of the algorithm establishing the tables, line 2 of the syntax structure table is updated:

Index	*Type*	*Ending?*	*Successor*	*Alternate*	(*Element*)
1	ii	NO	2		<*x*>
2	iii	YES	OK		<*y*>
3					

6. In the line which corresponds to the first element of the leftmost alternative set the "Alternate" entry to be the line number in the structure table of the first element of its alternate. Set all other "Alternate" entries to FAIL.

This step sets the links between the alternatives as shown by the curvilinear lines in the successor/alternate tree. Where there is no alternative, the last sentence of the step takes care of the appropriate entry. The structure table for the production <*s*> ::= <*x*><*y*> is finally:

Index	*Type*	*Ending?*	*Successor*	*Alternate*	(*Element*)
1	ii	NO	2	FAIL	<*x*>
2	iii	YES	OK	FAIL	<*y*>
3					

In steps 4 and 5, the entry headed "Ending?" was established. This entry is for the purpose of generating code from an analysis by indicating the point at which the total elements of a component have been recognized. This entry takes no part in the actual syntactic analysis itself.

Applying these steps to the other two productions in the simple grammar above, the tables eventually contain the following entries:

Type Table

Index	*Name or Character*	*Terminal?*	*Pointer to structure table*
i	<*s*>	NO	1
ii	<*x*>	NO	3
iii	<*y*>	NO	5
iv	a	YES	–
v	b	YES	–
vi	c	YES	–
vii	d	YES	–

Structure Table

Index	*Type*	*Ending?*	*Successor*	*Alternate*	*(Element)*
1	ii	NO	2	FAIL	$<x>$
2	iii	YES	OK	FAIL	$<y>$
3	iv	YES	OK	4	a
4	v	YES	OK	FAIL	b
5	vi	YES	OK	6	c
6	vii	YES	OK	FAIL	d

Note that in the case of lines 3 through 6, step 4 of the algorithm initially set the ending to NO whereas step 5 reset this entry to YES since these elements satisfy the conditions of both steps 4 and 5. Similarly, the successor entries in these lines were left blank by step 4 and set to OK by step 5.

The algorithm developed by Cheatham and Sattley performs the "tree-walk" through the successor/alternate trees, matching generated symbols with the characters in the string. For example, the walk which determines that the string **by** is contained in the language which is described by the syntax

$<s> ::= <w><x>$
$<w> ::= <a>|<b>$
$<x> ::= <y>|<z>$
$<a> ::=$ a|w
$<b> ::=$ b|x
$<y> ::=$ c|y
$<z> ::=$ d|z

is shown in Figure 3.3 where the dotted line indicates the progress of the walk. Note that the path from $<x>$ does not return to the root by way of the component $<w>$ since all the conditions necessary to satisfy the goal (prediction) of $<w>$ have already been satisfied and thus it is not necessary to report back to that node again. On the other hand, failure to satisfy a prediction (as in the case of $<a>$) requires a return to locate an alternative. Conversely, the confirmation of a prediction requires that the node from which the prediction was made is visited again, not only to report the confirmation but also to ascertain the next goal. This next goal could only take the form of a successor from a node already visited. It is interesting to note that the walk may be characterized by regarding the successor/alternate tree

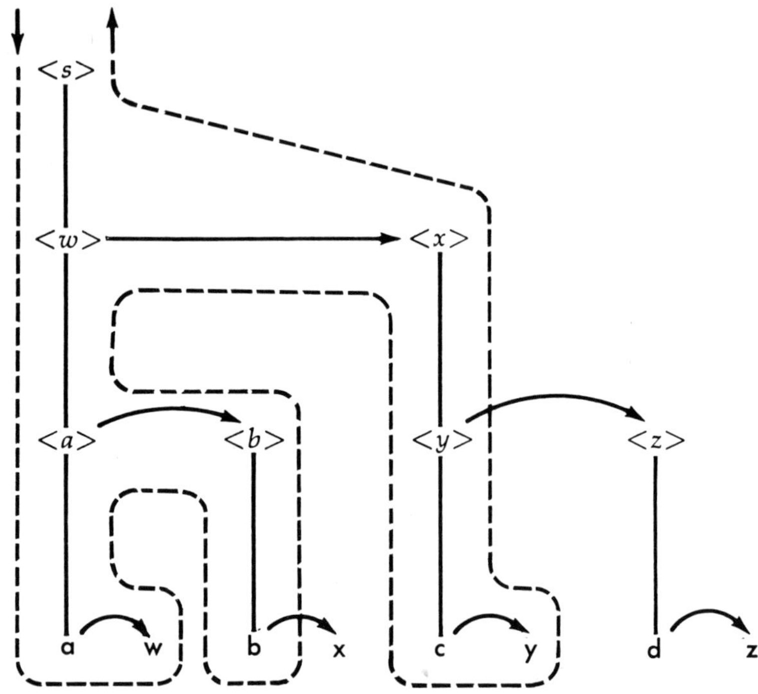

FIGURE 3.3 A walk through a successor/alternate tree.

as a map where the branches of the tree are walls to be followed and in which gates on alternate branches open only when a match has been found.

The formal algorithm for implementation of the Cheatham/Sattley analyzer is shown in Figure 3.4 (pp. 94, 95). This flowchart assumes the existence of three data structures over which it operates:

1. The string which is being investigated, which is stored in such a manner that each character may be referenced separately;

2. a set of pointers—a pointer to the string of characters (CHAR), a line pointer for the type table (TP), and a line pointer for the structure table (SP); and

3. LIFO stack, each element of which is composed of three parts corresponding to the pointer set elements.

Initially, the three components of the top stack element are set to indicate the first character in the string and the line in the type table corresponding to the root symbol. The structure table component is set to zero (0) indicating that no structure is being investigated currently. Assuming that the root symbol is described in the first line (line i) of the type table, then the structure of the root symbol is indicated by the structure table pointer in that line. Hence we may initialize the structure table pointer by use of this type table entry. In the structure table each line contains a pointer to the type table indicating the type of the leftmost component in that structure. This entry is the one which is set into the type table pointer. Finally, the character pointer is set to indicate the first character of the string.

The algorithm which follows this initialization process corresponds to the tree-walking discussed previously. The stack is used to store the sequence of suppressed goals, a goal being suppressed when it cannot be verified immediately—that is, when the goal is a nonterminal (component name). As portions of the string are recognized as being predicted from previous goals, they are removed from the stack. However, when a goal is only partially satisfied by a set of predictions, it may be "restacked." When total failure to correctly predict is recognized, the stack serves the purpose of supplying a set of alternatives to try as well as providing the pointer to the character immediately to the right of that last successfully predicted. Thus it will be noted that there is difference in the action taken in popping up the stack after either a successful predication or a failure in prediction. In the case of a successful prediction, only the table pointers are updated, indicating that the last character matched is an element of the goal which has been popped off the stack. However, after a mismatch, the old goal and the old character must be reexamined and thus all three pointers are reset. The test at point γ in the flow chart shown in Figure 3.4 is necessary for the successful recognition of left recursive specifications and will be discussed later.

As an example of the ability of this analyzer, let us consider the tables developed in the last section for the simple grammar

<*s*> ::= <*x*><*y*>
<*x*> ::= **a**|**b**
<*y*> ::= **c**|**d**

and the string **bc**⊢. The analysis of this string is shown, step by step, in Table 3.1 (p. 96).

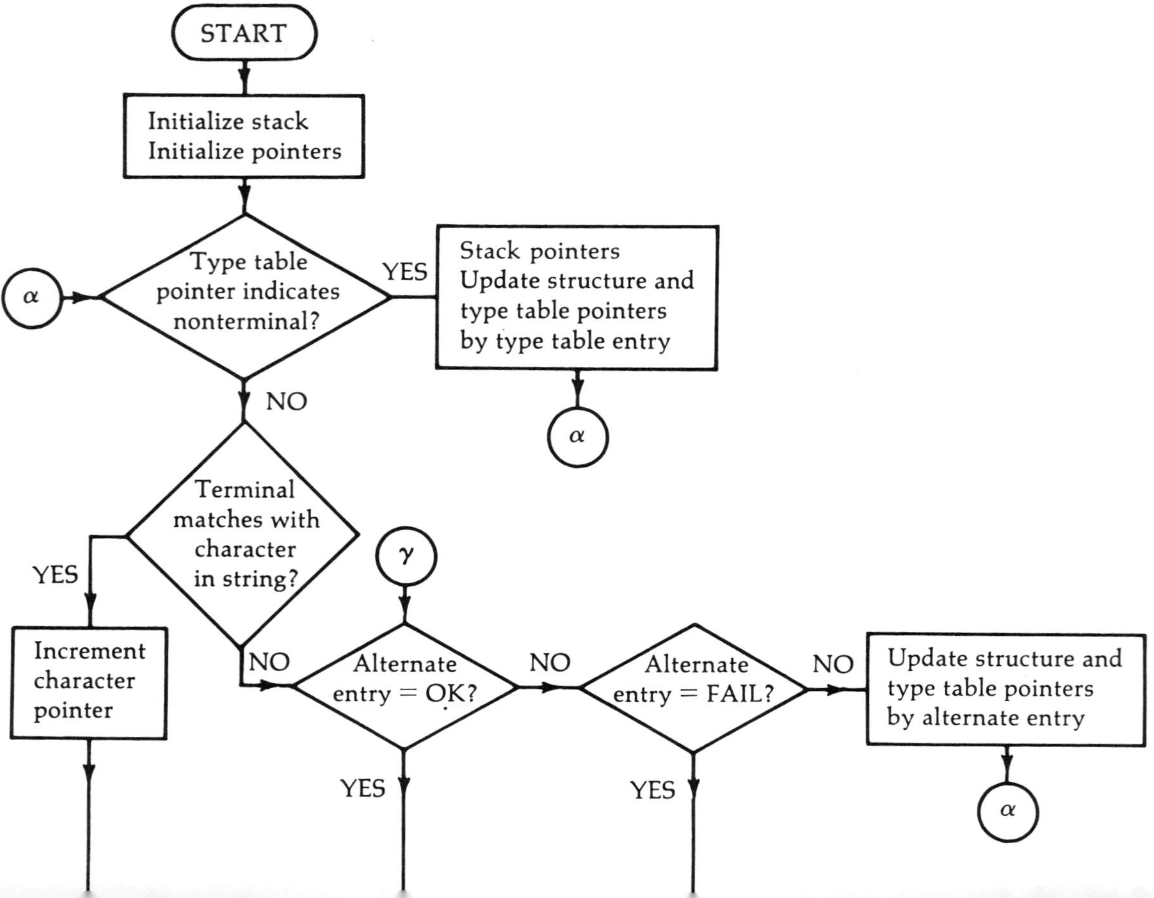
START
Initialize stack
Initialize pointers
α
Type table
pointer indicates
nonterminal?
YES
Stack pointers
Update structure and
type table pointers
by type table entry
α
NO
Terminal
matches with
character
in string?
YES
Increment
character
pointer
γ
NO
Alternate
entry = OK?
YES
NO
Alternate
entry = FAIL?
YES
NO
Update structure and
type table pointers
by alternate entry
α

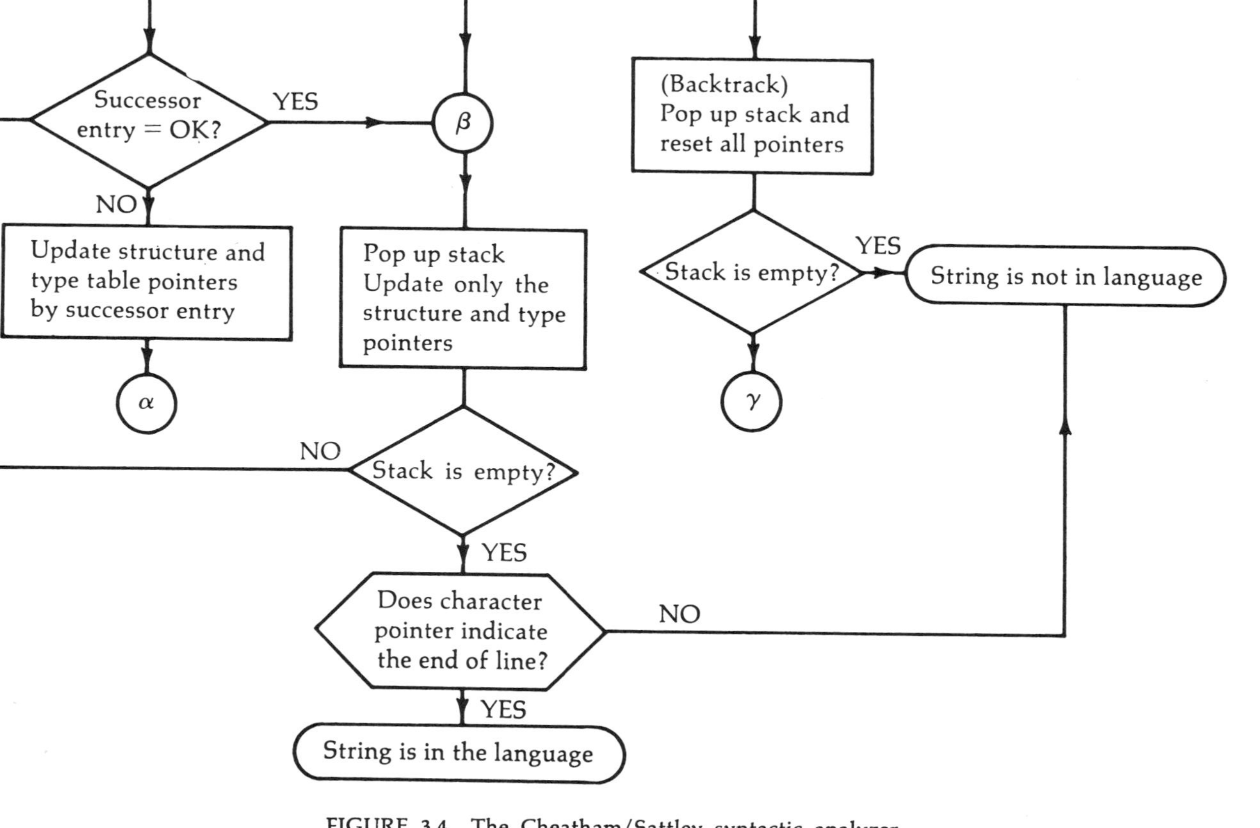

FIGURE 3.4 The Cheatham/Sattley syntactic analyzer.

TABLE 3.1

ACTION		*STACK*	*CHAR*	*TP*	*SP*
Initialize		*<1,i,0>*	1	ii	1
(α)nonterminal?	YES				
Stack and update TP/SP		*<1,ii,1>* *<1,i,0>*	1	iv	3
(α)nonterminal?	NO				
CHAR = **a**?	NO				
(γ)Alternate = OK?	NO				
Alternate = FAIL?	NO				
Reset TP and SP by alternate			1	v	4
(α)nonterminal?	NO				
CHAR = **b**?	YES				
Increment CHAR			2	v	4
Successor = OK?	YES				
(β)Pop up stack, reset SP and TP		*<1,i,0>*	2	ii	1
Stack is empty?	NO				
Successor = OK?	NO				
Reset SP and TP by successor			2	iii	2
(α)nonterminal?	YES				
Stack and update TP and SP		*<2,iii,2>* *<1,i,0>*	2	vi	5
(α)nonterminal?	NO				
CHAR = **c**?	YES				
Increment CHAR			3	vi	5
Successor = OK?	YES				
(β)Pop up stack and reset SP and TP		*<1,i,0>*	3	iii	2
Stack is empty?	NO				
Successor = OK?	YES				
(β)Pop up stack and reset SP and TP		(empty)	3	i	0
Stack is empty?	YES				
CHAR = ⊢?	YES				
STRING IS IN THE LANGUAGE.					

The Greek characters circled under the heading ACTION indicate the connection node in the flow chart (Figure 3.4) which was passed through to reach this action point. In the column headed ACTION, the name CHAR is to be taken to mean "The character in the string in question pointed to by the pointer CHAR."

This analysis is characterized by the walk through the successor/alternate tree shown below.

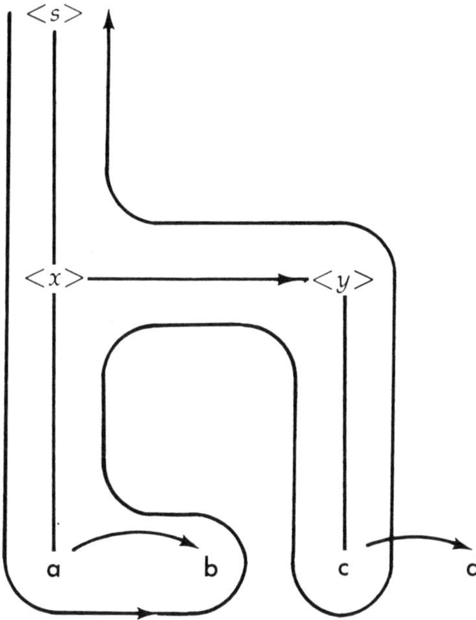

The problem of analyzing languages whose syntax contains productions which contain recursive references to the component being defined, is that it is possible to get into a predictive loop. In particular, if the recursive component is the leftmost component in the alternative, then the algorithm will enter an endless loop by repeatedly predicting that component. For example, consider the simple language which consists of all strings of the character **a**:

$$<s> ::= <s>\mathsf{a} | \mathsf{a}$$

which has the successor/alternate tree

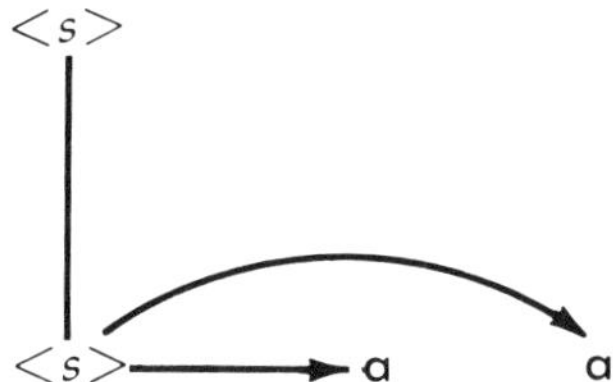

In the process of attempting to determine whether (say) the string **aaa** is contained in the language described by this syntax, the algorithm described above will never get to the point of generating a character and thus at no time will it be possible to match a character predicted with a character in the string. Hence, at least in the case of a recursive definition in which the recursive element is the leftmost in the alternative, special steps must be taken to remedy this potential flaw in the algorithm.

Primarily, it must be recognized that every meaningful recursive production must contain at least two alternatives—the alternative containing the recursive element and an alternative which is nonrecursive. Without the second alternative, there is no way in which a language can be generated which is composed only of characters, or, from the point of view of generating a string, there is no starting point in the definition on which other instances of the component can be based. For example, the production

$$<s> ::= <s>\mathsf{a}|\mathsf{a}$$

may be interpreted as:

> Given an instance of the component $<s>$, another instance may be formed by appending the character **a**. An instance of the component $<s>$ is the character **a**.

Without the clause which specifically describes (at least) one instance of the recursive component, the production (and hence the syntax) is incomplete. Let us assume that every left recursive production may be reduced by renaming and possible rearragnement of the alternatives to the form

$$<\substack{\textit{recursive}\\\textit{component}}> ::= <\textit{starter}>|<\substack{\textit{recursive}\\\textit{component}}><\textit{expander}>$$

Although the recursive component will occur in sentential forms of the language, it can be determined that the general form of string which will be generated by the above style of production is

$$<\textit{starter}><\textit{expander}><\textit{expander}> \cdots <\textit{expander}>$$

The successor/alternate tree for the generalized left recursive production shown above can be best visualized by considering the equivalent production which utilizes a repetitive group, that is

$$<\substack{\textit{recursive}\\\textit{component}}> ::= <\textit{starter}>\{<\textit{expander}>\}_0^\infty$$

In this case the successor/alternate tree might be represented by the following tree.

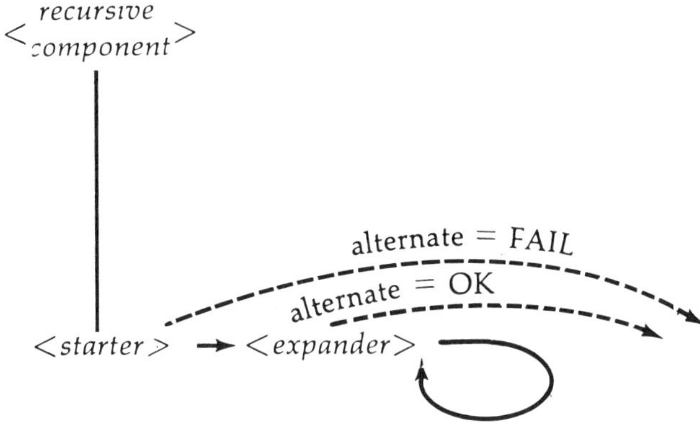

Using this knowledge we may establish a format for the entries in the structure table corresponding to left recursive productions.

In this description we wish to take into account the implied property of a recursive definition which states that a successor is known (that is, a definite line number can be entered under the heading "successor") but it will not necessarily be an error if this successor is not found, and whilst there is no definite alternative, a mismatch does not constitute a failure. Thus in the line of the structure table which corresponds to <*starter*> we shall define a successor (by line number) and indicate that there is no alternative to a starter (that is, the entry shall be FAIL). In the case of an <*expander*> line in the structure table, the successor will be this line itself and the alternate will be OK. Reference to the flow chart in Figure 3.4 will indicate that after a mismatch the alternate entry is checked and if found to be OK the side of the chart corresponding to successful matching is followed. However, in this case the character pointer is not incremented. In summary, the steps for establishing the structure table line entries for the starter and expander of a left recursive production are:

1. Assign a line in the structure table for <*starter*>.

2. Corresponding to the component on the left hand side of the production, set the structure table link in the type table to the line number of <*starter*>.

3. Set the "ending" to YES and the "successor" to the line number in the structure table of <*expander*>. Set the "alternate" to FAIL.

4. In the line corresponding to <*expander*> set the "ending" to YES, the "successor" to itself (that is, this line number) and the "alternate" to OK.

On the basis of this algorithm for the establishment of the entries in the structure table corresponding to left recursive productions, let us now consider the simple grammar:

<*s*> ::= <*x*><*y*>
<*x*> ::= a|<*x*>b
<*y*> ::= c|<*y*>d

From this grammar the tables are set up as follows:

Type Table

Index	*Name or character*	*Terminal?*	*Pointer to structure table*
i	<*s*>	NO	5
ii	<*x*>	NO	1
iii	<*y*>	NO	3
iv	a	YES	–
v	b	YES	–
vi	c	YES	–
vii	d	YES	–

Structure Table

Index	*Type*	*Ending?*	*Successor*	*Alternate*	(*Element*)
1	iv	YES	2	FAIL	a
2	v	YES	2	OK	b
3	vi	YES	4	FAIL	c
4	vii	YES	4	OK	d
5	ii	NO	6	FAIL	<*x*>
6	iii	YES	OK	FAIL	<*y*>

Based on these tables, let us now consider the step-by-step analysis of the string acd⊢ (see pp. 101, 102).

In general, recursive productions are potential problem generators in a predictive style analyzer only when the recursion involves the leftmost element in any production. In other cases, provided the starter is the first "type" specified in the structure table line corresponding to the recursive element and the alternative is the expander (whose successor is the recursive element), no special precautions need to be taken. In the case of an embedded recursive definition, that is of the type

<*r*> ::= <*starter*>|<*expander*$_1$><*r*><*expander*$_2$>

ACTION		*STACK*	*CHAR*	*TP*	*SP*
Initialize		*<1,i,0>*	1	ii	5
α nonterminal?	YES				
Stack and update TP/SP		*<1,ii,5>* *<1,i,0>*	1	iv	1
(α) nonterminal?	NO				
CHAR = **a**?	YES				
increment CHAR			2	iv	1
successor = OK?	NO				
reset SP and TP by successor			2	v	2
(α) nonterminal?	NO				
CHAR = **b**?	NO				
(γ) alternate = OK?	YES				
(β) pop up stack, reset SP and TP		*<1,i,0>*	2	ii	5
stack is empty?	NO				
successor = OK?	NO				
reset SP and TP by successor			2	iii	6
(α) nonterminal?	YES				
Stack and update SP and TP		*<2,iii,6>* *<1,i,0>*	2	vi	3
(α) nonterminal?	NO				
CHAR = **c**?	YES				
increment CHAR			3	vi	3
successor = OK?	NO				
reset SP and TP by successor			3	vii	4
(α) nonterminal?	NO				
CHAR = **d**?	YES				
increment CHAR			4	vii	4
successor = OK?	NO				
reset SP and TP by successor			4	vii	4
(note that since this is the line which corresponds to the recursive expander component there is actually no change in either SP or TP)					

ACTION		*STACK*	*CHAR*	*TP*	*SP*
(α) nonterminal?	NO				
CHAR = **d**?	NO				
(γ) alternate = OK?	YES				
(β) pop up stack, reset SP and TP		<*1,i,0*>	4	iii	·6
stack is empty?	NO				
successor = OK?	YES				
(β) pop up, reset SP and TP		(empty)	4	i	0
stack is empty?	YES				
CHAR = ⊢?	YES				
STRING IS IN THE LANGUAGE					

such as in the syntax which produces strings composed of equal numbers of characters **a** and **b**:

<*s*> ::= **ab**|**a**<*s*>**b**

it may be seen that the successor to <*r*> is to be the second expander and thus the structure table entry corresponding to the recursive element will carry a successor entry appropriately.

Whilst left recursive productions are (comparatively) easy to recognize, a sequence of productions which produces a cyclic definition is harder to recognize, but must be handled in the same manner as a recursive production. For example, the grammar

<*s*> ::= <*x*><*y*>
<*x*> ::= **a**|<*s*>**b**
<*y*> ::= **c**|<*s*>**d**

contains no recursive productions, but the combinations of productions develop a cyclical definition which is equivalent to recursive definition. In this case, the grammar must be rearranged so as to be in the form of a recursive definition; that is, in the above example:

<*s*> ::= <*starter*>|<*s*><*expander*>
<*starter*> ::= **a**<*y*>
<*expander*> ::= **b**<*y*>
<*y*> ::= **c**|<*s*>**d**

The last production (relative to the definition of <*y*>) is not included in this rearrangement since, although it produces a cyclic definition of the syntax, it does not produce a *left* recursive production on rearrangement. With these rearrangements, the organization of the tables for use by the Cheatham/Sattley algorithm is as described previously.

Problems

3.1
The Cheatham/Sattley algorithm reports that the string

$$\sigma\pi\pi\rho$$

is not in the language described by the syntax

$$\begin{aligned} <s> &::= <x><y> \\ <y> &::= \pi\rho \\ <x> &::= \sigma | <z> \\ <z> &::= \sigma\pi \end{aligned}$$

What is wrong and how can it be corrected?

3.2
Given the grammar

$$\begin{aligned} <s> &::= <x><y> \\ <x> &::= \mathsf{a} | <x>\mathsf{b} \\ <y> &::= \mathsf{b} | <y>\mathsf{c} \end{aligned}$$

set up the tables for the Cheatham/Sattley algorithm and attempt to determine if the string abc is in the language.

3.3
Given an ambiguous grammar such as

$$\begin{aligned} <s> &::= <x><y> \\ <x> &::= \sigma | <x>\pi \\ <y> &::= \rho | \pi<y> \end{aligned}$$

what happens when an attempt is made to recognize the string

$$\sigma\pi\pi\pi\rho$$

using the Cheatham/Sattley algorithm?

REDUCTIVE ANALYSIS

To provide a comparison of techniques for the syntactic analysis of computer-readable texts, let us now consider an example of a bottom-up, or reductive, analyzer. In this case we use the set of productions which compose the syntax of a language as a set of reduction definitions and attempt to match the right-hand sides into the string in question so as to determine some reduction that can be performed on the string so as to produce some reduced sentential form. Successive application of such reductive processes should eventually lead to a sentential form which is composed only of the root symbol. Using the analogy of the Cheatham game of dominoes, it may be seen that if the dominoes consist of a production, then it just as easy to play the game by starting at the bottom of the string and working up the playing area, as it is to play by a top-down (predictive) strategy.

The major problem in performing a bottom-up analysis is that every alternative of each right-hand side of the productions which compose the syntax is in the set of candidates for matching onto the string in question. While many of these alternatives clearly can be rejected in the game environment since they do not (say) contain any characters when the string is composed entirely of characters, the same procedure in a mechanical process is not as easy to implement. On this basis, the amount of pattern matching required even to determine on match can be excessive and that to develop the parse of one string may be very time consuming.

A particular algorithm developed by B. Domelki was first published in *USSR Computational Mathematics and Mathematical Physics* in 1965,[5] but was restricted to nonbacktracking grammars. This procedure was refined and amended to include backtracking by P. H. Frost. This latter work went unpublished and is referenced in a set of unpublished lecture notes by P. Wegner. The advantage of the method is that by the use of a logical matrix, the pattern matching of all alternatives in each of the productions which compose the syntax can be accomplished in a single operation. That is, the pattern matching can be achieved in parallel processing mode. Further, since almost all the operations of analysis involve only logical bit operations, the speed of analysis is comparatively fast. Gerhart[6] estimated that a machine with a memory of 48K bytes could "handle" a syntax consisting of a vocabulary of 300 elements and 250 elements in the alternatives of the productions, provided that there were no more than 200 characters in any string to be analyzed. This seems to be sufficient for most "moderate size" computer languages.

5. R. C. Glass, ed. and trans., "Algorithms for the Recognition of Properties of Sequence of Symbols," in *USSR Computational Mathematics and Mathematical Physics*, vol. 5, no. 1 (Oxford: Pergamon Press, 1967) pp. 101–130.

6. S. Gerhart, *The Domelki Syntactic Analysis Algorithm*, Publ. No. TN/CS/0003, Computer Science Program (Amherst: University of Massachusetts, Aug. 1968).

The Domelki algorithm utilizes a vector corresponding to each element (component or character) of the vocabulary of the language, which contains a bit string corresponding to every alternative in each production in the syntax. Looking upon the syntax as a *reductive* grammar, it may be seen that each sentential form may be matched with the component to which it reduces in a one-to-one relationship. Thus, writing out all the possible alternatives from the productions in the equivalent generative grammar, we obtain a set of reductions each of which contains *no* alternatives and more than one reduction may contain the same component as the reduction component. Thus each bit string in the vector corresponding to each element of the language corresponds to one of the reduction rules. If bit string i of vector v corresponds to reduction rule i, then a 1 (one) in the j-th bit position of the string indicates that the element related to vector v occurs as the j-th element of the reduction rule i. Since each bit string corresponds to a reduction rule then the length of the bit string is equal to the number of elements in the reduction rule, say n_i. Hence the total length of the vector is equal to the sum of the lengths of the bit strings. The composition of these vectors into a logical matrix will be referenced by the name M and the vector corresponding to element **t** of the language will be signified by M(**t**).

Together with the matrix M, several other vectors are required which contain the information relative to the reduction rules:

1. A vector U of the same length as the vectors in M contains a 1 (one) in the first bit of each bit string which corresponds to each reduction rule. Thus vector U marks the leftmost element in each rule.

2. A vector V of the same length as vector U contains a 1 (one) in the last bit position of each bit string, thus marking the rightmost element in each reduction rule.

3. A vector R contains the component to which each rule reduces if the elements of the rule match onto the sentential form being analyzed. The length of vector R is equal to the number of reduction rules.[7]

4. A vector L of the same length as vector R which contains the length of this reduction rule, and hence the number of elements which are replaced by the component when a reduction takes place.

On the basis of these directions for composing the matrix M and the "dope" vectors U,V,R and L, let us now consider the simple language

7. As will be shown later, we shall omit reduction rules which contain only one element from this count.

defined by the *generative* grammar

$$<s> ::= \text{abc}$$

The number of vectors (rows) in matrix M for the equivalent reductive grammar

$$\text{abc} \longrightarrow <s>$$

is 4 since the number of elements in the vocabulary of the language is 4; that is, $\{<s>, \text{a,b,c}\}$ contains 4 elements. Following the directions above, the following matrix and vectors are developed:

		a	b	c ⟵ (the reduction "pattern")
M	$<s>$	0	0	0
	a	1	0	0
	b	0	1	0
	c	0	0	1
	U	1	0	0
	V	0	0	1
	R			$<s>$
	L			3

The "core" of the analysis algorithm uses these vectors, matrix M, a working vector Q of the same length as U and V, a linked list S and a stack T which contains the string to be analyzed. The string is effectively accessible one character at a time from left to right.

The working vector Q is to be a status word in which the presence of a one-bit indicates that there exists a reduction which matches (at least partially) onto the string in question. By using the vector U we may inject into Q a one-bit in the position of the leftmost character in the reduction string. If the first character in T is also the first element of the reduction string, then Q & $M(\text{t})$ will be nonzero. Let us take the result of this logical operation to be the new value of Q. If we shift Q right by one bit position, then any bit remaining in Q will appear in the position to the right of where it was generated. The *and* of this value of Q with the next character in T will indicate whether the new character is matched in the reduction if the one-bit is not wiped out. This repeated shift and logical *and* with $M(\text{t})$ will move a one-bit across the Q vector so long as the characters in T match with the string in the reduction rule. If Q becomes all zeros, then a match has failed and the reduction cannot be applied.

The instant at which a reduction can be applied is determined by the V vector. Since the original one-bit was injected from the U vector, the successful transposition of that one-bit to the right hand end of the reduction rule indicates that a sequence of successful matches was made. Hence a reduction may be performed when $Q \& V$ is nonzero.

Working with the stack T and the linked list S, let us now follow the analysis (p. 108) of the string ⊣**abc**⊢ according to the grammar given opposite.

In this simple example, the possibility that a character in the unscanned string is an element of some rule is never in question and this technique will be satisfactory only in the case where the leftmost character is a component of a string which is reducible. Consider the case of a language which is defined in such a manner that the leftmost *reducible substring* which takes part in the first reduction does not encompass the first (leftmost) character. In this case the initialization of Q to the vector U sets a 1 into Q only at the point corresponding to the first character. If this character is not an element of a reduction rule then the one bit will be eliminated from Q. To simulate the condition that each character may be the leftmost character in some reduction rule, we shall inject U into Q as each character is scanned. By this means, the "anding" of Q with M(**t**) will retain only those one bits which are potential components of some reduction. For example consider the grammar[8]

$$<s> ::= \mathbf{a}<t>$$
$$<t> ::= \mathbf{b}<r>$$
$$<r> ::= \mathbf{c}$$

Initially considering only the productions (and hence the reductions) of length 2 (or greater), the matrix M has the value:

	a	$<t>$	**b**	$<r>$	
$<s>$	0	0	0	0	
$<t>$	0	1	0	0	
$<r>$	0	0	0	1	
a	1	0	0	0	
b	0	0	1	0	
c	0	0	0	0	⟵ changed to one eventually

Now obviously, this matrix does represent the total syntactic specifications since the reduction rule $\mathbf{c} \rightarrow <r>$ has not been included.

8. This grammar is termed right linear since the right hand sides contain no more than one component which is always at the right hand end of the rule. The problem discussed here is always encountered in attempting to analyze right linear grammars. On the other hand, left linear grammars can be used in the analysis without this special feature.

Step number	List S	t	String T	Q	M(t)	New Q = Q & M(t)	New Q & V	Next action
1	$\dashv$	(null)	**abc**$\vdash$					set $Q = U$
2	$\dashv$	(null)	**abc**$\vdash$	100				scan string
3	$\dashv$**a**	**a**	**bc**$\vdash$	100	100	100	000	scan string, shift new Q right[a]
4	$\dashv$**ab**	**b**	**c**$\vdash$	010	010	010	000	shift new Q right, scan
5	$\dashv$**abc**	**c**	$\vdash$	001	001	001	001	Q & $V \neq 0$, reduce[b]
6	$\dashv$**abc**$\langle s \rangle$[d]		$\vdash$					restart with reduced string
7	$\dashv$	(null)	$\langle s \rangle \vdash$					set $Q = U$
8	$\dashv$	(null)	$\langle s \rangle \vdash$	100				scan string
9	$\dashv \langle s \rangle$	$\langle s \rangle$	$\vdash$	100	000	000		terminate[c]

[a]There are two indicators that some action other than simply shifting new Q right and continuing to scan. These are that new $Q = 0$ and new Q & $V \neq 0$. In this case neither indicator is set.

[b]In this case new $Q \neq 0$ but new Q & $V \neq 0$. This indicates that all the conditions for matching some portion of the string against a reduction rule have been satisfied. By determining which bit in new Q & V is non zero, vector R may be referenced to determine the symbol to which the string is to be reduced. Similarly, reference to string L will indicate how much of the string is to be replaced by the symbol. In this case the chosen substring length from L is 3 and hence the reduced string is $\langle s \rangle$.

[c]At this line, the new Q has become zero, indicating that there exists no reduction which is being satisfied. However, in this case, the string is composed totally of the root symbol, identified by the fact that $M(t) = 0$ and the unscanned string consists only of the "right ender." Hence no further reductions are possible and the string is in the language.

[d]The arrow in this string indicates the "logically preceding" character in the string after reduction.

Analysis of the string **abc**, according to the grammar on page 106.

However, it is obvious that there is a one-for-one reduction possible here and thus we may include this reduction rule in M by merely placing a 1 (one) in row M(**c**) under the heading of <*r*>. This is equivalent to a modification of the grammar so that the reduction **bc** → <*t*> replaces the rule **b** <*r*> → <*t*>. The vectors U,V,R, and L corresponding to M above are

U	1	0	1	0
V	0	1	0	1
R		<*s*>		<*t*>
L		2		2

Using these values for M,U,V,R and L, the analysis of the string **abc** proceeds as shown on p. 110.

None of the grammars so far considered define a language in which at least one string can be recognized only after backtracking. In this method of analysis, where all reduction rules are matched against the string in question, several paths though the reducing tree are tested simultaneously. Two conditions can arise which may eventually require backtracking when some later matching process fails. First, it is possible that two reductions are applicable simultaneously since two one-bits in new Q "and" with corresponding one bits in vector V to produce a nonzero result. In this case, we may arbitrarily reduce by either of the elements in R which correspond to the nonzero bits in new Q & V. Since this may be the wrong choice, it may be necessary to back up to this point of reduction again and to reduce to the other symbol in R. To allow for this eventuality—we must leave a trail in the string S in order to perform the second reduction. Thus, if we store in S, along with every element either its generated new Q (to allow for reductions) or, in the case of a symbol placed in S by a reduction process, the generated new Q with the bit which initiated the reduction removed. In the latter case, any remaining bits will trigger subsequent reduction after backtracking.

The second case to consider is that of premature reduction. In this case, some substring of length (say) n may be reduced to some symbol in R, since new Q & $V \neq 0$. However, there may exist another one bit in Q which often function scanning moves into a location which produces a nonzero new Q and V. In this case, we need to backtrack to the point of premature reduction and, to find an alternative reduction, continuing the scanning process. The same contents of the trail as activated above will suffice for this case also.

Let us consider an example of the first case by analyzing the string

Step number	List S	t	String T	Q	Q ∨ U	M(t)	New Q = (Q ∨ U) & M(t)	New Q & V	Next action
1	⊣	(null)	abc⊢						set $Q = 0$
2	⊣	(null)	abc⊢	0000					scan string
3	⊣a	a	bc⊢	0000	1010	1000	1000[a]	0000	shift Q right, scan
4	⊣ab	b	c⊢	0100	1110	0010	0010[b]	0000	shift Q right, scan
5	⊣abc	c	⊢	0001	1011	0001	0001	0001	reduce
6	⊣abc<t>								restart with reduced string
7	⊣	(null)	a<t>⊢						set $Q = 0$
8	⊣	(null)	a<t>⊢	0000					scan string
9	⊣a	a	<t>⊢	0000	1010	1000	1000	0000[c]	shift Q right, scan
10	⊣a<t>	<t>	⊢	0100	1110	0100	0100	0100	reduce
11	⊣a<t> <s>								restart with reduced string
12	⊣	(null)	<s>⊢						set $Q = 0$
13	⊣	(null)	<s>⊢	0000[d]					scan string
14	⊣<s>	<s>	⊢	0000	1010	0000	0000		terminate

[a] At this point, the one bit indicates that the current character (a) is a potential element of some reduction. However, at line 4 this one bit is deleted showing a lack of total matching.

[b] In this case the one bit in the new value of Q indicates that b is matchable onto at least one reduction.

[c] After a restart such as just performed, it is obvious that some of the values generated previously must be regenerated. In fact line 9 is identical to line 3 indicating that the algorithm could be shortened by restarting at the line which corresponds to the "logical predecessor" rather than returning to the left hand end of the string again.

[d] As in the previous restart, line 13 has an identical predecessor—line 2.

⊣**abd**⊢ under the syntax

<*s*> ::= <*r*>**c**|<*t*>**d**
<*r*> ::= **ab**
<*t*> ::= **ab**

The corresponding reduction rules are:

<*r*>**c** → <*s*>
<*t*>**d** → <*s*>
ab → <*r*>
ab → <*t*>

The corresponding *M, U, V, R* and values are:

	<*r*>	**c**	<*t*>	**d**	**a**	**b**	**a**	**b**
<*s*>	0	0	0	0	0	0	0	0
<*t*>	0	0	1	0	0	0	0	0
<*r*>	1	0	0	0	0	0	0	0
a	0	0	0	0	1	0	1	0
b	0	0	0	0	0	1	0	1
c	0	1	0	0	0	0	0	0
d	0	0	0	1	0	0	0	0
U	1	0	1	0	1	0	1	0
V	0	1	0	1	0	1	0	1
R	<*s*>		<*s*>		<*r*>		<*t*>	
L	2		2		2		2	

All the examples which we have considered to this point in relation to analysis by the Domelki algorithm have involved reductions such that the logically preceding symbol was always the left-end symbol or the scanning was restarted with the left-end symbol. As an example of reductions which do not involve the left-end symbol as the logically preceding symbol and to show the power of this algorithm over the predictive techniques, let us consider the language

$$\{\sigma\pi\rho,\ \sigma\pi\pi\rho\}$$

defined by the syntax

<*s*> ::= <*x*><*y*>
<*y*> ::= $\pi\rho$
<*x*> ::= σ|<*z*>
<*z*> ::= $\sigma\pi$

from which may be generated the matrix and vectors shown on p. 113.

Step number	List S	t	String T	Q	Q ∨ U	M(t)	New Q = (Q ∨ U) & M(t)	New Q & V	Next action
1	⊣	(null)	**abd**⊢						Set Q = 0
2	⊣	(null)	**abd**⊢	00000000					Scan
3	⊣**a**	**a**	**bd**⊢	00000000	10101010	00001010	00001010	00000000	Scan, shift Q
4	⊣**ab**	**b**	**d**⊢	00000101	10101111	00000101	00000101	00000101	Reduce by left-most 1 bit
5	⊣**ab**<r>	<r>	**d**⊢				00000001		Reinstate ⊣
6	⊣**ab**<r>	<r>	**d**⊢	00000000					Scan
7	⊣**ab**<r>	<r>	**d**⊢	00000000	10101010	10000000	10000000	00000000	Scan, Shift Q
8	⊣**ab**<r>**d**	**d**	⊢	01000000	11101010	00010000	00000000		New Q = 0, backtrack to 5
9	⊣**ab**		**d**⊢				00000001	00000001	Reduce
10	⊣**ab**<t>		**d**⊢				00000000		Reinstate ⊣
11	⊣**ab**<t>		**d**⊢	00000000					Scan
12	⊣**ab**<t>	<t>	**d**⊢	00000000	10101010	00100000	00100000	00000000	Shift Q, scan
13	⊣**ab**<t>**d**	**d**	⊢	00010000	10111010	00010000	00010000	00010000	Reduce
14	⊣**ab**<t>**d**<s>		⊢				00000000		Terminate

Analysis of the string **abd**, according to the grammar on page 111.

	$<x>$	$<y>$	π	ρ	σ	π
$<s>$	0	0	0	0	0	0
$<x>$	1	0	0	0	0	0
$<y>$	0	1	0	0	0	0
$<z>$	1	0	0	0	0	0
σ	1	0	0	0	1	0
π	0	0	1	0	0	1
ρ	0	0	0	1	0	1
U	1	0	1	0	1	0
V	0	1	0	1	0	1
R	$<s>$		$<y>$		$<z>$	
L	2		2		2	

In these examples we have not considered the case of a string which is not in the language defined by the syntax provided. It may be noted that in the process of analyzing a string, the value of the vector Q contains bits which are propagated from the left hand end of each substring to the right hand end only so long as the elements which they represent match in both the string and the rules. When a reduction takes place (recognized by the fact that new $Q \mathbin{\&} V \neq 0$) the value of new Q stored in S with the last element scanned before reduction, is the value of new Q but with the leftmost bit which caused new $Q \mathbin{\&} V \neq 0$ removed. For example, the backtracking example on page 112, the value of new Q stored with character **b** at line 5 is 00000001, indicating that there still exists some reduction rule which has (at least partially) been matched with the string in question. On backtracking, this bit is used to either attempt some other reduction (if new $Q \mathbin{\&} V \neq 0$ even after the removal of the original one bit at line 5) or to continue the scan over more characters. In the case of string which is not in the language, either M(**t**) does not exist (since the character is not in the language) or, repeated backtracking will lead to a point at which there are no previous reductions to "undo" and thus no alternative paths to explore in attempting to generate the syntactic tree (or the parse) of the string in question.

The flow chart shown in Figure 3.5 (pp. 114, 115) is based on the organization of a linked list which has the following general format:

Element	Left logical link	Left physical link	New Q

In the elements of the link list, the left logical and left physical links are both set only in the case of a component which "covers" the ele-

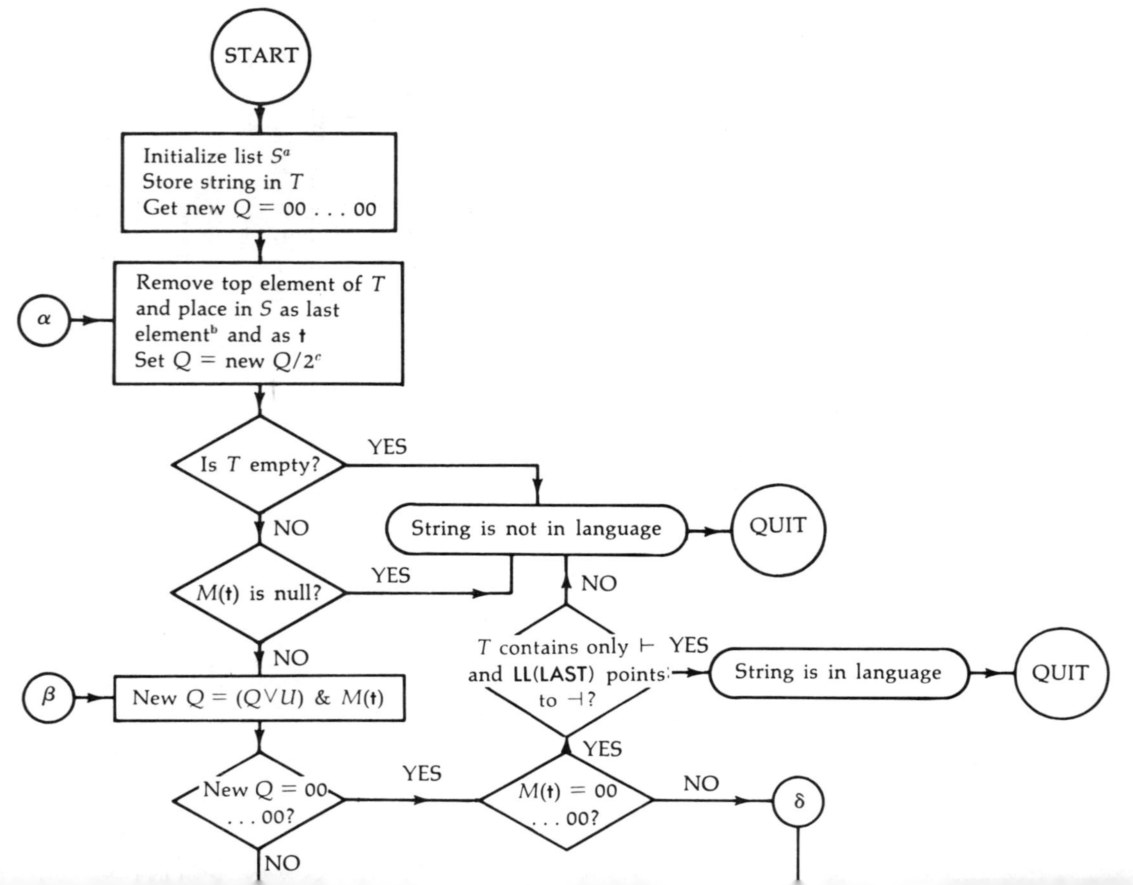
START
Initialize list S^a
Store string in T
Get new $Q = 00 \ldots 00$
α
Remove top element of T and place in S as last element^b and as †
Set Q = new $Q/2^c$
Is T empty?
YES
NO
String is not in language
QUIT
M(†) is null?
YES
NO
β
New $Q = (Q \vee U)$ & M(†)
New $Q = 00 \ldots 00$?
YES
NO
T contains only ⊢ and LL(LAST) points to ⊣?
YES
NO
String is in language
QUIT
M(†) = 00 ... 00?
YES
NO
δ

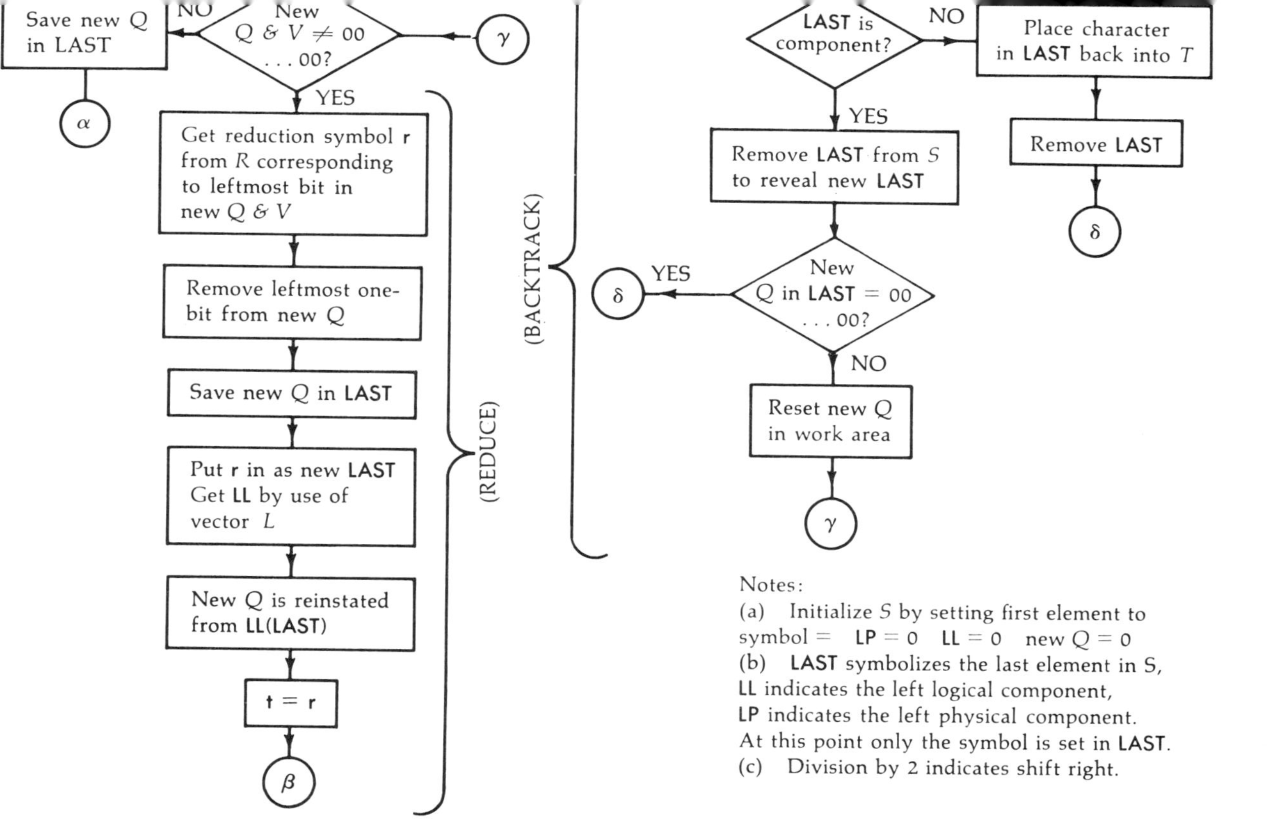

FIGURE 3.5 The Domelki reductive analyzer.

Step number	List S	t	String T	Q	$Q \vee U$	$M(t)$	New $Q =$ $(Q \vee U)$ $\& M(t)$	New $Q \& V$	Next action
1	$\dashv$	(null)	$\sigma\pi\pi\rho\vdash$						initialize $Q = 0$
2	$\dashv$	(null)	$\sigma\pi\pi\rho\vdash$	000000					shift Q and scan
3	$\dashv\sigma$	σ	$\pi\pi\rho\vdash$	000000	101010	100010	100010	000000	shift Q and scan
4	$\dashv\sigma\pi$	π	$\pi\rho\vdash$	010001	111011	001001	000001	000001	reduce
5	$\dashv\sigma\pi\langle z\rangle$	$\langle z\rangle$	$\pi\rho\vdash$				000000		reinstate, scan new char.
6	$\dashv\sigma\pi\langle z\rangle$	$\langle z\rangle$	$\pi\rho\vdash$	000000	101010	100000	100000	000000	shift Q and scan
7	$\dashv\sigma\pi\langle z\rangle\pi$	π	$\rho\vdash$	010000	111010	001001	001000	000000	shift Q and scan
8	$\dashv\sigma\pi\langle z\rangle\pi\rho$	σ	$\vdash$	000100	000100	000100	000100	000100	reduce
9	$\dashv\sigma\pi\langle z\rangle\pi\rho\langle y\rangle$	$\langle y\rangle$	$\vdash$				000000		reinstate $\langle z\rangle$, scan
10	$\dashv\sigma\pi\langle z\rangle\pi\rho\langle y\rangle$	$\langle y\rangle$	$\vdash$	010000	111010	010000	010000	010000	reduce
11	$\dashv\sigma\pi\langle z\rangle\pi\rho\langle y\rangle\ \langle s\rangle$	$\langle s\rangle$	$\vdash$				000000		reinstate $\dashv$, scan
12	$\dashv\sigma\pi\langle z\rangle\pi\rho\langle y\rangle\ \langle s\rangle$	$\langle s\rangle$	$\vdash$	000000	101010	000000	000000		terminate, OK.

The analysis of $\sigma\pi\pi\rho$, according to the grammar on page 113.

ments to its left. The left physical link is necessary in backtracking when the unscanned string must be reconstructed. For example, the final contents of the list S in the analysis of the string $\sigma\pi\pi\rho$ shown on page 116 will be represented in the form:

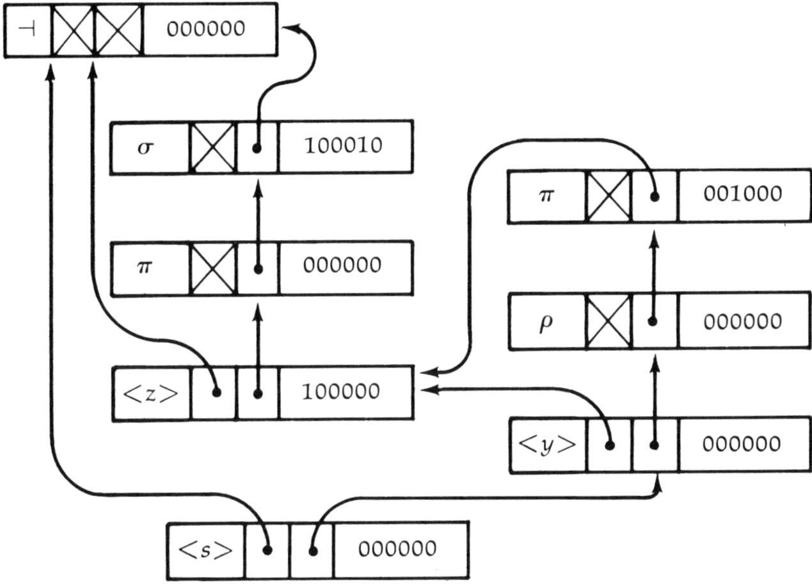

AD HOC ANALYZERS

The two methods of syntactic analysis which have been presented in this chapter typify the top-down and bottom-up techniques of analysis and, by themselves, are not unique in any way. Many other methods of analysis exist each having its own peculiar data set over which the analysis is performed. Some techniques are formally more precise while others take advantage of the idiosyncrasies of the language(s) to be analyzed. One particular class of analyzers has been omitted from this chapter. That is the class of analyzers which are designed to analyze languages which are themselves the generations of precedence grammars. Since precedence techniques of analysis are closely associated with the analysis of arithmetic expressions, the consideration of such techniques will be undertaken in the chapter dealing with the ASCAN section of a compiler.

It should not be inferred from the discussion here that "ad hoc" methods of textural analysis are not possible, or are not to be implemented in any "sophisticated" compiler. Rather, we have here emphasized the general technique applicable to most programming languages. It will be found however, that the specialized analyzer is far simpler to implement, and with some little thought can be more efficient, than the general analyzer. On the other hand, in a shop which is in the business of generating compilers (or interpreters), the generalized analyzer may be "taken off the shelf" and included in the compiler far more easily than a specialized analyzer can be built. Further the input to the generalized analyzer is the syntax of the language. To update such a syntax is obviously much simpler than patching the specialized analyzer.

The determination of statement type and the extraction of language components by parsing, using the guidelines of a syntax definition may be exhaustive and generally applicable, but it is inefficient compared to a specially designed analyzer. In a parse, the whole string of characters must be scanned regardless of the redundancy of this scanning. For example, a BASIC **READ** statement has the syntax definition:

$$<\text{READ statement}> := \textbf{READ} <\text{variable}>\{,<\text{variable}>\}_0^\infty$$

and to determine the validity and type of accretion, the whole string must be examined. However, due to the nature of all BASIC statements, the examination of only the first three characters will enable the type to be determined. The validity of the statement can then be checked as a by-product of the extraction of the variable names and during the subsequent compilation of the object code.

A close examination of the syntax of a language may reveal that each statement or class of statements has distinguishing marks that set it apart from all others. In other situations, the relationships of the marks within the string to each other determine the type of statement. In particular, the marks that are essential to a statement, such as a comma or parentheses, may be more reliable than variable components that are constructed from other marks and are not essential to the legal construction of a statement.

For example, consider the statements of basic FORTRAN. Although FORTRAN is generally taught as having two basic types of statement, that is, declaratives and executables, at compilation time the statements may better be classified as assignment and others. It would seem at first glance that the fundamental difference between these types of statements would be the presence of an = sign in assignment statements and the absence of that mark in other statements. However, an = sign is a standard occurrence in a **DO** statement, an indexed I/O statement, and a FORMAT declaration, for example:

```
DO 31 I = J, K, L
READ 100, A, B, (C(I), I = 1, 15, 2)
FORMAT(3HA= , I5)
```

Thus the = sign is not a unique characteristic of the assignment statement; but if an = sign is present, the set of possibilities for the identity of that statement has been reduced considerably. By observing the location of the = sign, one may see that in the cases of the READ statement and this particular FORMAT statement, the = sign is contained within a set of facing parentheses, whereas the = sign in both the assignment and DO statements is unparenthesized. While the = sign in an indexed I/O statement must have surrounding parentheses, this is not a *requirement* in a FORMAT statement. Consider the statement:

```
FORMAT(5HX) = (Y)
```

Another distinguishing mark in a DO statement, which may be present in assignment and FORMAT statements, is the comma. In the DO statement the comma is unsurrounded by parentheses, whereas in an arithmetic statement the comma can only occur within a subscript and is therefore always surrounded by parentheses. FORMAT has no such requirement.

Since FORMAT statements may contain unstructured character strings of any length (according to ANSI specifications), and the characteristic marks of the other statements could occur within the FORMAT statement, this statement must be removed from the list of possibilities at the outset of the sieve. This is achieved by using the only known characteristics of the FORMAT statement, that is, the characters F, O, R, M, A, T and (, as the first seven nonblank leading characters. Once this statement has been eliminated, the other statements that may contain an = sign can be distinguished from each other by the following decision table.

	Mark	
	=	,
Assignment statement	U	P[a]
DO statement	U	U
Indexed I/O statement	P	P

[a] if present
P = parenthesized
U = unparenthesized

TABLE 3.2 FORTRAN Keywords

ACcept	EQuivalence	PAuse	ReaL **FUNCTION**[a]
ACcept Tape	EXternal	PRint	STop
ASsign	Function	PRogram	SUbroutine
CAll	Go to	PUnch	Type **INTEGER**[a]
COMmon	Go to (	PUnch Tape	Type **REAL**[a]
CONtinue	IF	ReaD	Type
Dimension	INteger	ReaD Tape	Write
ENd	INteger **FUNCTION**[a]	ReaL	Write Tape

[a]These keywords require the total identification of the second word since the same keyword with one component can have a variable name in this position.

The other Basic FORTRAN statements may be recognized if their keywords, which must always occur in the leading position in the statement, are examined. The list given in Table 3.2 shows the characteristics within the keyword of each statement; the significant characters are upper case, while those that do not materially assist the sieve are lower case. Although the syntax of FORTRAN insists that the keywords must be present as defined, a sieve that only checks the significant characters and discards the other characters in the keyword can speed the process. In such a situation invalid keywords can be used without disturbing the compilation. In fact, knowledgeable programmers can concoct their own brand of FORTRAN keywords. For example, one programmer consistently used **DAMNITALL** as the keyword for **DIMENSION**.

In full FORTRAN, where many additional statements are present, a major difficulty arises from the inclusion of Hollerith constants in several statements. Thus the characteristic marks of an arithmetic statement, a **DO** statement and an indexed **I/O** are no longer unique. For example, the following two statements are, respectively, a legal **DO** statement and a valid arithmetic (replacement) statement:

```
DO1I = 1, 31, 2
DO1I = 5H,3,10
```

Similarly, the following are a legal **IF** statement and a valid arithmetic statement:

```
IF(I − 3H) = ( )1,31,2
IF(I − 3)  = 5H1,3,2
```

Thus if a statement contains the requisite marks, the keyword should also be examined to distinguish between possible statement types.

However, the presence of the requisite characters does not determine the type, but merely raises the possibility. If an arithmetic statement containing a Hollerith constant is restricted to be a simple replacement statement, as is recommended, then the DO statement may be distinguished by the following pointers:

1. Since no constant (and in particular a Hollerith constant containing an = sign) may occur to the left of a replacement sign as in an arithmetic statement or as in the index of a DO statement, then the first = sign must be either the replacement sign in an arithmetic statement or the delimiter between the index variable and the initial parameter in a DO statement.

2. When the first = sign has been located in a left to right scan, the first variable, function or constant in an arithmetic statement will be delimited by a parenthesis, an arithmetic operator or the end of the statement, whereas the first delimited in a DO statement must be a comma.

An = sign occurring in an IF statement is not mandatory, and thus no rule can determine the first distinguishing mark after the = sign. Thus, if one assumes that a particular statement is an IF statement (after checking the leading two characters) and this turns out to be a false assumption, an attempt can be made to compile the statement as an arithmetic statement. If this fails, the statement is not valid.

STRUCTURE WITHIN SYNTAX

Having discussed (in the previous chapter) the generation of text according to a set of rules (known as the grammar or syntax of the language) and the analysis of strings according to the same set of rules, we must hesitate to ask for what purpose we have analyzed a string and identified its elements with the components of the syntax. This association of substrings with syntactic components is expected to be used by the compiler (interpreter) to aid in the generation of code by which the presented program can be executed. Thus the analysis of a string which results in the identification of certain substrings with the component *<variable>* should lead the compiler system to (say) reserve storage for a data element which will be referenced by that name (substring) and in this particular context (say on the left hand side of a FORTRAN assignment statement) to generate an instruction which stores the current contents of the accumulator in the assigned storage location.

In the case of an arithmetic statement, where the textural material is not a simple linear list of operations to be followed, it is possible by the judicious use of syntactic specifications to mirror the order of execution of the various substrings in the statement. In the two analyzers presented here, little attention was attracted to the association of components and substrings. In the case of the Domelki algorithm, it is a fundamental part of the analyzer that the scope of components is maintained in the list for the possible need to backtrack at some point in the process. However, this list, at the time that the string is recognized as belonging to the language described by the syntax, is also a model of the syntactic tree, or parse, of the string.

In the case of the Cheatham/Sattley algorithm the equivalent stack is not maintained and thus a "trail" of the process of deciding that a string conforms to the syntax rules is lost. However, a simple modification to the algorithm can retrieve (or at least save) this information. If at the point that the stack is popped after a successful matching operation, the type table information in the stack is not discarded but rather is saved in a second stack together with the character count (which is the leftmost character of the substring which is associated with the component) contained in the stack and the current character pointer, then the domain of each component can be determined after the completion of the analysis. Where there are a number of successful matches before a backtrack, this stack can contain false information. Thus when the original stack is popped up after a mismatch and the character pointer is reset, the new stack should be emptied of all elements whose rightmost character pointer is at or to the right of the new character pointer. Based on the scope of each component as represented by the left and right character pointers in the second stack, it is a comparatively simple task to construct the syntactic tree for the analyzed string.

In considering the analysis of a string, certain assumptions must be made regarding the original generation of that string or else there can exist the possibility of there being more than one unique parse to the string. It is generally accepted that the process of text generation by the application of syntax rules is such that the leftmost component in each partially expanded string is replaced at each stage. In syntax sets which represent a simple list of elements (such as in a FORTRAN **READ** or **PRINT** statement) this ordering is of no significance. However, in a highly structured statement such as an assignment statement there may be a significant difference in implied meaning between two different forms of generation. For example, consider a simple arithmetic expression composed only of variables (represented by single elements of the roman alphabet) and the operation of diadic subtraction (represented by the horizontal bar −). The syntax for such an expression might take the form

<expression> ::= *<variable>*|*<expression>* − *<expression>*

Based on this syntax we might generate the string A−B−C by replacing the leftmost component at each stage. That is,

1. *<expression>*
2. *<expression>* − *<expression>*
3. *<variable>* − *<expression>*
4. A − *<expression>*
5. A − *<expression>* − *<expression>*
6. A − *<variable>* − *<expression>*
7. A − B − *<expression>*
8. A − B − *<variable>*
9. A − B − C

which corresponds to the syntactic tree shown in Figure 3.6.

Logically, this tree can be considered to represent not only the syntactic structure of the generated string but also its semantic represen-

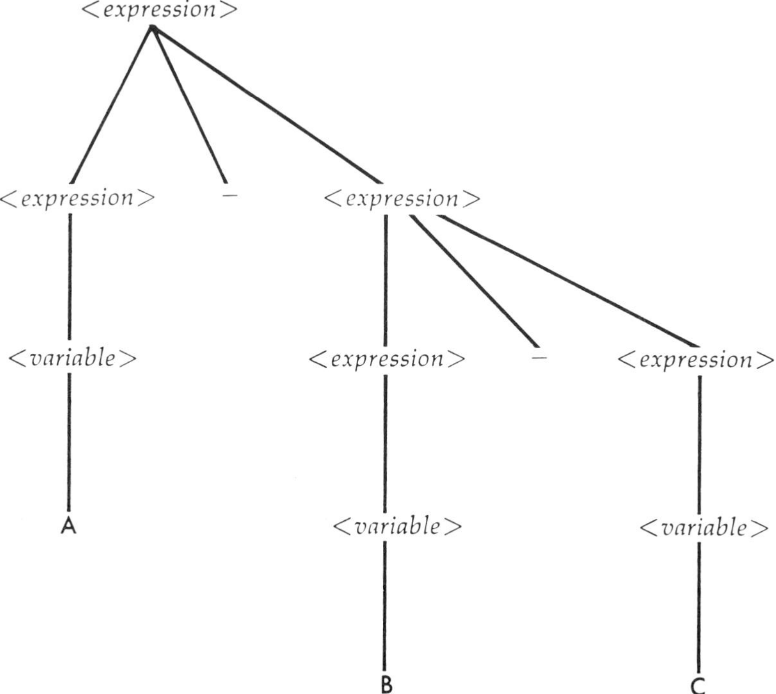

FIGURE 3.6 Leftmost generation of A − B − C.

tation. Based on this premise, it may be seen that step 4 in the generation may be taken to imply that one form of the string can be A−<*expression*> which can be construed as: "The value currently assigned to the variable A less the value of the string which replaces the component <*expression*>." Following this logical line of reasoning it may be deduced that by leftmost replacement generative process the string A−B−C is semantically equivalent to A−(B−C), since B−C is an independent phrase.

Conversely, with a rightmost replacement scheme, it may be seen that the generated syntactic tree is logically equivalent to the parenthesized string (A−B)−C.

However, in the syntactic analyzers which we have considered in this chapter the mode of scanning the string in question was from left to right and the first available substring for reduction to a component was recognized primarily. Thus irrespective of the manner in which a string was generated (since the syntactic tree is not carried forward with the string, and if it were there would be no need for syntactic analysis) the left to right scanning analyzers will reduce leftmost phrases to components (that is, associate leftmost substrings with component names), so that the string A−B−C will be reduced to <*expression*>−C at some intermediate stage. This we have logically deemed to be equivalent to the parenthesized form of the string (A−B)−C. Hence we may conclude that a left to right scanning syntactic analyzer will develop a parse of the string in question (or a syntactic tree relating the string to the root component) which is equivalent to the parse or syntactic tree which would be generated during a rightmost replacement system of generation.

As far as arithmetic expressions are concerned, it is expected that the string A−B−C, should be equivalent to the parenthesized form (A−B)−C, that in general, if ∘ is any operator (the replacement of which in any expression is consistently by the same symbol), then A∘B∘C is to be equivalent to (A∘B)∘C.

Consider an arithmetic expression composed only of single character simple variables. Any pair of variables may be connected with any one of the operators +,−,*,/ or ↑, or a single operand may be prefixed by a unary operator. However, no two operators may occur in juxtaposition, so that an infix operator may not be followed by a prefix operator, except when the prefix operator and its operand are enclosed in parentheses. Similarly, parentheses may enclose any operand to clarify or to define the hierarchy of calculation. According to these rules, an <*expression*> may be defined by the sequence:

<prefix operator> := +|−
<infix operator> ::= +|−|/|*|↑
<term> ::= *<variable>*|*<term><infix operator><term>*|
(*<expression>*)
<expression> ::= {*<prefix operator>*}$_0^1$*<term>*

This sequence of statements permits the construction of only legal *<expression>*'s and, in particular, does not permit the concatenation of two operators without the presence of enclosing parentheses. Consider the string **A** + (−**B**) * **C**, for which two parsings are shown in Figures 3.7 and 3.8. Both parsings conclude that the string is a legal *<expression>*, but one of them does not represent the correct ordering of the operations.

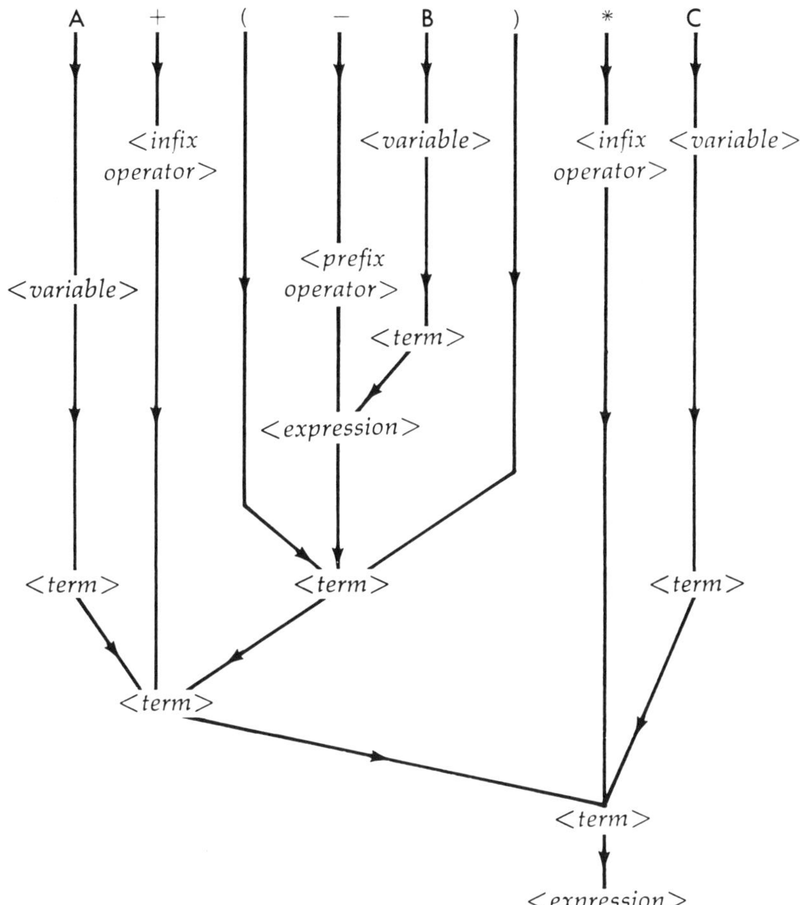

FIGURE 3.7

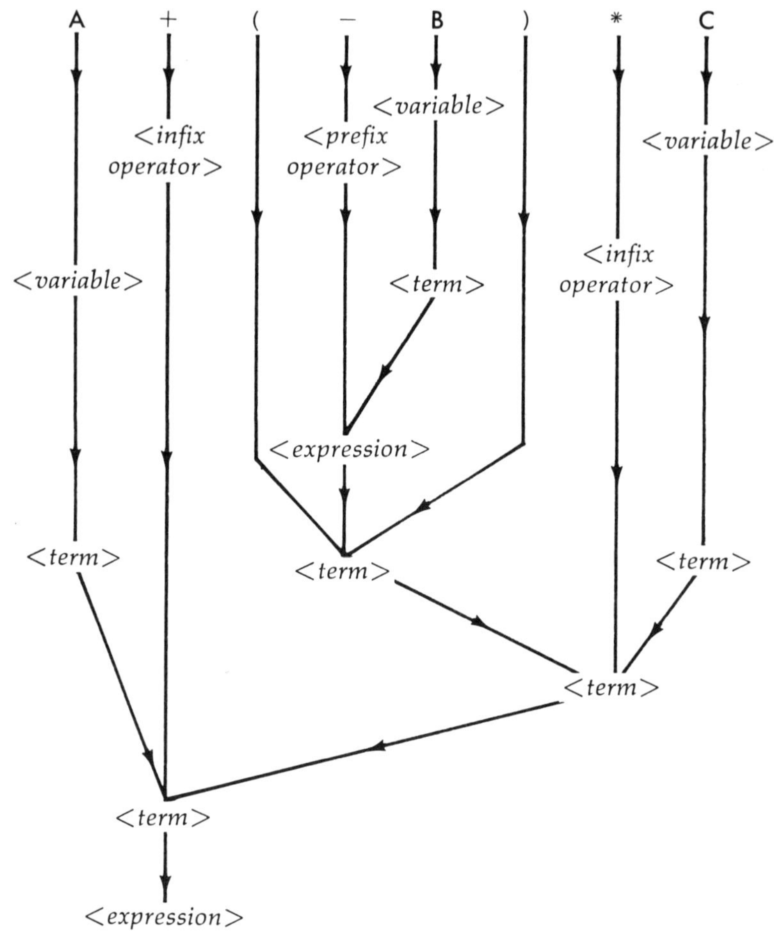

FIGURE 3.8

That is, according to the interpretation of syntactic structures (the ordering of components within the tree) the syntactic tree shown in Figure 3.7 is equivalent to the fully parenthesized expression ((A+(−B))*C) whilst that in Figure 3.8 is equivalent to (A+((−B)*C)). Our high school knowledge of the way in which an arithmetic expression should be evaluated is represented by the form shown in Figure 3.8. However, the form which is generated by a left to right scanning operation is the first (Figure 3.7) tree! Thus while our scanning system took care of one consistent level of operators (the reader may simply show that a mixture of + and −, or * and /, would parse correctly) the system fails when confronted with mixed levels of operators.

Give the same string to a high school student and he will have no problem in determining the correct order of computation, because he has been taught a set of rules that define the order:

1. Evaluate parenthesized expressions first.

2. Perform other operations in the order:
   (a) Involution
   (b) Unary minus (discard unary plus)
   (c) Multiplication or division
   (d) Addition or subtraction

With this ordering, the parsing should reveal groupings such that the order of recognition (and hence the order of compilation) is equivalent to the hierarchy of this set of rules. The development of a syntax that will permit the construction of all valid statements and which, at the same time will enforce the parsing by hierarchy of operators is complicated by the syntactical inconsistency of the reverse sign operation (that is, unary minus). By common practice, the syntax of the unary operator differs according to the location of the operator in the string of characters. Since the concatenation of two operators is not permitted, a unary operator and its operand must be enclosed in parentheses within the body of an expression. However, if the same unary operator and operand occur at the left-hand end of the expression, the parentheses may be omitted without the inference that the whole expression is the operand of the unary operator. Thus, though the following expressions are equivalent, the parenthesizing rules are different:

$$-A + B$$
$$B + (-A)$$

Initially therefore let us omit consideration of the unary operators and develop a syntax for arithmetic expressions which are composed of single character variables and the operators +,−,*,/ and ↑ involution). Irrespective of the scanning technique, we wish to force certain phrases which involve the operators to be reduced in advance of others. That is, according to the rules above, the phrase (if any) which includes the involution operator must be recognized (be reduced) prior to any phrase which includes the operators +,−,* or /. Similarly, in the reduced string (that is, having reduced the phrase including the involution operator) phrases including either the * or / should be reduced in advance of phrases involving the operators + or −. Thus in an expression which does not include parentheses, the following syntactic rules will force compliance with our wishes:

<term> ::= *<variable>*
<involution factor> ::= *<term>*|*<term>*↑*<involution factor>*
<multiply factor> ::= *<involution factor>*|
<multiply factor>$\{*|/\}_1^1$*<involution factor>*
<expression> ::= *<multiply factor>*|
<expression>$\{+|-\}_1^1$*<multiply factor>*

In this syntax it may be noted that the components whose replacement rules include the various operators are distinct by order of evaluation and that each such rule contains the higher level operator as its rightmost part. That is, by the definition the process of scanning a generated string from left to right will result in the proper ordering of phrases (factors or terms) so that the logical equivalence proposed in the previous section develops the desired parenthesized forms. For example consider the string A—B—C again. Since this grammar is not totally cyclic (starting at *<expression>*, for example, it is possible to develop *<expression>* again directly but *<multiply factor>* and *<involution factor>* can never reproduce a phrase containing either the symbols + or − or the component *<expression>*) strings which contain differing operators are parsed such that the structure levels are as desired and further, in a sequence of constant level operators (such as in the string A—B—C) the leftmost phrases are always the first and only phrases that can be reduced. Thus the string A—B—C has a unique parse as shown in Figure 3.9. Similarly the string A+B*C will be subject to a unique parsing (Figure 3.10, p. 130).

To include parentheses in the valid forms of a string which conform to the specifications with the root name *<expression>*, it is necessary to consider what role a parenthesized phrase plays in the meaning of an arithmetic expression. For our purposes here, it is convenient to consider a parenthesized phrase to be a sub-expression whose value is computed in advance of the phrase in which it is contained. Thus parentheses surround a phrase which conforms to the specification of an *<expression>*, the parenthesized phrase being both syntactically and semantically equivalent to a single valued variable. Thus the modification of the syntax by the replacement of the definition of the component *<term>* by the production

<term> ::= *<variable>*|(*<expression>*)

suffices to adequately specify both the generation of parenthesized strings and the correct analysis of such a string.

The problem of a unary operator still remains, however. Returning to the seemingly context-sensitive examples given previously where

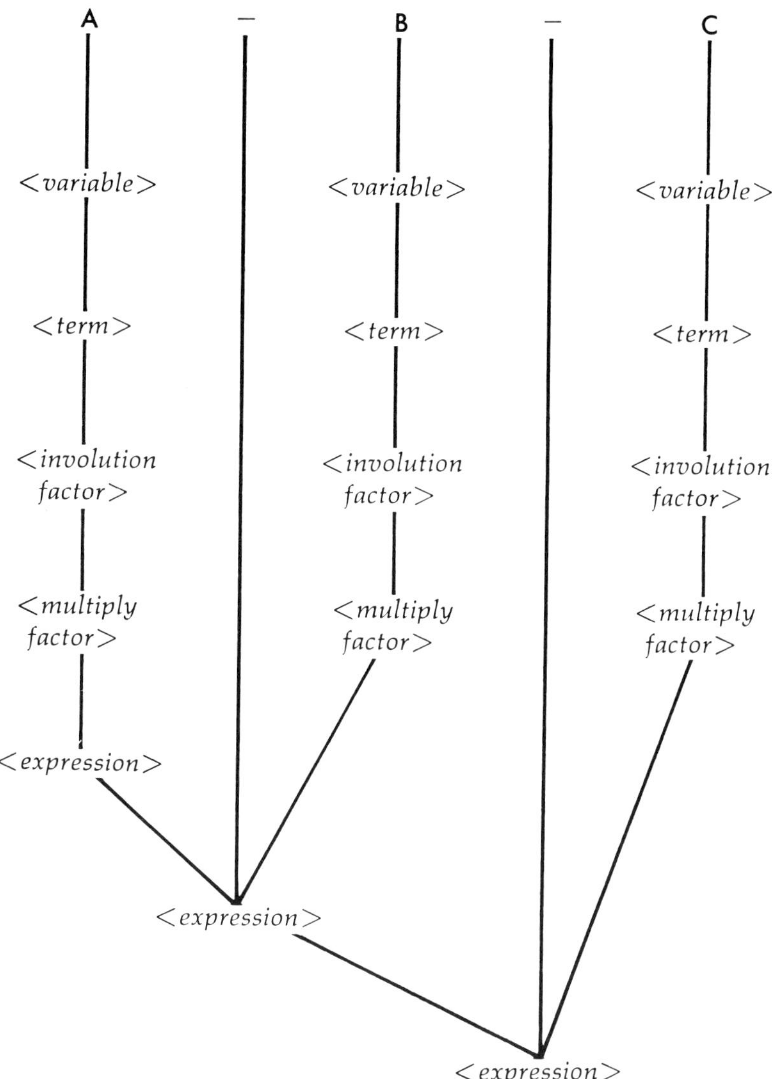

FIGURE 3.9

the necessity of enclosing a unary operator in parentheses depends on the location of the operator in the string, it may be seen that a unary expression is, like a parenthesized phrase, an independent subexpression. By redefining the component *<expression>* to include the option of a unary expression defined as a unary operator attached (prefix-wise) to the component *<multiply factor>*, it may be shown that the apparently context sensitive parenthesizing of a unary ex-

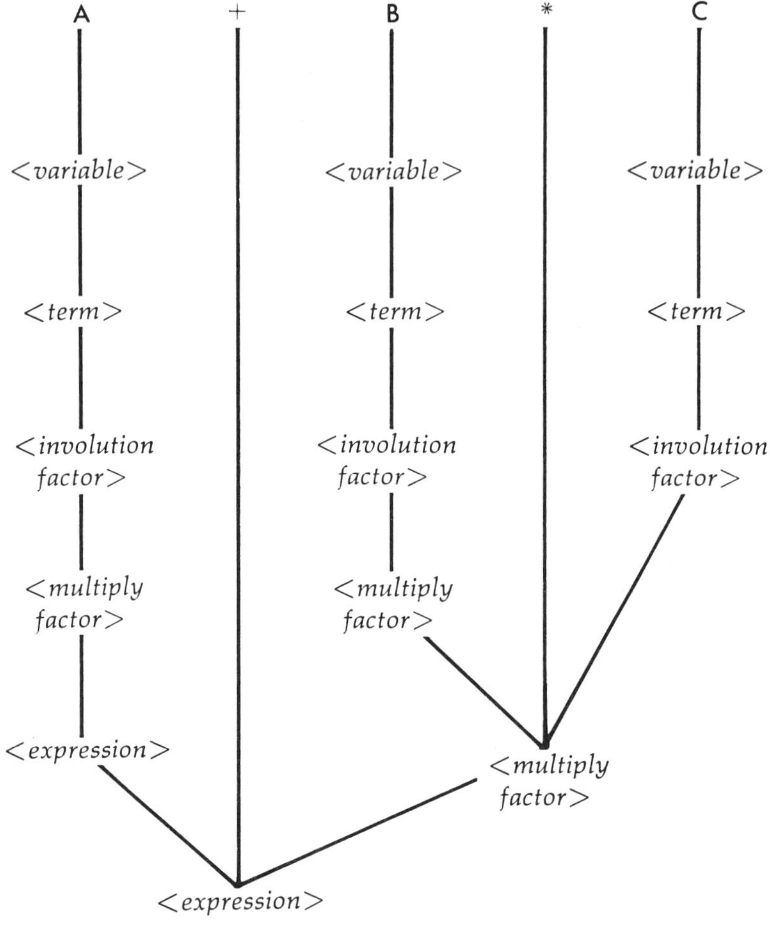

FIGURE 3.10

pression may be expressed in a context free form. That is,

$$<\textit{expression}> ::= \{+|-\}_0^1<\textit{multiply factor}>|$$
$$<\textit{expression}>\{+|-\}_1^1<\textit{multiply factor}>$$

By reason of the occurrence of the left recursive definition in this production, it is possible that an unparenthesized unary expression may occur as the leftmost phrase in a string. However, the only path from *<multiply factor>* to *<expression>* again is by the use of the definition of *<term>* which forces in the required parentheses. That is, once some intermediate sentential form has been reached, such as *<expression>* − *<multiply factor>*, then there is no way in which *<multiply factor>* can ever be replaced by an unparenthesized unary expression. It is important to observe that had the definition of *<expression>* been modified to include a definition of a unary expression as the concatentation of the unary operator and the component *<expression>*, this protection would not have been present. It is left for an exercise for the reader to show that the following syntax is not sufficient:

<term> ::= *<variable>*|(*<expression>*)
<involution factor> ::= *<term>*|*<term>* ↑ *<term>*
<multiply factor> ::= *<involution factor>*|
<multiply factor>$\{*|/\}_1^1$*<involution factor>*
<expression> ::= *<multiply factor>*|$\{+|-\}_1^1$*<expression>*|
<expression>$\{+|-\}_1^1$*<multiply factor>*

In order to verify at least the partial correctness of the syntax developed for arithmetic expressions, let us investigate the analyses of several possibly troublesome strings. Primarily let us consider the string −A↑B. Taking a scan from left to right, the first character encountered is the bar or minus sign. Looking down the list of possible reductions that are available it can be seen immediately that this symbol occurs only in one production (and hence in one reduction). Thus we may partially construct the syntactic tree as shown in Figure 3.11.

Continuing to the next symbol, A, it may be shown that A can be reduced directly to *<variable>*, *<term>*, *<involution factor>*, and

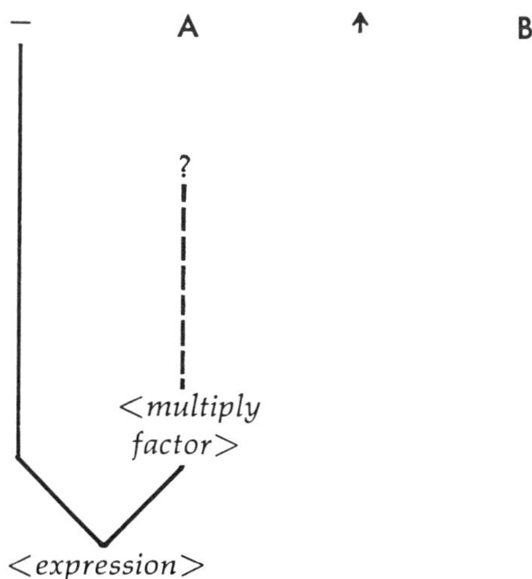

FIGURE 3.11

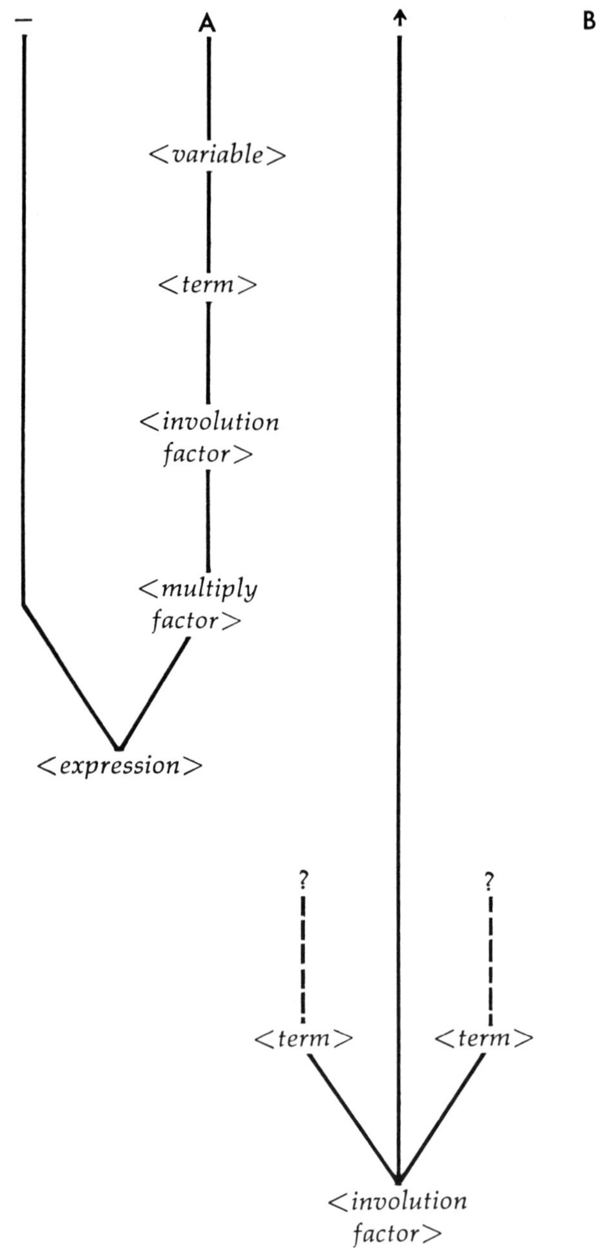

FIGURE 3.12

<multiply factor> in succession. That is, there does exist a relationship between the symbol **A** and the right hand component of the component *<expression>* as is tentatively predicated in Figure 3.11.

Passing to the right in the string, the next character scanned is ↑, which as in the case of the minus sign, occurs only in one reduction. Thus the predicted reduction of the string to include the involution symbol is as shown in Figure 3.12.

Without much logical reasoning it can be ascertained that in order for this predicted arrangement to be acceptable there must be some series (sequence) of reductions commencing at <*expression*> as the leftmost reducible string, terminating at <*term*>. However, this is not possible and thus this arrangement will not suffice. We point out that had there been a sequence of reductions between <*expression*> and <*term*>, the logical parenthesized equivalent form of the string would have been (−A)↑B which was not as intended by the rules of evaluation. The final analyzed form of the string −A↑B is shown in Figure 3.13.

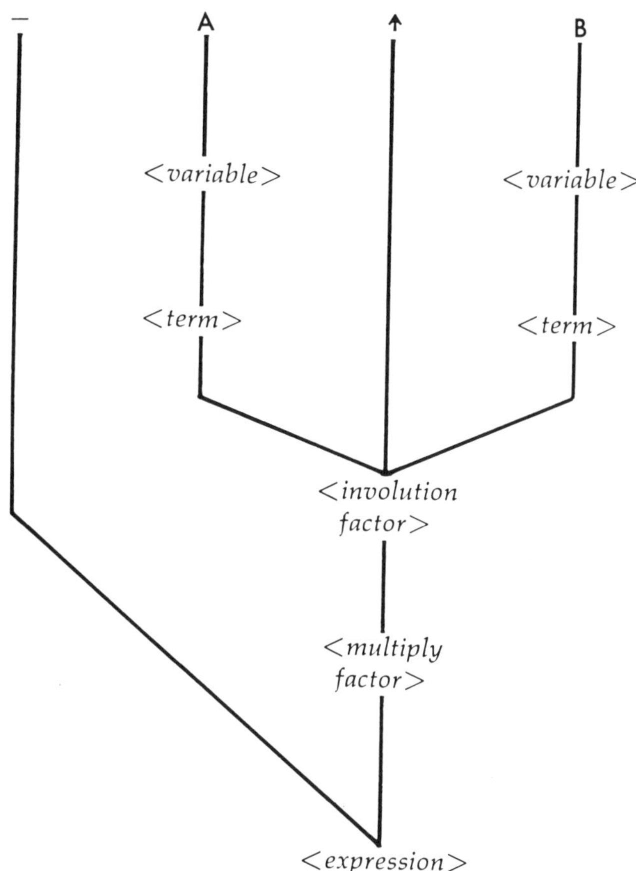

FIGURE 3.13 Reduced form of the string −A ↑ B.

Similarly in the case of the string −A+B, we should like to ensure that the subexpression −A is reduced before the phrase containing the addition sign (+) is reduced. That is, the parenthesized form should be (−A)+B. The result of analysis according to the syntax given here is shown in Figure 3.14.

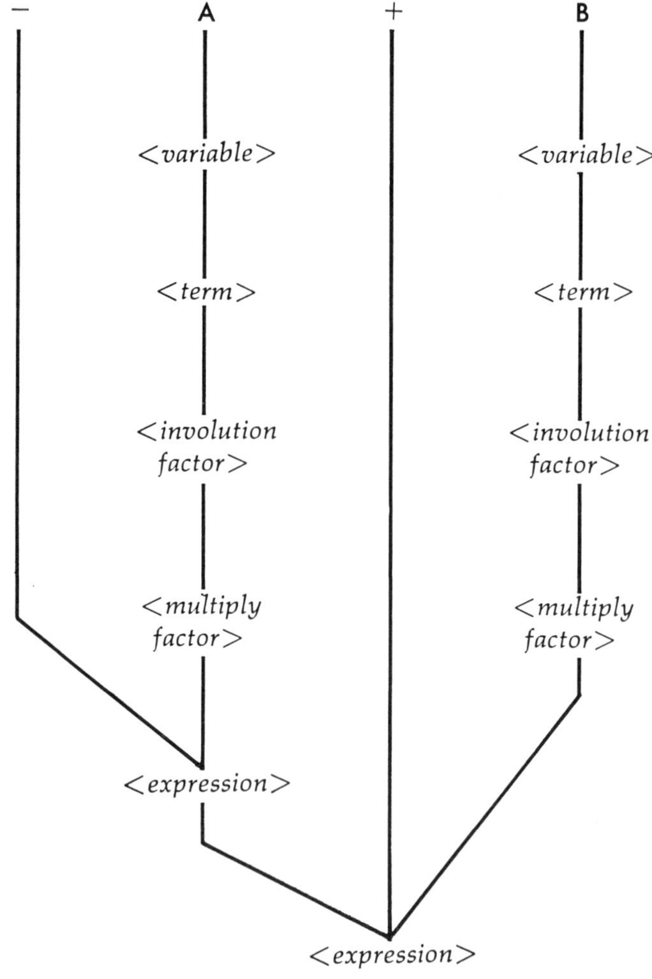

FIGURE 3.14 The result of the analysis of −A + B.

Problem

3.4
The examples given in the previous section refer specifically to the manner of presenting arithmetic expressions in FORTRAN, BASIC or scalar algebra. The APL programming system does not use this (or any) system of hierarchy of operators, but instead uses only parentheses and a *right to left* ordering of evaluation. That is, for example, the FORTRAN expression A + B * C would be expressed in APL as A + B × C and would, by coincidence, have the same meaning. However, the FORTRAN expression B * C + A would be translated into an APL expression in the form (B × C) + A or A + B × C. That is, the APL expression B × C + A would have the equivalent parenthesized form B × (C + A). Restricting the set of operators to {+,−,×,÷} in their diadic form (that is, two operands are required), develop a set of syntactic specification for APL expressions which correctly specify the ordering of the evaluation of those expressions.

SUMMARY

The analysis of nonnatural language statements by the use of parsing to determine the validity and type of statement can be achieved by the use of a generalized parsing routine or by a specific analyzer. The use of a general routine has the advantage that with the input of a language definition, there is no restriction on the language to be analyzed, and a single analyzer can perform the same task for many languages. Further, the intermediate results of the parse, if saved, can serve as indicators and pointers to the compiler generators. However, since parsing with respect to a set of syntax rules (which is akin to an interpretive process) must examine every component of the string to be analyzed, advantage cannot be taken of the inherent properties of each statement type without additional concepts. These are the topics of the next chapter.

4

Lexical Analysis and SYMTAB—The Symbol Table

As indicated in the chapter on syntactic analysis, the process of analyzing a string to determine the association of string elements (or substrings) with the components of the grammar of the language, can bog down when it is necessary to attempt to match, say, every alphabetical character against some character in the string merely to determine whether that character is alphabetic! Particularly in those cases where the alphabetic character in the grammar is the leaf of a long branch of the predicted syntactic tree, the amount of backtracking and subsequent stack manipulation may be sufficient to completely overwhelm the analyzer. Much of this inefficiency can be overcome by the careful design of a grammar so that the backtracking is minimized and so that the most likely (most frequently used) characters are used in the matching process at the earliest point in the algorithm. For example, a simple survey of BASIC programs collected from beginning programming students showed that the most frequently used single character variable was **X**, followed by **Y**, then **A**, and so on. Thus a syntactic specification of the form

$$\langle variable \rangle ::= \mathsf{X}|\mathsf{Y}|\mathsf{A} \cdots$$

is likely to improve the apparent efficiency of the analyzer over one which uses a definition which is ordered in the usual alphabetical manner. Similarly, in the description of statements, it will be more efficient to specify the most commonly used statements (the assignment statements) as the first alternative, and to order the alternatives in decreasing order of usage.

The alternative to this artificial reorganization of the grammar which drives the syntactic analyzer is to precede the syntactic analysis by a lexical analysis in which lexically recognizable language elements are identified. For example, in the majority of higher-level languages the identification of variable names can be achieved by a simple scanning scheme. That is, the syntactic rule for the formation of a variable name states that (say) the first character (in a left-to-right sense) shall be alphabetic and succeeding characters shall be alphanumeric. As a means of identification this is sufficient provided that the substring which is to be identified has already been delimited in the containing string. Thus we must be able to identify delimiting symbols in the string. Again, in most higher-level languages, these symbols are unique and belong to that class of symbols which are generally referenced as the special symbols, such as +,−,*,(,) and the punctuation marks.

In natural languages (particularly the written languages) the standard delimiting character is the space symbol. By use of this symbol we recognize (lexically) the groups of characters which compose a word in the language. In fact our eyes have become accustomed to this delimitation scheme and thus we find it very difficult to identify words in the absence of the space or its replacement by some other character. As a witness to the degree of difficulty involved in such a process of visual delimitation, consider the number of puzzles published in children's magazines which are composed of a "deblanked" story. Further, for those interested in crosswords, and anagrams in particular, consider the increase in complexity of solving an anagram problem when the result is to be composed of more than one word, particularly when the number of words in the answer is unspecified! If the blanks (spaces) were included in the character set of the anagram, the problem would be considerably simplified. Further, in natural language (and to some minor extent in synthetic languages) the space is an essential distinguishing feature between word sequences and their composition. Take, for example, the simple phrase *to get her* and the composition *together* which have entirely different meanings. Where such a compilation is truly an accretion of words this distinction is not so important, such as in the examples "over head" and "overhead" in the sense of (say) a roof being over one's head.

Besides variable names (which might include at first guess function names also), it is generally possible to extract lexically the representations of numeric values from statements in programming languages. There may be some confusion following a lexical analysis as to what the extracted string actually is intended to represent, but at this stage this is not necessarily disastrous. Out of context, the meaning of a string of numeric digits is impossible to ascertain, although a number of guesses are possible—an integer number, a statement number (or identifier), a logical unit number, or (given some format information such as the location of an implied radix point) a real number.

However, with the knowledge that a lexical analysis is to precede a syntactic analysis, it is possible to organize the grammar of the language such that components are grouped into lexically recognizable classes and thus to eliminate the repeated matching and backtracking that is an essential part of a practical syntactic analysis.

On another plane, it is possible that a presyntactic analysis can eliminate machine-dependent features from a text and thus permit the use of a machine-independent syntactic analyzer. For example, let us suggest that in some data collection system there are a number of differing collection devices which, unfortunately, do not all use the same character coding scheme, such as ASCII. It would be very inefficient to provide several copies of the same syntactic analyzer modified to take account of the differing coding schemes. Thus a simple scan would be able to transform the coding scheme into a common internal representation and, where necessary, to condense commonly occurring substrings into a single character (byte)[1] representation or to transform character sequences in one code into the one character code used by some other device. For example, in a time sharing system where there is a mixture of model 33 Teletypes and IBM 2731 terminals, the representation of some standard operators of the APL language is composed of several key strokes on the Teletypes (and hence a sequence of character codes at the receiving interface) and only one character on the communication line from the IBM 2731.

Similarly in APL, the programmer can "invent" new operators by combining characters using the backspace key. Thus a string of characters delimited in some definable fashion, every alternate character being the backspace code, may be condensed into a single character representation so as to aid in the recognition process in a syntactic analyzer.

THE LEXICAL EXTRACTION OF LANGUAGE ELEMENTS

Let us first consider the extraction of a digit string from a string of symbols. When any piece of data is to be extracted from a source

1. In this case the unit of representation should be that unit in the analyzer which is capable of being matched in a single instruction.

statement, the first consideration must be given to the delimiting characters of that data. As the source statement is scanned from left to right, the first character will generally give a clue to the type of element in hand (for example, in ALGOL and FORTRAN where a variable name is constrained to begin with an alphabetic character), but the last character of the element cannot be recognized until after it has been passed over and a delimiting character is noted. Since a digit string may contain only digits, any nonnumeric character will be a delimiting character. For the current purposes we shall disregard blanks (space characters) as delimiting characters.

If the source statement has been assembled into an area known as **CHI**, and there exists a word known as **CHINXT**, which contains the address of the character in **CHI** currently under consideration, the **SYMTAB** routine may start with that character and move toward the right. On returning from **SYMTAB** to the calling routine, **CHINXT** will contain the address of the delimiting character. Figure 4.1 shows the extraction process for a digit string.

Since this extraction routine can be useful to other routines than **SYMTAB**, provision must be made for more than simply the collecting string of characters. Similarly, the overzealous transmutation of the string, for example, to the internal representation can detract from the routine's general usefulness. The uses to which a simple digit string extraction could be put would include:

1. extracting an integer number representation,

2. extracting the logical unit number from a FORTRAN **READ** or **WRITE** command,

3. extracting the switch number from an **IF(SENSE SWITCH** *i*) statement,

4. extracting the display digits from a **PAUSE** or **STOP** statement, and

5. extracting numeric field widths and other specifications in **FORMAT** statements.

For example, the specification widths in a **FORMAT** statement may be extracted by using this routine repeatedly. Further, since neither part (*w* or *d* in an **F** or **E** specification) should exceed two digits; if the routine also returns the number of digits extracted, then a check for legality can be made.

If the terminating character of an integer extraction routine is **H**, one may assume that the following item is a Hollerith constant. Thus

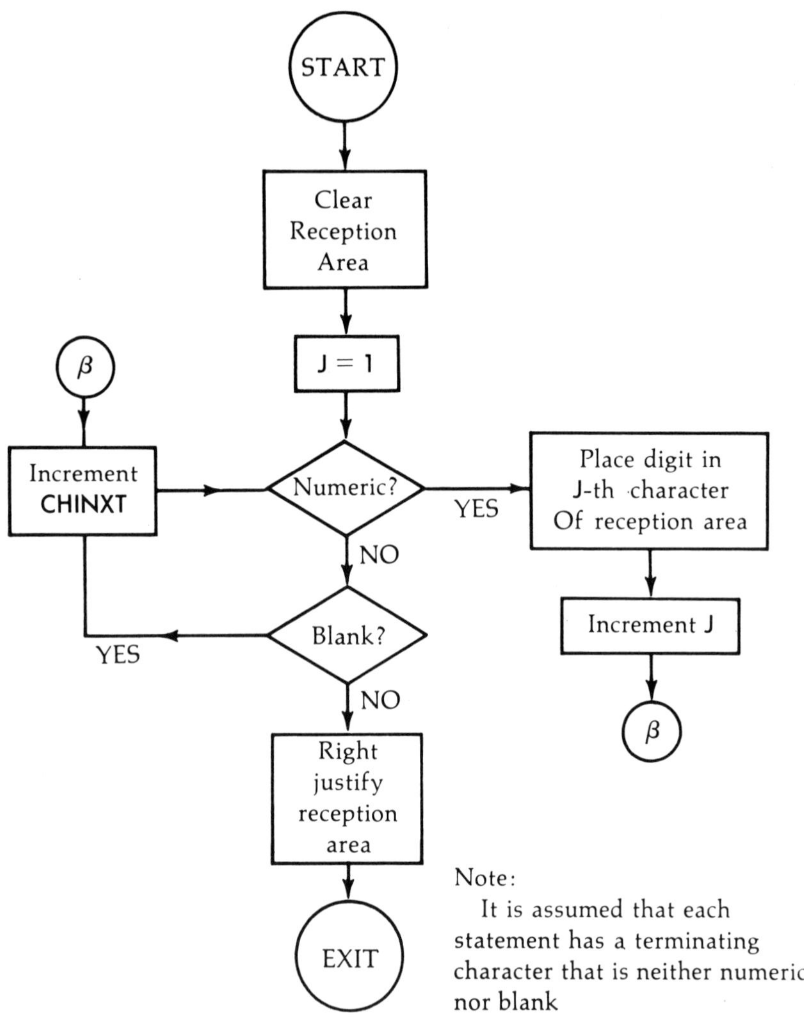

FIGURE 4.1 Integer extraction routine (**INTEX**).

the constant picked up by the routine is to be used by the generator as the count of the characters to be stored as the Hollerith constant. The characters to be extracted can then be extracted irrespective of their value. A constant such as **5H,1,38** would be extracted as **,1,38**.

The extraction of a decimal number (or **REAL** number in FORTRAN) involves more testing than for the extraction of an integer number since the number of valid forms is greater. Further, the internal representation of a real number is not a simple rearrangement of the source data, but a collection of three parts: the integer part, the fractional part, and the exrad. In a decimal machine, these parts may be collected sequentially, whereas in a binary machine, they must be kept separate in BCD form until a conversion from external to internal mode can be accomplished. However, if the compiler has a target language, such as an assembly code that accepts numeric data in external form, the task of conversion may be either postponed or handled by some other system. We shall consider the following techniques:

1. Source data to decimal internal real mode with a biased exrad and left-justified significand;

2. Source data to integer part, fractional part and exrad in external mode; and

3. External mode to internal binary.

First consider that a REAL number may be defined as:

<simple real no> := *<integer>*.|
<integer>.*<fraction>*|.*<fraction>*
<exponent no> := *<simple real no>*E*<sign><integer>*|
*<integer>*E*<sign><integer>*
<real no> := *<simple real no>*|*<exponent no>*

The significant characters in a real number are

. (radix point)
E (the symbol for "times 10 to the power")

and the right delimiting character, which in an assignment statement will be either an operator or the end of the statement. In a logical IF statement, the delimiter may be either an operator or a right parenthesis, or even an apparent second decimal point (e.g., IF(0.0.NE.X) . . .). In a DATA statement list the delimiter may be a comma.

In extracting a real number from a source statement, the technique of handling a zero must be considered in one of three manners:

1. After a leading nonzero digit, a zero should be treated as a digit.

2. Before a leading nonzero digit and prior to the radix point, a zero should be ignored.

3. Before a leading nonzero digit but following the radix point, a zero should be ignored, but with an adjustment of the exrad.

Figure 4.2 charts the routine for extracting a real number from a source statement and converting it to internal decimal real mode. For

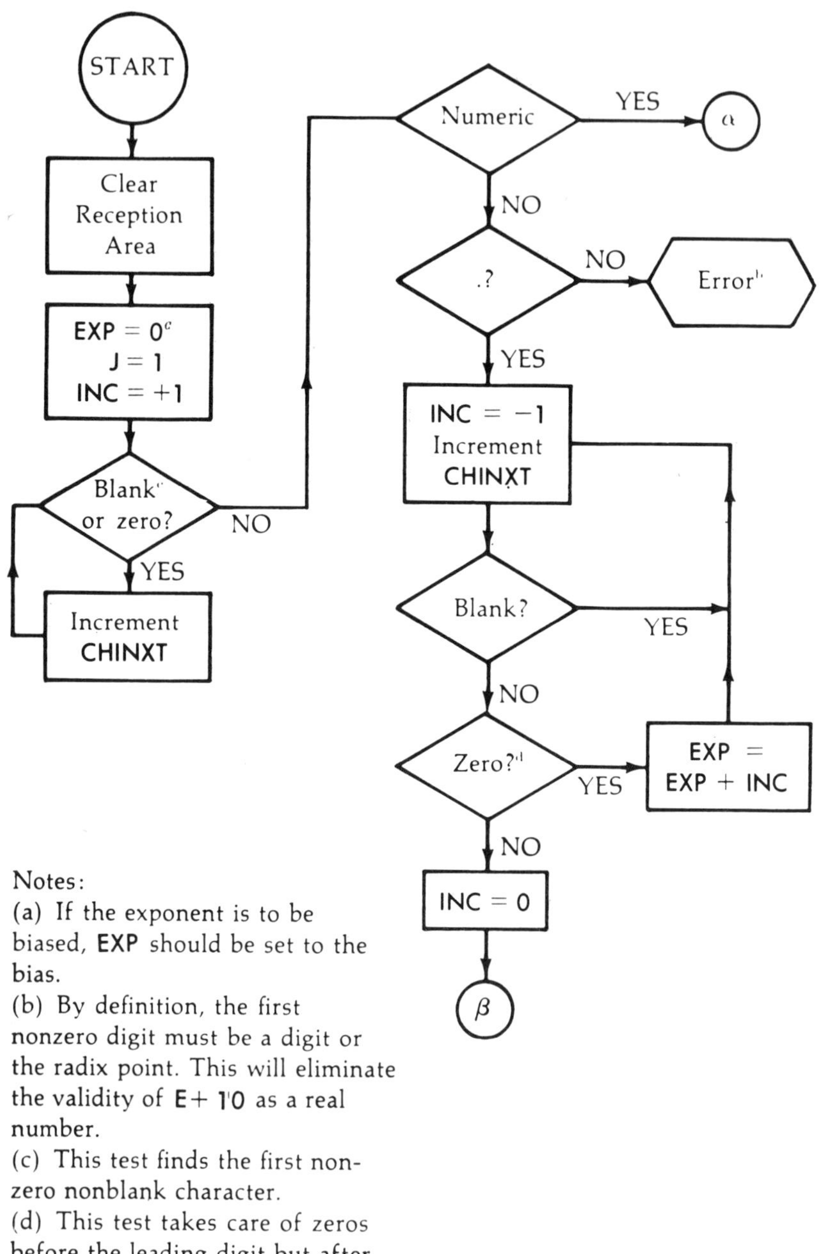

Notes:
(a) If the exponent is to be biased, **EXP** should be set to the bias.
(b) By definition, the first nonzero digit must be a digit or the radix point. This will eliminate the validity of **E+ 10** as a real number.
(c) This test finds the first nonzero nonblank character.
(d) This test takes care of zeros before the leading digit but after the radix point.

FIGURE 4.2 Real number extraction routine.

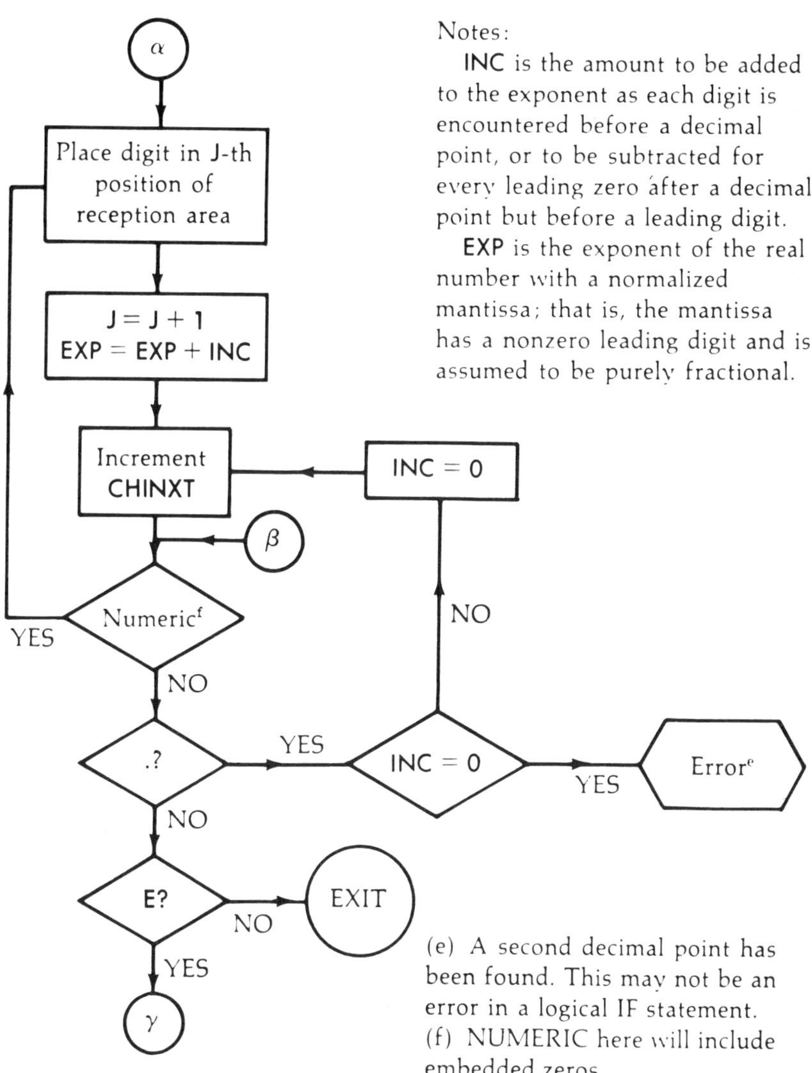

α
Place digit in J-th position of reception area
J = J + 1
EXP = EXP + INC
Increment CHINXT
INC = 0
β
Numeric[f]
YES
NO
.?
YES
INC = 0
YES
Error[e]
NO
NO
E?
NO
EXIT
YES
γ
Notes:
INC is the amount to be added to the exponent as each digit is encountered before a decimal point, or to be subtracted for every leading zero after a decimal point but before a leading digit.
EXP is the exponent of the real number with a normalized mantissa; that is, the mantissa has a nonzero leading digit and is assumed to be purely fractional.
(e) A second decimal point has been found. This may not be an error in a logical IF statement.
(f) NUMERIC here will include embedded zeros.

FIGURE 4.2 (Continued)

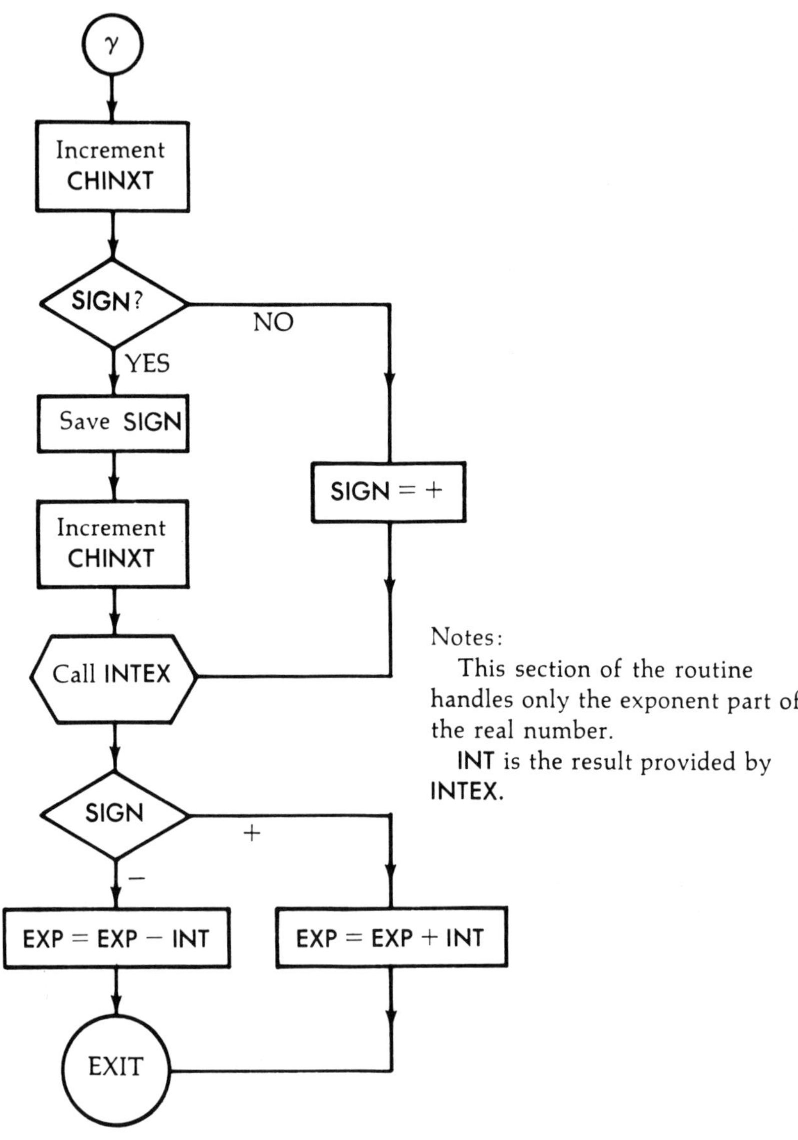
γ
Increment CHINXT
SIGN?
NO
YES
Save SIGN
SIGN = +
Increment CHINXT
Call INTEX
SIGN
+
−
EXP = EXP − INT
EXP = EXP + INT
EXIT
Notes:
This section of the routine handles only the exponent part of the real number.
INT is the result provided by INTEX.

FIGURE 4.2 (Continued)

the purpose of extracting a real number and maintaining the separate identities of the three parts, an alternative routine may be organized that utilizes the digit string extraction routine. This is shown in Figure 4.3.

These extraction routines have merely extracted numbers from a string of characters in the source statement and stored these numbers in their unadulterated form in a set of special bins. However, the form in which the data are read into the computer from the source document (tape, card, etc.) is not, generally, the form in which the information is to be manipulated at object time. For example, in binary machines the digits (0–9) can be represented as

Decimal	*Binary*
0	0000
1	0001
2	0010
3	0011
4	0100
5	0101
6	0110
7	0111
8	1000
9	1001

However, multidigit decimal numbers cannot be represented by the direct translation of digits according to the above table. For example, the decimal number 14_{10} does not code directly to 00010100_2, but rather to 00001110_2. To restrict the internal code of a character to merely 4 bits will restrict the allowable number of characters to 16, whereas in general we will wish to represent at least 48, or even 64, characters. For programming ease, most computers are arranged so that the memory words may be broken up into octal digits, since any binary number can be converted to an octal number if the bits are merely grouped into sets of three, to the left and right of the radix point. That is, $011{,}010{,}110.101{,}110{,}110_2$ is equivalent to 326.566_8. The representation of characters has been standardized in the U.S.A., as shown in Table 4.1 (p. 147).

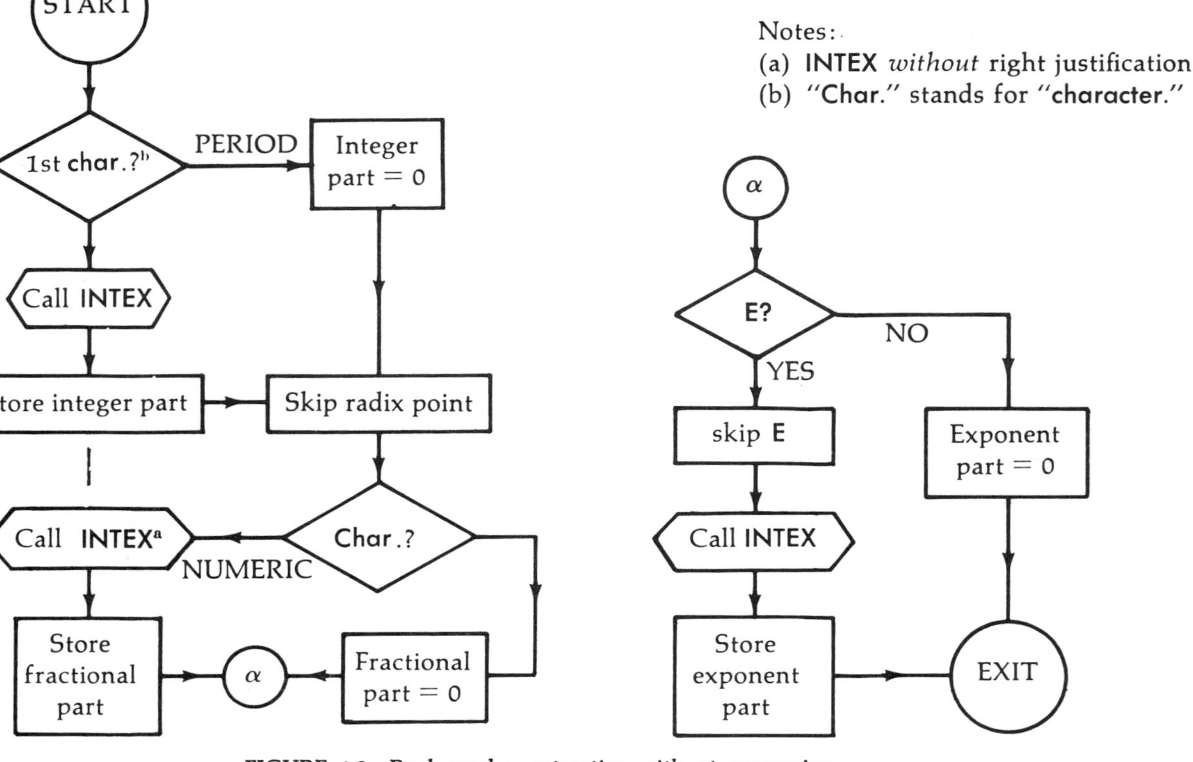

FIGURE 4.3 Real number extraction without conversion.

TABLE 4.1 Standard Code[a]

				b_7	0	0	0	0	1	1	1	1
				b_6	0	0	1	1	0	0	1	1
				b_5	0	1	0	1	0	1	0	1
b_4	b_3	b_2	b_1		**0**	**1**	**2**	**3**	**4**	**5**	**6**	**7**
0	0	0	0	**0**	NUL	DLE	SP	0	@	P	'	p
0	0	0	1	**1**	SOH	DC1	!	1	A	Q	a	q
0	0	1	0	**2**	STX	DC2	"	2	B	R	b	r
0	0	1	1	**3**	ETX	DC3	#	3	C	S	c	s
0	1	0	0	**4**	EOT	DC4	$	4	D	T	d	t
0	1	0	1	**5**	ENQ	NAK	%	5	E	U	e	u
0	1	1	0	**6**	ACK	SYN	&	6	F	V	f	v
0	1	1	1	**7**	BEL	ETB	'	7	G	W	g	w
1	0	0	0	**8**	BS	CAN	(	8	H	X	h	x
1	0	0	1	**9**	HT	EM	)	9	I	Y	i	y
1	0	1	0	**10**	NL	SUB	*	:	J	Z	j	z
1	0	1	1	**11**	VT	ESC	+	;	K	[	k	{
1	1	0	0	**12**	FF	FS	,	<	L	\	l	|
1	1	0	1	**13**	RT	GS	-	=	M	]	m	}
1	1	1	0	**14**	SO	RS	.	>	N	∧	n	~
1	1	1	1	**15**	SI	US	/	?	O	—	o	DEL

[a]This coded character set is to be used for the general interchange of information among information processing systems, communications systems, and associated equipment, according to American National Standard X3.4, 1968.

CONVERSION OF NUMERIC REPRESENTATIONS TO INTERNAL MODE

If one possesses a computer that stores its data in purely decimal form and that performs decimal arithmetic, the conversion from decimal to binary mode can be expressed as a simple algorithm. However, if one possesses such a machine, the need to convert from decimal to binary is of less importance than with other computers. As an aid to the consideration of conversion techniques, let us first consider the conversion from binary to decimal mode. Since both number systems are positional, a bit in a given position (with relation to the radix point) can be translated to its equivalent decimal number. For example, the presence of a bit three places to the left of the radix point may be converted to 4_{10}; a bit in the sixth place may be converted to the left to 32_{10}; and a bit in the third position to the right may be converted to 0.125_{10}. Thus one may translate a binary number to decimal mode by looking the positions of the bits up in a table and adding, in decimal mode, the results found in the table. For example, 10110111_2 is equivalent to $1\times2^7 + 0\times2^6 + 1\times2^5 + 1\times2^4 + 0\times2^3 + 1\times2^2 + 1\times2^1 + 1\times2^0 = 128 + 0+32 + 16 + 0 + 4 + 2 + 1 = 183_{10}$.

In general, the positional notation for the representation of a numeric value may be expanded, and with the appropriate base arithmetic any number representation may be transformed into some other base notation representation. That is, given an input string in base b_1 a conversion to base b_2 may be achieved by expanding the input representation and generating the representation of that number by arithmetic operations in base b_2. For example, any integer numeric representation N may be expressed in base b_1 by the sequence

$$N = a_n b_1{}^n + a_{n-1} b_1{}^{n-1} + \cdots + a_1 b_1{}^1 + a_0 b_1{}^0$$

where the subscript to the digits in the representation (a_i) is indicative of the location of that digit with respect to the radix point. Now realizing that a number, in its abstract sense, has no base of representation, then N represented in base b_1 must equal the representation of N in base b_2. Thus given the representation of the digits from base b_1 to base b_2, and the representation of b_1 in b_2, it is a straightforward task to develop the base b_2 representation of N given, as input, the representation of N in base b_1. Where b_1 is less than b_2 this task is comparatively simple (provided that base b_2 arithmetic is available), since the digits of the base b_1 system are directly representable as digits in the base b_2 system, and further, the base b_1 is representable is the b_2-system. On the other hand, when b_1 is greater than b_2, it may be necessary to "look up" the transformation of the digits in the b_1-system to the b_2-system.

For the purposes of example, let us consider the three arithmetic systems of binary, quinary and decimal notation. For ease of computation assume that we are given the addition and multiplication tables as shown in Tables 4.2 to 4.5. The transformations of digits between the three base systems is shown in Table 4.6.

TABLE 4.2 Binary addition.

+	*0*	*1*
0	00	01
1	01	10

TABLE 4.3 Binary multiplication.

×	*0*	*1*
0	0	0
1	0	1

TABLE 4.4 Quinary addition.

+	*0*	*1*	*2*	*3*	*4*
0	00	01	02	03	04
1	01	02	03	04	10
2	02	03	04	10	11
3	03	04	10	11	12
4	04	10	11	12	13

TABLE 4.5 Quinary multiplication.

×	*0*	*1*	*2*	*3*	*4*
0	00	00	00	00	00
1	00	01	02	03	04
2	00	02	04	11	13
3	00	03	11	14	22
4	00	04	13	22	31

TABLE 4.6 Digit conversion between binary, quinary and decimal representations.

Digit	*Binary*	*Quinary*	*Decimal*
0	0000	00	0
1	0001	01	1
2	0010	02	2
3	0011	03	3
4	0100	04	4
5	0101	10	5
6	0110	11	6
7	0111	12	7
8	1000	13	8
9	1001	14	9

Using these tables as a guide, let us now examine some conversion processes.

EXAMPLE 1. Convert 1101_2 to quinary.

Solution. Since the process of conversion starts with a representation whose base is less than that of the target representation, then the digits in the initial representation also exist in the same form in the target representation. Thus 1101_2 may be expanded to the sequence

$$1\times2^3 + 1\times2^2 + 0\times2^1 + 1\times2^0$$

Expanding the involution terms, this representation becomes

$$1\times2\times2\times2 + 1\times2\times2 + 0\times2 + 1\times1$$

Looking up the quinary multiplication table (Table 4.5) we find that

$$1\times2\times2\times2 = 02\times2\times2 = 04\times2 = 13,$$
$$1\times2\times2 = 02\times2 = 04$$
$$0\times2 = 00,$$

and

$$1\times1 = 01$$

Hence the representation is reduced to

$$13 + 04 + 00 + 01$$

Referring now to table 4.4 for the addition, we find

$$13 + 04 = 22$$

and

$$22 + 01 = 23$$

Thus we deduce that 1101_2 is represented by 23_5.

At this point, it is worthwhile pointing out that any programmer worth his salt should have been squirming in his seat to witness that evaluation of a power series by the expansion of the involution terms. Instead, the evaluation of a power series is most efficiently performed by factoring the terms so that the number of multiplications is minimized. In this manner, the generalized form of a positional notation may be written as

$$N = ((\cdots(a_n\times b + a_{n-1})\times b + \cdots a_1)\times b + a_0)$$

Using this sequencing for the evaluation of the quinary equivalent of the binary representation 1101_2 we find

$$N = (((1\times2 + 1)\times2 + 0)\times2 + 1)$$

That is,

$$\begin{aligned} N &= (((02 + 1)\times2 + 0)\times2 + 1) \\ &= ((03\times2 + 0)\times2 + 1) \\ &= ((11 + 0)\times2 + 1) \\ &= (11\times2 + 1) \\ &= (22 + 1) \\ &= 23_5 \end{aligned}$$

EXAMPLE 2. As an exercise in manipulation and as a check on the last example, convert the representation 23 in quinary to its equivalent in binary.

Solution. In this case the target base is less than that of the initial representation and thus we shall have to make use of the table of representation equivalents for digits (Table 4.6) to convert the individual digits of the representation. That is,

$$23_5 = (2\times10 + 3)_5$$

in binary is equal to the expression

$$(10\times101 + 11)_2$$

Evaluating this expression in two steps:

$$\begin{aligned} 23_5 &= (1010 + 11)_2 \\ &= 1101_2 \end{aligned}$$

EXAMPLE 3. Convert the decimal representation 38 into its equivalent representation in quinary.

Solution. As in the previous example, the target base is less than the initial base and hence digit conversions may be necessary. After digit conversion,

$$38_{10} = (3\times10 + 8)_{10}$$

is equal to

$$(3\times20 + 13)_5$$

Evaluating term by term,

$$(3\times20 + 13)_5 = (110 + 13)_5 = 123_5$$

As a quick check on this evaluation, let us exand 123_5 and develop the decimal representation again.

$$123_5 = ((1\times5+2)\times5 + 3)_{10} = (7\times5 + 3)_{10} = 38_{10}$$

Problems

4.1 Convert the following representations to decimal mode:

(a) 110110_2 (b) 110110_5 (c) 101010_2
(d) 101010_5 (e) 011011_2 (f) 011011_5
(g) 4201_5

4.2 Convert the following decimal numbers to both binary and quinary representations:

(a) 3902 (b) 223 (c) 7001
(d) 1920 (e) 1101

4.3 Having "desk run" the algorithm for the conversion of numeric representations between various bases, now write a program to perform the same task. Obviously one part (a subprogram ?) will be that portion of the program which will perform arithmetic in the target base. It is suggested that either the arithmetic tables are provided, or modulo arithmetic is used to simulate the appropriate base system.

The input to the program should consist of the representation of the number to be converted, the initial base (that is, the base of the initial representation) and the target base. The output should be the representation in the target system.

Another method of numeric representation conversion is based not on the positional notation but instead on the value represented. That is, given some internal representation (as opposed to a positional notation which we shall consider to be an external representation) we may determine a positional representation based on the ability to maximize the degree of representation for a set of diminishing place values. For example, given a number (rather than its representation), it is possible to determine a representation by counting the number of place values which compose that number. Now since place values determine the representation, then it is possible to convert any number into any representation system without having to perform arithmetic in the target system. In fact, provided that the initial representation conforms with that of the available arithmetic system, any mode of conversion is possible. Thus in a binary machine given a binary representation it is possible to generate any other base representation system, and given a decimal machine it is possible to convert from a decimal representation to any other representation.

For example, consider the case of converting from decimal notation (in a decimal machine) to a binary representation. The algorithm consists of finding that decimal number which is an integer power of 2 (the base of the target system) which is smaller than the number represented, put a one bit in the corresponding place value position of the target representation, subtract the located value from the number being converted, and repeat until there is no remainder.

Consider the decimal number 173_{10}:

$$
\begin{array}{rl}
173 & \\
\underline{-128} & = 1\times 2^7 \\
45 & \\
\underline{-32} & = 1\times 2^5 \\
13 & \\
\underline{-8} & = 1\times 2^3 \\
5 & \\
\underline{-4} & = 1\times 2^2 \\
1 & \\
\underline{-1} & = 1\times 2^0 \\
0 &
\end{array}
$$

Thus the binary equivalent of 173_{10} is $1\times2^7 + 1\times2^5 + 1\times2^3 + 1\times2^2 + 1\times2^0$, or in positional form, 10101101_2 Although this conversion process is correct, it is somewhat clumsy.

Expanding the positional binary of a number to its power series, one may write a number in the nested form:

$$B = ((\cdots((b_n\times2 + b_{n-1})\times2 + b_{n-2})\times2 + \cdots b_2)\times2 + b_1)\times2 + b_0$$

where b_i is the $(i+1)$th digit to the left of the radix point.
Now if D is the decimal representation number to be converted into binary mode such that $B = D$, one can write:

$$D = ((\cdots((b_n\times2 + b_{n-1})\times2 + b_{n-2})\times2 + \cdots b_2)\times2 + b_1)\times2 + b_0$$

Dividing both sides of this equality by 2 in integer[2] mode yields:

$$D'[+ R] = (\cdots((b_n\times2 + b_{n-1})\times2 + b_{n-2})\times2 + \cdots b_2)\times2 + b_1[+ b_0]$$

where D' is the integer quotient of the left-hand side, and R is the remainder, which obviously will be either 1 or 0. The remainder of the division of the left-hand side must be the same as the remainder on the right-hand side, that is, b_0. Thus the low-order digit of the binary equivalent may be determined by a simple division by 2 in decimal mode. The quotient of the division (D') is equivalent to the higher order bits in the binary number, and thus continued division and extraction of the remainder will produce the whole binary equivalent. Such a process is shown in Figure 4.4 (p. 154).

This process can be generalized so that the target representation may be expressed in any base. It is fortuitous that in the case of a binary target representation that the only available digits are 0 or 1, but in general the developed digits may be outside of this very limited range. For example, consider the case of converting from decimal representation in a decimal machine to hexadecimal, where the representation of the digits is shown in Table 4.7 (p. 155).

Conversion between decimal and hexadecimal of the number 173_{10} would then correspond to the sequence of steps shown below:

$$\frac{173}{16} = 10\times16 + 13 = 10\times16 + \mathrm{x}$$

ux

$$\frac{10}{16} = 0\times16 + 10 = 0 + \mathrm{u}$$

2. Integer mode as in FORTRAN.

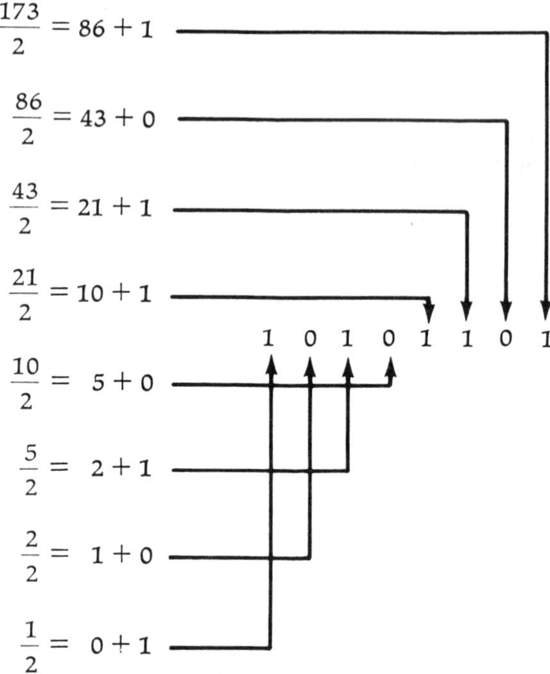

FIGURE 4.4 Decimal to binary conversion by division by 2.

This process of conversion is shown algorithmically in Figure 4.5.

Consider the following cases of conversion from binary to quinary using binary arithmetic.

EXAMPLE 1. Convert 11010_2 to quinary.

Solution. First, we must express the target base in the initial base; $5 = 101_2$

$$\frac{11010}{101} = 101 + 1$$

$$\frac{101}{101} = 1 + 0$$

$$\frac{1}{101} = 0 + 1$$

101

Hence, $11010_2 = 101_5$

In this example, the generated digits were also digits in the target system and hence no code conversion was necessary.

TABLE 4.7 Correspondence between decimal values and hexadecimal digits[a]

Decimal value	*Hexadecimal digit*
0	0
1	1
2	2
3	3
4	4
5	5
6	6
7	7
8	8
9	9
10	u
11	v
12	w
13	x
14	y
15	z

[a]So as not to show any preference, this set corresponds to the notation which was available on the Bendix G-15, now obsolete!

EXAMPLE 2. Convert 11101_2 to quinary.
Solution.

$$\frac{11101}{101} = 101 + 100$$

$$\frac{101}{101} = 1 + 0$$

$$\frac{1}{101} = 0 + 1$$

$$10(100)$$

Now the generated digits are still represented in the binary system and thus it is necessary to convert the result into the target base. That is, $100_2 = 4_5$ and hence the result is

$$11101_2 = 104_5$$

While this method seems simple and straightforward, it is in fact only of use for the purpose of converting from internal mode to some external mode. That is, since the initial representation is assumed to be in the mode of the available arithmetic system and internal repre-

N = Number to be represented in base **B**

B = Target base

D = Generated integer part of quotient

R = Generated remainder part of quotient

T = Digit conversion table (see Table 4.9, for example)

S = String of digits which is representation in target base

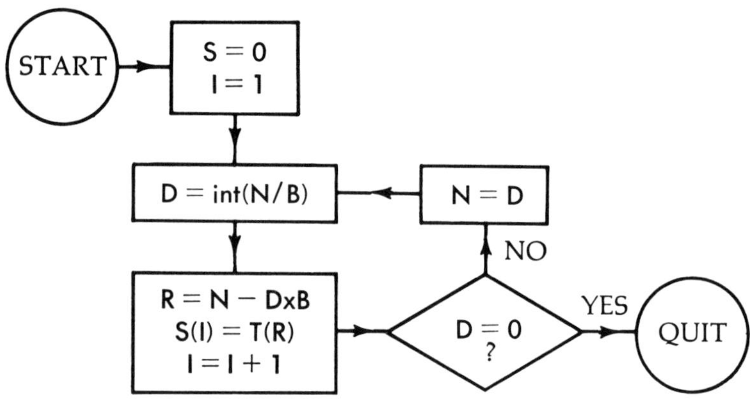

FIGURE 4.5 Conversion of representations.

sentations are usually in the same system as the available arithmetic system, this method of conversion has little usefulness in a compiler system. It would find a place on the other hand in the I/O control subsystem (IOCS) of the host environment in which the code generated by the compiler is placed. Further, as a means of conversion from external (source text) mode to internal mode in the environment of (say) simulated decimal arithmetic, there exists another practical problem which will hamper this conversion process. For example, in a binary machine the character string passed by the IOCS is not a correct representation of the number which was represented in the source text.

Consider a 4-bit representation of digits. The source language internal representation of 173_{10} will be 000101110011_{bcd}. Now dividing by 2 is equivalent to a shift to the right of one place, so dividing the **BCD** representation by 2 gives a quotient of 00010111001_{bcd}, with a remainder of 1 (which is shifted off). This quotient is equivalent to the number

$$0(11)9_{10}$$

where the middle digit is greater than 10. In reality, a 4-bit internal representation can only truly represent a hexadecimal number (base 16) in which a division by 2 would produce the correct quotient and remainder. Thus, in terms of the previous algorithm, unless special technique are used to divide by 2 in decimal mode using hexadecimal or **BCD** data, the algorithm is inapplicable to a binary machine.

Such an algorithm may be developed, though it is extremely tedious and time consuming. For example, a **BCD** character set using six bits to allow the acceptance of all characters in the language can contain at least two leading zeroes in the representation of the digits which may be made use of in the following algorithm. If an integer number is maintained in **BCD** input form, then a shift right is almost equivalent to a division by 2, and any bit shifted off the right-hand end is the true remainder. Consider each **BCD** character to be a separate entity which is shifted right as a whole. Then the movement of a low order bit of an internal byte to the high order position of the next lower byte is an indication of adding 5 to that lower byte. Thus if we add 5 to each byte in which a high order bit has occurred, and remove the high order bit, we can simulate the borrow feature of a decimal divide. This process is shown in Figure 4.6.

				Digits Shifted Off
173_{10}	000001	000111	000011	
Shift right	000000	100011	100001	1
Remove H/O bits and add 5 as appropriate	000000	001000	000110	1
Shift right	000000	000100	000011	01
No H/O bits occurred	000000	000100	000011	01
Shift right	000000	000010	000001	101
No H/O bits occurred	000000	000010	000001	101
Shift right	000000	000001	000000	1101
No H/O bits occurred	000000	000001	000000	1101
Shift right	000000	000000	100000	01101
Remove H/O bits and add 5	000000	000000	000101	01101
3 shifts right	000000	000000	000000	10101101

FIGURE 4.6 Conversion from **BCD** to binary using a simulated decimal division by 2.

This technique is time consuming, but it does show that decimal division of a **BCD** string is possible. It must be anticipated that the number of one-bit shifts is equivalent to the word size and that the number of tests after each shift to recognize the existence of high-order bits is equal to the number of **BCD** characters to be translated. Also, a computer with bit and byte manipulation instructions is necessary.

It should be recognized that each **BCD** byte is a true representation in binary mode of the decimal digit and *on its own* can be treated as a binary field. Now a decimal number is merely a representation of the true number, the position of each digit implying its power of 10 exponent. That is, 253_{10} is a representation of:

$$2\times10^2 + 5\times10^1 + 3\times10^0$$

If a decimal number takes the form:

$$d_n d_{n-1} d_{n-2} \cdots d_2 d_1 d_0$$

where

$$<d_i> ::= 0|1|2|3|4|5|6|7|8|9$$

then the number can be written in nested form:

$$(((\cdots((d_n\times10 + d_{n-1})\times10 + d_{n-2})\times10 + \cdots d_2)\times10 + d_1)\times10 + d_0)$$

If each **BCD** character of the input decimal number is stored in a separate word or addressable byte in memory, then the binary equivalent may be constructed by evaluating the nested polynomial from left to right. For example, the decimal number 104 will be stored in memory in separate words as:

d_2 000001
d_1 000000
d_0 000100

The binary equivalent of decimal 10 is 1010_2; so evaluating the polynomial:

$$\begin{aligned} d_2 \times 10 &= \quad 0000001010 \\ + d_1 &= \quad 0000001010 \\ + 10 &= 00000001100100 \\ + d_0 &= 00000001101000 \end{aligned}$$

that is, 104_{10} is equivalent to 1101000_2. As a check, the result may be converted back to base 10. In terms of base 10 numbers, the binary number is the summation:

$$2^6 + 2^5 + 2^3 = 64 + 32 + 8 = 104_{10}$$

Problem

4.4 Assume that the following decimal numbers are input, so that each digit is stored in a separate word in its BCD equivalent coding, and convert the following to binary mode:

(a) 93
(b) 176
(c) 256
(d) 1000
(e) 577
(f) 19
(g) 901

We shall not consider the conversion of fractional numbers from decimal (or BCD) to binary since a little internal processing before conversion can always ensure that each number is primarily converted to an integer significand and an accompanying exrad. Thus the number can be extracted in integer form, the exrad being supplemented by the appropriate amount. During the extraction of the number from the source document, the initial conversion may be accomplished so that prior to conversion to internal mode (probably binary) the number appears in the form of an integer significand and an exrad. However, the external base or radix is not the same as that for the internal storage, and further, it is usually found that significands are stored as pure fractions. Therefore although the initial conversion produces an integer and an exrad of, for example, base 10, the subsequent conversion must be to a pure fraction and an exrad of base 2. The conversion from an integer of base 10 to a fraction of base 2 is not difficult. If one converts from the external integer to the internal mode integer, internal conversion to a fraction may be accomplished merely by supplementing the 2's exrad by the amount the radix point is shifted. At this stage of the algorithm, the number 0.104 would be converted through the following steps:

$$0.104 = 104. \times 10^{-3}$$
$$104. \times 10^{-3} = 1101000._2 \times 10^{-3}$$
$$1101000._2 \times 10^{-3} = 0.1101000_2 \times 2^7 \times 10^{-3}$$

One problem still remains: The number now contains two exrads which are not in the same mode. That is, the multiplying factor of base 10 must be converted to base 2 with the appropriate adjustment to the significand. Suppose one is given a multiplying factor of 10^n where n is an integer by definition. This is to be converted to the multiplying factor 2^m where m is not necessarily an integer. If

$$10^n = 2^m$$

then

$$\log_2 10^n = \log_2 2^m$$

that is

$$n \log_2 10 = m$$

Now n can be converted to binary by the techniques described above and then multiplied by the constant $\log_2 10$ in binary mode. However, in general m will not be an integer and may be represented in the form $(i + f)$ where i is an integer and f is a fraction. If the original decimal number is written as

$$d \times 10^n$$

then its binary equivalent is $b \times 2^{(i+f)}$, that is, $b \times 2^i \times 2^f$. Thus before the number can be stored, the factor $b \times 2^f$ needs to be evaluated since the exrad must be an integer. This may cause some consternation as one would not expect a compiler to include a routine for such a complex operation as involution unless the operation is a load-and-go one with the compiler, library routines and compiled program resident together. As an alternative, this process may be simulated by a table look up procedure based on the powers of 10.

For example, FORTRAN 3600 (for the CONTROL DATA 3600) contains a table of the integer and fractional exponents in base 2 for the base 10 powers of 1 to 20, 40, 60, . . . 300. With this table, the integer powers of the base 2 exponents may be summed and the fractional parts successively multiplied into the significand. Once this task has been completed, the significand may be normalized and the exrad adjusted appropriately.

Problem

4.5 Using logarithmic tables if necessary, convert the following decimal representations to normalized binary representations:

(a) 800.46×10^{20} (c) -59.381×10^{-45}
(b) 331.24×10^{8} (d) 3.03×10^{24}

THE LEXICAL EXTRACTION OF NAMES

The lexical extraction of character strings which represent the names used to identify variables, functions, subroutines and procedures (Figure 4.7) is by no means as complex as that for the extraction of numeric representations, since a conversion between external and internal mode is not required. In fact, the internal representation of a name may often be the bit string which is encountered during the lexical scan. More often however, the internal form will be some condensed representation so as conserve on space in the symbol table.

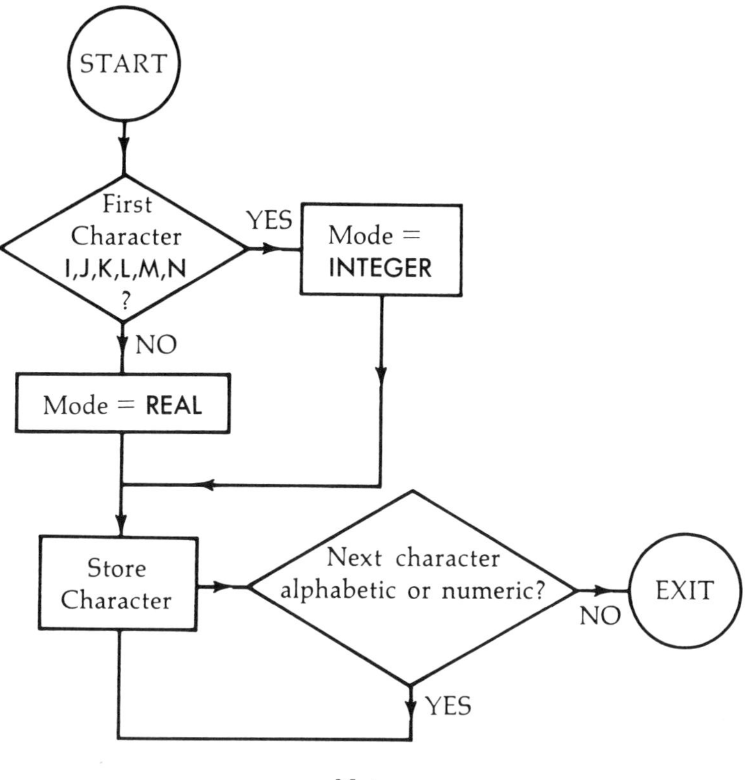

Note:
On entry to this routine, **CHINXT** is pointing at the primary character of the name. On exit, the pointer is set to the delimiting character.

FIGURE 4.7 Routine **VAREXT**: A routine to extract character strings.

The delimiting characters of names are generally characters which represent operators, punctuation characters such as commas, periods or parentheses or statement delimiters. Of these classes of characters only the opening parenthesis requires special attention. If the delimiting character of a character string which represents a name is the opening parenthesis, then it may be anticipated the name extracted has the attribute relationship of an array variable, a function name, or a subprogram identifier. The means for distinguishing these types will be discussed later. At this point, given that the extraction routine is referenced as a subprogram, it is sufficient to say that the data returned should include not only the extracted character string (or some condensed form of it) but also some indicator of the delimiting character.

Problem

4.4 Write a program that will read a FORTRAN assignment statement that does not include Hollerith constants and will output a list of all the variable names occurring in that statement. For example, the input statement

```
AJ1 = B(I+3,J) + 3.0 * (X/(C(K) + 5.0))
```

should output the following list:

```
AJ1  B  I  J  X  C  K
```

Note: The name extraction routine may be written as a subprogram and this routine will be useful in later problems. If a variable occurs more than once in a statement, it will be permitted to output the name more than once.

THE DATA IN THE SYMBOL TABLE

In the organization of any translatory system in which several processes of translation take place, such as lexical analysis, syntactic analysis, code generation etc., the vehicle for the transference of extracted or deduced information regarding the text is the symbol table. Also the symbol table provides a base for the coalescence of data relating to the various elements of the source text and possibly for describing certain relationships between the text and the target machine, such as the (possibly relative) addresses assigned variables. In a static environment, the symbol table will serve the purpose of providing (say) assigned addresses to the compiler's code generator for substitution into instruction masks, while the symbol table in a dynamic environment may exist also at run time to provide a key to currently allocated memory space. At the instant between the end of compilation and the beginning of execution of the generated program (assuming that the generated code is not resident), the symbol table will provide necessary data to the loader for the acquisition of library-provided subprograms and will, in turn, during run time, act as a transfer vector for the linkage of the generated code and those subprograms.

The compile-time symbol table of an algebraic language processor will contain entries pertinent to the various data elements which may occur within the source text. In general these may include variables (both simple and *n*-dimensional), statement identifiers, subprogram (or block) names and constants. Amongst this data will appear not only the deduced (or defined) attributes of the language element but also data pertinent to the compilation of the statements in which they either appeared or are expected to appear.

The purpose of a symbol table in a translatory system is best explained in the context of the functions which it must support. Besides being a repository for information between the various phases of a compiler or interpreter, the symbol table is the manifestation of the mapping function between language elements and their allocated elements in the executable form. That is, the symbol table is a *function.* The mappings which the symbol table can perform are symbolized in Figure 4.8. In this diagram, the language element (*id*) is the primary argument for the mapping functions "possesses" and "associated with" which select, respectively, the attributes (*attr*) possessed by the element and the name of the cell (*cell name*) with which the element

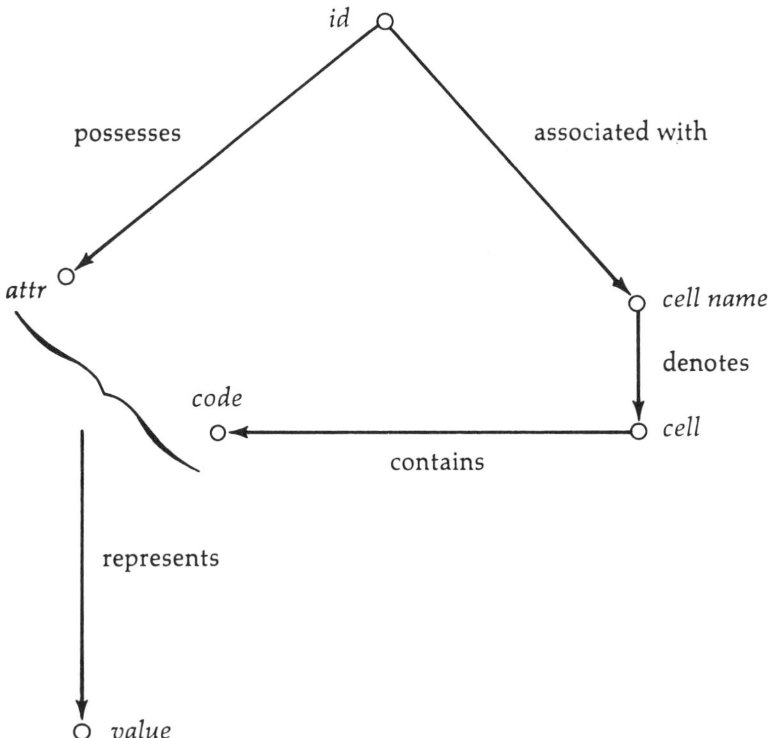

FIGURE 4.8 Symbol table mappings.

is associated. In turn, the cell name denotes a (physical) cell which is part of the storage system over which the translatory system is operating (or is to operate, in the case of a compile/execute system) which contains a code. When used as the arguments to the mapping function "represents," the attributes (*attr*) transform the code into a value. Of course the function "represents" may be a composite function, one portion of which exists in the translator as part of the code generator which produces an appropriate instruction which is executed later.

In an interpretive system (Figure 4.9) where the data store and symbol table are coexistent, the symbol-table function contains the mapping from the language element *id* onto the cell and the attributes, whereas in a compiler (Figure 4.10) the mapping is from *id* onto the cell name and the attributes. In the latter case, the cell is not existent at the time of compilation. Thus, in the loader, the mapping from cell name to cell is accomplished. It is important to note that in a system which involves relocatable code (either generated by the compiler or as a function of the host system) the mapping from cell name to cell is not fixed.

Similarly, in a one-pass compiler where forward references to labels, or references to subprograms, are accomplished by the use of a run-time transfer vector, this vector (or run-time symbol table) is representative of the mapping from cell names associated with a particular subclass of language elements onto the allocated cells.

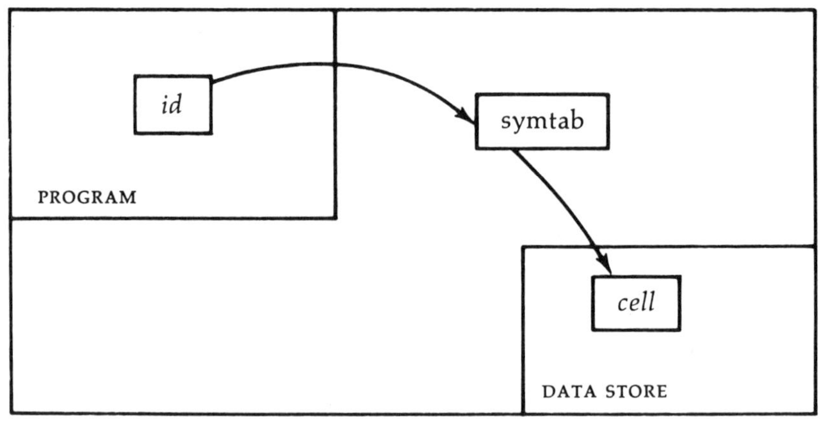

symtab: *id* → *cell*

FIGURE 4.9 Symbol table mappings in an interpretive system.

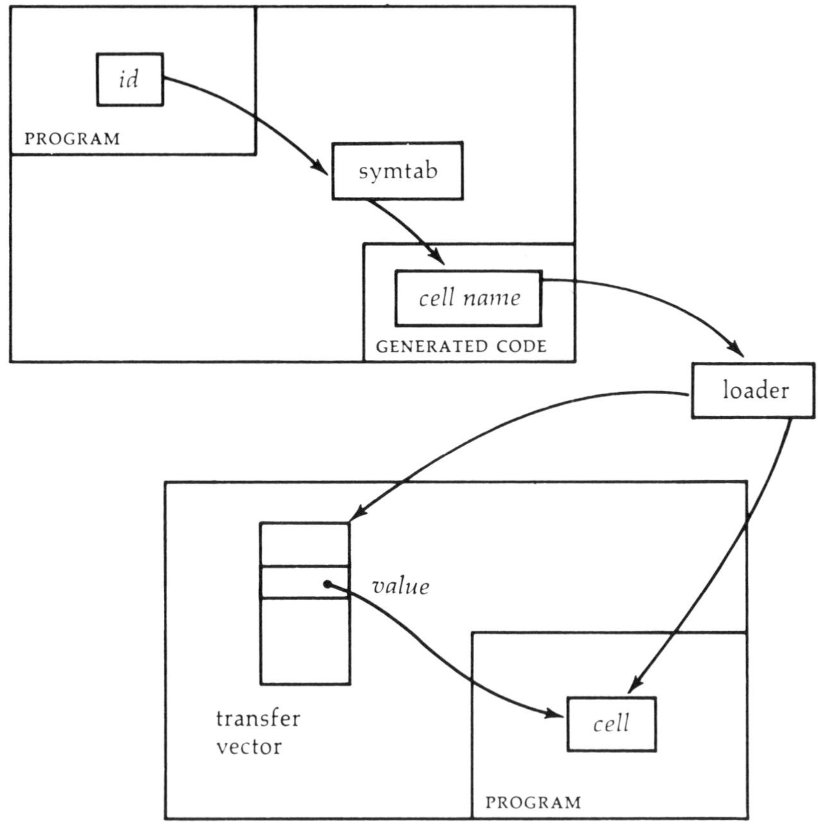

FUNCTIONS: symtab: *id* → *cellname*
loader: *cellname* → *cell*
transfer vector: *value* → *cell*

FIGURE 4.10 Symbol table functions in a compile/execute system.

The following table lists some of the information which is passed to the various generators in a compiler system or which is present at run time in an interpretive system:

Variables:

Mode? Real, integer, complex, etc.

Dimensioned? If so, what are the dimensions and how many?

Did the variable name appear as a formal parameter?

Did the variable appear in a COMMON statement or was it forced into COMMON by way of an EQUIVALENCE statement?

Has the variable been defined[3] within the subprogram; that is, is there a statement which will assign a value to this variable?

In the case of a compiler without the intermediate stage of translation to an assembly language, that is, a one- or two-pass system, what is the object time address of this variable?

In the case of an interpreter or a system with dynamic run-time storage allocation facilities, what is the current location assigned to this variable?

Subprograms:

Is it implementation defined as a subprogram to be provided by the host system or is it user defined?

Is it global? That is, is the subprogram referenceable by all subprograms (except possibly itself unless otherwise defined by the language)? If it is not globally referenceable, what restrictions exist on its referenceability? For example, in FORTRAN, an arithmetic statement function is referenceable only by the subprogram in which it is defined, but is referenceable by all other arithmetic statements functions also defined in that subprogram. Similarly in the block structure of ALGOL, a procedure defined in a block is referenceable in that block and to all encompassed blocks and defined procedures.

What is the mode of the subprogram? That is, in the case of FORTRAN functions and ALGOL procedures, what are the attributes of the result which is to be passed back to the referencing statement? This is particularly important where the name of the function or procedure is used as a variable in the description of the subprogram. In a FORTRAN-style SUBROUTINE, no distinction is made between results and arguments, thus this data element has no significance in this case.

What is (or are) the attribute(s) of the argument(s)?

Statement Identifiers:

Numeric or symbolic? If numeric, is there any significance in the numeric ordering? If symbolic, is there any value relationship? That is, does the statement identifier also exist in the domain of the operators of the language?

What is the starting address of the associated statement in a one-pass system or a system in which there is a direct relationship between the source text and the allocation of run-time memory?

In an interpretive system, at what address is the associated statement to be found?

3. See the next section for an amplification of the use of the term "defines."

Constants:
It is anticipated that in most languages, user-described constants are classed as being globally referenceable. That is, there exists in the target system only one copy of a constant.[4] In fact, a numeric value, in this sense may occur only in its positive form, any attached negative sign being interpreted (or compiled) as a unary minus.[5]

In some system other than an algebraic processor, the symbol table may play an extremely important part of the run-time characteristics of the system. For example, in any system which includes the ability to allocate and free storage or a system which is implemented so that storage is dynamically controlled (and yet is transparent to the user), the symbol table is the key between the executable code and the data set.

In the previous section on the lexical extraction of character strings, there was mention made of the distinctions between variable, function and subroutine names. Syntactically and lexically there are no distinguishing features of these three entities. There may exist some contextural features which enable some distinctions to be made. For example, if the translatory system has access to all subprograms which are being composed into the program being translated, it might be possible to search for name occurrences in the header statements of each subprogram to ascertain the usage of a certain character string. That is, by having the ability to examine header statements, it would be possible to match character strings which are possible subprogram references with the specified names (character strings) of subprograms. However, this is not always (and usually) possible, feasible or practical. A "good" translator system should be capable of compiling the composing subprograms in any order, taking advantage of any predefined names (in a temporal and local sense) but also being capable of deducing the attributes of undefined strings where necessary. That is, the first attempt to identify should be the "easy" route attempting to match the string with some predefined string and hence the associated attributes. Failing that, the deductive (and more cumbersome) process should be entered. This process applies not only to subprogram names as character strings but also to array names. In

4. There may exist many source text representations of the same number, such as 13, 13.0, +0.13E+2 and 15B. Depending on the definition of the language these might be combined into a single representation in the object time data set.

5. This may not be true in APL since the language explicitly distinguishes between the sign appended to a numeric representation and the unary minus sign as a prefix operator.

FORTRAN when the name has previously occurred in a **DIMENSION** statement (and therefore is already existent in the symbol table) or has had dimensions assigned to it in a **COMMON** statement, the name extracted refers to an array or an element of that array. If, in the context of an assignment statement or expression (within an arithmetic **IF** statement or an expression in a **CALL** list), and the name has not occurred previously in either a **DIMENSION** or **COMMON** statement with dimension, then the name must refer to a function. If the name is a reference to a library function, then the symbol table should have this information; the absence of such information would lead the compiler to assume that the reference is to a user-defined function. Thus whilst this may in fact be an error on the part of the programmer who has omitted to list this array in a **DIMENSION** statement, the compiler has a logical alternative which masks the error. However, at the time that the compiler has completed its task and control is turned over to the loader (possibly with a considerable hiatus in-between), the loader will attempt to locate within the system library a subprogram of the appropriate name. In the majority of cases this will not be successful and hence the loader can report back that the named subprogram was not available. This will undoubtedly cause the programmer some concern, but with a little experience he will realize the logical alternative that the compiler took and will look towards the declarative portion of the various subprograms to recognize the absence of a dimensioning statement.

In systems such as APL, where there exists no declarative part, this logical alternative is not present for the translator to fall back upon. In this case, however, it is to be expected that the translator is a portion of an interpretive system and therefore there exists a listing of the available subprograms, both system and user defined. Thus the absence of a name from this list must imply that the name is to be used as the name of an array. However, in APL itself this ambiguity does not exist since the functions act as either monadic or dyadic operators, and array references utilize the square brackets to enclose the subscript expressions. For example, the equivalent statements in APL of the FORTRAN expressions

BF(X,Y) and **X(I,J)**

would be

X BF Y and **X[I,J]**

between which no ambiguities occur. This is a patent example of designing a language so as to eliminate such amphiboles.

Since the entry key to each element in the symbol table is some representation of the name or the value of the string which was located in the source text (such as BCD for names and binary for constants), the recovery of any item together with its relevant information can be severely impeded by the necessity to compare the item in hand with every other item. Therefore to speed this search, each entry should be equipped with another secondary key that will describe the type of information being stored. For example, if one knows that the item in hand is a constant and the object time storage location needs to be determined from the table, it is pointless to compare the item in hand with the variable names in the table. Furthermore, there is a possibility that a constant stored in binary mode (in a one-pass system) will have a pattern of bits that is identical to the BCD representation of a name. The presence of the secondary key will obviate the possibility of a confusion arising in this case.

CONDITIONS THAT "DEFINE"[6] A QUANTITY

Part of the task of the compiler should be to give diagnostics to the programmer to indicate that a program is, for example, in error as a result of a variable being undefined within the source document. Thus the attempted execution of this program may fail due to the absence of a meaningful value for this variable. Similarly, an undefined statement number can cause the compiler difficulty in generating code corresponding to branch statements.

In FORTRAN, *variables* are defined by:

1. Appearance in a COMMON statement. This is not a foolproof test for definition, but when programs are to be overlaid, the compiler cannot check for the existence of a value for each variable.

2. Appearance in an EQUIVALENCE statement. However, if a set of lists describing the variables that have appeared in EQUIVALENCE groups is maintained during compilation, the possibility of undefined equivalenced variables may be checked further.

3. Appearance as a single-entity argument in a CALL statement. This also is not an absolute test of definition, since there is no way to determine within the subprogram which elements are to be used as input to the subroutine and which are to be given values by the routine.

6. "Define" in this sense is a poor use of the word, to be taken to mean "is assigned a value before it is referenced." The FORTRAN standard (X3.9–1966) also misuses the word.

4. Appearance as a formal parameter (dummy argument) in the defining statement of a subprogram.

5. Appearance on the left-hand side of an assignment statement.

6. Appearance as the second variable in an ASSIGN statement, that is, as the variable to which the statement number is assigned; for example, in the statement

ASSIGN 19 TO K

K would be taken to be defined.

7. Appearance in a DATA statement.

8. Appearance as an element of an input statement.

None of these tests for value definition are completely foolproof since only one (the appearance in a DATA statement) assures that a variable is assigned a value before it is to be used as a source of information and the assignment of a value to an element of an array (even in the DATA statement) does not ensure that all other elements have values. However, if none of the above conditions applies, then the compiler may emphatically issue a diagnostic warning. In certain instances, this lack of definition should be disastrous enough to prevent execution, whereas in others the programmer is merely given due warning of impending failure.

As a special case, the index parameter of a DO statement is taken to be defined within the range of the DO. Although it would appear that the index parameter (or control variable) of a DO loop is defined within the range of the DO and will take on the value of the last passage through the loop plus the increment, except when the range is exited abnormally, the specifications for FORTRAN state (with regard to the conditions which terminate the repeated execution of a DO range):[7]

> If the value of the control variable is greater than the value represented by its associated terminal parameter, the DO is said to have been satisfied and *the control variable becomes undefined.*

This situation results from the original implementations of the FORTRAN compiler. In these versions the DO range was controlled from a set of index registers in which the various parameters were stored. However, because of the limited number of registers it was necessary to reuse registers outside the range, and thus there was no guarantee

7. Sec. 7.1.2.8, American National Standard FORTRAN, Document X3.9–1966.

as to the current value of the index parameter (or control variable). Thus rather than leave the value of the parameter to the wiles of the compiler writer, it was felt better to state that the value of the parameter became undefined. Further, since the value of the parameter was stored in a register instead of direct access memory, its value was not available without considerable programming difficulty and subsequent loss of computer time.

Statement numbers are defined by appearance in columns 1–5 of a source statement.

Subprogram names are defined by appearance in a **FUNCTION**, **SUBROUTINE** or **PROGRAM** statement, by appearance on the left-hand side of an arithmetic statement function, or by implication as a standard library subprogram.

Constants are always defined.

In a block-structured language such as ALGOL or PL/I, the definition of a variable, a procedure, or a statement identifier depends not only on the factors listed above but also on the block within which that language element is located. The scope of variables is normally determinable at compile time and thus, though there may be some semantic ambiguity in the name applied to some storage location at a given instant, the knowledge of scope, determined on activation of a block, removes any ambiguity. In this case, the determination of definition is local to each block during compilation, each block being provided with its own separate symbol table which is manipulated at compile time in a manner similar to those acting over the directories for the storage assignments on block activation and release. The means for determining scope and the procedures followed on the activation and release of blocks will be discussed in detail in Chapter 5.

ORGANIZING THE SYMBOL TABLE

In any procedural or block-structured language there may exist, during the various phases of compilation or interpretation, several differing symbol tables, each relating to a particular block or procedure. Whilst the raison d'être and the means of establishment of each symbol table may be distinct, the means by which symbol tables in general are organized is common to all.

The purpose of a symbol table is to provide a common data source to the various components of a translatory system relating to the elements of the source text, and in particular to provide a source of data pertinent to the specified or deduced attributes of those elements. The symbol table is thus being accessed by many routines during the process of translation and thus must be amenable to rapid access and data retrieval. The **SYMTAB** routine is assigned this task of symbol table organization. Among the tasks which **SYMTAB** directs are:

1. Post an item and its associated data.
2. Retrieve the data associated with any item.
3. Delete an item and its associated data.

All these activities involve searching the table either to locate the item or to recognize the absence of that item, and hence the efficiency of this search affects the efficiency of the whole compiler.

The obvious technique of arranging the symbol table is to divide the memory into a distinct number of cells and to assign each entry to the next available cell in the table vector. To retrieve the data associated with any item, or to locate an item for deletion, the in-hand item must be checked against the table from the top down. Thus to retrieve an item, the average number of comparisons will be equal to half the size of the present table. Similarly, determining that an item is present requires the same number of checks.

If certain character strings in the language are to be reserved for special purposes, then the number of comparisons will be increased by this number each time. Thus the search time in a compiler with a set of reserved names can increase substantially, compared to one without such restrictions.

An alternative manner of symbol table organization[8] is that which was originally used in the **SOAP** assembler for the IBM 650. Instead of assigning compile time cells to an item in the order of their presentation to the symbol table, this technique uses the internal representation of the item as input data to a routine that creates an address within the available symbol table area. This address is then checked to verify the existence of the item. If the location is blank, the item does not exist in the table and may be posted at that position. If the location is already in use, the item that is stored and the item in hand must be compared. If they match, the search is complete. If they are not equal, then a further search must be made. This may be done by

8. J. Field, D. A. Jardine, E. S. Lee, J. A. N. Lee, and D. Robinson, *Kingston FORTRAN II*, 1620 Users Group Conference, Chicago, 1964; also A. Batson, "The Organization of Symbol Tables," *Comm. ACM*, vol. 8, no. 2, 1965.

one of two techniques: Either a sequential search can be initiated or a link can be formed to a separate list ordered by appearance of the item. The former technique has two advantages: Only a single table is required, and if a blank cell is located during the sequential search, then the item in hand does not have a match within the table since an entry would have had to take the same route. However, when the table is reaching the saturation point, the number of comparisons either to locate the matching item or determine the absence of that item approaches that of a standard sequential search (Figure 4.11a). Further, the sequential search must be so organized that the table is considered to be cyclic. That is, since the starting point for the sequential search is not the first item in the list, special arrangements must be made to cycle from the last item in the physical table to the first item in the table and also to stop if the cycle continues up to the cell onto which the name of the item was originally mapped. If the latter situation occurs, then the table is full and the item has not been included in the table.

A second method uses a primary table which is linked into a secondary table such that each entry is supplemented by an address defining the location of the next entry in this string. Thus if a match is not made in the primary table, the link address is checked to determine whether there is a list emanating from that point. If the address is blank, then such a list is not present and a match will never be accomplished. The item may be posted at the next available cell in the secondary table. If a link address exists, then the item at that address must be checked, and if a match is made, then the search is complete. If not, the link address at this location is to be tested, and the search will continue through the secondary table. The checking of reserved words in a random search technique does not detract from the overall efficiency of the system since a single mapping of the word into the primary table will suffice to determine whether the item is reserved. Thus in the worst case, only one cell must be checked to determine that an item is not a reserved word as opposed to the necessity to check every reserved word in a sequential search. The linkages of this pseudo-random addressing technique are shown in Figure 4.11b.

This technique is much faster than the sequential search system, provided the table is not approaching the saturation point. Table 4.8 shows some experimental results.

This "random" posting and retrieval technique affords substantial time-saving advantages but also has some inherent disadvantages:

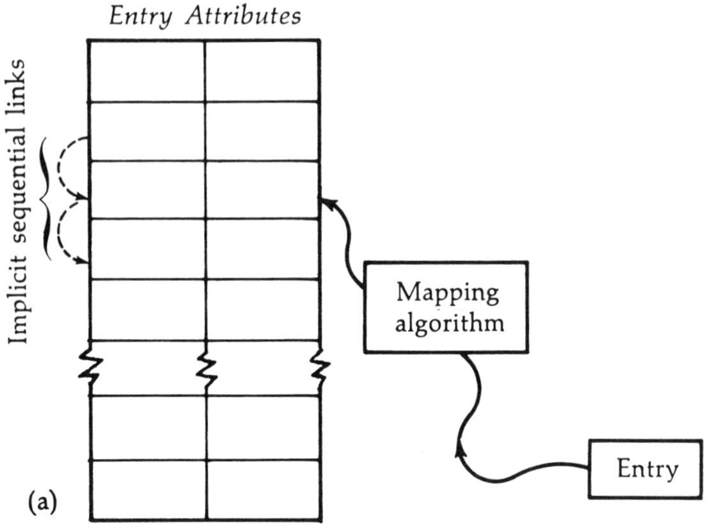

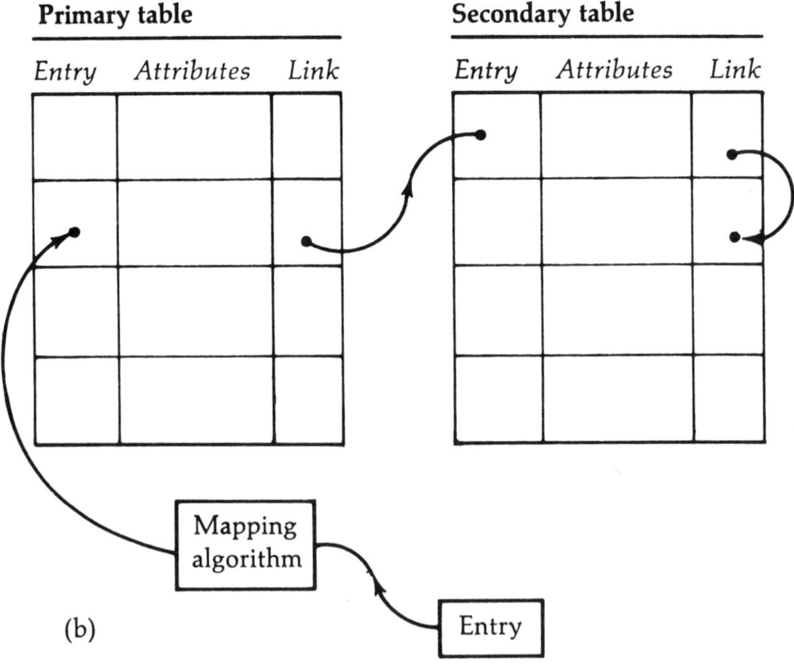

FIGURE 4.11 (a) A sequential table system; (b) a linked secondary table system.

TABLE 4.8[a]

No. of items in table	*Sequential search*	*"Random" search*
20	40	2.14
50	55	2.25
100	80	2.37
200	130	3.14
To locate a reserved-word	15	1.08[b]

Retrieval time: τ/T[c]
Table size: 400 cells
No. of reserved words: 30

[a]From A. Batson "The Organization of Symbol Tables," *Comm. ACM*, vol. 8, no. 2, 1965.

[b]This time is not exactly 1.00 since some reserved words mapped into the same location in the primary table and thus had to be stored in the secondary table.

[c]T is the time to examine a single entry in the table; τ is the total search time.

1. The tables must be arranged so as to be cyclic.

2. Although it is obvious when the secondary table is full in a linked secondary system since items are posted sequentially, vacant cells may be present in the primary table, and only a sequential search through the primary table will reveal these cells. Thus the table may appear to be full when the secondary table becomes full, and only special action can determine the validity of this assumption.

3. If the programmer requires a symbol table mapping, the table together with any imbedded blanks must be searched, whereas in a sequential table the table is dense and can be mapped more rapidly.

4. In a FORTRAN-style language, that is, a language without intrinsic block structure, the completion of compilation of a single subprogram is also a signal for the deletion of the symbol table, in preparation for the compilation of the next subprogram. This is almost 100% possible since the relationships between subprograms are not expressed in terms of the names of the language elements. Only one particular type of symbol table entry is to be saved by the compiler through the compilation of the next subprogram—the names of referenced subprograms and the locations assigned to the indirect entry point to those subprograms. It is not necessary that the next subprogram compilation take advantage of this residual information, but it is possible that the compiled code can be enhanced by recognizing the

existence of this information. For example, it would be wasteful of both time and space to have a separate entry point for each reference to a single subprogram; wasteful of both time in the loader (which will be forced to "fill in" the actual entry point addresses in several places) and wasteful of space due to the multiple storage of the same address. The location of these entries in the symbol table in order to have the information will not be insubstantial since the speedy table accessing is accomplished by the use of the entry key. Lacking the key, the table must be searched sequentially.

The same problem will occur in relation to the generation, activation, and deactivation of the symbol tables relating to block-structured languages. In this case, the symbol table for an inner block is to be generated from the existing symbol table of the encompassing block. Thus whilst a copy of the outer block symbol table is stacked (see Chapter 5) any variables which do not have scope in the inner block must be deleted and the local variables must be added to the table. This too will turn out to be a sieving operation for which the tables are not well organized.

Depending on the whims of the implementer, constants may or may not be passed between procedures and blocks. That is, it is an implementation decision as to whether a constant is to be regarded as in the same class as global variables, and thus there will exist only one copy in the system of each representation of any number. If the data relating to constants is maintained within the symbol table, the task of preserving their attributes on exit from a procedure or upon entry to (or exit from) a block is similar in complexity to that for preserving the appropriate table entries between subprograms or procedures. This line of reasoning would lead us to the proposition that separate symbol tables might be established for constants and subprogram entries so that it is not necessary to search for their corresponding entries in a general table.

Besides the manner in which the symbol table is organized, the efficiency of the SYMTAB routine will also depend on the ability of the mapping algorithm to discriminate between the various anticipated entries. That is, if the mapping algorithm is so poorly organized (in the extreme) that every entry maps onto a single cell in the primary table, then the organization of the symbol table degenerates into an equivalent sequential table system. At the other end of the scale, given sufficient space and an efficient mapping algorithm, the secondary table would not be necessary, and thus all symbol-table references would be accomplished in a single reference cycle (see T in Table 4.8). The practicality of symbol table organization obviously lies between these two extremes. In the report by Batson (see Table 4.8) on the relative efficiency of a table organized on the basis of "random" search versus a sequential search, no mention is made of the actual algorithm of mapping between the given entry and the location of the corresponding data in the primary table.

To give some indication of the differences in "efficiency" of various mapping algorithms, the author developed a program for the posting system using the two-table method, leaving undefined a function which computed the address (subscript, index) in the primary table which was to be matched initially. The students in a data structures course were then invited (in fact, assigned) to develop their own mapping algorithms. The efficiencies of using the tables were then compared.

Although many students took part in the project, some algorithms were identical and thus only 11 different algorithms were recorded. These may be classified into four groups according to the means of computing the basic data for the algorithm or the means of computing the address from this value. In the first group of algorithms (the summation methods), the starting value for the method was computed by summing the binary (BCD) representations of the individual characters of the data items. In the second group (the equivalence methods), the initial value was taken as the integer value equivalent to the binary representations of the string of characters in the data item. In each of these two classes, the address was computed either as the modular function of this value or by direct proportioning of the value into the range of the primary table. The third technique, of which there were two examples, also used the characters of the data item as a starting value for the algorithm, but then utilized one of the classic pseudorandom number generator routines to compute the address. The final method used a mapping function based on the distribution of words in an English dictionary.

The original data set up on which the students tested their algorithms was the concordance of the Rubaiyat of Omar Khayyam. This choice resulted from a previous assignment in which the students were given the task of preparing a program to extract words from a prose text prepared in free form with spacing and punctuation. The Rubaiyat was chosen as the text for that assignment due to its exotic punctuation. However, since the vocabulary of the Rubaiyat is not typical of that of standard English prose, a different text was chosen as the validation text for the algorithms. By chance, (i.e. picking a book at random from a bookshelf) the preface and introduction of *Academic Freedom and Tenure* by Louis Joughin (University of Wisconsin Press, 1967), was chosen as the test prose. This section of the book contains 1405 data items (words, abbreviations and numerical values) of which 545 are distinct. These were contained on 142 standard 80-column cards. Seven tests were made on each algorithm using 20, 40, 60, 80, 100, 120 and 142 cards. The number of distinct words in each set of cards were 113, 197, 289, 412, 479 and 545 respectively.

During the testing of each algorithm, records were maintained with respect to the secondary list length which emanated from each primary table element. Since the majority of the hashing techniques "sprayed" the data over the primary table without respect to the actual alphabetical contents, no comparative data are available concerning the effect of the distribution of the data on the different algorithms. For example, it might be found that certain algorithms are more efficient with data sets in which the words are evenly distributed over the alphabet. However, if such algorithms are to be used in connection with the storage of the distinct words from a prose corpus, then it cannot be expected that such ideal distributions will be presented. The only algorithm which attempted to take into account the distribution of words in the English language also produced a listing which was semiordered (alphabetized). The original posting algorithm provided as the basis for these experiments utilized a primary table of one hundred elements. Since the data provided exceeded 100 items, any remaining memory (after the loading of the program and space for a primary table of 100 elements) was available for the construction of linked lists emanating from the primary table. Thus if more than one data item were mapped into a single element of the primary table, succeeding items were to be stored in the elements of the linked list. Organizationally, the secondary table consisted of a one-dimensional array, each element of which consisted of a location for the data element itself and an address pointing to the position of the sequential item in the table. Similarly, each primary table element consisted of two parts, a location for the data item and the link address.

If the mapping algorithms had the capability of evenly distributing the data elements over the primary table, then each and every secondary linked list would be of equal length. Since the total number of distinct words in the text was 545, then it would have been expected that the linked list[9] lengths would have been 5.45. In fact, the

9. A linked list consists of the entry in the primary table and the entries in the secondary table.

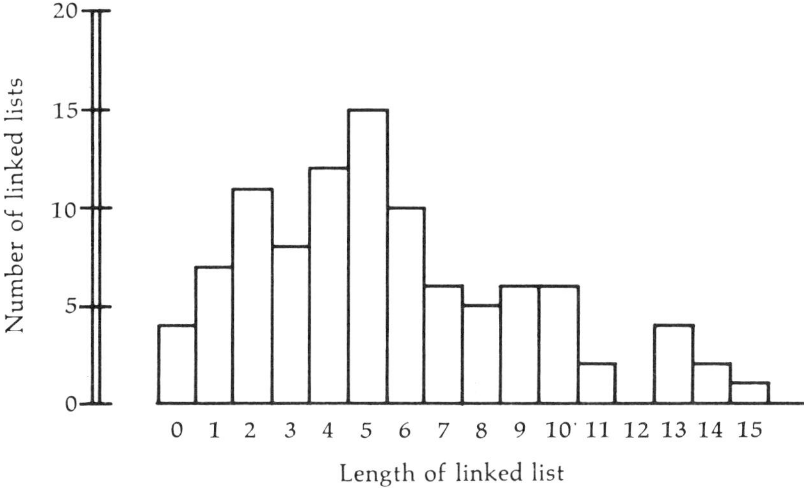

FIGURE 4.12 Distribution of lengths of linked lists.

distribution of list lengths averaged over all algorithms (Figure 4.12) shows that the most frequently occurring list length is 5.

The average primary table utilization for each class of methods is shown in Figure 4.13. From these plots it may be seen that the summation methods are consistently superior in their utilization of the primary table. Although the pseudorandom methods have an average performance comparable to that of the character equivalence, the different performances between the two methods is so large as to discount the average values. Comparing the pseudorandom methods with the summation methods, it may be seen that the percentage utilization of the primary tables are within 15%. However, the extra effort in computing the primary table address by the pseudorandom technique (and hence the additional time utilized during each posting or retrieval) does not appear to have improved on the efficiency of storage usage.

Similarly, for the summation methods, the results are not significantly different from those of the equivalence method to justify the additional computer time needed to extract the individual characters of the data item and to produce a starting value for the address from the sum of the binary representations of those characters. Figure 4.14 shows the cumulative relative frequencies of list lengths obtained by using the equivalence method to store the various portions of the data of the text containing 545 distinct words.

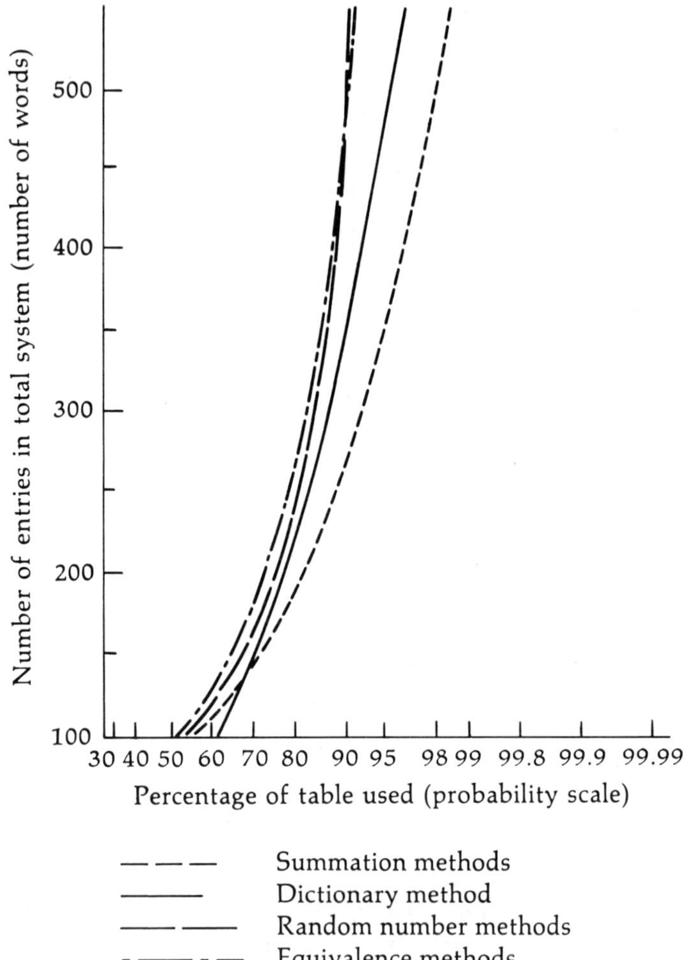

FIGURE 4.13 Average primary table utilization.

These techniques of symbol table organization together with a secondary or even a tertiary table have the advantage that where there is variable amount of pertinent data to be stored with each entry the subsequent table can be used for these variable data strings, whereas the primary table(s) which contain the keys and fixed-length names may be of standard cell sizes. For example, a dimensioned variable must be stored in the symbol table not only by name and type but also with the dimensions. Thus the name may be stored in the primary table (if space exists) together with a link to a subsequent table in which the dimensioning information is stored. Thus if a single word is reserved for the storage of the next available address in the subse-

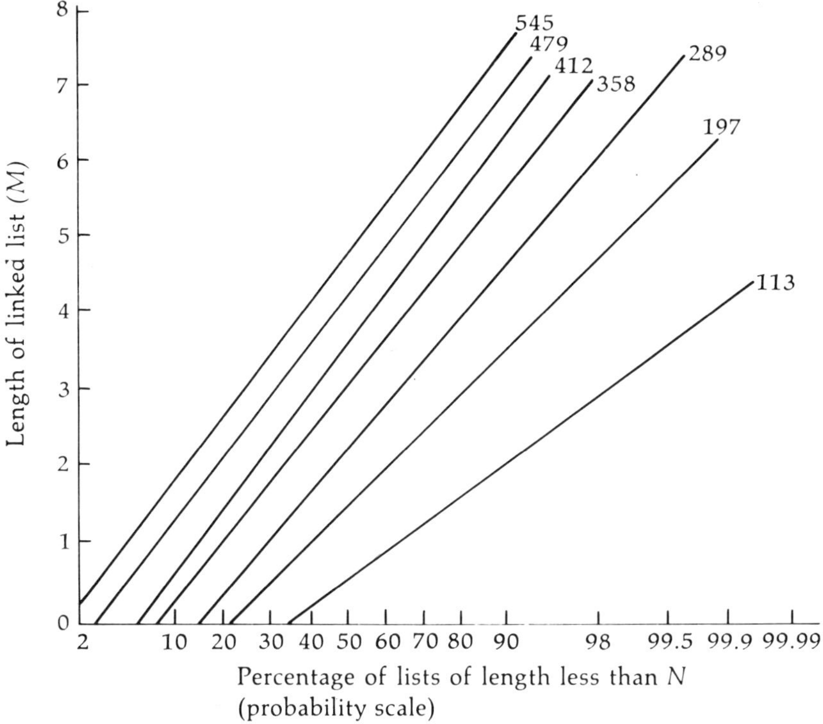

FIGURE 4.14 Lengths of linked lists for the equivalence method.

quent table, variable numbers of words may be reserved for the dimensioning information without upsetting the whole organization of the symbol table and at the same time only using space as required without leaving blanks in cells that were originally set at a size equal to the maximum required for any string of data.

Such a technique can be utilized for the construction of the symbol and occurrence table of an indexer.[10] An indexer is a program, the input to which is the source language of, for example, an assembly system, and the output of which is a table of the statements in which each variable is either used or defined. For example, the following COMPASS (Control Data 3600) listing includes the names of 10 variables, some of which are actually defined in this portion by their appearance in the first eight character positions. Thus the output of the indexer for this partial program will show that some variables are undefined.

10. R. Pratt, *Referencer and Indexer.* IBM 1620 Program Library No. 1.1.014.

```
        STA     CACHE          001
A       IF,EQ   CACHE,STORE    002
        ENI     99,1           003
B       IFU                    004
AB      RAO     AA,1           005
        IJP     AB,1           006
        ENI     49,2           007
C       IFU                    008
        ENDIF   B              009
        ENI     49,2           010
AB      RAO     AA,1           011
        IJP     AB,1           012
        ENDIF   C              013
BC      RSO     BB,2           014
        IJP     BC,2           015
        ENDIF   A              016
        LDA     NEXT           017
```

The indexer output for this program would be:

```
002   A       016
      AA      005   011
005   AB      006   012
004   B       009
011   BB      014
014   BC      015
008   C       013
      CACHE   001   002
      NEXT    017
      STORE   002
```

where the first column of figures denotes the statement in which the variable is defined, and the figures to the right of the variable denote the statements in which that variable name appears. Thus the variable AB is defined at statement number 005 and used in the statements numbered 006 and 012. Similarly, the variables AA, CACHE, NEXT and STORE are not defined.

Such a table is extremely useful in the debugging or updating of programs, for the change in action or effect of a single variable at several points in the program or the execution of a program may require the checking of each occurrence of that variable. Similarly, in reading a program, the index is an aid to the tracing of the logical flow of the execution of the program.

When a program is prepared to perform the task of an indexer, both the number of references to each variable and the total number of variables are unknown. Thus given a sufficiently large portion of memory, the hashing technique, with a subsequent table for the storage of the references, is a suitable system. The primary table may be used to post the name of the variable and three addresses:

1. The address of the storage location of the next variable which maps into the same position in the primary table.

2. The address of the word in which the occurrence of the first use of the variable is noted.

3. The address of the last word in the subsequent table at which the number of the statement in which the last (or latest) occurrence has been noted.

Within the occurrence list associated with each variable will be: (a) the number of the statement at which the variable was found, (b) a tag to indicate whether the occurrence was merely a use or a definition and (c) an address linking this posting with the word in which the next occurrence is noted. This system is shown graphically in Figure 4.15. The address of the last (or latest) occurrence in the primary table is merely a luxury which enables the posting or retrieval routine to locate the last entry without chaining through all previous occurrence postings. This address is continually updated as new postings are made. The posting routine is shown in Figure 4.16.

Problem

4.6 Literary critics have taken to using a computer to automate many of the techniques of literary analysis and, as a result, have been able to authenticate the authors of several important works. For example, using a computer to analyze the metric form of the *Odyssey*, researchers concluded that the whole work was written by one person, and since there is other evidence to ascribe certain portions to Homer, the evidence as a whole leads to but one conclusion. Similarly, the authorship of the *Federalist Papers* was determined by an examination of the frequency of such key words as *upon*, *while*, and *whilst*. The technique of word counting and listing all occurrences in context is known as forming a concordance. Such a program involves the reading of a text in machine-readable form (cards, tape etc.), extracting each word and keeping track of each occurrence of that word.

Assume that a text has been prepared on cards and may contain punctuation. Write a program to extract the words, to count the num-

	Name	Next name	First occurrence	Latest occurrence
01	A	04	11	15
02	AB	00	12	14
03	B	05		
04	AA	00	16	16
05	BB	00		
06				

	Address of occurrence	Tag[a]	Next occurrence
11	002	D	15
12	005	D	13
13	006	U	14
14	012	U	00
15	016	U	00
16	005	D	00

[a]D = definition
U = a use

Note:
In this example all two-digit addresses refer to entries in either table, while three-digit addresses refer to statement numbers. The primary table is incomplete.

FIGURE 4.15

ber of occurrences and, eventually to output both an alphabetized listing of the words and counts and a second listing in the order of frequency of occurrence, commencing with those words of least frequency. Do not overlook the fact that some of the text words may not fit into a single computer word.

For this particular example, the following symbolism may be used

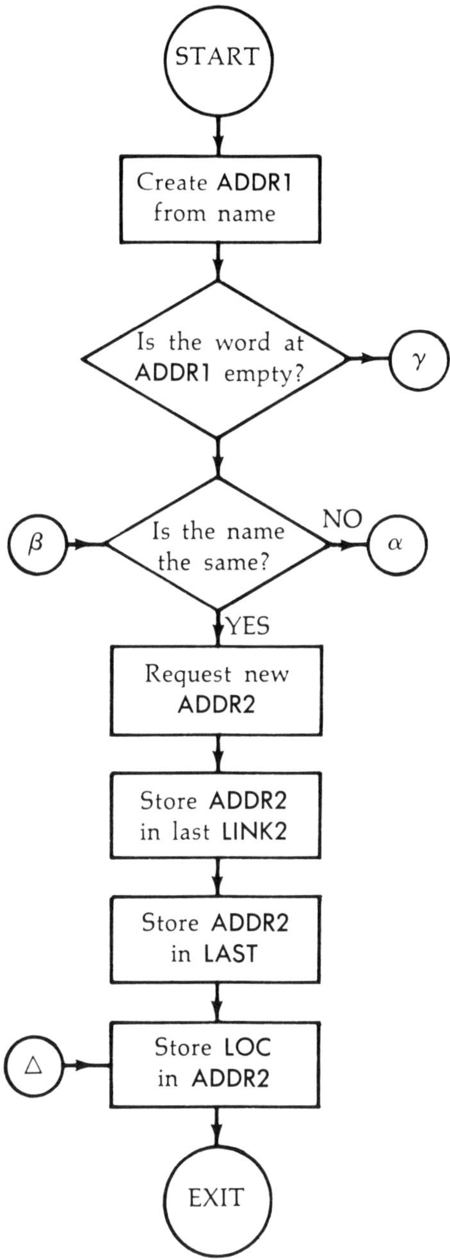

FIGURE 4.16 Occurrence posting: Input parameters include name and location of occurrence.

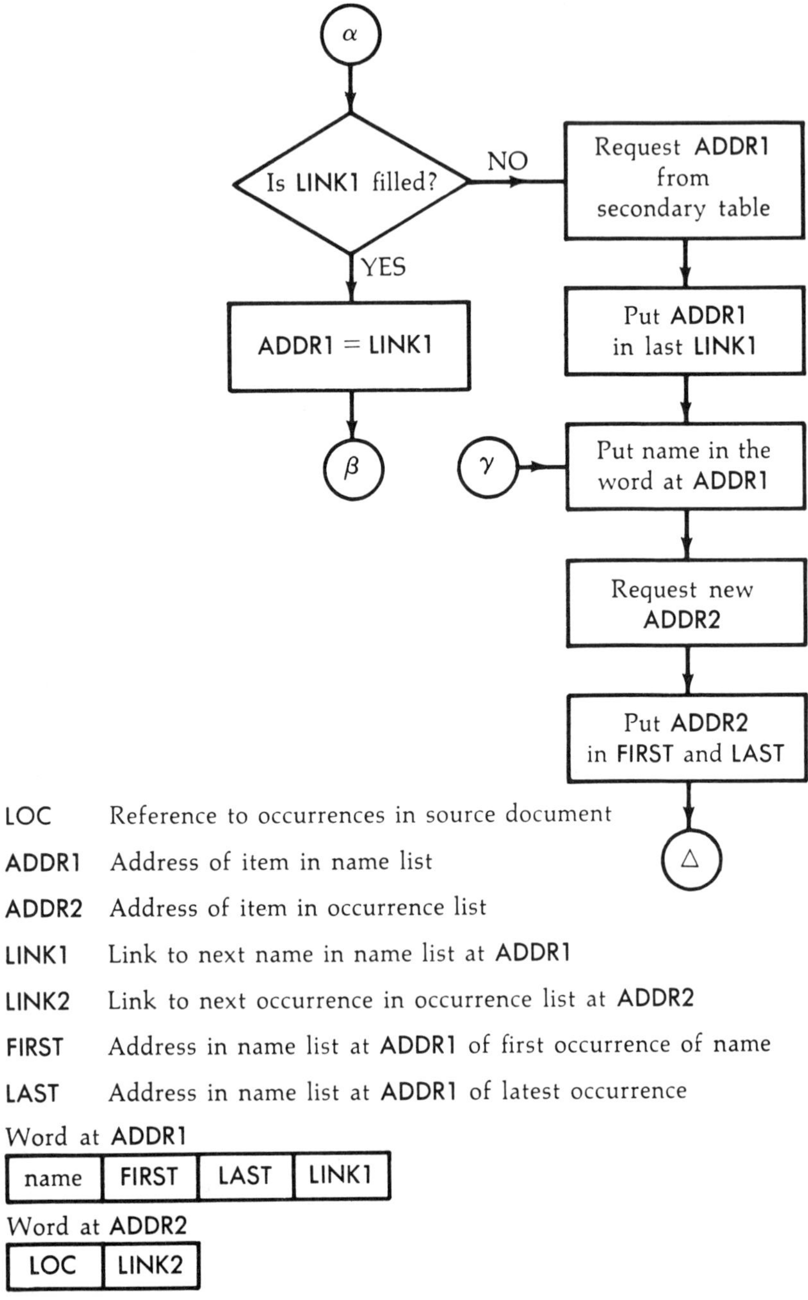
α
Is LINK1 filled?
NO
YES
Request ADDR1 from secondary table
ADDR1 = LINK1
Put ADDR1 in last LINK1
β
γ
Put name in the word at ADDR1
Request new ADDR2
Put ADDR2 in FIRST and LAST
△
LOC Reference to occurrences in source document
ADDR1 Address of item in name list
ADDR2 Address of item in occurrence list
LINK1 Link to next name in name list at ADDR1
LINK2 Link to next occurrence in occurrence list at ADDR2
FIRST Address in name list at ADDR1 of first occurrence of name
LAST Address in name list at ADDR1 of latest occurrence
Word at ADDR1
name
FIRST
LAST
LINK1
Word at ADDR2
LOC
LINK2

FIGURE 4.16 **(Continued)**

to represent those characters that do not exist in a standard 48 character set:

!	exclamation mark	/.
?	question mark	@.
:	colon	..
;	semicolon	.,
'	quote and unquote	*
'	apostrophe	/
-	hyphen	- (minus sign)
—	dash	-- (repeated minus)

Note the following: (a) Poets and writers of prose may use shortened words such as *'twas* or *'t*. The apostrophes should be included as part of these words. (b) A hyphenated word should be regarded as a single word. (c) When the last character in a sentence is an apostrophe, the text should be prepared so that there is a blank between this character and the period. In this manner there can be no confusion between this combination and an exclamation mark.[11]

LINKED LISTS AS TREE STRUCTURES IN SYMBOL TABLES

As an alternative to the schema in which a prescribed portion of memory is delineated as the space available for the construction of a symbol table, and in which there exists some linear table which is the potential first element list of a number of linked lists, let us consider the case of tree structures, represented as linked lists. In this case there will exist only one single-entry point to the symbol table, namely, the root node of the tree, but from that point there will emanate several (if not many) linked lists in which the successive components of the symbol table are stored. A tree, in the sense in which we wish to discuss trees here, can be considered to be a set of nodes (symbol table entries) and connectors (links, pointers) between nodes. We shall assume that there exists only one node in a tree which has no connectors terminating at it (that is, the root node) and that each connector has associated with it a direction of connection. We shall also assume that the paths which may be formed by the sequences of connectors and intermediate nodes do not interconnect and in particular there exists no path such that it is possible to "move" from any node through other nodes and return to the original node. In terms of *representations* in a storage system, there may exist pointers

11. For further information see J. A. Painter, "Computer Preparation of a Poetry Concordance," *Comm. ACM*, vol. 3, no. 2, (Feb. 1960), pp. 91–95.

by which it is possible to traverse a circuit in the tree (such as from node *a* to node *b* and back). However, pointers and connectors are not one for one representations of each other, as will be seen later.

In order to accomplish the "tree-walking" operations which are necessary, the representations of tree structures may include pointers which are in opposition to the expected direction of connection of the nodes. That is, we shall consider a tree in which it is possible only to enter at the root node, and once having reached a node it is not possible to return to any predecessors of that node. However, in the representation system with a limited number of pointers certain tree traverses may be accomplished (simulated) only by locating certain predecessors (such as the *father* node).

Given any particular node in a tree, we term all the nodes which are connected by arcs emanating from that node to be the *successors* of that node, and in turn, all the nodes of which a particular node is a successor are the *predecessors* of that node. By selecting any connector emanating from a given node, the node selected by that connector and all its successors compose a *branch* of the tree. To carry this arboreal analogy further, those nodes which have no successors are termed the *leaves* of the tree.

In utilizing a tree structure as the storage system of a data set (and in our particular case of the data in a symbol table), it is necessary that there exist some relationship between the data elements so that the tree can provide a meaningful storage and retrieval system. In the worst case, a tree could be composed of a single nonsplitting branch wherein each node was connected to only one other node. In this sense the tree might represent the data in its order of arrival at the storage mechanism, and the retrieval system would be a simple sequential search through the tree to locate any item.

Such a degenerate representation is no better (if not somewhat worse) than storing the data in a linear (one-dimensional) array. That is, given that the representation of a node must contain not only the data item but also information regarding its relatives (in the form of pointers), it is obvious that a storage scheme in which the relationships are implied is at least better from the point of view of storage utilization, and there is an implication that retrieval should be more efficient in the implied linkage case, since no retrieval of linkages is necessary. That is, in the latter case, the implied organization requires only a single "look-up" to retrieve a value, whereas the linked system will require at least two fetch operations. Discarding the worst case, let us focus on the "best" case where the tree is so organized by virtue of the relationships between the values contained at the nodes so that the number of nodes to be examined to identify a particular value is minimized. The best case then corresponds to the situation in which there exists a root node and from that node all other data items are accessible in a branch composed of a single connector and the desired node. This corresponds roughly to the tabular structure used in the previous section, where the primary table was large enough to contain all values without secondary lists.

In between these two extremes exists reality. First, the notion of relationships has been almost ignored, since in the degenerate case (the single branch tree) the only relationship was one of arrival time, and the second case related values to some universe rather than each other. As a first step to realizing a practical organization, let us consider the binary tree.[12] If we were to restrict ourselves to the storage of numeric values, it would be possible to develop a relationship scheme whereby the choice of which connector to select to travel through the tree would be determined by a "greater than" or a "less than" relationship. That is, for example, if the data which is associated with some given numeric key is desired, a succession of comparisons with the keys at the nodes of the tree (starting from the root node) the left or right connector being chosen as the route to the next node depending on whether the "in-hand" key was "less than" or "greater than" the value of the key at each node respectively.

When information is stored in the form of a tree structure, the accessibility of any single item depends on the length of the longest branch within the tree. For example, an ordered list may be considered as a tree which contains a single branch and within which each parent has only a single child. Thus the retrieval time of any piece of data will be proportionate to the length of the single branch. However, in a binary tree where the length of all branches does not differ by more than one node, the average retrieval time may be shortened enormously.[13] For example, a tree containing 1,000,000 items may be constructed so that no more than 20 comparisons are necessary either to locate an item or to determine its absence. Thus if a tree contains n levels, that is, the length of each branch is n, then the maximum number of items in the tree will be 2^n-1, whereas in an

12. That is, a tree in which each node (except the leaves) has no more than two connectors emanating from it.

13. See the references in C. C. Foster, *A Study of AVL Trees*, Proceedings of the A.C.M. Conference, Cleveland, Ohio, August, 1965, and W. A. Martin and D. N. Ness, "Optimizing Binary Trees Grown with a Sorting Algorithm," *Comm. ACM*, vol. 15, no. 2 (Feb. 1972).

TABLE 4.9

n	*Maximum no. of entries*
1	1
2	3
3	7
4	15
5	31
10	1023
15	32767
20	1048575

unbalanced tree (that is, one in which the branches or subtrees within one node need not be of equal length), the minimum number of stored items is n. The maximum number of items stored in a balanced tree is shown in Table 4.9. Conversely, the same table indicates the maximum number of comparisons necessary to locate a single item in a balanced tree.

The efficient retrieval of information from a balanced tree may also be accomplished by use of a binary search technique on an ordered list of items. That is, given an ordered list the number of comparisons necessary to retrieve an item cannot exceed $\log_2(m+1)$, where m is the number of items in the table. A binary search technique compares the in hand item with that at the center of the table and then makes one of three decisions: (1) The item is at that location; (2) The item is above this point (that is, it must occur in the upper portion of the table); or (3) The item lies in the lower half of the table. If the item is not located immediately, then the portion of the table within which it would appear to lie is regarded as a new table and the search procedure repeated. If the table is successively halved until one item remains and that item does not compare equally with that in hand, then the item does not exist within the table.

In a compiler, the order of presentation of variable names and other symbol table data to **SYMTAB** is purely random, and thus maintaining an ordered list is wasteful of time. Further, the unrestricted formation of a tree will not necessarily produce a balanced tree from which data may be extracted rapidly. Foster[14] has shown that trees may be kept balanced by a simple routine, but the posting and retrieval time, together with that for maintaining balance, far exceeds that for the same procedures in a pseudorandom table.

14. C. C. Foster, ibid.

5

Storage Allocation and Management

Most multipass compiler systems take no direct part in the allocation of memory to the language elements of the program which they are operating over. This task is left to the assembler which is already available in the total computer system (or operating system). Many of the features of storage allocation are transparent to the programmer and some may be transparent to the implementer. In some cases the language defines the most logical organization of memory by providing hints for the implementer to recognize, whilst other languages are totally independent of the storage schemes. In this chapter we shall consider both the systems of storage organization and the methods of storage allocation.

ALLOCATION OF LANGUAGE ELEMENTS TO OBJECT TIME MEMORY

Given a program in (almost) any language and the derivation therefrom of the set of identifiers, constants, references and other language elements, at some instant there must occur a mapping from this user's set of elements onto the available memory locations of the computer which is to execute or which is executing the generated program. The majority of high-level computer languages do not provide the programmer with the ability to describe explicitly the organization of memory at object time (except in the case of FORTRAN **COMMON**, see later) and rarely (with the exception of FORTRAN **EQUIVALENCE**, see later) allow the user to specify relationships between identifiers and other language elements. Thus the implementer is free to devise some mapping algorithm between the language elements and their assigned storage locations (at object time) provided that certain criteria are met. That is, very simply, that the values assigned to some identifier (variable, array element, statement identifier, etc.) are retrievable at some later (possibly restricted) time.

The instant at which all the information necessary to permit the allocation of object time memory to some language element is one of the bounds on the binding time of that element. That is, there must exist two bounds (which in certain instances may be identical) on the time during which memory may be assigned to a language element. The latest time (bound) available to assign a memory location to a language element is obviously the instant prior to its first usage in the program. Conversely, if all the attributes of a language element are not only known but are also known to be fixed, then it is possible to assign (allocate) memory at this earliest time. This period may be further subdivided by considering the type of memory referencing to be performed. That is, if the earliest binding time is taken as that instant when an absolute address can be assigned to a language element, then binding time might be defined as load time (that is, the time at which the program is loaded into memory). However, to leave all memory assignments to the loading routine may be a severe overload on the loader. In an environment where the loader determines which portion (bank, page, segment, etc.) of memory is available for the particular program to be loaded, it is anticipated that at least the memory assignment system would be able to develop a mapping scheme by which language element locations could be referenced to some base address provided by the loader. In this instance, we should define the earliest binding time as that time at which the offsets in the relative addressing system may be assigned to the language elements. By this definition, the binding time of language elements in a time sharing system with relocatable roll-in and roll-out would not be affected. Similarly in a language system, such as ALGOL, where storage is allocated to some portion (a block or procedure) of the program as that subprogram is invoked, binding time need not necessarily be delayed until the invocation time since relative addressing is still possible. The same logical argument can be used to show that the binding time of local variables in (say) FORTRAN subprograms is compile time rather than invocation time. On the other hand, the binding time of parameters in subprograms must be invocation time since it is not possible to relate parameters and their values until invocation time. In particular where a parameter relates not to a value but to an address (the address of the argument in the invoking statement), the binding time is invocation time. Binding time may be a language feature or it may be implementation defined. For example, in APL, the left arrow (assignment operator ←) operation has the side effect[1] of assigning the attributes of the expression to its right to the operand on its left. Thus the instant at which all the information is available to enable the assignment of storage to the operand on the left is the instant of executing the assignment operation. Thus APL has dynamic attribute specifications and binding time (earliest and latest) is execution time. Lacking explicit (and fixed) declarations of attributes, APL itself determines attributes at execution time. Conversely, BASIC, in the case of missing (omitted) array size declarations inserts the missing attributes so as to permit compile-time binding of variables.

It should be pointed out that there can exist three different concepts of binding time depending on the point of view of the observer. As far as the user of a programming language is concerned, the binding time of language elements is the instant that he writes the element into the program. Transferring this to the execution of the program, the user is unconcerned about the actual (physical or logical) binding time but rather assumes that language elements are bound by the time they are used.

At the intermediate stage, the implementer of a translatory system (compiler, assembler, or interpreter) sees only a logical binding time being that instant when sufficient information about the language element is known so as to fix its relationship to other language elements in the generated program. This binding may take the form of locating the language element within a "template" or "map overlay," the actual location of the physical manifestation of the elements located in the template being determined at execution time.

For the point of view of the implementer of the host system (within which both the translatory system and the generated program are expected to reside), the binding time of the storage elements of the generated program may never be fixed but rather will depend on the storage management scheme which the hardware resources dictate. For example, in a time sharing system, the binding time of a program element (and hence a language element) initially will be the load time of that segment of the program, the elements being "unbound" (released) at the end of the time slice and then being "rebound" at the beginning of the next time slice. Within each time slice, the actual (absolute) address assigned to any language element is expected to be

1. Truly this should be classified as an "initial effect."

fixed, but between two time slices, any language element having a logical existence in both time slices may have differing absolute addresses.

In the discussion here, we shall consider only the implementers' point of view, the physical aspects of binding being transparent to the implementer and being controlled by some host system external to the translatory system which he is developing. Also, since the user's point of view determines a latest binding time, and it is anticipated that the implementer will use the earliest binding time wherever possible, there will be no conflict in restricting our considerations to the logical binding time only.

To instigate binding within the bounds of binding time, the implementer is free to choose any particular instant. However, the later that binding takes place the greater the difficulty in generating effective code and more time it will take to both store and retrieve the values of language elements. That is, if an absolute address can be assigned to a variable then all references to that variable in the generated code may be made directly. However, if the binding time is delayed until (say) the last moment, then each reference to that variable will require the system to look up the assigned location. Thus the work of the symbol table is delayed until execution time and may be performed repeatedly rather than just once as would be the case for compile time binding of variables. In any case, it should be a general principle that the earliest possible binding time should be used. In the discussion of memory allocation which follows here, all memory references can be considered as being relative to some base address (explicit or implicit), and thus the methods are generally applicable to binding times which occur in either the compile-time cycle or the execution period of the process. The exception will be the case of arrays with dynamic dimensions which will be considered separately.

As a general policy, compiler writers choose to allocate object time data storage in the high-order end of the memory on the basis that generated programs must be placed in sequentially increasing memory locations. Subprograms which are relocatable may be fitted into any available space. Data must be organized in at least some reasonable fashion, thus beginning at the highest available location, data are allocated space in descending sequence, arrays being stored backwards[2] with respect to their storage addresses. However, given a tar-

2. The history of allocating arrays to memory such that the successive elements (as defined by the numerical ordering of the subscripts) are placed in descending order of addresses, is intimately related to the method of index modification in the IBM 704 which was a *decrementing* system.

get machine which possesses base registers, or a decision on the part of the implementer to utilize one of the index registers as a base register (so that *all* addressing is relative to the address stored in that register by the loader), or placing the burden of address modification on the loader, it is possible to develop a schema in which the compiler develops a storage template in which locations are assigned in ascending address order and array subscripts increase as do their memory locations. These two organizations are shown in Figure 5.1 and 5.2 (pp. 196, 197).

STORAGE REQUIREMENTS

The following list describes the storage needs of various language elements.

Simple variables (scalars) and constants:

1. Real-type variables are allocated one word[3] of memory, the format of assigned values being two parts; a biased exponent (exrad) and a normalized mantissa (significand).

2. Integer-type variables are allocated one word, the assigned value being expected to be in the usual internal integer form for the target machine.

3. Complex-type variables are allocated two contiguous words, the format of each word being equivalent to a real type variable. In effect, a complex-type variable is treated as a one-dimensional array of two elements.

4. Logical- or Boolean-type variables require only one bit to represent an assigned value. Depending on the whims of the implementer, logical-type variables may be packed into a single word with many other logical variables or constants, or assigned a whole word independently. Logical arrays may also be packed into words so as to conserve storage.

5. All constants in the language are allocated storage in the same manner as their respective variables. However, the value of the constant must be loaded into memory before execution of the object program, whereas locations assigned to variables (except as defined in DATA statements) are unaffected by the loading operations.

3. In the sense used here, "word" should be taken to mean the minimum aggregate of memory elements (bits, bytes, etc.) which are required to provide a reasonable degree of precision over the operations defined in the language, or in the target machine. A word might also be constructed as the minimal addressable storage element.

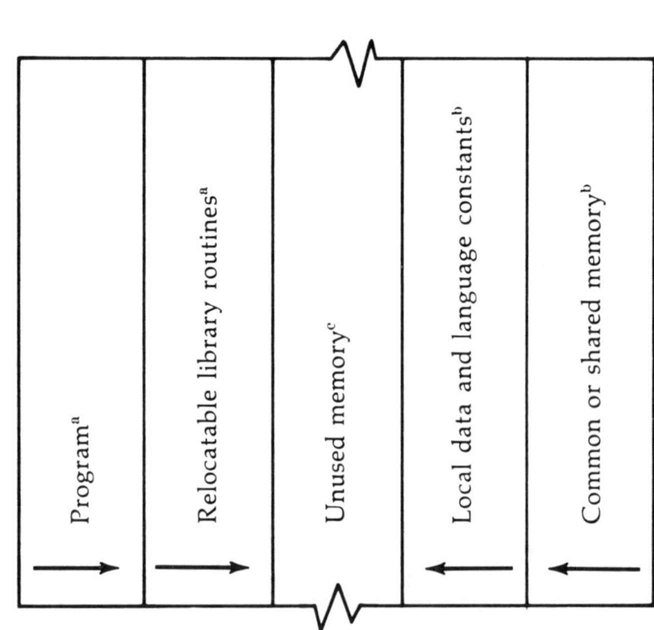

Notes:
(a) Due to the nature of these programs, their assigned locations are allocated in ascending address order.
(b) Since base registers are not available, the storage for these sections is allocated in descending address order.
(c) It is important to note that both portions of the storage allocation scheme "feed" on the common set of unused memory locations.

FIGURE 5.1 Memory organization without base register usage.

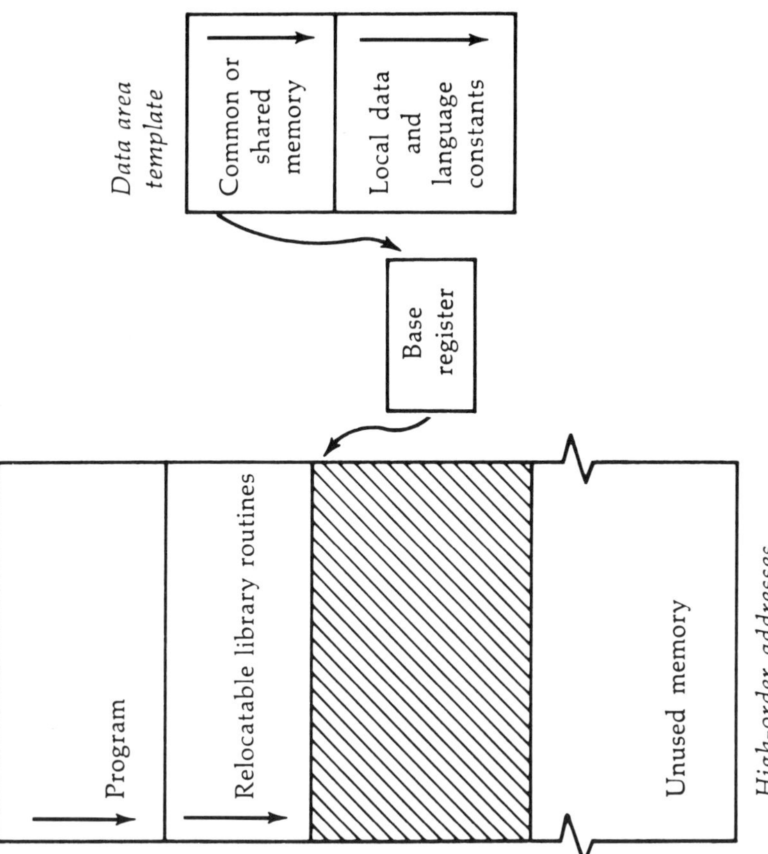

FIGURE 5.2 Memory organization with base register usage.

Dimensioned variables:[4]

6. One-dimensional arrays are stored such that their first element is located at the currently highest numbered available address and with succeeding elements at progressively lower-numbered addresses. That is, the vector dimensioned A(10) would be stored in the order A(1), A(2), A(3) . . . A(10) at successively lower memory locations. The address of element A(I) may be calculated from:

Address of A(I) = Address of A(0) − I

where the address of A(0) is called the *base* address of the vector A. Note that

Address of A(0) = Address of A(1) + 1

7. Two-dimensional arrays are stored with the first element, for example, B(1,1), stored at the highest numbered address available. The rest of the elements are stored at progressively lower-numbered addresses. Let us propose that the order of storage is such that the first subscript changes most rapidly in passing through sequentially lower storage locations:

B(1,1), B(2,1), B(3,1) . . . . .

If the matrix B is dimensioned as B(IMAX,JMAX), then the address of the general element B(I,J) may be computed from the expression:

Address of B(I,J) = Address of B(0,0) − (J*MAX+I)

where the address of B(0,0) is called the *base* address of B and

Address of B(0,0) = Address of B(1,1) + (IMAX+1)

Note that if the compiler or object time routines do not check for subscripts outside the range of the dimensions declared in the DIMENSION statement, and in particular for zero or negative values of those subscripts, then such subscripts will work properly in the second subscript position but not on the first. For example, if B is dimensioned B(3,3), then B(3,1) and B(0,2) will refer to the same element, a condition which may be undesirable. That is,

Address of B(0,0) = Address of B(1,1) + 4
Address of B(3,1) = Address of B(1,1) + 4 − (1*3+3)
= Address of B(1,1) − 2
Address of B(0,2) = Address of B(1,1) + 4 − (2*3+0)
= Address of B(1,1) − 2

4. We assume here that all arrays have 1-indexed origins. A simple modification of the mapping functions will permit 0-indexing if necessary.

However, the location of B(2,0) will be two words higher than B(1,1). Since zero and negative subscripts are extremely useful in the manipulation of data that occur in the COMMON area, the facility to refer to elements outside the range of the DIMENSION statement is important. However, the programmer must be warned to know what he is doing and to obtain the storage allocation algorithm. As an example of memory layout, consider the following COMMON statement:

COMMON X, A(4), B(2,3)

The memory layout would be:

Variable name	*Memory location (base 10)*
X (also base of A)	3999 (for example)
A(1)	3998
A(2) (also base of B)	3997
A(3)	3996
A(4)	3995
B(1,1)	3994
B(2,1)	3993
B(1,2)	3992
B(2,2)	3991
B(1,3)	3990
B(2,3)	3989

8. Three and higher dimensional arrays are stored in the same manner as simpler arrays; thus elements are stored at progressively lower-numbered addresses with the first subscript of the array varying most rapidly and the final subscript least rapidly. For example, an array with dimensions A(2,3,3,2) is stored in the following order (from highest numbered memory address to lowest address):

A(1, 1, 1, 1) Highest numbered address
A(2, 1, 1, 1)
A(1, 2, 1, 1)
A(2, 2, 1, 1)
A(1, 3, 1, 1)
A(2, 3, 1, 1)
A(1, 1, 2, 1)
A(2, 1, 2, 1)
A(1, 2, 2, 1)
A(2, 2, 2, 1)
A(1, 3, 2, 1)
A(2, 3, 2, 1)

```
A(1, 1, 3, 1)
A(2, 1, 3, 1)
A(1, 2, 3, 1)
A(2, 2, 3, 1)
A(1, 3, 3, 1)
A(2, 3, 3, 1)
A(1, 1, 1, 2)
A(2, 1, 1, 2)
A(1, 2, 1, 2)
A(2, 2, 1, 2)
A(1, 3, 1, 2)
A(2, 3, 1, 2)
A(1, 1, 2, 2)
A(2, 1, 2, 2)
A(1, 2, 2, 2)
A(2, 2, 2, 2)
A(1, 3, 2, 2)
A(2, 3, 2, 2)
A(1, 1, 3, 2)
A(2, 1, 3, 2)
A(1, 2, 3, 2)
A(2, 2, 3, 2)
A(1, 3, 3, 2)
A(2, 3, 3, 2)      Lowest numbered address
```

The decision as to the ordering of subscript changes is not one which can be logically debated. In the example given here (and later in Chapter 7), we have chosen to vary the subscripts through the storage area so that the first subscript varies most rapidly, the second subscript the next most rapidly, and the last (the rightmost) varies most slowly. This is merely a matter of convenience based on the scheme used for storing the dimensions in the symbol table which was assumed to be left to right also and the algorithm for creating the address of a subscripted array element, which also was a left to right system. As may be seen from an examination of the addressing algorithm (Chapter 7) if insufficient subscripts are provided in an array element reference, the reference is equivalent to the case where the unspecified subscripts take the value of zero. This may be regarded as a convenience. In any case the algorithm will not abort due to insufficient information. On the other hand, if a subscript mapping scheme were developed in which the subscripts varied in the same manner as an automobile odometer (that is, in the usual positional numeric right to left sense) a left to right scanning system would not be aware of the insufficiency of subscripts until some code had been generated, thus possibly causing some consternation within the compiler. On the other hand in a right to left scanning environment such as that specified for APL, a right-to-left subscripting scheme[5] is satisfactory. In this case, minor variations in the algorithms given here will satisfy the rearranged addressing system.

There is a tendency in the business of language specifications to specify only the barest minimum of the semantics of languages and to leave as much of the organization of the language features as possible to the whims of the compiler (interpreter) implementer. That is, provided that the implementation does not directly affect the meaning of the language statements, the specification of the language should not range over topics which are in the domain of implementation. Thus it is unexpected to find that the 1966 ANSI specifications for FORTRAN do in fact specify the algorithm of mapping multidimensional arrays onto a one-dimensional medium. In the standard, this is called the *array element successor function.* This algorithm is given in Table 2 of the standard and is shown here in Table 5.1 as modified to use the notation of Chapter 7.

TABLE 5.1 Array element successor function.

Dimensionality	*Dimensions*	*Subscript values*	*Array element successor function*
1	d_1	s_1	s_1
2	d_1,d_2	s_1,s_2	$s_1 + d_1(s_2-1)$
3	d_1,d_2,d_3	s_1,s_2,s_3	$s_1 + d_1(s_2-1) + d_1d_2(s_3-2)$

While this does differ slightly from the algorithm developed here, the difference is only in the assumed ascending storage scheme as opposed to the descending scheme used in the previous section.

Statement identifiers:

9. In a one-pass system there can be references to a statement identifier that is not yet defined. In this case, an object time word is needed to allow indirect references to the statement identifier. The address of the statement can then be filled in when the statement is encountered. After that statement has been compiled, all references to that statement can be compiled directly, and therefore the object time

5. See the APL ravel operator, and the index sequence specified for the language in S. Pakin, *APL/360 Reference Manual* (Chicago: Science Research Associates, Inc., 1968).

word is no longer needed. The address of the statement may be loaded into the reserved location before execution of the program.

In order to save data storage space at the cost of loading time and at the cost of a larger amount of data emanating from the compiler, a list which describes the location of each reference in the object program to the undefined statement identifier may be maintained in the compiler and provided to the loader. The loader must then overlay these addresses onto the object program. Although this increases the loader time, the branches may now be executed directly, thus saving execution time.

In a multipass system or even a one-pass system where all references are made after the referenced statement has been encountered, no object time storage is required.

Subprogram Entries:

10. In a system that compiles an object language and data onto an external medium and then reloads for execution, only user-defined and selected library routines need to be loaded, thereby saving both time and memory space. In this situation, library subprograms must be written in a relocatable form and do not occupy a fixed location in the memory. Similarly, the location of user-defined subprograms is indeterminate since their lengths are undefined.

A simple method for linking the mainline program to library subprograms which are relocatable and of which there is a predefined number, is to reserve a singly dimensioned array into which, at object time, will be stored the absolute address of the entry point to each subprogram. With this *transfer vector*, links may be made to library subprograms indirectly, each subprogram having a fixed address location in the vector. Thus if there are *n* library routines provided with the system, then the transfer vector should have the same number of entry locations. For example, ANSI Basic FORTRAN requires that each compiler be provided with seven external functions: **EXP, ALOG, SIN, COS, TANH, SQRT** and **ATAN**; whereas the full FORTRAN must contain 24 external functions: **EXP, DEXP, CEXP, ALOG, DLOG, CLOG, ALOG10, DLOG10, SIN, DSIN, CSIN, COS, DCOS, CCOS, TANH, SQRT, DSQRT, CSQRT, ATAN, DATAN, ATAN2, DATAN2, DMOD** and **CABS**.

On the other hand the specification lists a number of intrinsic functions (six in Basic FORTRAN, including such functions as **ABS** and **IFIX**, and 31 in full FORTRAN), but does not state the number of these which are required in a system. Thus it would appear that the compiler writer can choose those to be included. However, the standard does specifically state (in Sec. 8.2) that: "The symbolic names of the intrinsic functions are predefined to the processor. . . ." A similar linkage technique may be utilized in connection with user-defined subprograms if transfer addresses provided in the object time data area are used. In essence, referring to a subprogram is similar to the task of referring to an undefined statement identifier and the same techniques of linkage apply.

In particular, since subprogram names are not deleted from the symbol[6] table between subprograms, a transfer address location may be assigned at the first reference to the subprogram if it has not yet been compiled. If the subprogram is compiled before any other subprogram makes a reference to it, then the transfer address location must be reserved on recognition of the subprogram definition statement.

STORAGE ALLOCATION IN BLOCK-STRUCTURED PROGRAMS, PROCEDURES, AND SUBPROGRAMS

In considering the storage allocation schemes as related to the various manners in which programs are either subdivided or structured, it is important to separate these schemes from those which may be imposed on the operating program by the host system. That is, we shall assume that the effects of paging, segmentation, relocation and multiple-level memory management systems are transparent to the translatory system implementer. Thus we shall assume that all portions of the code which compose a program, both compiled code and that collected from a library, are existent in the memory during execution. It would be possible to develop a means by which only those portions of the program which were active were assigned storage at any given instant, but we shall restrict this discussion to considering only the allocation of storage to satisfy the data storage requirements of the program being executed.

Within any portion of the program (be it represented either as the user's text of the program or the compiled code) there can exist three types of variable data reference: through shared memory (compare the FORTRAN-style COMMON and ALGOL global concepts); through the use of parameters which themselves reference a user provided argument; and through the use of language elements which

6. For a discussion of the interaction of symbol tables between subprograms, see page 210.

have an existence only within the current portion of the program. Leaving aside, for the moment, the means by which parameters are related to their corresponding arguments, except to recognize that there must be provided by the storage allocation system some storage which contains a quantity such as the address of the argument of the parameter (or even the current value of the parameter), we shall consider the effects on storage allocation of the activation of portions of a composite program.

By activation of a portion of a program we mean the process of executing a portion of a composite program by direction of the programmer. If such portions of the program utilized all the same variables as the program from which the portion was activated, there existed no arguments to pass to the portion (and hence no matching of arguments and parameters was necessary) and there existed no shared memory, then the problems of storage management and allocation would be nonexistent. For example, the BASIC **GOSUB** statement merely transfers control to a portion of the program without implying any of the above three types of storage references. On the other hand, ALGOL through its use of block structures uses two means of referencing identifiers—local and nonlocal (that is, locally global) references. In ALGOL and in FORTRAN, subprograms can be activated (procedures in ALGOL, **SUBROUTINES** in FORTRAN) which require local storage, have the ability to reference shared memory and contain references to arguments through a parameter list. On activation of a program portion it is necessary not only to transfer control to that portion of the program, and possibly to leave a trail for return to the activating program, but also to establish the storage for that portion.

With a little imagination it is possible to conceive of a system of storage allocation for local entities which is based on the use of a storage template so that when the program portion is activated, the template can be laid over some unused portion of the available memory. Similarly on exit from the portion (deactivation) the template can be removed and the memory space returned for use by some later activation of this or another portion of the program. In this sense activation implies some execution-time storage allocation system (which may be as simple as setting a base register to the address of the next sequentially available memory location and updating the next available memory location address to clear the template). However, there can exist programs and there exist languages in which it is possible to determine portion activation sequences at compile time. FORTRAN is inherently such a language, and all programs written in FORTRAN possess a compile time binding time. Certain programs can be written in ALGOL so that their storage can be allocated at compile time, and further, it is possible to determine that the storage can be allocated at compile time, but these are special cases and rare enough not to include a determination algorithm within the compiler and hence not to allocate storage at compile time.

Although it is possible to allocate storage for all FORTRAN storage at compile time, it is not necessary that this be implemented. That it, it is not a language feature (and hence imposed on the implementer) that FORTRAN storage be allocated at compile time. In certain environments, particularly the environment of limited storage, it is not possible to allocate storage in such a manner that all addressing in all portions of a compiled FORTRAN program be in absolute addresses. There simply does not exist enough memory for all storage templates to cover discrete portions of the storage system simultaneously. In this case it is necessary to consider storage allocation at execution time.

As an initial example of storage allocation, let us consider the case of a program composed of nonrecursive nonstructured[7] subprograms in an unbounded memory in which any arrays (local, or in shared memory) are fixed in dimension at compile time.

The subprogram structure which we wish to investigate can be exemplified by the simple language defined by the following syntax:

<*program*> ::= <*subprogram sequence*>

<*subprogram*> ::= <*head*>;<*body*>;<*tail*>

<*subprogram sequence*> ::= <*subprogram*>{;<*subprogram*>}$_0^n$

<*head*> ::= **subprogram**<*name*>{;**parameters**<*identifier list*>}$_0^n$

<*name*> ::= a|b|c|d|e| ··· |x|y|z

<*identifier*> ::= A|B|C|D| ··· |X|Y|Z

<*identifier list*> ::= <*identifier*>{,<*identifier*>}$_0^n$

<*body*> ::= <*statement sequence*>

<*statement sequence*> ::= <*statement*>{;<*statement*>}$_0^n$

<*statement*> ::= <*assignment st*>|<*execute st*>

<*assignment st*> ::= <*identifier*> := {<*identifier*>| <*constant*>}$_1^1$

<*execute st*> ::= **execute**<*name*>{**with**<*argument list*>}$_0^n$

<*argument*> ::= <*identifier*>|<*constant*>

<*argument list*> ::= <*argument*>{,<*argument*>}$_0^n$

<*tail*> ::= **end**

7. That is, non-ALGOL-style block structures.

This program structure is similar to that used by FORTRAN. For simplicity we shall not consider the case where subprogram arguments are linked to their corresponding parameters by name, though we shall consider the implications on the storage allocation scheme of passage by value or by location (address). The subprogram which is activated first (presumably by the host system) is the physically first subprogram. We shall require that this subprogram have no **parameters** statement (see <*head*>). The simple assignment statements of the language are to be executed in the usual fashion, the identifier defined on the left hand side of the statement being assigned the value of the right hand side, where the value of the right hand side is defined either as the value of the constant or the value assigned to the identifier on that side, depending on which syntactic element is present. The **execute** statement causes the named subprogram to be activated and the appropriate associations to be made between the specified arguments and the parameters listed in the **parameters** statement of the named subprogram. All statements within a subprogram are executed in strict physical sequence until the **end** statement is encountered. This statement causes the deactivation of the subprogram and control to be transferred back to the subprogram which caused the activation at the statement immediately (physically) following the **execute** statement which initiated the activation. The execution of a program must be so arranged that only one activation of a subprogram exists at any instant in time (time being assumed to progress steadily as statements are executed). In particular, the initial subprogram (that activated by the host system) can never be activated by any subprogram. When the **end** statement of the initial subprogram is reached the program is completed and control is returned to the host system.

The number of arguments in an **execute** statement must exactly equal the number of parameters (identifiers) listed in the **parameters** statement of the named subprogram. Any identifiers in a subprogram which are not listed in the **parameters** statement are local identifiers which have no association with any identifiers outside that subprogram and no preset values assigned to them.

In this style of organization it is possible at compile time to develop a template for each subprogram, for the shared memory, and for the vectors which represent the data linking parameters and their arguments. Further, since there can exist at the most only one activation of any subprogram since recursive subprograms have been omitted in this example, then it is possible to develop an absolute storage allocation scheme in which each template is placed over the memory so that no two templates overlap and all templates are allocated space. By virtue of the restriction that arrays have fixed dimensions, the templates themselves are fixed in size and their components are fixed in place within the template with respect to each other.

Let us propose, for the purpose of example, that each template is composed of two components: the dope vector for parameter mapping, and the storage for local entities. During compilation of each subprogram it will be possible not only to develop the template but also to determine (or more likely, specify) the relative position of that template with respect to the templates corresponding to other subprograms. That is, it will be possible to develop absolute addresses for local entities, or at the very least, addresses relative to a single base address provided for the whole program by the loader. Given the restriction (as in FORTRAN) that the shared memory area is of a constant size, and that the number of parameters of a subprogram is fixed, it is also possible for the compiler to develop absolute (or relative to a single base address) addresses for all language elements. Consequently all addressing may be in terms of absolute addresses or, at the very worst, relative to a single base address.

Even in the case where the various subprograms are compiled separately, the amount of additional work given to the loader is small. Since, in practice, the template is merely an abstract notion, the data required by the loader in order to allocate memory and to ensure that there exist no overlaps, is simply the initial base address for the first subprogram (the bound of available memory) and the size of each template. In a system where the data areas are laid out commencing at the upper bound of available memory towards successively lower addresses, the loader can allocate the data area relative to each subprogram as the code for that subprogram is loaded, and thus at the same time the loader can convert relative addresses in the generated code to absolute addresses in one pass. Alternately, the loader may place the initial address for the template for this subprogram into a mailing box within that portion of the subprogram which initializes the machine on activation. On activation, this initialization routine could place this address into a base register (saving the previous value for reloading on exit from this subprogram) or into a particular general index register which modifies all addresses within the subprogram.

In the case where the data storage area is to be allocated to memory immediately following, and in ascending storage locations, the generated code, the modification of addresses by the loader or the posting of base addresses in individual mailboxes will have to be delayed until all subprograms have been loaded, since only at that time can the initial base address be determined. In such a situation it would be advantageous to allocate memory to the mailing boxes in some system area, possibly directly associated with the transfer vector which also contains the entry address(es) for each subprogram.

A third alternative would be to allocate memory for the code for a subprogram and for its data area in contiguous portions of memory. That is, on loading, two data items can be provided to the loader: the size of the data area template, and the size of the generated code for the subprogram. Knowing the initial address for the loading of the generated code, the base address for the data area may be deduced, thus providing the loader with sufficient information to adjust the relative addresses within the code being loaded or to place in the mailing box.

Using this method of allocation, the ordering of the data area as either an ascending or descending sequence would not be significant. Such a scheme is shown in Figure 5.3.

In this static system of memory allocation, the placement of shared data elements is of some concern. That is, since all data elements are existent in the memory for the totality of the execution time and simultaneously, it is possible for there to exist single copies of constants which are not collected into a single data area. In a system (as will be developed in the next section) where data areas are not permanently resident in memory, it is advantageous to develop an implied shared-memory area in which are maintained copies of constants and locations reserved for temporary storage purposes. It is obviously possible to include copies of constants and temporary storage locations within the data area for each subprogram. However, this can be wasteful of space. In the case of dynamically allocated data areas (see the next section) it is important to ensure that such constants exist in a static data area.

In this case, however, since all storage allocation is static, the location of the single copy of a constant is influenced only by the means of accessing that constant. Maintaining the premise that there should be only one copy of a constant in the whole system is feasible provided all the subprograms are compiled in an unbroken sequence. Thus we should modify our stand to expect that there should be only one copy of a constant for each set of subprograms compiled in a single sequence. Thus each compiled sequence of subprograms may be expected to possess its own shared memory area for constants and temporary storage locations. The existence of a location (for either a

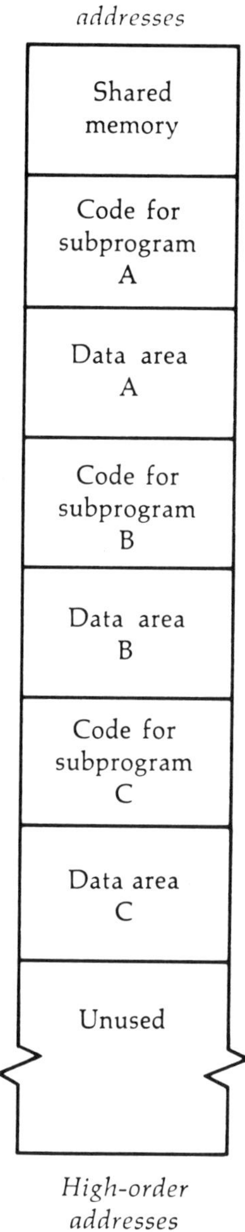

FIGURE 5.3 Memory layout for a collection of nonrecursive, nonstructured subprograms in an unbounded memory with fixed-attribute language elements.

constant or as temporary storage for intermediate results) in the data area of some other subprogram than that which is accessing that location does not also imply that the mechanism of access is straightforward. In a storage allocation scheme where data areas can be assigned absolute addresses (or addresses relative to a single base address over the whole compiled code) then this type of addressing is similarly absolute and simple. However, where the loader is given the responsibility of placing the templates over the available storage area, the linking of the template address and the absolute address cannot take place until execution time, and will require a modicum of code to realize. This style of addressing will be necessary in developing addresses which are associated with nonlocal identifiers in block-structured program, as will be seen in the next section. However, outside the particular case of a master template which encompasses all the subprogram templates (and therefore uses only one base address for all relative addresses) *and* subprograms which are compiled together, the saving on space by not having multiple copies of constants and providing private sets of temporary storage for each subprogram is outweighed by the code necessary to develop the absolute address from the address relative to the base address of some other subprogram.

In the subprogram type of organization of a program, there exist no relationships between the names used for identifiers in any of the subprograms. Thus the usage of (say) A in any subprogram does not imply any relationship with the usage of the name A in any other subprogram. Even in the usage of a shared storage area (COMMON) there are no implications of name sharing, but merely the overlaying of names onto an fixed (static) storage area which may already contain data values. There is no implication that the state of this shared storage area is to remain unchanged during the execution of the statements within any subprogram, but there is an implication that the values assigned to identifiers associated with this shared storage area will be altered when the storage element with which they are associated is modified. With reference to constants and temporary storage locations, there can exist, depending on the implementation scheme used, an association between constants in one subprogram and some other subprogram. For example, by implementation we may imply that the integer representation 57 in the first (physical) subprogram is directly related to all other occurrences of the integer representation 57 in both this subprogram and all others. Similarly, the reservation of a temporary storage location by a subprogram may, by implementation, imply that location is available for use by all other subprograms.

As far as the compiler is concerned in this storage allocation system, the data to be passed between compilations of subprograms may be insignificant. That is, in the scheme where constants and temporary storage locations are regarded as being local to that subprogram, the only information to be passed between the compilations of two subprograms is the location(s) of the entry point(s) to the subprograms. Since this can be expected to take the form of a commonly accessible transfer vector within the host system or within the shared memory area, this may be a simple name/address directory. Further since most compilers are organized so as to process subprograms sequentially without any reference back to an already compiled subprogram, this directory may contain anticipatory entries to which addresses in the transfer vector have already been assigned. Although there are no name to name connections between language elements which exist in the shared memory, the subprograms need to know the base address of the shared storage area, and the size of the area, if checks are to be included which ascertain that the various shared memories areas defined in the subprograms do actually fit together. In the case where absolute storage areas are allocated as the subprograms are compiled, the "next available address" is also an item to be passed from one compilation to the next. In the case of storage allocation at load time, a data set must be built up during compilation which will provide the information required by the loader in order to perform its tasks. That is, the size of each area, the location into which the base address of each area is to be placed and the transfer vector locations into which the entry addresses of each subprogram are to be entered.

We shall consider the means of linking subprograms at execution time in a later chapter, but it suffices at this point to assume that there exists an argument-passing algorithm and that parameter storage locations are part of the local storage for each subprogram.

Using the template system for each portion of a program, this system of static storage allocation can be extended to a block-structured program. Let us consider the case of a simple block-structured language where blocks exist merely to define the scope of the language elements. Such a language is exemplified by a form of Ledgard's[8] Mini-language 1. In this language, there exist only simple replacement statements of the syntactic form

$$<identifier> ::= \{<identifier> | <constant>\}_1^1$$

8. H. F. Ledgard, "Ten Mini-Languages," *Computing Surveys*, vol. 3, no. 2 (September 1971).

where <*identifier*> is restricted to being represented by single characters from the roman alphabet:

<*identifier*> ::= A|B|C ··· |X|Y|Z

and <*constant*> is represented as integer number representations:

<*constant*> ::= <*digit*>|<*digit*><*constant*>

Two other statements exist in the language which define and delimit blocks, and which also declare the local identifiers in that block:

<*declaration*> ::= **begin local**<*identifier list*>

where

<*identifier list*> ::= <*identifier*> {,<*identifier*>}$_0^n$

and

<*end delimiter*> ::= **end**

Ignoring the elementary transfer of control and the existence of statement labels, a program in this mini-language is defined as follows:

<*program*> ::= <*block*>
<*block*> ::=
    <*declaration*>;<*statement sequence*>;<*end delimiter*>
<*statement*> ::= <*block*>|<*assignment*>
<*assignment*> ::= <*identifier*> := {<*identifier*>|<*constant*>}$_1^1$
<*statement sequence*> ::= <*statement*>{;<*statement*>}$_0^n$

This mini-language is intended to demonstrate the scope of identifiers in block-structured languages. The existence of an identifier in any block may be determined by a simple algorithm: Given any identifier, its scope (period of being bound) is the block in which it *last* appeared in a <*declaration*>. On activation, a block will appear to require the allocation of storage to those identifiers which are listed in the declaration at the head of the block and the stacking of any similarly-named identifiers existing in the block from which this block was entered. On exit from a block (through the **end** statement) all local identifiers (that is, those listed in the head statement of the block) are eliminated from storage and the identifiers which were stacked on activation of the block are reinstated. Where the names of identifiers in the outer block and the inner block do not conflict, the identifiers of the outer block still have an existence in the inner block. By this manner, values can be transferred between blocks without the formal use of argument and parameter lists, and without the associated matching operations necessary.

Consider the following program written in this minilanguage:

```
begin local  A,B,C,D;
   A = 3;
   B = 2;
   C = A;
   begin local  A,B;
      A = 4;
      C = A;
      D = 5;
      ←——— point α
   end;
   ←——— point β
end;
```

Within this program we may identify two sets of identifiers, each set being related to the block in which it has scope. Let us, for the purposes of discriminating between these two sets, give the subscript 1 to those identifiers which have scope in the outer block, the subscript 2 to those of the inner block. The set of identifiers of the outer block may be shown to be $\{A_1, B_1, C_1, D_1\}$, assuming that there is no outermost block not shown here, or if there is such a block, there exist no identifiers in that outermost block. Within the inner block is a set of identifiers which are local to that block (since they are defined in the **begin local** statement): $\{A_2, B_2\}$. Since these identifiers bear the same names as identifiers in the outer block, then the identifiers in the outer block $\{A_1, B_1\}$ have no scope in the inner block and their assigned values must be saved on entry into the inner block for the time at which the outer block is reinstated. However, identifiers $\{C_1, D_1\}$ are not preempted by the declaration in the inner block, and thus they have scope in the inner block. Consequently, the set of identifiers which have scope within the inner block is $\{A_2, B_2, C_1, D_1\}$. Executing this program would develop the following results:

At point α: $A_2 = 4$, (A_1 has no scope in this block),
B_2 is undefined, but has scope,
$C_1 = 4$, and
$D_1 = 5$

At point β: $A_1 = 3$,
$B_1 = 2$,
$C_1 = 4$, and
$D_1 = 5$

Developing a storage allocation scheme for such a language is comparatively simple in an unbounded memory system. That is, since the local identifiers of each block are distinct from those of outer blocks, a storage template for each block can be developed which is distinct from that of any outer block. Although the program itself is structured, this does not imply that the storage areas must be similarly structured. In fact, the data storage areas may be allocated sequentially, in exactly the same manner as for nonrecursive subprograms with fixed attribute elements.

The only difference here is the existence of locally global (or nonlocal) identifiers, which must be referenced from within the block. In a static storage allocation system where data areas are bound to absolute addresses (or relative to one base address) it will be possible to relate locally-global identifiers to their original allocation without ambiguity.

The relation between a program in this block structured language and its corresponding data areas is shown in Figure 5.4.

Comparing the problems of compilation of the structured program[9] with those of the subprogram organization, it may be seen that the problems of storage allocation are no more complex, but the task of determining scope is now present. If block-structured languages were written in such a manner that each block were distinct from its enclosing block, in the same manner as subprograms in the previous section were considered to be separate, it would be necessary for the programmer to provide a list of identifiers which were nonlocal in scope and to associate each with its appropriate block.

Even in this (seemingly) simpler organization, it would be necessary to possess, at the same time, copies of large portions of all the symbol tables of all blocks, in case of references from the block currently being compiled to those other blocks. However, in the structure used in the language used here, it may be seen readily that at the very most, the number of symbols tables to be retained is equal to the depth of embedding of the block currently being compiled. It can be expected that this number is far less than the number of blocks in the program.

Based on the structure of the program and assuming (for example) that storage is being allocated absolutely, we may develop a symbol table scheme by which both the necessary information is passed to the new block and the old table is retained. Using a simple stack process (LIFO) the symbol table for the enclosing block can be saved. The new symbol table initially will be a copy of the table for

9. As constrasted with structured programm*ing*.

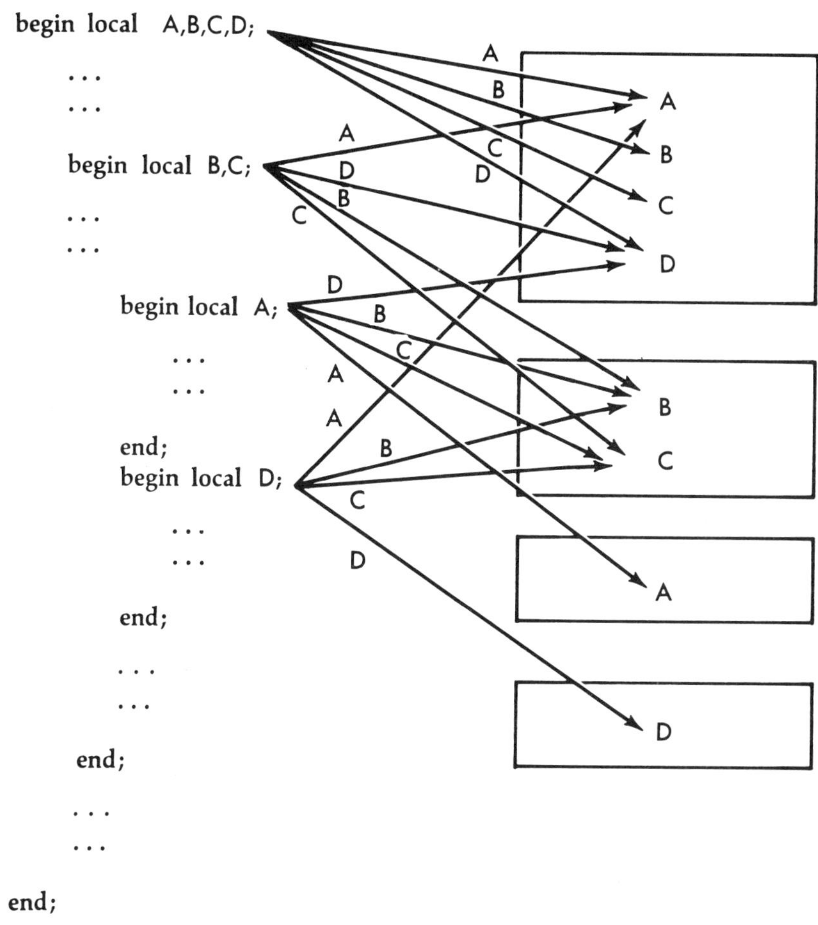

FIGURE 5.4 Relation between program and storage.

the enclosing block. On compilation of the declaration statement of the new block, the storage for local identifiers will be allocated, thus replacing references to the identifiers of the same name in the encompassing block. On completion of the compilation of the code for the new block, its symbol table can be discarded and the table on the top of the stack becomes the current symbol table, thus reinstating the environment of the encompassing block. Since storage is being allocated absolutely, all references are also absolute and direct, and there is no necessity to "juggle" base registers, as will be necessary in later organizations.

The organization of memory as a static system brings with it advantages of implementation of features which are "messy" in dynamic (nonstatic) situations. Firstly there exists the problem of value retention by local identifiers over two activations of a program portion, as typified by the ALGOL **own** feature. In this feature the value assigned to a local identifier is to be retained after deactivation of the program portion so that on reactivation the value is also reactivated. This style of feature is useful in the cases where the first activation of a program portion is intended merely as an initialization phase, subsequent activations being predicated on the preset values. For example, a subprogram which computes pseudorandom numbers will usually utilize the last generated number as the basis for the production of another number, the first generation being developed from some number provided by the user. In this type of subprogram there is a requirement to retain internal values between activations. In the static storage scheme which we have presented here, such values will be retained, but not as a matter of intentional design but rather as a free bonus of the implementation. This also implies that the FORTRAN-style DATA statements can be permitted easily, the loading of the values being invoked only once; that is, immediately prior to the loading of the whole program. In a dynamic scheme it would be necessary to load these values on each activation. On the other hand, if the language is defined to mean that the elements of a DATA statement are part of the initialization of each activation, then the loading will be necessary on each and every activation and the static storage scheme shows no advantages in this feature implementation.

One further feature which may be provided as a free bonus is the feature of implied argument passing, wherein the "old" values of arguments are retained and thus the absence of an argument in a calling sequence is taken to mean "the last defined entity." For example, in the case of parameter passing by value[10], where neither the compiler nor the object code is checked for the matching number of arguments and parameters, it is possible to initialize a routine by the use of the last few arguments in the calling sequence, thus assigning values to the corresponding parameters in the routine. In later activations of that routine, the absence of arguments corresponding to these parameters will leave their values unchanged. Thus **execute a with 3,56,19** as the first activation of the routine a followed by **execute a with 9** would be equivalent to **execute a with 9,56,19** provided that subprogram a did not alter the values of the parameters corresponding to the values 56 and 19 in the original activation.

10. See the later section on parameter passing.

In a situation where parameter passing is accomplished by the use of address passing,[10] **execute a with A,B,C** followed by **execute a with R,S** would be equivalent to the second activation being written as **execute a with R,S,C**. Both of these forms of implied arguments are available since the storage area for the parameters in the subprograms is statically allocated and not destroyed on the deactivation of the subprogram.

Similarly in the case of block structured programs in a statically allocated storage system, the values of local identifiers will not be lost on deactivation even if the **own** attribute has not been attached to those identifiers. In fact, this may be an embarrassment in some cases.

Let us now consider the same two types of program structure with similar limitations of array dimensioning in a bound environment. In particular, let us consider the case where under no circumstances can a data area be available for each and every portion of the program simultaneously. Obviously, we must develop some scheme by which the templates can be placed in memory and addressing into those areas be accomplished with the minimum of address modification.

Primarily let us consider the program with a subprogram structure. In this style of programming language, although the set of identifiers for each active subprogram are bound, the ability of a particular subprogram to reference identifiers in some other subprogram is extremely limited. In fact, if we disregard the arguments which are associated with the parameters of each subprogram for the time being, we may see that the subprogram can reference only two memory areas: the area assigned for shared memory locations (that is, the COMMON area in FORTRAN) and the local storage area. Since the shared memory area is permanently resident in memory and is not liable to modification any time during execution of the subprogram, then memory references to that area may be made either directly (as an absolute address) or relative to a base register whose contents are set by the loader. In the case of local references, the template may be set with respect to a second base register and thus are equally straightforward. In fact since no other references are permitted (we shall take care of parametric associations shortly), only two base registers are required at any instant, say BR1 and BR2. However, on activation of a subprogram and the establishment of its storage area, the contents of the base register used by the activating subprogram must be saved for reactivation upon the return from this subprogram being entered. Thus we shall propose the introduction of a base register stack which will be used to save the contents of BR2. This stack will be organized as a LIFO stack since our organization of the structure of the program in this language does not allow a "parent" (antecedent) subprogram to "die" before the activated subprogram has been executed to completion. Thus we can never get into the situation where the top element of the stack is not the base address of the data area of the subprogram to which control is being returned on deactivation of subprogram.

The allocation of memory to a data area can proceed in a purely sequential manner by the use of a mailbox in which is kept the next available address. On activation of a subprogram, the current contents of BR2 are added to the BR stack, the next available address is placed into BR2 and a new next available address is computed by adding to the current value the size of the template for this subprogram. Similarly on deactivation, the new next available address is the current contents of BR2, the base address of the reactivated subprogram is on the top of the stack and thus is removed to BR2. This style of organization, together with the permanently resident shared memory area and the generated code is shown in Figure 5.5. If one were to possess only a single base register or there was only one index register available for this use, it would be possible to organize an addressing scheme where all references were related to that one register. In fact, it would be advantageous to use that register for all local references, since they are expected to occur most frequently, and then to compute addresses in the shared memory area by in line code.

Let us now consider the case of references from within a subprogram to the data of another subprogram through the use of parameter associations. Again omitting the case of pass by name, it is obvious that pass by value can be taken care of by the linkage mechanism between the subprograms so that the parameters act as local identifiers and thus do not enter into our considerations at this point. Remaining, then, is the problem of pass by location (or address). In this case, the address which is to be passed to the subprogram being activated is related to the base address of the subprogram in which it was initially defined. That is, the address of an argument being passed to a parameter must contain two addresses: the address within the template and the base address of the data area. Alternatively, since the calling programs are neither volatile nor relatively relocatable, the address of the argument can be related to the base address of the shared memory area by a simple calculation at the instant of linkage between the two subprograms. It will be necessary for the compiler to distinguish between arguments which are local identifiers and those which are parameters, so that double shifting of addresses is not attached to parameters in the calling subprogram. This scheme is shown in Figure 5.6.

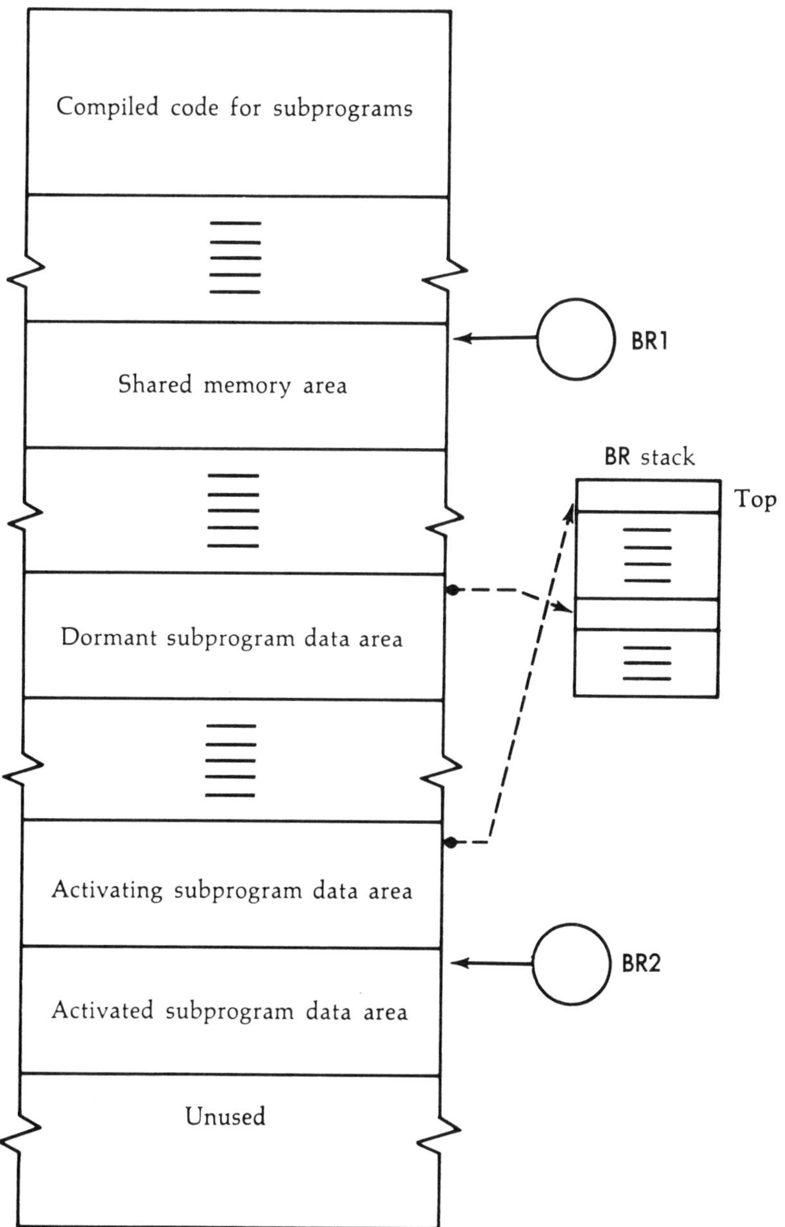

FIGURE 5.5 Storage as allocated on activation of subprograms.

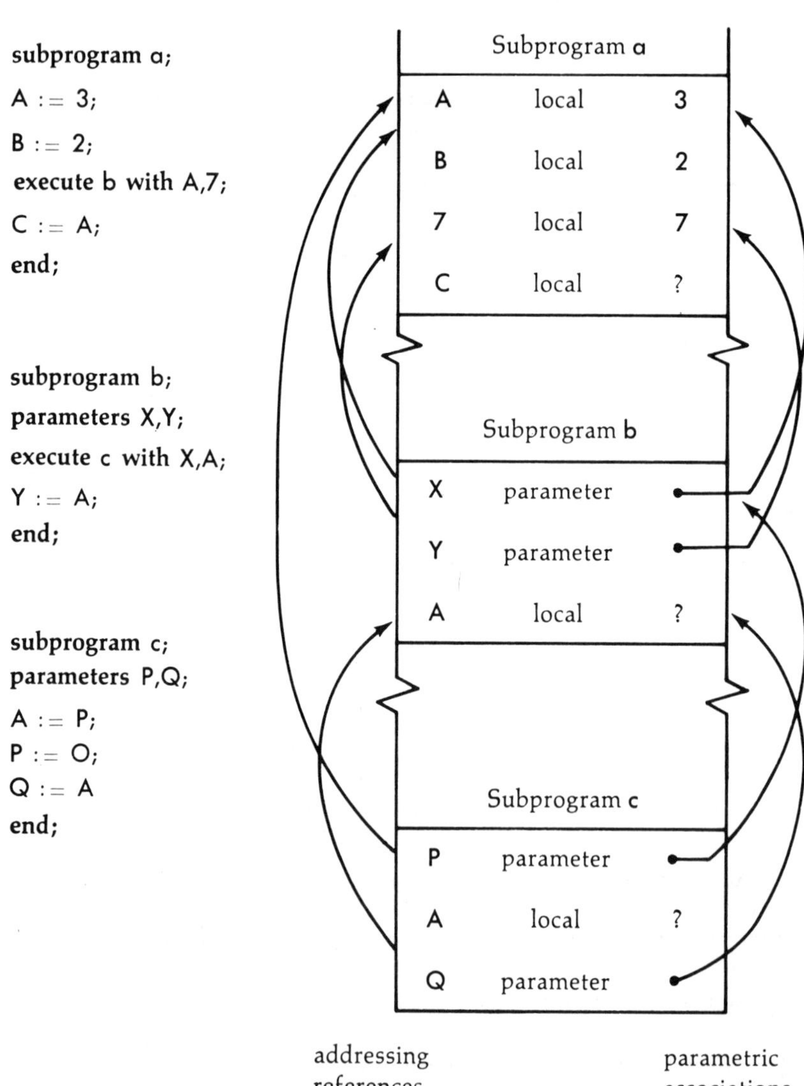
The state of memory immediately following the activation of subprogram c.
subprogram a;
A := 3;
B := 2;
execute b with A,7;
C := A;
end;
subprogram b;
parameters X,Y;
execute c with X,A;
Y := A;
end;
subprogram c;
parameters P,Q;
A := P;
P := O;
Q := A
end;
Subprogram a
A local 3
B local 2
7 local 7
C local ?
Subprogram b
X parameter
Y parameter
A local ?
Subprogram c
P parameter
A local ?
Q parameter
addressing references
parametric associations

FIGURE 5.6 Parameter associations and references.

The actual process for the referencing of entities which can occur in any of the previously activated subprograms (procedures, blocks, etc.) is by the use of a display. This is composed of a vector which contains information on currently active subprograms and the means by which they can be referenced. At each level of subprogram activation, the display must contain two entities: the return address of the calling subprogram and the base address of its own (local) storage area. These two elements permit the subprogram to reference its own local elements and to return control to the calling program on completion. If the display also includes a list of the data area addresses (base addresses) of the currently active subprograms, in the order of activation, reference to inherited elements can be accomplished by knowing two features: the relative depth of nesting of the current subprogram with reference to the subprogram in which the element was originally specified and the location in the template of that element. Thus addressing to elements which are nonlocal can be accomplished by the evaluation of the expression

$$(\text{template address}) + C(\text{display}[i])$$

where i is the depth of nesting, display[i] is the location of the base address related to the i-th outer level subprogram, and $C(x)$ indicates the contents of location x. Thus in the compilation process, the nesting level can be accumulated in the symbol table together with the template address.

In this style of storage allocation, the deactivation of a subprogram implies that the associated data storage area is freed for other use, possibly for the next subprogram which is activated. There is never any problem related to the management of the available storage due to the execution time allocation and release of the storage areas. Since storage is allocated sequentially in the same order as subprograms are activated, and are released in *exactly* the reverse order, the released storage areas always immediately abut the unused storage area. Thus there is never any need for *garbage collection.*

In the static form of storage allocation considered in the last section, the maintenance of values related to local identifiers between successive activations of subprograms was taken care of without any special action on the part of either the implementer or the compiler. Thus the ALGOL style **own** attribute of an identifier was an automatic feature of that implementation. However, in the case just considered the storage area relative to local identifiers is not maintained between activations and thus the **own** feature is not automatically implemented. Furthermore, there are two other "free" features of the static style of storage allocation which do not exist automatically in the *allocate on activation* storage system; these are the ability to default the relationships between parameters and arguments and the ability to preset values into identifiers.

Let us consider the latter case first. Several languages have a feature which allows the user to preset the value assigned to a particular identifier by the use of a statement of the syntactic form:

<initialize st> ::= **initialize***<data list>*
<data list> ::= *<data pair>*{,*<data pair>*}$_0^n$
<data pair> ::= *<identifier>* : *<constant>*

This list specifies the values to be assigned to the identifiers (which must be local). Two methods of definition are possible: the values are assigned to the identifiers at each activation of the subprogram, or the values are assigned to the identifiers at the first activation only and thereafter those identifiers have the **own** attribute. In the original static style of storage allocation the latter meaning of the **initialize** statement is simple to implement. In the storage scheme just considered, this meaning of **initialize** would be equivalent, after the initial value assignments, to the **own** problem.

In the case where the values are to be assigned to the identifiers on each activation, it will be necessary for the compiler to generate the appropriate code to preset the contents of the locations associated with each identifier as part of the initialization routine (activation routine) for that subprogram. Thus the storage allocation system in the compiler can assign these identifiers locations within the template for the storage area. However, the presetting values of those identifiers must be stored in an area which, to all intents and purposes, has the **own** attribute!

The major advantage of the **initialize** statement in programming languages over a sequence of assignment statements is in the time that can be saved by a judicious use of contiguous storage and machine commands which permit the transference of data records. That is, if the machine has a command which moves data in blocks such as MOV A_1, A_2, CNT, where CNT sequential words are to be copied from memory starting at location A_1 into an equal size block commencing at address A_2, and the compiler's storage allocator carefully assigns the identifiers in an **initialize** statement to contiguous storage, then the assignment of initial values to identifiers can be substantially faster than the use of successive loads and stores which would be generated from successive assignment statements. Irrespective of this implementation technique, which is obviously machine dependent, the initial values must be stored in a storage area which has the **own** attribute.

Two basic systems of storage allocation to **own** identifiers is possible. First, we may attach a statically allocated storage area to the area of shared memory locations for these special identifiers. Since this is static storage the same base register (**BR1**) as was used for the shared memory area can be used for these identifiers also. The advantages of the static storage allocation system then automatically apply to these special areas. Another static storage area is that associated with the compiled code for each subprogram. Thus a second method of implementing the **own** attribute will be to associate a static storage area with the compiled code. This has the advantage that the loader may then place the values into the locations assigned for **own** identifiers and further, all references to those identifiers can be made of the same address base as instruction references. Thus an additional base register is not required.

Conversely to the design of the subprogram style of program structure, the block-structured language does not specify the set of identifiers which are nonlocal to the block or which are to be associated with arguments in the activating block, but rather specifies the local identifiers. With some little work on the part of the compiler, it would be possible to convert the program written in the block structured language into an equivalent program in the subprogram style of organization, with unique names added to identify the subprograms which correspond to the blocks. For example, the example used earlier can be transformed as shown in Figure 5.7.

There could be minor (but nontrivial) variations in this transformation scheme depending on the manner of parameter passing used in the subprogram organization; that is, pass by value or address. However, a closer examination of the semantics of the block-structured language will reveal that since all references from within a block to nonlocal identifiers are accomplished in terms of addresses, then the pass by address method of parameter passing will develop an equivalent program in the structured organization. While this transformation is possible, and we can satisfy ourselves that there exists a semantic equivalency between the original program and its transformation, we shall continue to examine the methods of compilation of block structured languages and the allied storage allocation schemes. It is important to our discussion here that the scope of identifiers in programs written in the block-structured language is statically determinate; that is, determinable by the compiler without reference to the logical execution sequences of the program. Thus at the point that a header statement of a block is encountered in the physical sequencing of the program, the compiler can determine from the cur-

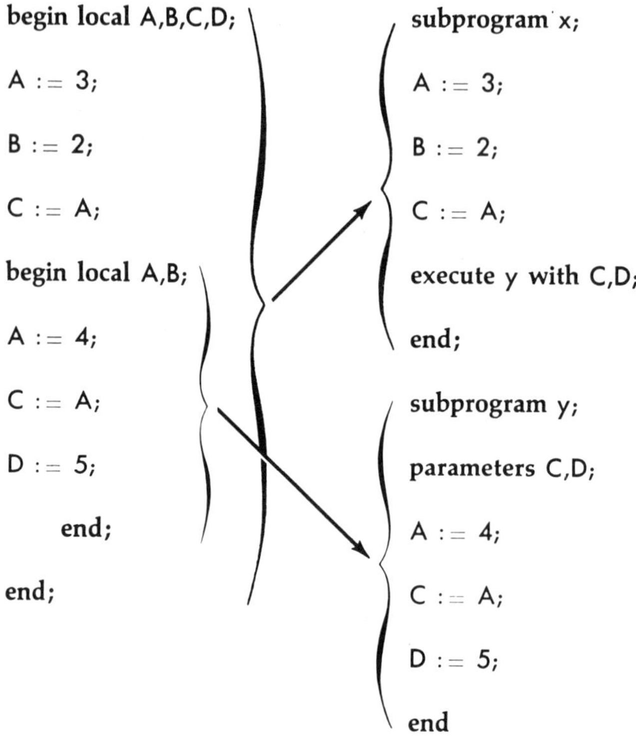

begin local A,B,C,D;
A := 3;
B := 2;
C := A;
begin local A,B;
A := 4;
C := A;
D := 5;
end;
end;
subprogram x;
A := 3;
B := 2;
C := A;
execute y with C,D;
end;
subprogram y;
parameters C,D;
A := 4;
C := A;
D := 5;
end

FIGURE 5.7 Transformation of a block-structured program.

rent state of the symbol table and the declarations of local identifiers, the scope of all identifiers. Furthermore, the scope of identifiers following the incidence of the **end** statement also must be determinable. As we discussed in the previous discussions with respect to the static storage allocations schemes in the environment of block-structured programs, a simple symbol table stacking procedure will accomplish this scope determination. At execution time we can easily see that the life of an activating block cannot be ended while an inner block is being executed. Thus, the storage relevant to an activating block cannot be released while an inner block is being executed. This restriction does not necessarily imply that the storage associated with an outer block must be currently allocated to memory at the time of execution of the inner block, as would be possible in the case of a subprogrammed program structure where all parameter passing was to be accomplished by value passing only.

Even in the case of parameter passing by address it would be possible to envisage a scheme by which the storage area associated with an outer block could be saved externally to the immediately accessible storage system, without requiring accesses to that external storage each time the inner block referenced a nonlocal identifier. Such a scheme would be composed of activation and deactivation routines which, working over the local store only, would transfer values into locations and return values from the local store respectively to satisfy the nonlocal language features. Thus, the local template would encompass all identifiers irrespective of their scope, and the code generated for the statements within the block would contain local address references only. The activation and deactivation routines would then bring in and pass out the values for nonlocal identifiers. The flowchart of this scheme is shown in Figure 5.8.

This scheme implies the reuse of storage areas dynamically, and the possible reactivation of a storage area into another area of memory than it was originally allocated. However, this is not necessarily required. By allocating memory initially in a purely sequential manner since the storage for an inner block must be allocated prior to the release of the storage for the outer block, a "hole" will exist in the storage map until the activation of the next inner block. At that time, a decision can be made as to whether the hole can be used or whether more space is needed elsewhere. Where the size of the template for the subsequent block is less than or (coincidentally) equal to that of the released area, then the hole can be used; otherwise two alternatives are open. Either another sequentially addressed storage area can be requested or the storage layout be reorganized so as to leave no holes.

The former scheme can lead to a storage layout in which there exists some unused storage and thus the possibility that storage will appear to be used up before all the existing storage has actually been used. However, a simple examination of the storage allocation scheme and the order of activation of blocks will show that there exist at the most two unused storage areas. Such a demonstration of storage allocation is shown in Figure 5.9. Even in the case where storage is allocatable on a relocatable basis, as shown in Figure 5.10, only two unused storage areas can exist simultaneously.

As a further alternative to the scheme for allocating storage for a block structured program, let us consider a semistatic system similar to that last proposed for the subprogram structured programs, with the additional usage of dope vectors for the linkage of subprograms and nonlocal identifiers. In this type of organization we shall maintain copies of the storage areas for activated (though not necessarily

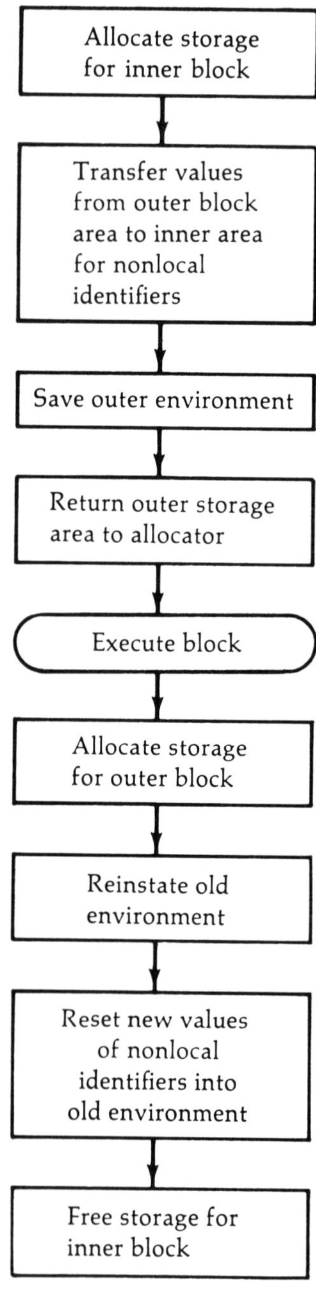

FIGURE 5.8 Activation and deactivation processes in a nonresident storage system.

Block structure

a b c d e

time

Available storage

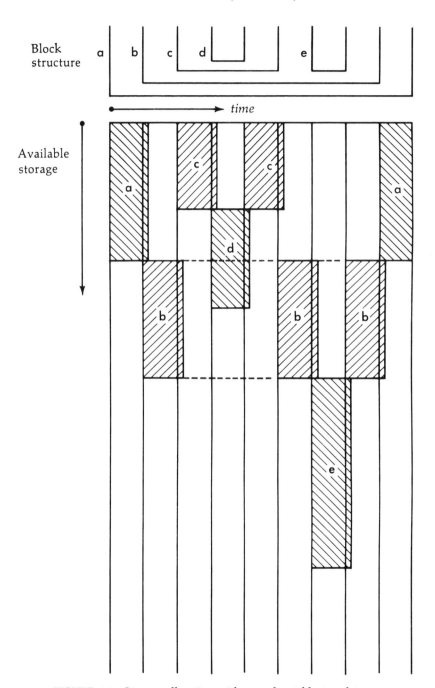

FIGURE 5.9 Storage allocation with nonrelocatable templates.

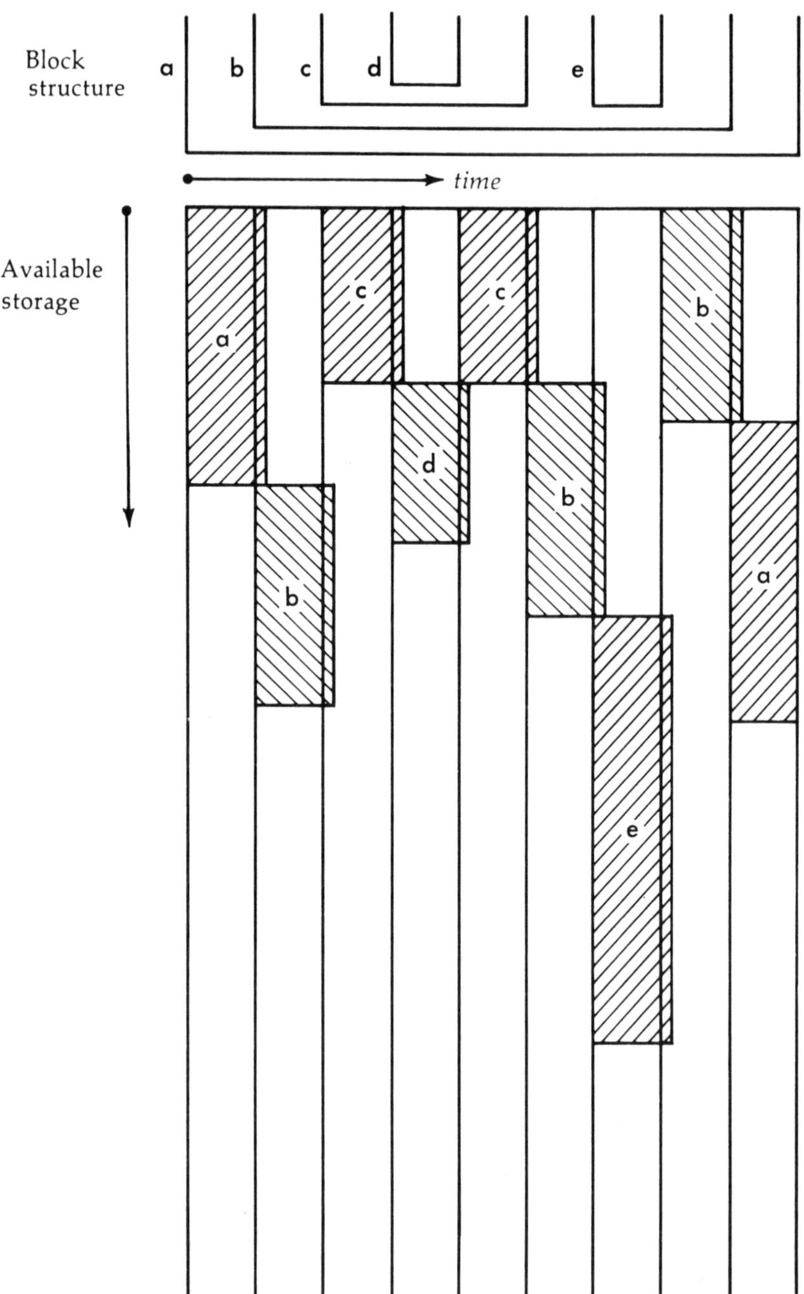

FIGURE 5.10 Storage allocation with relocatable templates.

active) blocks in the directly accessible store, so that there is no necessity to pass values back and forth as was used in the nonresident scheme considered above.

In this schema, each storage area will have associated with it an execution time symbol table or dope vector through which all referencing is accomplished. Since the storage system is static with respect to activated blocks and since blocks cannot "evaporate" before their descendents have been executed to completion, then the locations of nonlocal identifiers are fixed, or at least can be referenced with respect to a system base address. Using two base registers again and a stack for base addresses of nonactive blocks, local references can be made with respect to the local base address (**BR2** in the previous discussion) and nonlocal references can be based on the system address base. Thus on activation of a block the dope vector for the activating block is to be copied on to the top of the stack of vectors. All addresses within that vector which refer to local identifiers must then be modified to be based on the system base address, since these identifiers are candidates for use as nonlocal identifiers in the block being activated. Then, *in the same vector,* the entries for local identifiers will be introduced with the local tag (see Figure 5.11) set to indicate their local attribute. Through this dope vector all addressing can be accomplished.

Storage allocation can proceed on a strictly sequential basis, the last block activated being assigned space following the storage for the activating block. In order to adequately protect storage from appearing to be full prematurely, we shall propose that the stacks be allocated storage in a descending order from high order memory, so that memory will actually be totally utilized when the space for the templates and the stacks overlap. Alternatively, the dope vectors can be assigned a fixed area within each template, the only stack being needed for the base addresses.

Finally, let us consider the problems related to the ability of language elements to alter their attributes during the execution of the program. In both the subprogram and block-structured program organizations, there can exist only one program portion which is active at a single instant, though many other portions may be only temporarily dormant. It is important, however, in the discussion which follows that the attributes of the elements of dormant program elements are unchanged during the execution of descendent portions. Thus, for this discussion we shall insist that the attributes of nonlocal identifiers in block-structured programs and the arguments associated

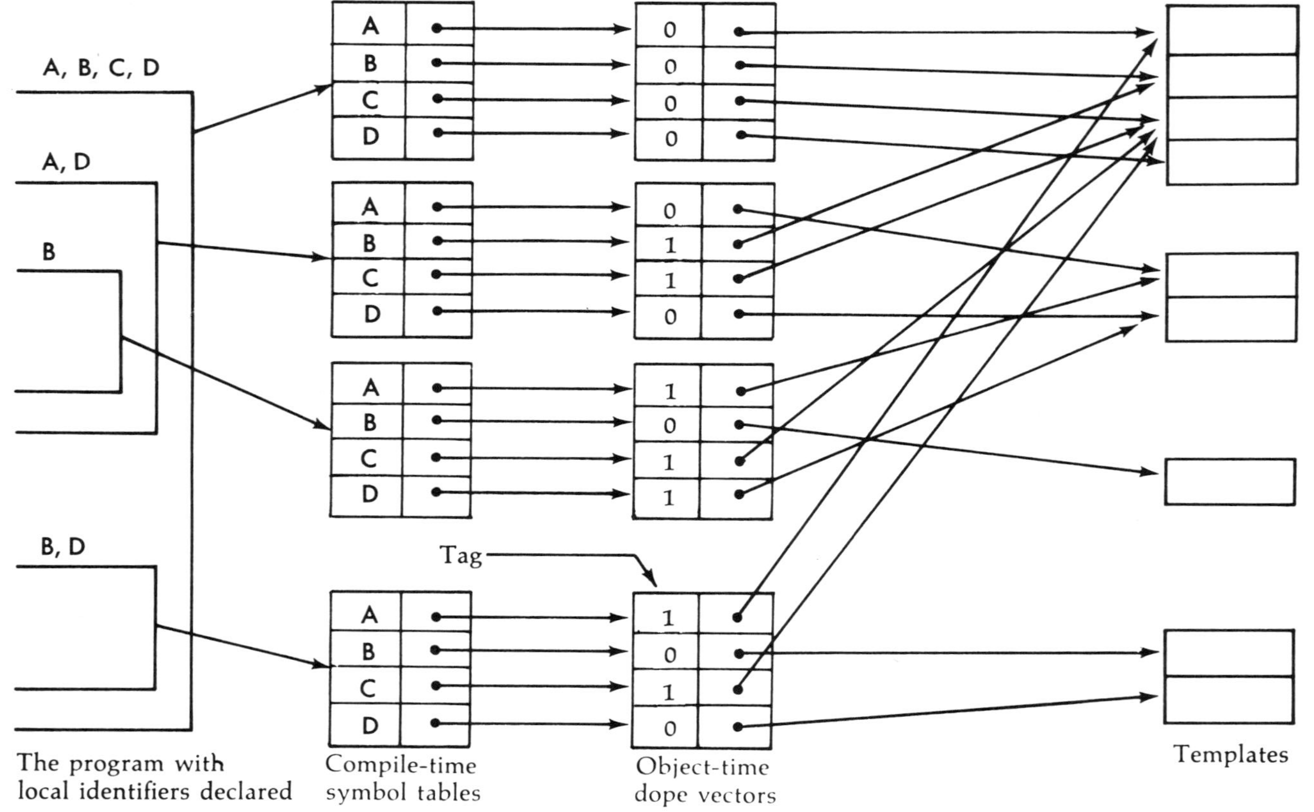

FIGURE 5.11 **Semi-static storage allocation.**

with parameters in subprogram structured programs do not alter. In particular we shall restrict our considerations of attribute changes to those which will require some alteration in storage allocation. For example, we shall omit for the purpose of discussion those alterations which can be made in situ without affecting storage allocation.

As a first step let us consider the case of program portions in which the attributes (in particular the dimensions of arrays) can be specified on activation of the portion (block or subprogram) but remain static for the execution of the portion. This differs considerably from the problem of specifying the array size of a parameter of a subprogram since the latter problem is merely related to the arguments of the subscripting algorithm not to the allocation of storage. In this case the storage for the argument has already been allocated in the activation of the subprogram in which the argument was originally defined. Apart from the problem of implicit equivalences which may be undesirable, this language feature introduces no new compile-time difficulties. On the other hand, the ability to specify the dimensions of a local array at the instant of activation of the block or subprogram will cause some difficulties with respect to the establishment of the storage template for that program portion. In all our previous considerations, the size of the template was assumed to be fixed at compile time; not so in this case. To minimize the storage referencing time over the whole program portion, we shall assume that simple identifiers (scalars) remain forever as one-element items and can be collected into a static portion of the template so that their references are relatively direct. The remainder of the template must then be organized at the instant of activation of the program portion. To facilitate referencing these elements, an object-time dope vector will be required in which the base address of each array is stored by the activation (and storage allocation) routine. Further, this dope vector must contain the information relative to the addressing of elements of these arrays since this information is not available at compile time for insertion into in-line code.

Once dope vectors have been introduced into the storage allocation system and into the language element referencing procedures, there is no reason why this same mechanism cannot be used for the implementation of totally dynamic storage schemes. That is, schemes in which the size attributes of arrays vary during the execution of the program portion. Very simply, if array dimensions are linked into identifiers, the subscripting procedures can be similarly linked to those identifiers.

However, the storage allocation scheme is much more complex. Typical problems encountered in such a dynamic storage allocation system can be identified in the problems of executing APL programs. APL contains no specific declaration statements, but the attributes of any language element can be implicitly specified in any statement. In fact, the assignment operator (←) has the effect of assigning values and also specifying attributes. The only restriction currently part of the APL language with respect to arrays is that no element of a n-dimensional array can be referenced (either to assign a value or to retrieve a value) until *all* elements in that array have been assigned values. Thus it is not possible to extend arrays by merely referencing an element currently outside the domain or to add a dimension by merely adding a subscript. Thus the following two programs are invalid:

```
A ← 25
A[6] ← 6
```

and

```
A ← 25
A[;1] ← 9
```

The use of memory by APL for the storage of temporary (or intermediate) results is far more intense than in other languages due to the basic tenet of the language that the fundamental element in data is the n-dimensional array. Thus instead of requiring one word temporary storage locations APL requires storage for n-dimensional arrays! Thus at almost every step of the evaluation of an APL expression, storage is requested and must be allocated. In fact, APL is so intimately involved in storage allocation that most implementations do not bother to test for changes in element attributes but instead allocate storage on each and every assignment. As in other languages, the use of temporary storage for intermediate results is limited to the particular statement being executed, and thus all intermediate storage can, without question, be freed (released) following the completion of the execution of a statement. If storage is in short supply, intermediate storage can be released during the execution of a statement and be reused again during that statement. To facilitate this highly dynamic storage allocation system, there must exist a symbol table to relate identifier names with their currently allocated storage areas and their current attributes. All operations over the data and references to memory must then be interpretively executed through this table.

For the purposes of simplification, we shall consider here only those aspects of storage allocation which are relevent to the execution of one portion of a program. The relationships between program portions will be overlooked for the time being, the storage allocation processes for such an environment being obvious extensions of the previous proposals.

In APL, every time a language element occurs on the left hand side of an assignment operator (which may be embedded within a larger assignment statement), storage for that element must be allocated and any previous allocation can be released. In an interpretive system the organization of a symbol table progresses as the interpretation of the program progresses and thus the previous allocation of storage to an element is identifiable simply by the occurrence of that element in the symbol table. Part of the problem of storage allocation in this style of programming environment is the knowledge of the available data areas. Whereas in our previous considerations either storage was allocated on the basis of one unused area (as in the static allocation case or the semistatic case for resident allocation of activated program portions) or two areas (in the case of resident storage for only the currently active portion), in this case there may exist at any time numerous unused, noncontiguous storage areas. We shall assume that in the event that a storage area is released that is contiguous with an already unused area, the two areas will be combined into a single unused area. The record of unused storage will be maintained as a linked list, each element of which is composed of the low order address of the area and the size of the area. A scan through this list on storage allocation will enable the allocator to choose an appropriate unused space for the new allocation. There are two organizations of this linked list which we must consider. One organization would be to maintain the list so that it is ordered with respect to the addresses of the unused areas. In this manner it will be simple to combine contiguous areas and moreover there will be a tendency to use the low-order portions of memory primarily, thus concentrating the usage of the available space. On the other hand, a second manner of organization can give some advantages; that is, an organization in which the list is maintained in the order of the size of the available areas. It would be more difficult to combine contiguous storage areas by this method, but by using the first available area into which the requested space will fit (assuming that the ordering is by ascending size), there will be less tendency to break up large areas into smaller pieces and thus require the eventual combining of blocks when apparently there is no space large enough to accept a new allocation. Several other questions then remain. Should any leftover area from a space not used by a current allocation be returned to the space available list? One can argue that in most programs there is a tendency for data structures to grow as the program progresses and thus any process which divides memory into smaller and smaller pieces is to be abhorred. As a rough figure, an implementation could decide not to return any storage remainders to the available storage list when the remainder is (say) less than 15% of the total available space. Thus the remaining 10 words from a 100 word space into which a 90 element array has been placed would not be returned to the available space list. When should the seemingly expensive task of combining areas be initiated, if it is not done on every allocation? Should memory ever be totally reorganized so that all used memory and all unused memory are together in two wholly contiguous blocks? Which is it better to do: combine blocks to find a large enough space, or totally reorganize storage? Should one system be tried in preference to the other? If so, what are the criteria for their choice?

Obviously, total storage reorganization will be very costly, since all the currently stored data values will have to be moved physically to their new locations. On the other hand, the combining of areas is an administrative task not directly affecting the storage areas themselves. The cost of storage combination will be in the searches through the available storage list to locate contiguous areas. Thus both styles of linked list organization are useful. To simplify this latter task whilst at the same time enhancing the storage allocation scheme by the use of a size ordered list, it should be possible to develop a doubly-linked list whereby both orderings are implied. The process of storage allocation can then proceed as follows:

1. Compute the size of the area required, S.
2. Using the size ordered linking system, examine the list to locate an unused area of sufficient size.
3. If such an area exists, remove it from the available space list and return any unused portion to the list, subject to the conditions discussed above.
4. If no area on the space available list is of sufficient size, initiate the routine which combines areas (step 5).
5. (Note since this routine has been initiated, it is decided to combine *all* contiguous areas, irrespective of their suitability to this particular allocation). Using the address linkages, combine contiguous areas and place the newly generated area in the size linked list in the correct position. Maintain a record of the largest block generated, G, and the sum of the block sizes, M.[11]

11. With little extra work in step 3, a running total of available space can be maintained at all times. Thus in step 1, if S is greater than M, control can be transferred directly to step 7 to attempt to retrieve the unused areas which were not separated out in step 3.

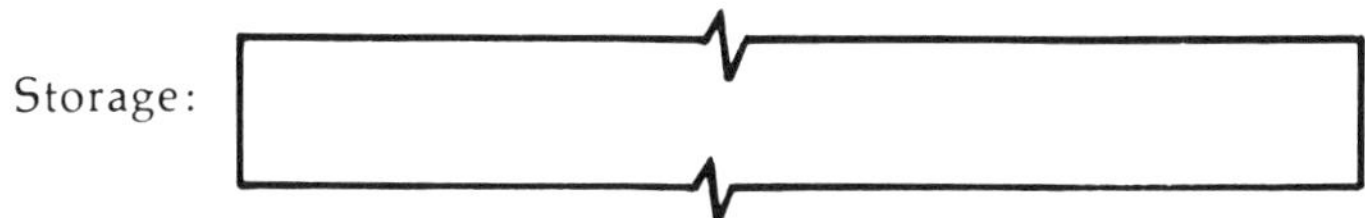

List of available space (**FREELIST**): Doubly linked list, 4 Components per element

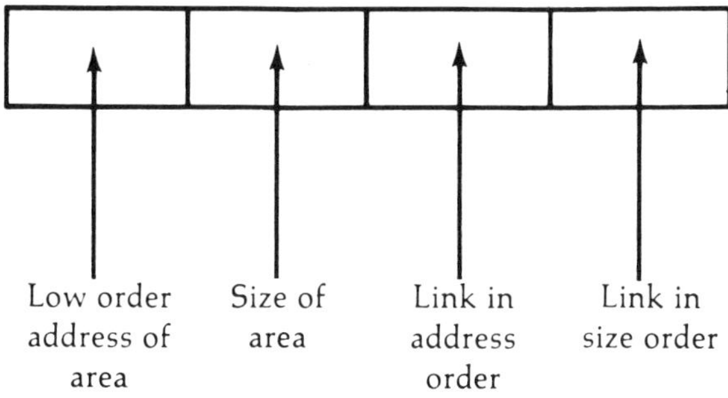

MAXSIZE: Size of largest area in **FREELIST**

FREESUM: Sum of area sizes in **FREELIST**

SIZE PTR: Pointer to first (smallest) area in **FREELIST** in size order

ADDR PTR: Pointer to first (low-order) area in **FREELIST** in address order

DIRECTORY: (symbol table) For the purposes of the algorithm; a list of two component element address of first (low order) word size used.

Initially, **FREELIST** contains one element showing that the whole space is one available area. **MAXSIZE** and **FREESUM** are set to the storage area size.

FIGURE 5.12 **Dynamic storage allocation algorithm.**

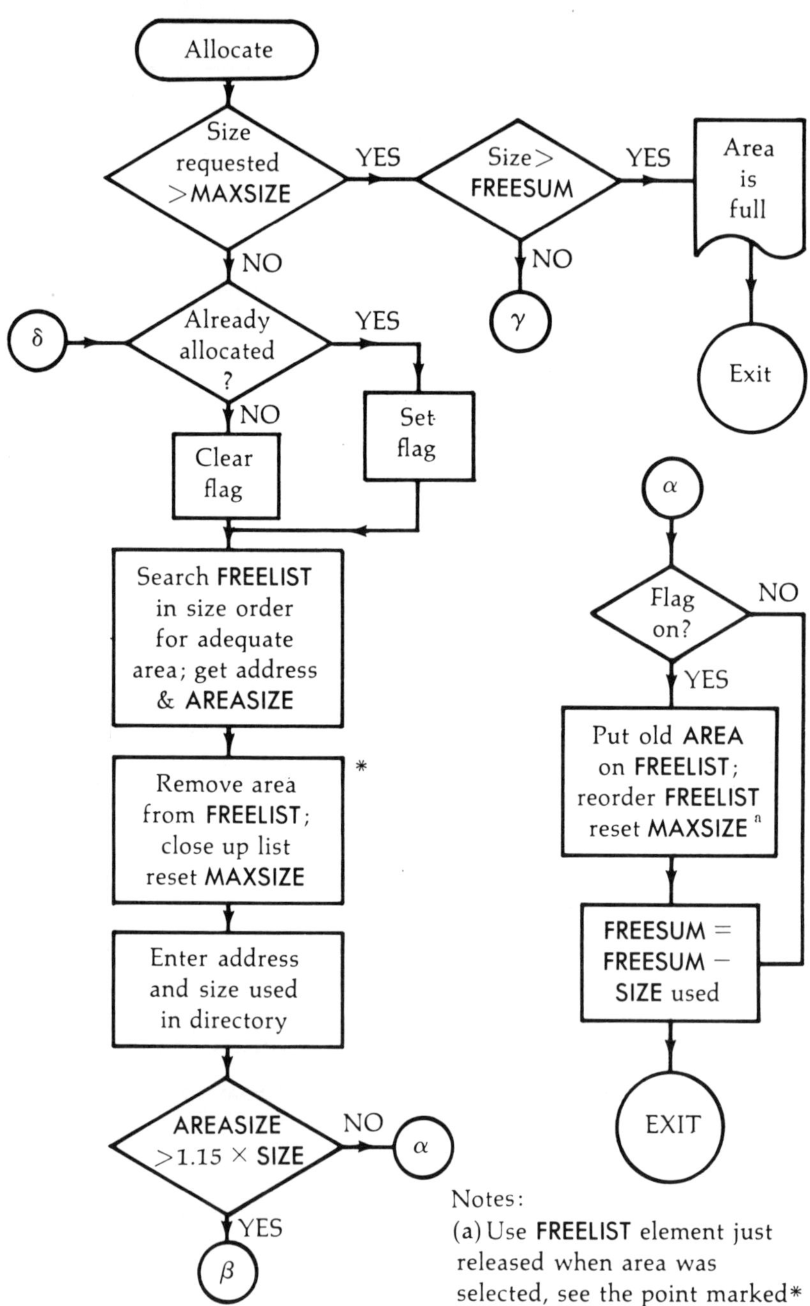

FIGURE 5.12 (Continued)

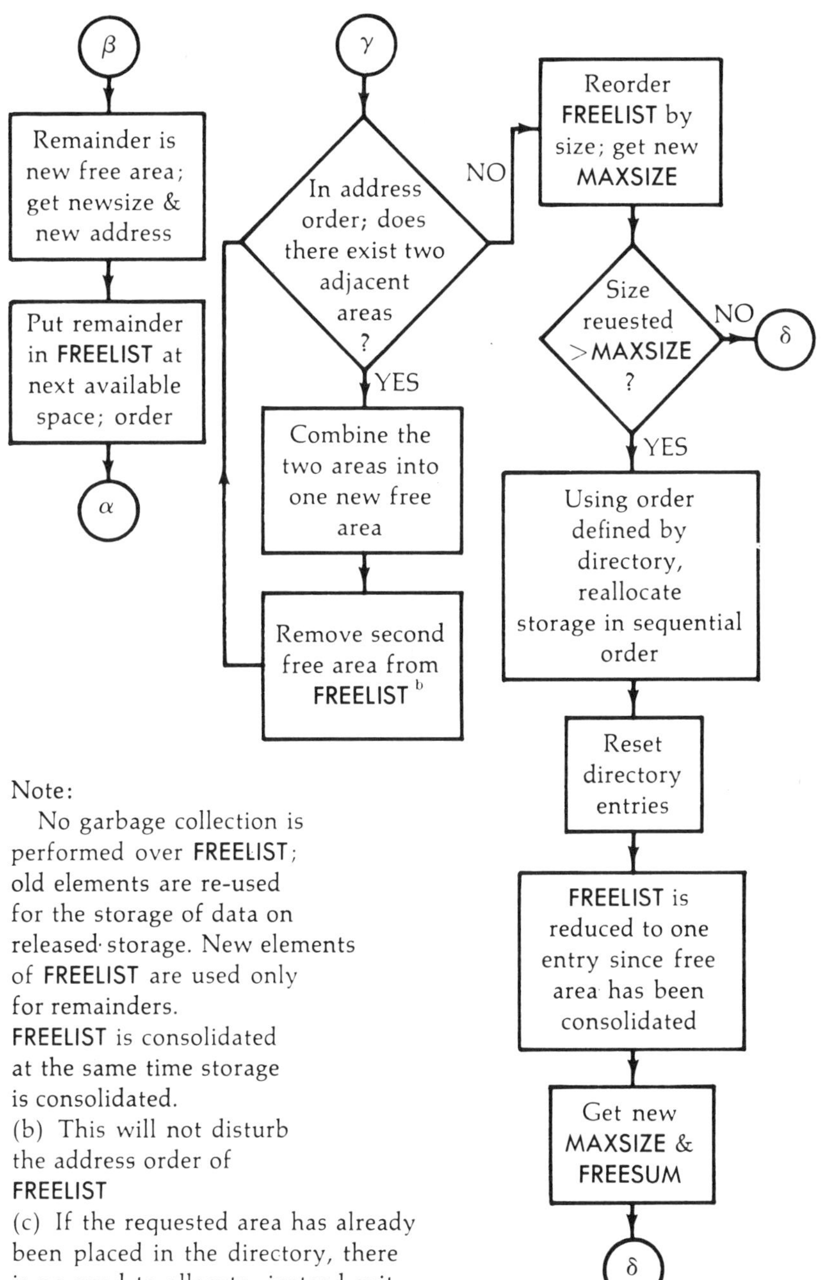

FIGURE 5.12 (Continued)

6. Is S greater than G? That is, has a space been generated which is of sufficient size to accommodate the requested allocation? If G is greater than S, return to step 2, with an assurance of success. Otherwise, initiate the total reorganization scheme (step 7).

7. There can exist at the most $M + .15T$ available space in the memory, where T is the total used space. Thus if S is greater than $M + .15T$, the working space is full and no further action need be taken other than to abort the interpretation of the program.

8. The address linked list specifies the available space in the correct order, but there does not exist a list of used space in order. Obviously such a list can be generated from the symbol table, but again it will be more efficient if such a list can be generated during the execution of the program, and maintained in the symbol table. Thus on each allocation (step 3), a space-used list will be updated. Using this list, the memory usage can be consolidated into a single area, and the available space list reduced to a single entry representing the remaining space which is also contiguous. Following this process, control can be returned to step 2 with an assurance of success.

THE CONCEPTS AND ORGANIZATION OF SHARED MEMORY

FORTRAN contains a memory organization facility which is extremely powerful, is utilized in a very large number of complex programs, and which provides the programmer with program properties present in few other programming systems; that is, shared memory facilities. While it could be argued that the pass by address system of parameter passing is a form of shared memory facility, we shall specifically omit parameter passing from consideration in this section. FORTRAN provides two declaratives (COMMON and EQUIVALENCE) which together with DIMENSION enable the programmer to share memory between subprograms and between local identifiers. Further, these facilities permit the user to develop an environment for a memory location such that the manner of reference defines the usage. That is, the reference prescribes attributes rather than declarations. Although FORTRAN does not allow for dynamic attribute referencing, the application of multiple names and correspondingly multiple attributes to a single location (or array space) is feasible. These applications transverse the boundaries of subprograms as well as applying to local entities.

FORTRAN is not unique in the availability of memory sharing features, since PL/I contains the concept of CELL, but the author feels that such concepts are not in common usage since their applicability is both implementation dependent and machine dependent. That is, depending on the algorithm for mapping between arrays and linearly addressed storage, the correspondences between elements of arrays will vary; depending on the numeric representation of language values, the correspondences between the attributes of elements will vary. In the discussion here we shall omit consideration of attribute variances.

COMMON, DIMENSION, AND EQUIVALENCE

The layout of the object time data area is greatly influenced by the declarative statements COMMON, DIMENSION and EQUIVALENCE. In general, the FORTRAN programmer has no control over the absolute locations of data and variables, though by the use of COMMON and implicit dimensioning, certain items may be placed in a template in a prescribed order. In particular, a DIMENSION statement, while declaring arrays and requesting a certain number of locations, cannot force upon the compiler the manner in which the array is to be stored. As mentioned, the elements of the array may be stored in some random order and, provided that the object time routines could unwind this order to provide a certain requested element, the programmer would not be aware of the mapping algorithm. Further, the definition of several arrays in a single DIMENSION statement does not imply that these arrays have any connection to each other. In fact, if the compiler does place these arrays in memory in that order, this is a peculiarity of the system, not of the language.

A COMMON statement, or a collection of COMMON statements, does imply contiguous placement of the variables and arrays. Blocked (numbered) COMMON, on the other hand, does not imply contiguous blocks.

To complicate this abstract concept, the programmer has the ability to equate identifiers by the use of the EQUIVALENCE statement. However, an EQUIVALENCE statement is doubly defined, or at least has two algorithms of organization depending on the data to be equated. Let us review some of the rules that control the use and meaning of the EQUIVALENCE statement.

1. Each pair of parentheses in the statement encloses the names of two or more identifiers that are to share the same memory location at object time.

2. Each language element not mentioned in an EQUIVALENCE statement is assigned a unique location, except when that element appears in a COMMON statement.

3. Identifiers brought into the COMMON block by means of an EQUIVALENCE statement may increase the size of the COMMON block as originally specified in the COMMON statements. That is, if an array is brought into COMMON in such a fashion that some elements would fall outside the already established bounds of COMMON, then the size of the COMMON block must be increased to encompass the whole array.

4. Since the elements of an array are stored in consecutive locations from high-order address to low-order address, an array may not be brought into the COMMON block in such a way as to cause the array to extend beyond the upper bound of the block. In particular, as is a frequent occurrence, when the COMMON block is arranged to be the uppermost portion of memory, this protection ensures that some elements of the array do not lie in fictitious memory.

5. EQUIVALENCE may not rearrange COMMON. That is, two items already specified as existing in the COMMON block may not be equivalenced.

6. Subprograms may not extend COMMON. Thus the COMMON block defined in a main program shall always be of a length greater than or equal to the COMMON blocks in subprograms. For this reason the location of the END OF COMMON must be communicated to all subprograms.

Certain effects implied in these rules must be observed. By rule 2, any variable not in COMMON and not specifically mentioned in an EQUIVALENCE statement must have a separate entity. Thus if the following statements appeared in a single subprogram,

```
DIMENSION A(10),B(3),I(2,3)
EQUIVALENCE (A(1),B(1))
```

memory would be arranged in the form:

```
A( 1) ≡ B(1)
A( 2) ≡ B(2)
A( 3) ≡ B(3)
A( 4)
A( 5)
A( 6)
A( 7)
A( 8)
A( 9)
A(10)
I(1,1)
I(2,1)
I(1,2)
I(2,2)
I(1,3)
I(2,3)
```

However, if the EQUIVALENCE statement were replaced by

EQUIVALENCE (A(10),B(1))

and the arrays A and I were left in the same locations as previously, the array B would overlap the array I. This would imply EQUIVALENCE, such that I(1) and I(2) would share memory locations with B(2) and B(3), respectively. Thus a violation of rule 2 would exist. Hence the array I will have to be relocated.

```
A( 1)
A( 2)
A( 3)
A( 4)
A( 5)
A( 6)
A( 7)
A( 8)
A( 9)
A(10) ≡ B(1)
        B(2)
        B(3)
I(1,1)
I(2,1)
I(1,2)
I(2,2)
I(1,3)
I(2,3)
```

There may be implicit equivalence of *elements* in those arrays that appear by name in the **EQUIVALENCE** statement, such that

```
EQUIVALENCE (A(5),B(2))
```

also implies

```
EQUIVALENCE (A(4),B(1)),(A(6),B(3))
```

but undeclared implicit equivalences of distinct language elements are invalid—except in **COMMON**. Given the statements

```
COMMON (A(3),X,K
EQUIVALENCE  (A(2),B(1))
DIMENSION B(3)
```

the **COMMON** block will be arranged as the sequence **A(1),A(2),A(3), X,K** and the following implicit equivalences will be permitted

$$B(2) \equiv A(3)$$
$$B(3) \equiv X$$

Consider the statements:

```
COMMON A(3),X,K
DIMENSION B(5)
EQUIVALENCE  (X,B(5))
```

Now after the compilation of the first statement, the **COMMON** block would be allocated in the form:

```
A(1)
A(2)
A(3)
X
K
```

Making the fifth element of **B** equivalent to **X** would imply the following equivalences, which are all valid since all identifiers are within the **COMMON** block: **A(1)** ≡ **B(2)**, **A(2)** ≡ **B(3)**, **A(3)** ≡ **B(4)**, *but* element **B(1)** is now before (has a higher memory address) than **A(1)** in violation of rule 4.

By rule 5, the **EQUIVALENCE** statement may not cause a rearrangement of the variables in the **COMMON** area; that is, in effect, two items that already appear in **COMMON** may not be elements of an **EQUIVALENCE** statement group. This would seem to say that within one parenthetical group, there may appear only one item which is in **COMMON**. While this is true, the statement is not strong enough to prevent some implied equivalences. The interaction of **COMMON** and

EQUIVALENCE can cause a violation of rule 5 that is not apparent in the statement, but that appears after the compilation of certain groups in the **EQUIVALENCE** statement. For example,

```
COMMON A(3), X, K
DIMENSION B(5)
EQUIVALENCE (X,B(1)),(B(2),A(3))
```

would require the following arrangement of **COMMON**:

```
A(1)
A(2)    X    B(1)
A(3)         B(2)
K            B(3)
             B(4)
             B(5)
```

which is illegal, as **COMMON** has been rearranged since the first definition of the area in the **COMMON** statement. To overcome this obstacle, it is stated (rule 3 implicitly) that an identifier brought into **COMMON** must be regarded as having been declared as an element of **COMMON** after its first equivalencing. Thus group 2 of the above **EQUIVALENCE** statement is invalid.

Whilst rule 3 states that an identifier may be brought into **COMMON** in such a fashion that the length of the **COMMON** area is increased, rule 6 will prevent implicit overlap with variables not in **COMMON** (rule 2). For example, consider the following statements in a main line program and a subprogram:

```
PROGRAM MAIN          SUBROUTINE SUB
COMMON X,Y(3),K       COMMON A,B,C
                      DIMENSION X(2)
```

Such statements would implicitly equivalence the following variables:

Main Program	*Subprogram*
X	A
Y(1)	B
Y(2)	C

If the **X** array in the subprogram were placed immediately following the variable **C** in the subprogram, the following equivalences would be in effect:

Main Program	*Subprogram*
Y(3)	X(1)
K	X(2)

That is, the X subprogram array would effectively be in COMMON. Thus the END OF COMMON must be used to determine the object time addresses of non-COMMON variables in subprograms.

Conversely, if we allowed COMMON to be extended by a subprogram without recourse to extending COMMON in the main program, then some local variables in the main program would be implicitly in COMMON, hence violating rule 2. Rearranging COMMON as a result of an extension in a subprogram is not practical when subprograms may be compiled without reference to the main program. That is, where a subprogram may be compiled for use with several main programs, the compiler has no way to determine the size of the original array.

When the implementer is constrained to conform with the standard so that all the elements of the language are present (a reasonable request) and to permit all those features that have been overlooked (a questionable request), and thus is required to permit the extension of the COMMON area by a subprogram, he must follow one of two courses. He must either cause the examination of all COMMON block lengths to determine which is largest before assigning other memory space or ignore the rule stating that no implicit equivalences are permitted between variables that are outside of COMMON and the COMMON block, giving the programmer a diagnostic warning that this may cause some unusual results. In this instance, the insistence of not extending the COMMON area would seem to be a valid variance from the standard.

As a result of these intricacies, the "execution" of EQUIVALENCE statements at compile time is not straightforward and cannot necessarily be performed in the order set out by the programmer. For example,

```
COMMON A(3),X,K
DIMENSION B(5),C(2)
EQUIVALENCE (B(5),C(1)),(B(1),A(3))
```

would require a number of steps. Initially (before the EQUIVALENCE statement is encountered), the COMMON area would be set out as:

```
A(1)
A(2)
A(3)
X
K
———————— END OF COMMON
```

```
B(1)
B(2)
B(3)
B(4)
B(5)
C(1)
C(2)
```

Then after the first **EQUIVALENCE** group has been executed, the following arrangement would exist:

```
A(1)
A(2)
A(3)
X
K
———————————— END OF COMMON
B(1)
B(2)
B(3)
B(4)
B(5)      C(1)
          C(2)
```

In practice, the only operation necessary to make this memory rearrangement would be to alter the addresses of the variables in the symbol table.

The next group within the **EQUIVALENCE** statement places **B** into the **COMMON** area, bringing with it the array **C** (adjusting the base addresses of both arrays), and shifts the **END OF COMMON** down by three words to encompass the whole set of variables and elements of arrays of which at least one element is now in **COMMON**. To remember that **C** is equivalent to a portion of the array **B** requires special handling. The final layout of memory will be:

```
A(1)
A(2)
A(3)      B(1)
X         B(2)
K         B(3)
———————————————————— Initial END OF COMMON
          B(4)
          B(5)      C(1)
                    C(2)
———————————————————— Final END OF COMMON
```

In processing COMMON, DIMENSION and EQUIVALENCE statements it is both uneconomical and frustrating to organize blindly the memory layout in the order of occurrence of the statements and variables within those statements. Consider Figure 5.13. If all COMMON statements are collected primarily and processed, then a temporary END OF COMMON (EOC) may be computed and permanent address assignments made to all variables that appear in that area since COMMON may not be rearranged. Next DIMENSION statements must be considered since the proper "execution" of the EQUIVALENCE statement depends on this knowledge. However, it is not known at this point which of the variables in the DIMENSION statement will eventually be brought into COMMON by equivalencing, and hence only the names and dimensions may be posted in the symbol table. To enable the later assignment of addresses to variables that do not appear in the COMMON area, a list of the variables occurring in the DIMENSION statement must be formed (DLIST) and reserved until the EQUIVALENCE statements have been processed. Having collected the dimensions of the arrays that may appear in the EQUIVALENCE statement, we must now collect EQUIVALENCE groups (that is, parenthesized groups declaring that the variables are to be stored in the same computer word) in ELIST and scan these for the names of variables that have already appeared in the COMMON statement. Once these variables are recognized, all other variables in that group must be considered to be in COMMON and hence can be assigned permanent object time addresses on the basis of the original COMMON declaration and with reference to the preceding DIMENSION statement. Also these should be deleted from the list of variables (DLIST) not yet assigned addresses that was set up when the DIMENSION statements were scanned. Once such a group has been processed, *all* other groups must be scanned for variables that are now in the COMMON area. That is, if the first located COMMON variable in the first scan was found in the third and last group, the other two groups must be rescanned after the third group is processed in case any one of their variables is now in COMMON.

Once all groups in the EQUIVALENCE statement that contained either an explicit or implicit variable in COMMON have been eliminated, and the END OF COMMON has been adjusted, then all other groups must contain non-COMMON variables.

Since these groups have no fixed address on which to base their absolute address and much reshuffling may take place, each group must be scanned to determine its *spread*. The spread is the number of words that are affected by the arrays and variables in the group after the appropriate elements have been assigned to the same storage location. For example, if we have the statements

```
DIMENSION A(10),C(5)
EQUIVALENCE (A(8),C(2))
```

then regardless of the absolute address of each element, the group template would be laid out as follows

```
A( 1)
A( 2)
A( 3)
A( 4)
(A 5)
A( 6)
A( 7)    C(1)
A( 8)    C(2)
A( 9)    C(3)
A(10)    C(4)
         C(5)
```

and the *spread* of the group would be 11 words. The uppermost element in this template is A(1); thus if we were to place this group into memory from the top down, A(1) would be the element that would determine the placement of all other elements since it would have to fit into the next available location. Let us assign this key element the relative address of 000. The element C(1) would then have a relative address of −006, and the last element in the group (C(5)) would have the relative address of −010. Subsequent to these relative assignments, all other groups would have to be scanned to locate other occurrences of the same variables. Thus with the statements

```
DIMENSION A(10),C(5),X(3),Y(10)
EQUIVALENCE (A(8),C(2)),(X(1),Y(1)),(C(5),Y(3))
```

which contain the same dimensions of A and C as before with the same equivalence group, we would find that after relative addresses have been assigned to A and C, the third group also contains a reference to the array C. Thus the Y array can be brought into relation with the elements of the first group and may be assigned relative addresses. Thus Y(1) will have a relative address of −008, and the lower limit of the group will be at −017.

The variables A, C and Y are now in a single grouping. A further scan shows that the only remaining group contains a reference to Y, and thus its associated variable (X) is also part of the grouping. Since the first element of the X array is equivalent to the first element in the Y array, their relative addresses must be the same; that is, the relative address of X(1) is −008. Further, since the X array does not extend the spread of the grouping, the lower limit relative address is still −017. The final arrangement of these arrays is

000	A(1)			
−001	A(2)			
−002	A(3)			
−003	A(4)			
−004	A(5)			
−005	A(6)			
−006	A(7)	C(1)		
−007	A(8)	C(2)		
−008	A(9)	C(3)	Y(1)	X(1)
−009	A(10)	C(4)	Y(2)	X(2)
−010		C(5)	Y(3)	X(3)
−011			Y(4)	
−012			Y(5)	
−013			Y(6)	
−014			Y(7)	
−015			Y(8)	
−016			Y(9)	
−017			Y(10)	

At this point, all groups in the EQUIVALENCE statement that were interconnected have been eliminated, and a list of variables whose permanent addresses may be assigned has been built up. Scanning the temporary relative addresses of the arrays in this list, we find that the highest address has been assigned to the first element of A. Thus this element can be placed in the next available address, and all other elements and arrays can be given permanent addresses. The next available location for subsequent assignments may be computed from the lower limit relative address.

It may appear unnecessary to search for the largest temporary address since that first one assigned happened to be the largest; however, if the EQUIVALENCE statement had been written as

EQUIVALENCE (C(2),A(8)),(X(1)(Y(1)),(C(5),Y(3))

then

C(1) would have been assigned the relative address of	000
A(1)	+006
Y(1)	−002
X(1)	−002

and the lower limit address would be −011. It would be possible to adjust all relative addresses so that the highest address is 000 at all stages of the process, but such repeated adjustment would be wasteful of time and can be easily omitted and replaced by the final search for the maximum relative address.

This procedure of finding the implicit groups in an EQUIVALENCE statement and assigning relative addresses can be repeated until all groups have been eliminated and, in effect, the EQUIVALENCE statement is empty.

Once all variables mentioned in the EQUIVALENCE statement have been assigned permanent addresses, the list of DIMENSIONed variables must be scanned to assign addresses to the remaining arrays. These may be arranged sequentially through the available memory. The process is shown in Figure 5.13.

Problem

ANSI standard FORTRAN specifically states (Sec. 7.2.1.4) that the element in an EQUIVALENCE group may not be a parameter of a subprogram. This is mainly because of the difficulty in implementing a routine capable of handling all the possible cases that could arise if an EQUIVALENCE statement in a subprogram were able to contain a parameter wherever a simple variable is permitted by the standard. Further, the mention of the elements associated with or equivalenced to this parameter in other statements within the subprogram would require special handling. Among the situations to be considered are:

1. A local scalar variable is equivalenced to a non-dimensioned parameter.

2. Two non-dimensioned parameters are equivalenced.

3. A local scalar variable is equivalenced to an element of an array which is in the parameter list of the subprogram.

4. A non-dimensioned parameter is equivalenced to an element of a local array.

Investigate the problems of storage allocation and reference associated with each of these situations and determine the manner in which the EQUIVALENCE concept can be extended readily.

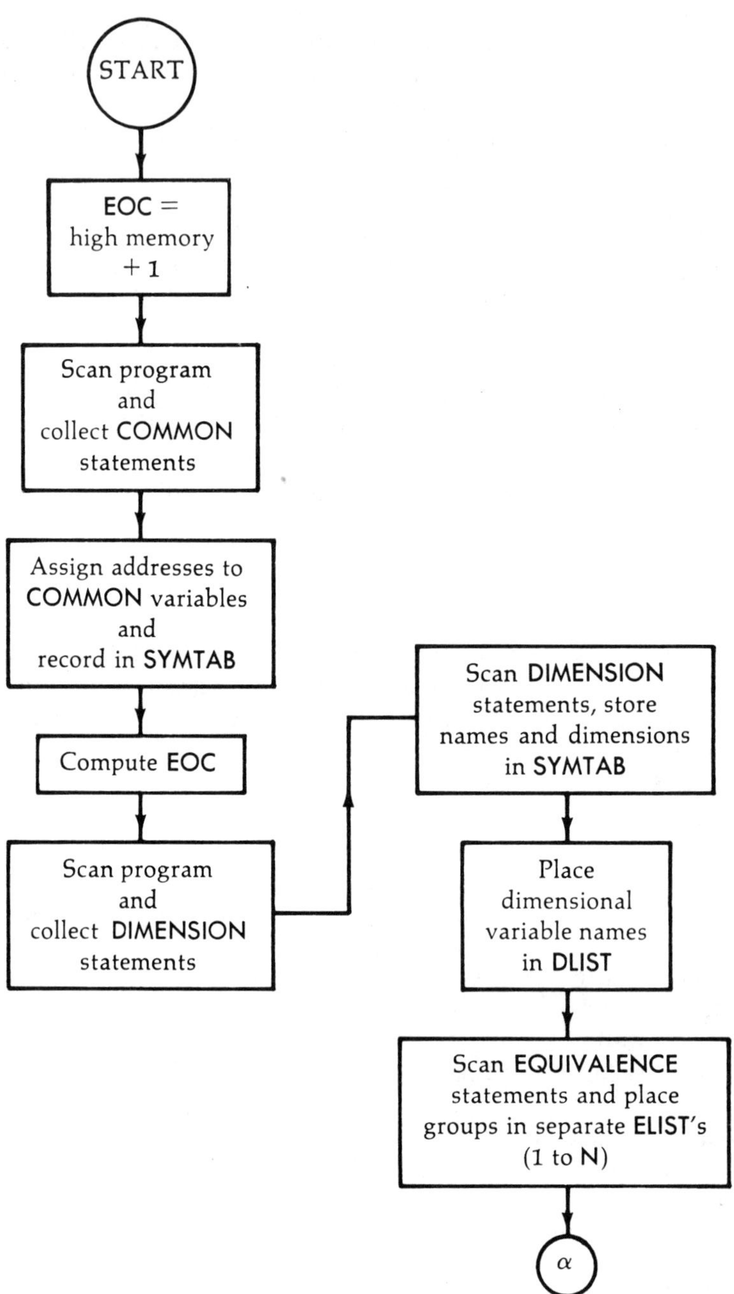

FIGURE 5.13 The equivalence algorithm.

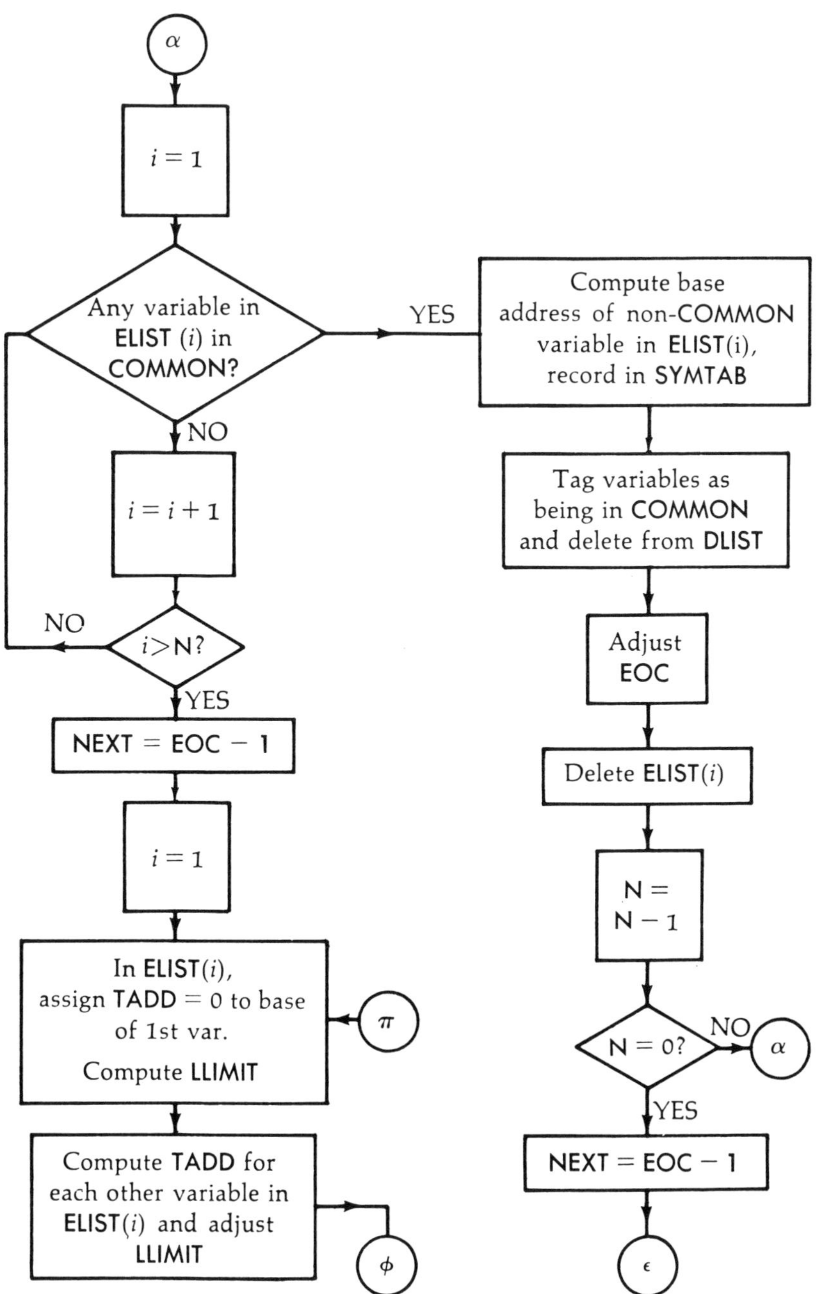

FIGURE 5.13 (Continued)

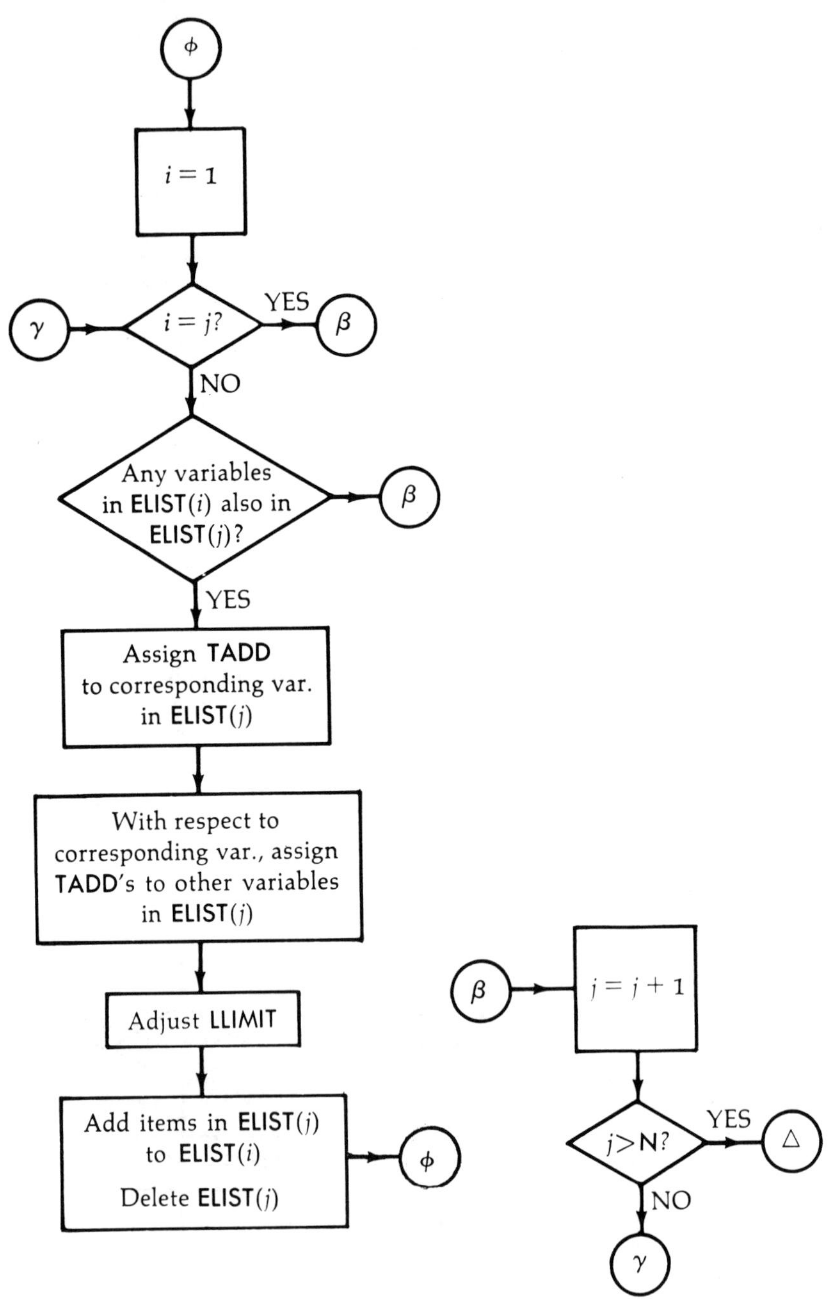

FIGURE 5.13 (Continued)

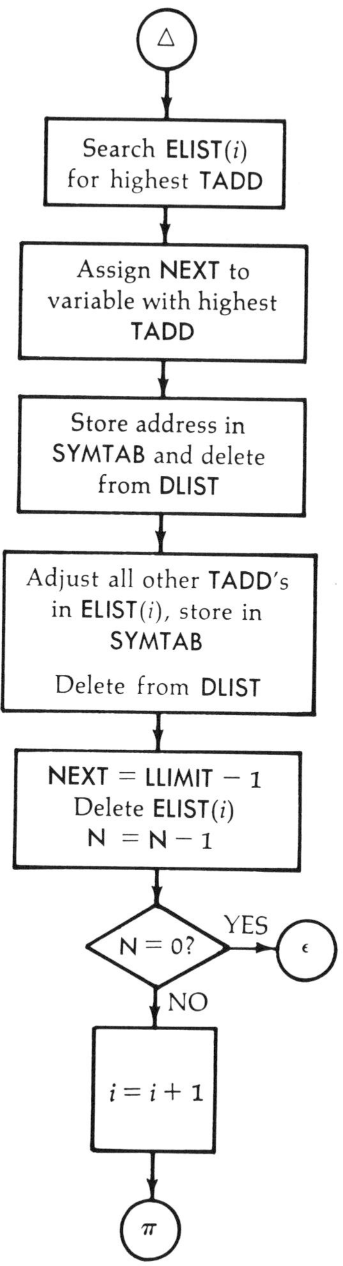

FIGURE 5.13 (Continued)

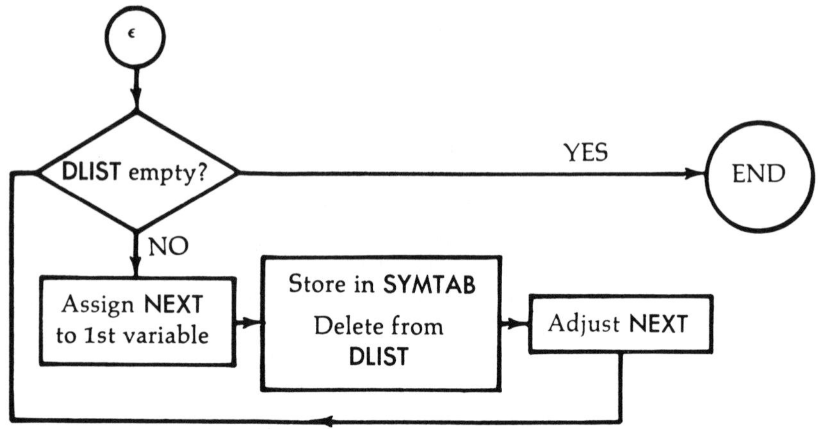

EOC The address of the last element in **COMMON**, that is, the address of the **END OF COMMON**.

DLIST A list of variable names that are mentioned in the **DIMENSION** statements. This list is used after the execution of the **EQUIVALENCE** algorithm to assign unique addresses to these variables.

ELIST A set of lists containing each group of the **EQUIVALENCE** statement.

ELIST(i) The i-th sublist in **ELIST**.

NEXT The next unused word in the available memory.

LLIMIT The lower limit address in the algorithm.

N The number of sublists in **ELIST**.

TADD Temporary address.

SYMTAB Symbol table.

Note:

Since no element in an **EQUIVALENCE** group may be a formal parameter, all address assignments may be completed at compile time, and thus no object program is output from the algorithm for object time address computation.

FIGURE 5.13 **(Continued)**

SUMMARY

The solutions to the problems of either storage organization or storage allocation are rarely defined by the language in which the programs are written. We have decided, as an industry, for better or for worse, that such controls should not be apparent to the "everyday" user. Even in the simple case of an identifier which references a scalar, there is little concern on the part of the user as to how the name maps onto the available storage and almost no concern as to the relationships (spacial or otherwise) between different parts of the storage system. Even in the case of FORTRAN **COMMON** or PL/I **CELL**, the user looks upon the provided feature of shared memory more as a convenient renaming or double attribute facility. Only the implementer is required to think in terms of the actual physical meaning of such language features.

6
Source Text Manipulations

So far in this text, none of the portions of a compiler considered have led directly to the generation of code which would be executed to solve the problem posed by the source text. The next sequence of chapters will cover this aspect of the process of compilation.

In this chapter we shall begin a study of arithmetic expressions with a view to their compilation in an efficient manner. It can be seen readily that expressions are fundamental to the majority of statements that occur in any program. Whereas some languages will contain restrictions as to the type (or complexity) of expression that may occur in certain statements, we shall release those restrictions here so as to maintain generality. In fact, we shall consider all references to be of one of two types: loadables or executables. That is, as far as compilation is concerned, a reference which is to be used as the location into which a value is to be "loaded" or a reference from which a value is to be obtained. In the majority of cases a loadable will be represented as a reference to a single location in memory such as a simple variable or an array element. Conversely, the executable reference can be any expression which yields a value, the degenerate case being a single memory reference to a constant.

For the time being we shall not consider the generated code from either of these two situations, but instead we shall look at the source code for means of generating some intermediate text from which it will be more convenient or more efficient to generate target code, or a form which will lead to improved (optimized) code.

EXPRESSION STRUCTURE

The usual form of expressions used in mathematics represents not only a series of operations (such as addition, multiplication, etc.) but also an ordering of execution. The idiosyncrasies of such expressions are in the main due to our methods of written communication which are based on linearized sequences of characters. If we could standardize on two-dimensional communications, then the embedded structure of expressions could be specified without the use of parentheses, without the use of rules of hierarchy, and without rules for scanning direction (usually left to right). That is, if expressions were presented to us as diagrams, the process of deciding which portion of the expression can be evaluated (or compiled, in the environment of this text) would be minimized. We have already seen that by the use of syntactic specification, syntactic analyzers can be used to develop this picture of expression structure.

Working from the base of a parsed text, or a syntactic tree, it is possible to generate other intermediate forms which are highly susceptible to either evaluation algorithms or compilation schema. Let us consider, initially, the case of syntactic trees.

In Chapter 3 we developed the following syntax for arithmetic expressions which included only the usual operators for addition, subtraction, multiplication, division, involution, negation (unary subtraction), and unary addition:

<term> ::= *<variable>*|(*<expression>*)
<involution factor> ::= *<term>*|*<term>*↑*<involution factor>*
<multiply factor> ::= *<involution factor>*|
  <multiply factor>$\{*|/\}_1^1$*<involution factor>*
<expression> ::= $\{+|-\}_1^1$*<multiply factor>*|
  <expression>$\{+|-\}_1^1$*<multiply factor>*

Using this syntax and a left to right scanning system, we find that the linear expression **A + B * C** may be analyzed uniquely into the tree form (Figure 6.1).

Based on these trees, a simple evaluation scheme can be established for the evaluation or compilation of the represented expressions. Let us consider evaluation at this point. The object of the exercise will be

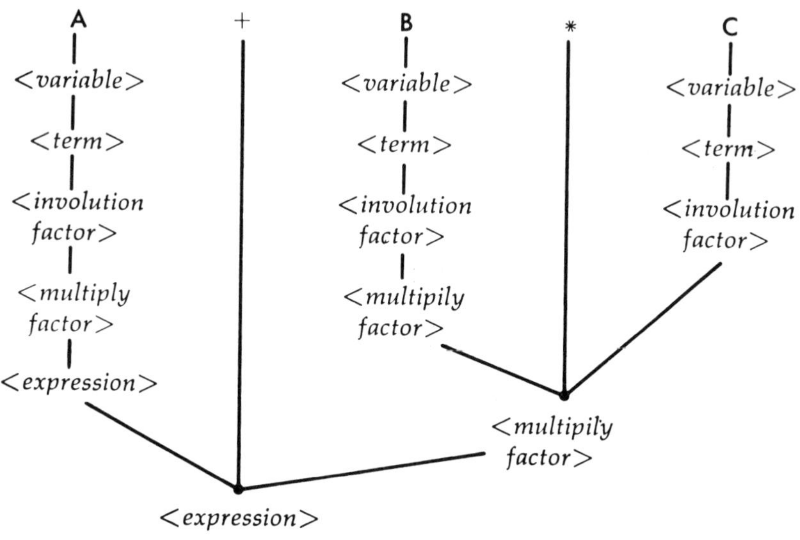

FIGURE 6.1

to generate a value for the expression, represented in this case by the syntactic term *<expression>*, which resides at the base (root) of the tree. Syntactically, *<expression>* is composed of three elements, all of which must be evaluated in order to evaluate *<expression>*. Working up each branch of the tree in this manner, "values" can be passed through each level until the tree is reduced to the form of Figure 6.2, where the overstrokes indicate "evaluation."

If we represent $\overline{\overline{B},*,\overline{C}}$ as the value of *<multiply factor>* then this tree can be further reduced to Figure 6.3.

Finally we can represent the generated value of expression as $\overline{\overline{A},+,\overline{\overline{\overline{B},*,\overline{C}}}}$. Obviously, the overstrokes are equivalent to parentheses and we can recognize that the original meaning of the expression A+B*C is maintained through the syntactic analysis and subsequent "evaluation."

A further modification that can be made would be to replace the syntactic names by their first level operators to signify the scope of the operators over the operands. In this modification, the first reduced tree above will take the form of Figure 6.4.

This tree-structured representation of an expression is obviously superior to the syntactic tree form, adequately expressing the structure and order of evaluation of the expression. Further the algorithm of

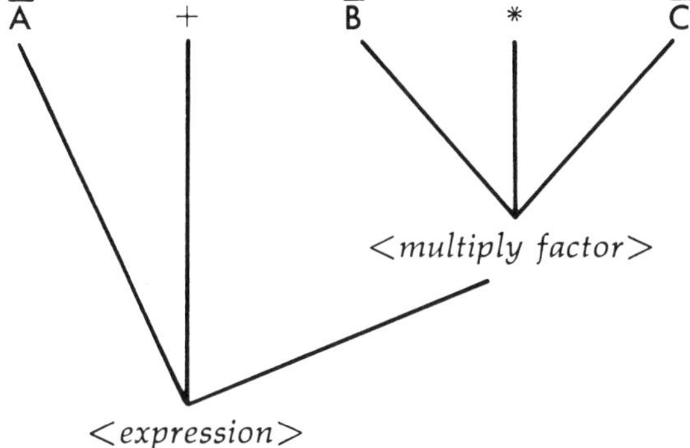

FIGURE 6.2

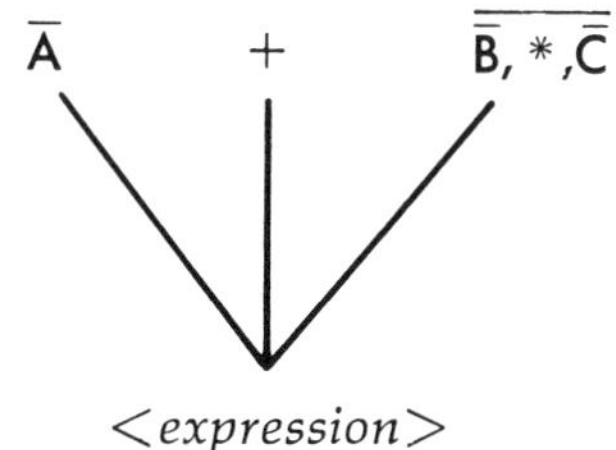

FIGURE 6.3

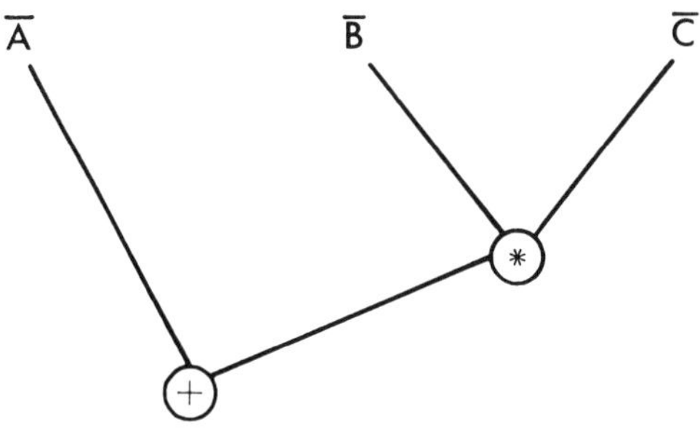

FIGURE 6.4

transformation of a syntactic tree to the structured expression is simple and requires little decision making.

However, even with these seemingly simple diagrams, their representation and manipulation within the memory of a computer is not quite so straightforward. Let us then consider the linearized representations of these forms.

One linearized form of representation of syntactic trees is known as the *phrase marker* of the string. This form uses a functional notation to associate the syntactic element with its components. Thus the subtree

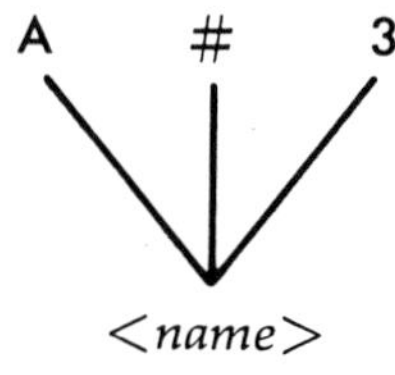

FIGURE 6.5

would be linearized to the string <*name*>(A,#,3). Using this scheme, the phrase marker of **A** + **B** * **C** would be

$$e(e(mf(if(t(v(\mathbf{A}))))),+,mf(mf(if(t(v(\mathbf{B})))),*,if(t(v(\mathbf{C})))))$$

where

$e =$ <*expression*>
$mf =$ <*multiply factor*>
$if =$ <*involution factor*>
$t =$ <*term*>
$v =$ <*variable*>

and the symbols in the source text stand for themselves. Using the scheme of evaluation over syntactic trees specified previously, we may see that we can move "values" through these phrase-marker forms, so that by direct substitution of the inner "value" for the syntactic name where there is only one component inside the parentheses, we obtain the functional form

$$e(\overline{\mathbf{A}},+,mf(\overline{\mathbf{B}},*,\overline{\mathbf{C}}))$$

where, again the overstrokes indicate evaluation. If $mf(\overline{\mathbf{B}},*,\overline{\mathbf{C}})$ evaluates to $\overline{\overline{\mathbf{B}},*,\overline{\mathbf{C}}}$ and, in general, $e(\mathbf{X},\circ,\mathbf{Y})$ evaluates into $\overline{\mathbf{X},\circ,\mathbf{Y}}$, then the "value" generated from the original phrase marker form of the source statement expression will be $\overline{\overline{\mathbf{A}},+,\overline{\overline{\mathbf{B}},*,\overline{\mathbf{C}}}}$, which is identical to the result obtained previously.

Let us now look at the equivalent phrase marker form of the modified trees in which the syntactic names have been replaced by the prevalent operators. In this form the syntax of a subtree will be <*operator*> (<*operand list*>) so that the original string **X** + **Y** will be represented by $+(\overline{X},\overline{Y})$. In the case we have been considering, the original string A + B * C will be represented by the string $+(\overline{A},*(\overline{\overline{B}},\overline{\overline{C}}))$.

This functional representation can also be recognized as one of the forms of *Polish string notation* (see the next section) except for the presence of the parentheses. Where there exists no ambiguity between the operand symbols and those of the operators (as is usual in expressions), the parentheses can be omitted without losing the meaning of the string. Further, where the symbols are distinct, the punctuation can be omitted also. Thus the functional form above can be reduced to[1] +A*BC.

The functional representation, however, has one drawback: the ordering of the operator and its operands is not precisely the same as that required in an evaluation process. That is, in scanning from left to right (our normal order) the operator appears before its operands and thus must be saved until its operands have been evaluated. A right to left scan does not suffer from this feature. Thus for a left to right scan, a postfix (as opposed to prefix) notation is preferable. In this, the operands are followed by their operator, the evaluation of the operands preceding the scanning of the operator. Thus the usual string A + B * C is represented in postfix notation as the string ABC*+.

The use of a syntactic analyzer and the subsequent transformation processes for converting the parsed text (syntactic tree or phrase marker) into a more manipulable form, while generally applicable, is a form of overkill which a specific system may not be able to afford. In the subsequent sections of this chapter we shall consider more direct transformation schemes.

POLISH STRING NOTATION

The notation employed by a Polish logician, J. Lukasiewicz (and generally known as Polish string notation since most people fail to pronounce or remember the name) is a means of representing arithmetic or logical expressions that is unambiguous, does not need parentheses to enforce the hierarchy of operations, and may be broken down to a set of operations and operands in a single scan. There are, in fact, several forms of Polish string notation. The particular form to be described is known as Reverse or Postfix Polish. In this notation, each operator is preceded by its two operands. Thus the string $ab+$ is the Polish string form of the usual arithmetic expression $a+b$, it

1. We shall omit the overstrokes from this point on.

being assumed in this particular instance that each variable name is only one character in length.

Once an expression has been reduced to Reverse Polish, its translation back to the usual algebraic form is accomplished by scanning the string from left to right until the first operator is located. This is then placed between the two preceding operands, all three items becoming a parenthetical group or, in other words, a term in the string. For example, consider the string

$$xabc*d/+ =$$

1. In a left to right scan, the first operator is *, which is placed between the two preceding operands:

$$bc* \rightarrow (b*c)$$

The string becomes

$$xa(b*c)d/+=$$

and the term $(b*c)$ is regarded as an operand from this point on.

2. The scan is continued for the next operator to the right of the asterisk, which is /. This is placed between the term $(b*c)$ and the operand d:

$$(b*c)d/ \rightarrow ((b*c)/d)$$

3. The scan is continued further and the next operator is +. This is placed between the two preceding operands, and the string is transformed to

$$x(a+((b*c)/d))=$$

4. Finally, the last operator in the string is =; the completely transformed statement is

$$(x=(a+((b*c)/d)))$$

or

$$x = a + \frac{bc}{d}$$

THE CONVERSION FROM ALGEBRAIC TO POLISH NOTATION

Performing the translation from normal algebraic notation to Reverse Polish is not quite as simple as the above procedure (which could be programmed easily), since normal notations are not explicit.

For example, an order of execution dependent on the hierarchy of operators may be recognized in any algebraic statement, whereas Reverse Polish is independent of hierarchy. For example, the scalar expression

$$a + b(c-d)e - f$$

may be executed several ways, but with some implicit rules of the form:

1. Parenthetical phrases are to be evaluated primarily.

2. Multiplication or division operators are to be executed before addition or subtraction.

3. When several operators of the same hierarchical level exist simultaneously in a statement, they are to be executed from left to right.

To overcome the handicaps of needing to refer to a set of rules of execution order, an expression that is to be translated should be fully parenthesized. That is, it should be written in a form that is a valid instance of the rules:

<expression> ::= *<variable>*|(*<variable>* = *<expression>*)|
(*<unary operator><expression>*)|
(*<expression><dyadic operator><expression>*)
<unary operator> ::= −|+
<dyadic operator> ::= −|+|*|/|↑

If these rules are used, no pair of parentheses contains more than one operator at the same parenthetical level, where the parenthetical level of an operator is defined as the number of parentheses between it and the outside of the statement. For example, the parenthetical level of each operator is written beneath each operator in the following statement:

$$\begin{array}{ccccccccc} (x & = & (a & + & ((b & * & c) & / & d))) \\ & 1 & & 2 & & 4 & & 3 & \end{array}$$

This particular syntax will permit the generation of strings of the type

$$(x = (a + (y = (-b))))$$

or

$$(x = (y = (z = (a + b))))$$

we shall permit in our generalized considerations of expressions. The latter style of statement is permitted in FORTRAN (without the parentheses) and the former style is typical of APL. In either case the recognition of the replacement sign (=) as a dyadic operator (albeit a special case) will add to the generality of our discussion.

Once an expression has been fully parenthesized, it may be translated to Reverse Polish by working from the innermost parenthetical phrase toward the outside of the statement. Taking the first example above, the innermost parenthetical group is

$$(b * c)$$

which is transformed into

$$bc*$$

Let us use { ··· } to distinguish that portion of the expression which has been translated and may now be regarded as a single term; then the statement becomes:

$$\underset{1}{(}x = \underset{2}{(}a + (\{bc*\} \; / \; d\underset{3}{)}))$$

The symbol "/" appears at the next level:

$$\underset{1}{(}x = a + \underset{2}{\{}bc*d/\}))$$

Continuing to level 2:

$$\underset{1}{(}x = \{abc*d/+\})$$

and, subsequently, at the lowest level:

$$\{xabc*d/+=\}$$

Since no other untranslated parenthetical groups remain, the { ··· } may be dropped. Translation from an arithmetic statement to Reverse Polish does not necessarily result in a unique string. The result depends on the parenthesizing. Automatic parenthesizing routines that recognize the hierarchy of a leftmost operator in a string of equal hierarchical level operators will produce the same string consistently, whereas manual parenthesizing which takes advantage of the associativeness of + and * can produce differing Reverse Polish strings. For example, the algebraic string

$$a(b-c)d$$

may be parenthesized to two manners:

$$((a * (b - c)) * d) \qquad \text{and} \qquad (a * ((b - c) * d))$$

which translate to

$$abc-*d* \qquad \text{and} \qquad abc-d**$$

respectively. A more startling result is found when a normal string contains many commutative operators of the same level:

$$a + b + c + d$$

$$(((a + b) + c) + d) \qquad (a + (b + (c + d)))$$

$$ab{+}c{+}d{+} \qquad abcd{+}{+}{+}$$

Although a pair of parentheses may not contain more than one operator at the same level as the parentheses themselves (that is, no more than one unparenthesized operator), there may be as many as two operators at the next level, three at the next, and so on. For example, the statement

$$a + b * c + d + e * f$$

may be wholly parenthesized in the form

$$\begin{array}{c} ((a + (b * c)) + (d + (e * f))) \\ 2 \quad 3 \quad 1 \quad 2 \quad 3 \end{array}$$

Thus in translation to Reverse Polish, there are two possible starting points for the conversion process: the two operators at level 3. In fact, the order of conversion is irrelevant, since all orders of hierarchy are dissipated by the inclusion of parentheses. However, no operator can be involved in a conversion process until all other operators of higher parenthesis level have been eliminated. In a perfect situation, it would be advisable to convert all equal level operators with their operands to Reverse Polish simultaneously. For example,

$$(a * b - (c + d)/ e) * f$$

$$\begin{array}{c} (((a * b) - ((c + d) / e)) * f) \\ 3 \quad 2 \quad 4 \quad 3 \quad 1 \end{array}$$

$$\begin{array}{c} (((a * b) - (\{cd+\} / e)) * f) \\ 3 \quad 2 \quad 3 \quad 2 \end{array}$$

$$\begin{array}{c} ((\{ab*\} - \{cd+e/\}) * f) \\ 2 \quad 1 \end{array}$$

$$\begin{array}{c} (\{ab*cd+e/-\} * f) \\ 1 \end{array}$$

$$\{ab*cd+e/-f*\}$$

The unary operators, and, in particular, the unary minus, must hold a special place in Reverse Polish notation since only one operand is associated with this operator. Thus, whereas the production rule of converting between Reverse Polish dyadic operators and normal notation may be described as

<operand><operand><dyadic-operator> ↔
(*<operand><dyadic operator><operand>*)

the production rule to be used in connection with a unary operator is

<operand><unary operator> ↔ (*<unary operator><operand>*)

Another drawback to the use of unary operators (which, incidentally, are merely a shorthand method of denoting an operation involving the zero operand) is the use of the same symbolism for unary plus and minus as binary plus and minus, respectively. A unary operator may be recognized because:

1. It is the first character in an algebraic string, for example,

$$-a - b$$

2. It is the first character following an opening parenthesis, for example,

$$a * (-b)$$

In the following discussion, the unary plus will be ignored, and a unary minus will be represented by the special symbol ~. Thus in the translation, $(-a)$ becomes $\{a^{\sim}\}$. According to the rules of total parenthesizing, a unary minus must be surrounded by parentheses; thus $((-a) * (-b))$ becomes $(\{a^{\sim}\}* \{b^{\sim}\})$ and, finally, $a^{\sim}b^{\sim}*$.

Problems

6.1 Convert the following Reverse Polish strings to normal algebraic strings:

(a) $a^{\sim}cd*+bc-/zk^{\sim}\uparrow+$
(b) $xcd\uparrow e/ab*+=$
(c) $ab+cd*/egf^{\sim}+*-^{\sim}$

6.2 Convert the following algebraic statements to Reverse Polish notation:

(a) $-a + b * c * d / e^{f}$
(b) $(a - b - c) / d / e$
(c) $a(b/c + d/e) * f(-g - h)$

PARENTHESIZING EXPRESSIONS

The translation from normal algebraic statements to Reverse Polish notation depends on the existence of a fully parenthesized statement. Since this is not the form in which statements are generally presented, let us consider an algorithm for the parenthesizing of unparenthesized or partially parenthesized statements. Basically, the parenthesizing of an expression defines the order of execution of each operator without regard for the hierarchy of these operators. However, the technique of parenthesizing must depend on this hierarchy. If each expression is delimited by two pseudo-operators, $\vdash$ and $\dashv$, which define the beginning and end of the statement, respectively, then the hierarchy levels may be tabulated as follows:

$\vdash$	$\dashv$	0
$=$		1
$+$	$-$	2
$*$	$/$	3
$\sim$		4
$\uparrow$		5

Using this hierarchical table, we may plot the values of the operators in each statement (Figure 6.6).

By examination of a number of graphs of this type one will be able to ascertain that the operator which is first to be used in an evaluation and hence first to be enclosed in parentheses is that operator which occurs either on the peak of a graph or is the leftmost operator on a plateau. Furthermore, it is easily recognizable that the associated

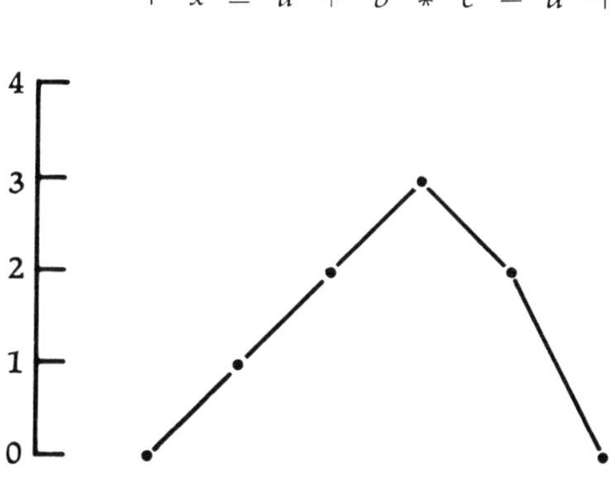

FIGURE 6.6

operands are always those immediately abutting the operator. Thus, if at each stage, the expression is reduced so that a parenthesized group is regarded as a single operator, the process of parenthesizing is comparatively straightforward. Where there exist more than one peak in an expression, the routine has a choice in which may be parenthesized first. Normally, this will be the leftmost peak, since we choose to scan statements from left to right. Using this graphical method, let us parenthesize the above expression. In the sequence of graphs shown in Figure 6.7, the "peak operator" is indicated by the circle in each case. Figure 6.8 shows an example which contains two peaks.

Based on this system, we now develop a scanning system over expressions which simulates the graphical method in locating either peaks or plateau edges. The parenthesizing process consists of the following steps:

1. Add the beginning and end delimiters to the statement.

2. Place the operator hierarchy values under each operator. Note, we shall use the term $\mathsf{V}(\mathsf{op}_{i}.)$ for the hierarchical value of operator i, where i is the position number of the operator from the left-hand end of the statement. That is, the beginning operator $\vdash$ always has a position number 1.

3. Starting from the left-hand end of the statement, ($\mathsf{op}_1 = \vdash$), set the counter at $n = 1$.

4. Scan along the statement by incrementing n to the right until the hierarchical value of the operator n is found to be greater than or equal to that of operator $n+1$, that is,

$$\mathsf{V}(\mathsf{op}_n) \geqslant \mathsf{V}(\mathsf{op}_{n+1})$$

5. Place a closing parenthesis to the left of op_{n+1}.

6. From op_n move left until op_i is found, so that

$$\mathsf{V}(\mathsf{op}_i) \leqslant \mathsf{V}(\mathsf{op}_n)$$

7. Place an opening parenthesis to the right of op_i.

8. Remove $\mathsf{V}(\mathsf{op}_n)$.

9. If op_{n+1} is the end delimiter and op_{n-1} is the beginning operator, then the parenthesizing is complete. Otherwise, set the pointer to op_{n-1} (that is, decrease the value of the pointer by 1). Go to step 5 if $\mathsf{V}(\mathsf{op}_n) \geqslant \mathsf{V}(\mathsf{op}_{n+1})$; otherwise, go to step 4.

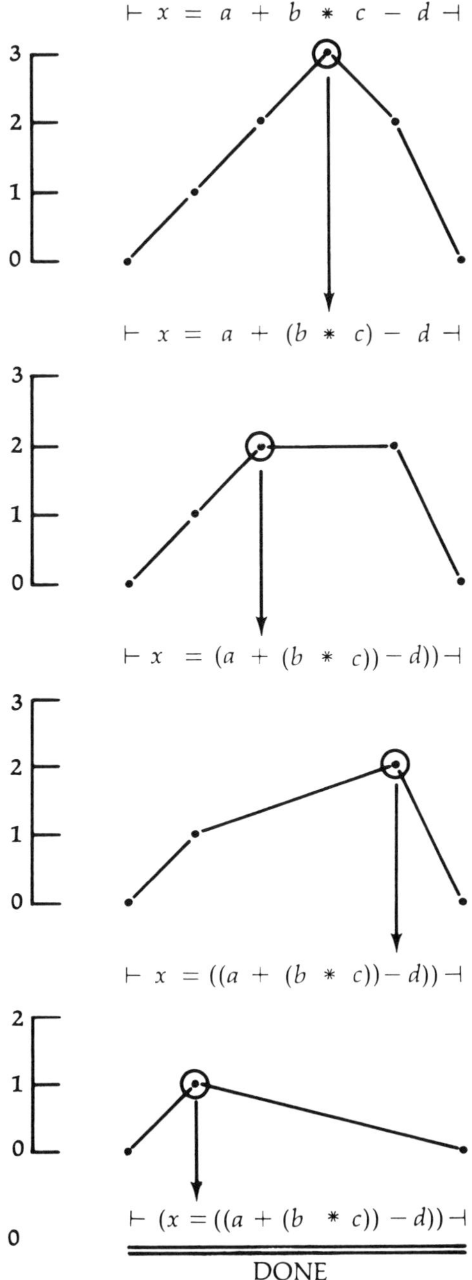

FIGURE 6.7 Parenthesizing—I.

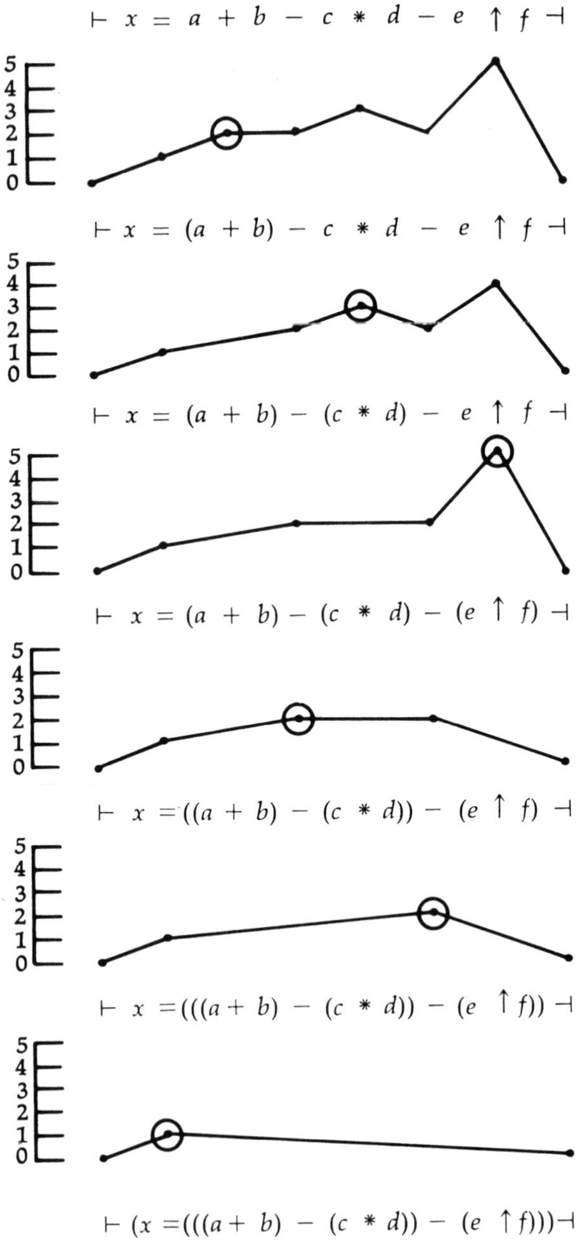

FIGURE 6.8 Parenthesizing—II.

For example, consider the delimited string:

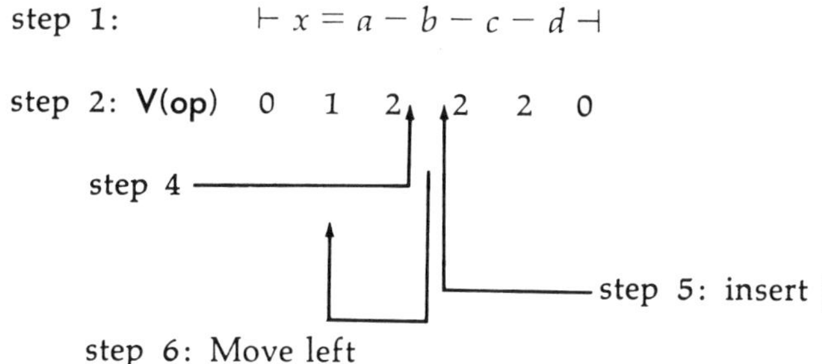

step 6: Move left
step 7: Insert (
step 8: Remove V (op_3)
step 9: op_4 is not the end delimiter.

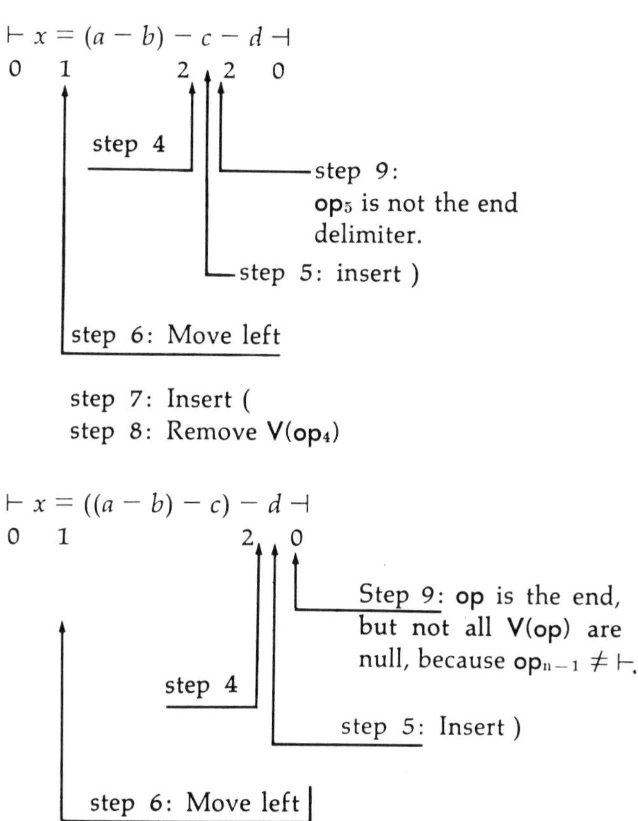

step 7: Insert (
step 8: Remove V(op_5)

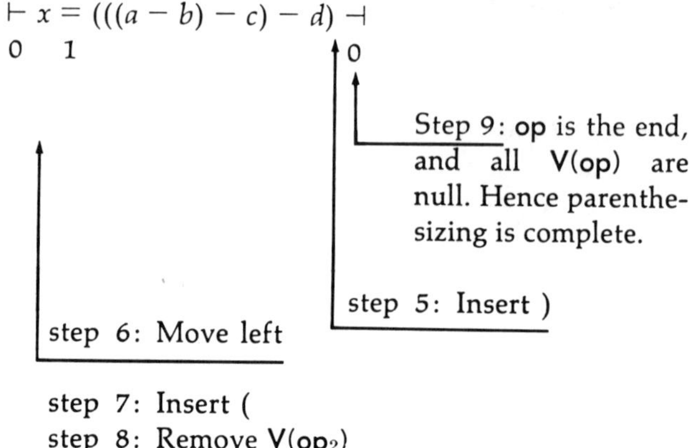
⊢ x = (((a − b) − c) − d) ⊣
0 1 0
Step 9: op is the end, and all V(op) are null. Hence parenthesizing is complete.
step 5: Insert)
step 6: Move left
step 7: Insert (
step 8: Remove V(op₂)

The resulting string is:

$$\vdash (x = (((a - b) - c) - d)) \dashv$$

In the following example, the individual steps are not shown, but an arrow indicates the operator chosen in step 4.

$$\vdash x = a * b \;/\; c * d \dashv$$

$$\vdash x = a * b \;/\; c * d \dashv$$

0 1 3 3 3 0
↑ (under the first 3)

$$\vdash x = (a * b) \;/\; c * d \dashv$$

0 1 3 3 0
↑ (under the first 3)

$$\vdash x = ((a * b) \;/\; c) * d \dashv$$

0 1 3 0
↑ (under the 3)

$$\vdash x = (((a * b) \;/\; c) * d) \dashv$$

0 1 0
↑ (under the 1)

$$\vdash (x = (((a * b) \;/\; c) * d) \dashv$$

0 0
↑ Complete

If a statement is already partially parenthesized, the above procedure must be modified slightly. In particular, if a left parenthesis is encountered during a left to right scan, the string following that operator up to the closing right parenthesis may be regarded as an entirely separate statement. Once that inner statement has been parenthesized, the outer statement may be parenthesized.

Returning to the graphical concept of determining the parenthesizing order, it can be seen that the parentheses can be regarded as end delimiters, the mapping of hierarchical values being to another graph, as shown in Figure 6.9. This second graph must be used primarily for the purpose of parenthesizing, the original parentheses in the expression being *ignored!*

For example, after the inner groups of the string:

$$\vdash x = (a + b + c) \ / \ (c + d * e) \dashv$$
$$0 \quad 1 \quad 2 \quad 2 \quad 3 \quad 2 \quad 3 \quad 0$$

have been parenthesized, the statement is of the form

$$\vdash x = (((a + b) + c)) \ / \ ((c + (d * e))) \dashv$$
$$0 \quad 1 \qquad\qquad 3 \qquad\qquad 0$$

After the next two steps, the parenthesizing of the multiplication and replacement operators, respectively, the statement takes the form

$$\vdash (x = ((((a + b) + c)) \ / \ ((c + (d * e))))) \dashv$$

This technique adds an overabundance of parentheses since each group within a parenthesis pair is reparenthesized. The technique may be improved by using the opening and closing parentheses to alter the hierarchical order of the enclosed operators. In particular, if the hierarchical values associated with the enclosed operators were so

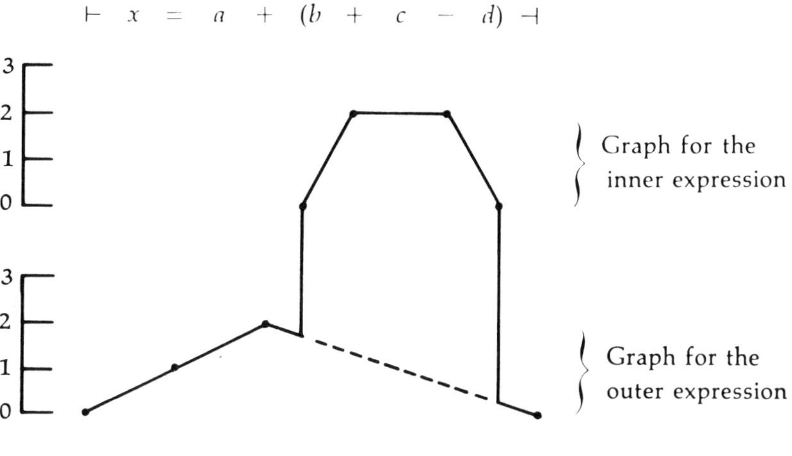

FIGURE 6.9

changed as to ensure their inclusion in the parenthesizing operations before those of the outer expression, then the purpose of the originally provided parentheses would be accomplished. This is simply achieved by increasing the hierarchical values of all enclosed operators above the maximum value possible outside the parentheses. For example, one may add 10 to all V(op)s when a left parenthesis is encountered in a left to right scan, and subtract 10 when a right parenthesis is found. At the same time, parentheses are dropped (or omitted) from the string. When, in the above example, hierarchy values are added as affected by parentheses and the parentheses are dropped, the expression becomes

$$\begin{array}{ccccccccccccccccc} \vdash & x & = & a & + & b & + & c & / & c & + & d & * & e & \dashv \\ 0 & & 1 & & 12 & & 12 & & 3 & & 12 & & 13 & & 0 \end{array}$$

This scheme eliminates the necessity to make an exception to the algorithm for the recognition of parentheses and also provides two other features:

1. Unpaired parentheses exist in the statement when the value of the level of the end delimiter is not zero.

2. Extra unneeded parentheses are eliminated. For example, if in the statement:

$$x = (a) + b \ / \ (c)$$

the level values are added and the parentheses dropped,

$$\begin{array}{ccccccccc} \vdash & x & = & a & + & b & / & c & \dashv \\ 0 & & 1 & & 2 & & 3 & & 0 \end{array}$$

parenthesizing gives:

$$\vdash (x = (a + (b \ / \ c))) \dashv$$

Problem

6.3 Given the following operator hierarchy table (from lowest level to highest),

$\vee$ (or)
& (and)
$< \; > \; \leqslant \; \geqslant \; = \; \neq$
~ (not)
$+ \; -$ (both dyadic)
$* \; /$
$+ \; -$ (both unary)
$\uparrow$
functions

parenthesize the following expressions:

(a) $y > 3 \vee b$
(b) $x \uparrow 2 - |x * y| > y \,/\, x$
(c) $a \wedge b \vee c \wedge d \neq {}^{\sim}(a \vee b)$
(d) $\sin(x) \uparrow 2 + \cos(x) \uparrow 2 = 1$
(e) $\sinh(x) = (\exp(x) - \exp(-x)) \,/\, 2$

THE FORTRANSIT PARENTHESIZING METHOD

A parenthesizing process of historical interest is that utilized in the FORTRANSIT system of the IBM 650. In this process, the hierarchical table is used as a basis for the insertion of parentheses around each operator. If an operator and its operands are to be enclosed properly in parentheses, the highest level operator must be imbedded most deeply in a nested set of parentheses and the lowest operator enclosed by the fewest parentheses. Thus the FORTRANSIT parenthesizing routine places opposite-facing parentheses about each operator, the number of parentheses being in the inverse ratio to the hierarchical level. Consider the set of expressions that may be formulated from the restricted set of operators with the following hierarchical levels:

(binary)	$+ \ -$	level 1,	inverse level 3,
	$* \ /$	2,	2,
	$\uparrow$	3,	1.

Consider the particular expression

$$a * b + c$$

If a set of parentheses is placed around each operator so that the number of parentheses is equal to the number of the inverse level, the expression becomes

$$a))*((b)))+(((c$$

Obviously, this expression is invalid since the number of parentheses that closes a group exceed the number that opens a group at at least one point in the string. To overcome this, the opening and closing delimiters must be added with (in this case) a hierarchical level of 0 and an inverse level value of 4. Further, since delimiters are one sided, parentheses need only be added between the delimiter and the expression. The above expression then becomes

$$((((a))*((b)))+(((c))))$$

At this point, an overabundance of parentheses has been created, making it difficult to determine whether or not the parenthesizing is complete or sufficient. If the matching parentheses surrounding each operand are removed, the expression is reduced to

$$((a * b) + c)$$

When operators of the same hierarchical level occur in sequence, this simplified system breaks down. For example,

$$a - b - c$$

is parenthesized to

$$((((a)))-(((b)))-(((c))))$$

and reduces to

$$(a - b - c)$$

which is not satisfactory. Thus when the operator being surrounded is of the same level as that parenthesized immediately beforehand, the inverse levels in the whole table must be increased by 1, and an extra parenthesis added to the opening delimiter. Thus the above expression is parenthesized to the string

$$(((((a)))-(((b))))-((((c)))))$$

which reduces to

$$((a - b) - c)$$

Consider the expression

$$a + b + c \uparrow d - e$$

which parenthesizes to

$$(((((a))) + (((b)))) + ((((c)) \uparrow ((d)))) - ((((e)))))$$

Canceling the matching parentheses around each variable reduces the expression to

$$((a + b) + ((c \uparrow d)) - e)$$

This reduced expression (which still has two extra parentheses surrounding the involution operator) still has two operators at the same level, namely an add and a subtract. This is because the intervening involution operator masked the fact that, in the order of execution, the add and subtract would be in sequence. To overcome this object, the rule regarding the increase in the hierarchical level (inverse) should be amended to read that the inverse hierarchical level should be increased after each subsequent usage of the same operator level. That is, the inverse hierarchical level should be increased at the second and all subsequent occurrences of an operator from a single hierarchical level. With this rule the above expression would parenthesize to the following string:

$$((((((a))) + (((b)))) + ((((c)) \uparrow ((d))))) - (((((e))))))$$

which would reduce to

$$(((a + b) + ((c \uparrow d))) - e)$$

and further to

$$(((a + b) + (c \uparrow d)) - e)$$

This particular technique is an interesting approach to the problem of parenthesizing, but as will be shown later is a redundant operation in the arithmetic generator. However, in those specialized systems (such as FORMAC) where parenthesizing is one of the primitive operations, it may be worthwhile.

Problems

6.4 Extend the above algorithm to include the occurrence of parentheses in the original expression.

6.5 Write a program to read in a partially parenthesized expression, to parenthesize the expression, and to output the result. The program may include the replacement sign, unary operators and the operators +, −, *, / and ↑; each variable consists of a single letter, and no constants are included. If the FORTRANSIT method is used, discard any redundant parenthesis pairs.

DIRECT CONVERSION

After a statement is parenthesized, the next stage of translation is that described previously for converting a fully parenthesized expression to Reverse Polish notation. Let us now consider the techniques of combining these two processes. The process of converting from a parenthesized group to Reverse Polish notation may be described by the production

(<*operand*><*operator*><*operand*>) →
{<*operand*><*operand*><*operator*>}.

Thus if one knows where the parentheses are to be added in a string, that group may be immediately converted to Reverse Polish notation. However, the FORTRANSIT parenthesizing routine is not satisfactory for this purpose, since the parentheses are added before the groups are defined.

Using the parenthesizing routine discussed on page 268, we may proceed to step 4, locating the highest level operator before altering the algorithm. It may be shown that in the first pass of the scan, the chosen operator is adjacent to its operands which are simple variables. Thus, these three items may be converted to Reverse Polish notation immediately. In fact, the operator and right-hand operand merely change places, and the three items form a new operand. If, for the purposes of demonstration, the operator and operands currently being converted to Reverse Polish notation are enclosed by { and }, then, unless one or other of the operands is already enclosed, the process of conversion may be described as follows:

1. Choose the operator and operands to be converted (by the same rules used for the parenthesizing algorithm) and surround each operand and the operator by { and }, if not already enclosed.

2. Within the string, exchange the positions of the operator and its right-hand operand, carrying the enclosing braces with each item.

3. Scan the string and remove any adjacent braces. After this operation, only two braces will remain in the string. These braces will surround the converted string which is considered henceforward as an operand.

4. Repeat the above steps until the string is totally enclosed in braces, at which point the string has been converted.

Consider the string

$$\begin{array}{ccccccccc} \vdash & x & = & a & + & b & / & c & \dashv \\ 0 & & 1 & & 2 & & 3 & & 0 \\ & & & & & & \uparrow & & \end{array}$$

where the arrow denotes the first chosen operator by the rules of the parenthesizing algorithm. Enclosing the operator and its operands in braces and exchanging the positions of the operator and right-hand operand, we obtain:

$$\begin{array}{ccccccccc} \vdash & x & = & a & + & \{b\} & \{c\} & \{/\} & \dashv \\ 0 & & 1 & & 2 & & & & 0 \end{array}$$

Cancel the adjacent braces

$$\begin{array}{ccccccc} \vdash & x & = & a & + & \{bc/\} & \dashv \\ 0 & & 1 & & 2 & & 0 \end{array}$$

The next operator to be included in the grouping is the addition sign which has a left-hand operand of a and a right hand operand $bc/$. When braces are added to the string, the right-hand operand is not affected since it is already enclosed. At this stage the string is of the form

$$\begin{array}{ccccccc} \vdash & x & = & \{a\} & \{+\} & \{bc/\} & \dashv \\ 0 & & 1 & & & & 0 \end{array}$$

Exchanging the positions of the right-hand operand and the operator gives:

$$\begin{array}{l} \vdash x = \{a\}\ \{bc/\}\ \{+\} \dashv \\ 0 \quad 1 \qquad\qquad\qquad\quad 0 \end{array}$$

Removing the adjacent braces:

$$\begin{array}{l} \vdash x = \{abc/+\} \dashv \\ 0 \quad 1 \qquad\qquad\quad 0 \end{array}$$

The last three steps are

$$\begin{array}{l} \vdash \{x\}\ \{=\}\ \{abc/+\} \dashv \\ 0 \qquad\qquad\qquad\qquad\quad 0 \end{array}$$

$$\begin{array}{l} \vdash \{x\}\ \{abc/+\}\ \{=\} \dashv \\ 0 \qquad\qquad\qquad\qquad\quad 0 \end{array}$$

$$\begin{array}{l} \vdash \{xabc/+=\} \dashv \\ 0 \qquad\qquad\qquad 0 \end{array}$$

An input string containing embedded parentheses may be handled in the same manner provided the hierarchical levels are adjusted within the parenthetical groups and the parentheses dropped before the conversion is attempted. For example, consider the input string

$$x = (a + b)\ /\ (c \uparrow d)$$

Using a bias of 10 within the parenthetical groups, and dropping the parentheses, we obtain the input string:

$$\begin{array}{l} \vdash x = a + b\ /\ c \uparrow d \dashv \\ 0 \quad 1 \quad 12 \quad 3 \quad 14 \quad 0 \end{array}$$

↑ chosen operator

The steps in the conversion process are

$$\begin{array}{l} \vdash x = a + b\ /\ \{cd\uparrow\} \dashv \\ 0 \quad 1 \quad 12 \quad 3 \qquad\quad 0 \end{array}$$

$$\begin{array}{l} \vdash x = \{ab+\}\ /\ \{cd\uparrow\} \dashv \\ 0 \quad 1 \qquad\qquad 3 \qquad\quad 0 \end{array}$$

$$\begin{array}{l} \vdash x = \{ab+cd\uparrow/\} \dashv \\ 0 \quad 1 \qquad\qquad\qquad 0 \end{array}$$

$$\begin{array}{l} \vdash \{xab+cd\uparrow/=\} \dashv \\ 0 \qquad\qquad\qquad\quad 0 \end{array}$$

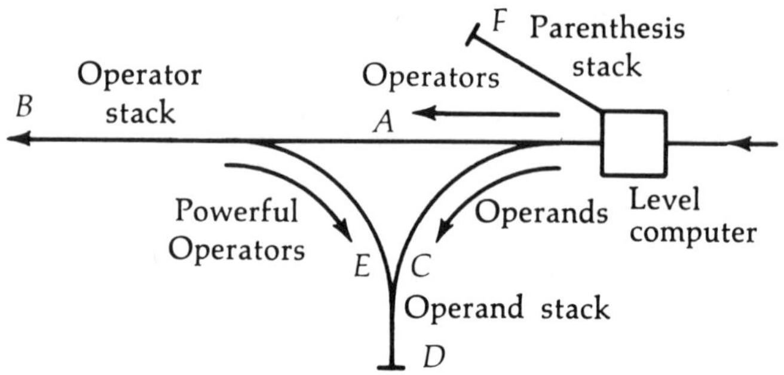

FIGURE 6.10 A railroad model of the process of expansion and conversion.

The process of conversion from an algebraic to a postfix form of expression can be further visualized by the use of a model railroad. This model is composed of a set of interconnected **Y** switches in the form of a triangle (Figure 6.10). Consider that an algebraic expression is represented by a train of cars preceded by a locomotive (representing the left hand end symbol ⊢) and succeeded by a caboose which represents the right hand end of the expression. The cars represent the individual elements of the expression (operands, operators and parentheses). The purpose of the shunting operation which occurs at the triangle is to accept a train at entry (top right hand corner of the switch triangle) which represents the normal algebraic form and to leave at the left with a train representing the Polish form of the expression. The level computer at the top right hand corner performs several tasks; distinguishes between operators and operands and selects the correct switch setting, computes the level value (**V(op)**) associated with operators and compares the "strength" of the operator on the right with that which is stacked on the left.

The process of conversion can be described as follows:

1. The locomotive (left-hand marker ⊢) moves along track *A* to stack point *B*;

2. The next element is examined;

3. If the element is an operand, the switch is set to move the operand to stack *D* through track *C*;

4. If the element is a parenthesis, the internal bias is incremented (or decremented as necessary) and the element is removed from the system by being shunted into siding F, from which it is never retrieved;

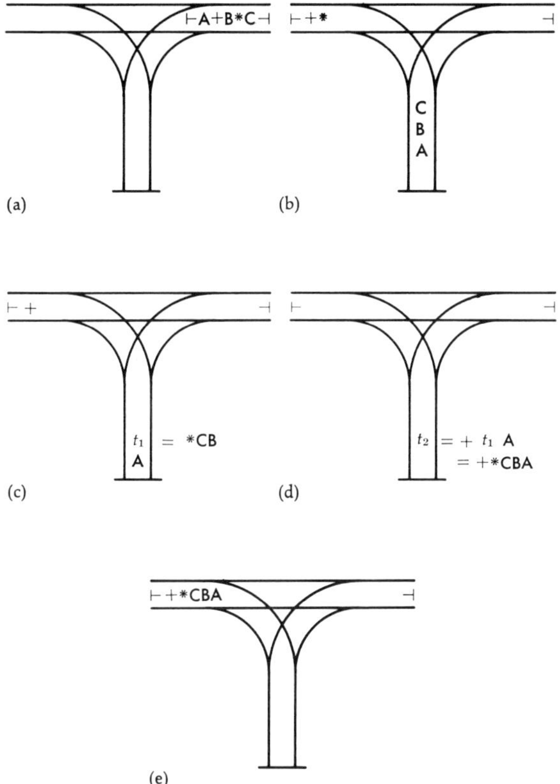

FIGURE 6.11 Analysis and conversion of **A + B * C**.
(a) The initial state.
(b) A later state. This state has been reached in a sequential manner since operands and operators have been divided between the two spurs. In this state the operator exposed on the left-hand spur (*) is powerful enough (in comparison with the one on the right) to force its way down onto the operand stack and to combine with the operands as shown in (c).
(c) The next state, after combining the operator "*" with its operands. The removal of the operator "*" from the operator stack reveals the operator "+" which is also more powerful than the operator remaining on the right-hand side (input area). Thus in the next step this "+" will move onto the operand stack and combine with operands.
(d) The penultimate state, following the combination of the operator "+" with its operands. In this state, the operator is of equal hierarchical power with that of the operator on the right; hence it can move onto the operand stack. This particular operator merely "couples" with the top element on the operand stack and "steams away," as shown in (e).
(e) The final state. The left-hand end operator pulls away with the string.

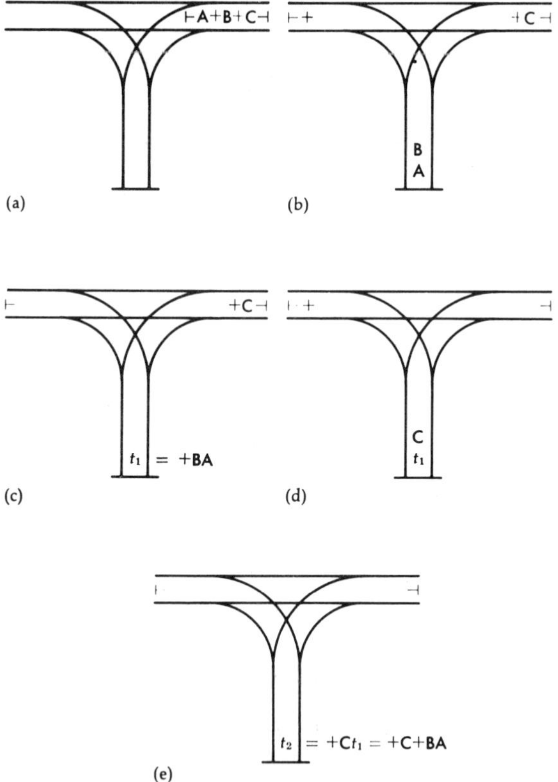

FIGURE 6.12 The analysis of conversion of A + B + C.
(a) The initial state.
(b) Sometime later. The left- and right-hand operators are of equal hierarchical value. In this state the operator on the left can force its way down onto the operand stack and combine with the proper number of operands.
(c) The next state. At this point the operator exposed on the right is more powerful than the one on the left; in the next step the right operator will move to the left across the upper track.
(d) The state following the transposition of the right-hand operator. The operator on the right is now in a position to move onto the operand stack.
(e) The penultimate state.

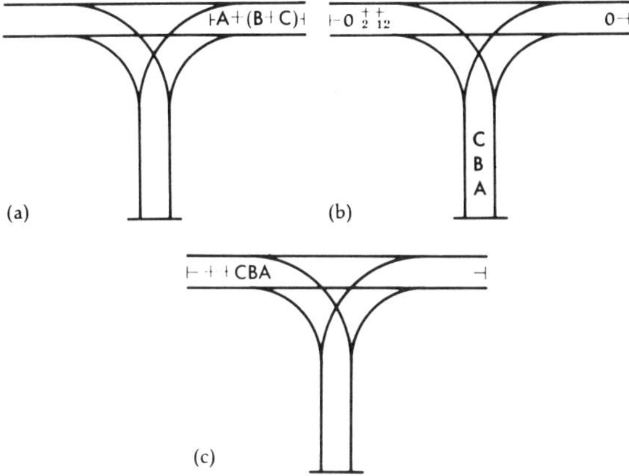

FIGURE 6.13 Analysis and conversion of A + (B + C). The actual operator level values are indicated in the operator stacks.

(a) The initial state.

(b) Much later. In this state the parentheses themselves have been discarded, but their effects are still present. The hierarchical level value of the exposed "+" operator in the left-hand stack has been elevated by the presence of a left parenthesis. The level associated with the right-hand end operator is 0, showing that there were matching parentheses in the expression.

(c) The final state.

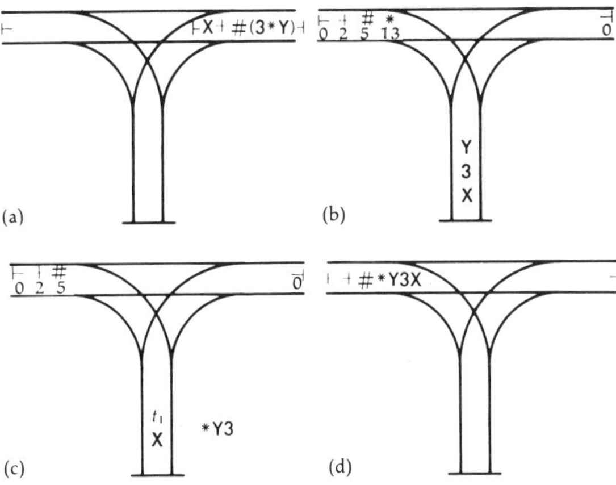

FIGURE 6.14 Analysis and conversion of X + SIN(3*Y). (Here the function "SIN" is represented by the single character "#.")

(a) The initial state.

(b) The parentheses have been discarded, but their effects are evident, as in the previous example.

(c) The next state. To this point, the function "#" has been treated as another operator; the only potential difference which will be recorded is the number of operands it needs. (In this case the number is 1.)

(d) The final state.

5. If the element is an operator, the next step is to compute its level value (with due reference to the current value of the bias). This computed level value is then compared with the level value of the operator which is on the right hand end of the operator stack at point B. If the operator on the right is of higher value it is considered to be stronger than that on the left and so it forces its way over to the operator stack at point *B*. Otherwise (that is, the operator on the right is either weaker or of equal strength with the operator at *B*), the rightmost operator at *B* forces its way down track *E* to stack *D*, and there combines with the appropriate number of operands to form a new operand which remains as the top element of stack *D*. (This may be regarded physically as the coupling of these elements.) This process (of the left-hand operator forcing its way onto the operand stack) continues so long as the operator on the right is not able to force its way to the left. Eventually, there must come a time when either the right hand operator moves to the left and the sieving starting at step 2 is repeated, or the operator which forces its way onto the operand stack is the locomotive. In the latter case, the locomotive couples onto the top element in the stack and drives off through track *E*, and point *B*, the train now being correctly assembled. One small point though: the caboose (right-hand end) remains at the point of entry. This anomaly can be removed by arranging for a spare caboose to be originally stored at point *D*.

LANGUAGE-DEPENDENT OPTIMIZATION

In our discussion of the composition of a compiler in Chapter 1, we alluded to two levels of optimization which can be undertaken. The most common form of optimization is that directly related to the generated code wherein certain code sequences (such as store; load) may be eliminated or replaced by more efficient code sequences. Such optimization, which operates over the generated code and which, in general, is applicable to any form of code, be it generated by a compiler or by hand, is machine dependent optimization. Included in this type of optimization is the allocation of index registers, a topic we shall consider later. At this point we shall restrict our attention to language-dependent optimization which is possible over the original language text. Irrespective of the generated code, this type of optimization seeks to recognize those aspects of the written program which may be consolidated in order that there be generated less target code. The classical example of language-dependent optimization is the recognition of common subexpressions in statements so that the result of one evaluation of a subexpression can be saved and reused rather than recomputing the value.

Another aspect of this optimization is the reduction of an expression to its "minimal form." The work of the mid-1960s in connection with symbol manipulation under the auspices of SIGSAM[2] failed to lead to any concensus on minimal expressions, the minimum being highly dependent on the environment of the expression. There exist certain sequences of code which in the environment of bounded word lengths (and hence precision) give differing results although they are mathematically equivalent.

Other optimization that can be undertaken within a statement includes the compile time evaluation of expressions whose operands are known and the replacement of complex time consuming operations by simpler, faster, mathematically equivalent operations.

On a larger scale, programs themselves can be optimized by examination of the logical flow of the program. Some work is being conducted in this area but little real progress has been made which is practically implementable. On the other hand, the identification of redundant operations within loops is feasible and can be used to advantage. In this form of optimization we seek to examine closed loops and discover those operations which are executed on each pass through the loop and which yield the same result. These operations may then be moved into an initialization block for the loop and be executed once rather than on each pass through the loop.

The amount of code included within a compiler to accomplish optimization is highly dependent on the environment of the compiler and the whims of the implementer. In the environment of an educational institution where the load-and-go compiler is supreme (witness the popularity of WATFOR and even WATFIV), the saving of two milliseconds at run time is of minor consequence, provided the compiler can churn through source texts at a high rate; that is, the compiler, but not necessarily the generated code should be highly optimized. Similarly in a time-sharing environment where the majority of programs are small, one-time runs, the efficiency of the target code is of secondary importance, particularly if the time needed in the compiler (and hence the space used by the optimization routines) is disproportionate to the saving at run time. On the other hand, where a production program is to be the mainstay of a system and two

2. Special Interest Group for Symbolic and Algebraic Manipulation, ACM, New York.

extra seconds at compile time to optimize the generated code can save considerable time over the long run of program executions, optimization is important.

Like optimization or minimization in many other endeavors, there exist simple, straightforward processes, easy to implement, inexpensive to use and effective in their intended task which will achieve (say) 50 per cent of the recognizable optimization possible. The other 50 per cent saving will require enormous expenditures of energy (by the implementer), of code to implement, and machine time to execute. Only in the case of large production programs is the latter worth considering.

The ultimate optimal program is an ideal which is hard to realize simply because we have no yardsticks by which to measure optimization. The "minimal" program in physical terms is not necessarily the "minimal" program in logical execution terms. The code which is minimal (uses a minimum of space for itself) may use a gross amount of storage for the data over which it operates. One can become very pessimistic about the ability of compilers to achieve a satisfactory level of optimization in the generated code. Cocke[3] saw some possibilities that he expressed in this statement:

> It is clear . . . that there will never be techniques for generating a completely optimum program. These . . . results, however, do not preclude the possibility of ad hoc techniques for program improvement or even a partial theory which produces a class of . . . programs optimized in varying degrees.

In the remainder of this chapter we shall consider in detail some of the techniques of language dependent optimization that have the scope of single statements in a program. The optimization over the structure of a program will be considered in somewhat less detail being considered to be in the class of the "last 50 percent" improvement achievable.

LOCAL OPTIMIZATION

Although the intent of any optimization is to reduce the execution time and storage of the generated target-language program, and hence is at least conducted with an eye towards the machine of execution,

3. J. Cocke, "Global Common Subexpression Elimination," in *Proc. of Symp. on Compiler Optimization*, SIGPLAN Notices, vol. 5., no. 7, (New York: ACM, July 1970).

language dependent (or machine *in*dependent) optimization anticipates a general Von Neumann target machine to justify the optimization. That is, if the number of operators in the source language text can be reduced, then it is a fair assumption that the number of instructions in any generated target language will be similarly reduced. From the point of view of storage, if the number of isolated peaks in the graph of the hierarchical values of the operators in an expression can be reduced, then the amount of intermediate temporary storage locations can be similarly reduced as well as the number of store instructions.

At another level, if we know that, independent of the machine on which the target code is to be run, the execution of any operator of higher level hierarchy takes significantly longer than an operator of lower level, then the transformation of operators to lower levels in certain contexts may be advantageous. Similarly expressions (or subexpressions) that can be evaluated at compile time will reduce the amount of execution time required in the long run.

As mentioned previously, the zealousness with which expressions are modified by the compiler must be tempered with some degree of respect for the intentions of the programmer. Modifications of the ordering of operator application to the evaluation of expressions can have serious effects on the resulting precision of the results.

DEFAULT CONDITIONS

Before considering the manipulation of any expression, the real meaning of that expression must be ascertained, particularly with respect to any language defaulting conditions. In particular, let us examine the modification of expressions by the inclusion of mode conversion operations. In a system where the attributes of language elements are statically defined, it is possible for the compiler to determine the mode of an expression or some subexpression, and to insert into the text the mode conversion functions necessary to explicitly define the expression. For example, consider the scalar FORTRAN assignment statement:

$$X = A + B$$

Under the normal defaulting conditions, all the identifiers in this statement are assumed to be associated with **REAL** values. On this basis we may conclude that the addition operation indicated by the symbol + is to be performed in the **REAL** mode, that the result of the evaluation of the right hand side is in the **REAL** mode, and that there is no mode conversion necessary in the assignment of the value of the right hand side to the location associated with the identifier X. On this basis, we may conclude that the statement is equivalent to

X = A r+ B

where r+ indicates real-mode (floating-point) addition. Similarly for the other operators in expressions, mode decisions can be made.

If in connection with the program in which the above assignment statement appeared, the identifier X was explicitly declared to be of a mode not equal to that of the value of the right hand side, then it would be necessary to perform mode conversion prior to the storage of the value. If we assume that the assignment symbol = is to be associated with the target language operation of store (STO) where no mode conversion is implied, then the right hand side must be modified to include a mode conversion function. For example, if X has been declared to be INTEGER, then the statement can be expanded to

X = INT(A r+ B)

where INT is the function of conversion from REAL to INTEGER mode.

The determination of the mode of an operator is dependent on the mode associated with its operands. Given a table of modal hierarchy, the mode of an operator is simply that of the operand with the highest level hierarchical value. Thus in mixed mode expressions, conversions may be necessary to raise the mode level of an operand to that of the operator. For example, in the case of FORTRAN, there exist several mode levels:

LOGICAL	1
INTEGER	2
REAL	3
COMPLEX	4

where the mode levels are indicated in the associated numeric value in this list. Thus given a set of operands over which an operator is to apply, the mode of the operator and all mode conversions can be determined. Associated with the hierarchical levels, there must also exist a series of mode conversion functions, some of which may be a part of the language available to the programmer (such as INT and FLOAT) whilst others are transparent to the programmer. For the purposes of example, the diagram (p. 289) indicates the conversions and the associated function names.

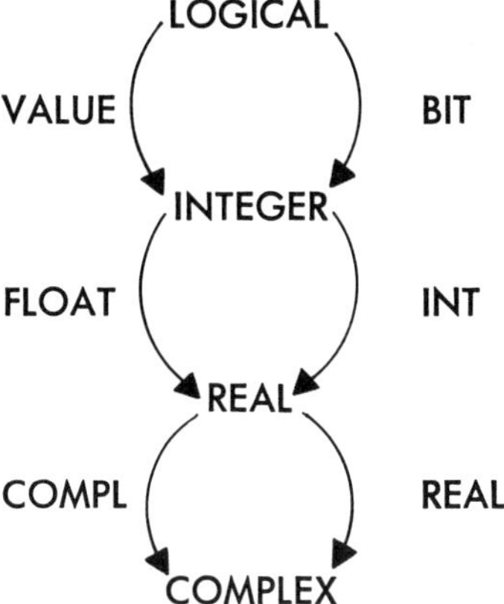

Thus in the case of the statement above (X = A + B) in the environment

LOGICAL X
INTEGER A
REAL B

the expression can be qualified completely by expansion to the form

X = BIT(INT(FLOAT(A) r+ B))

In the cases where such qualifications are inserted into an expression the possibilities for local optimization are reduced somewhat unless compile time evaluations can eliminate the conversion functions. For example, the simple expression

2 + 3.

must initially be qualified to the form

REAL(2) r+ 3.

This expression would seem to hold no possibilities for optimization but compile time evaluation of REAL(2) will permit the reduction of the expression to 2. + 3. and the eventual reduction to 5.

EXPRESSION SIMPLIFICATION

As pointed out earlier, the concept of expression minimization is an issue which is still being debated, the minimum for one purpose not necessarily equaling the minimum for some other use. In this part we shall only consider the question of operator reduction thereby aiming for at least partial optimization.

Let us first consider the manipulation of expressions such that there will be a reduction in the number of storage instructions and storage locations required. Both a store instruction and a storage location are required when the expression being evaluated contains two subexpressions, separated by at least one operator of low level, both of which must be evaluated (or compiled) and their values stored before the intervening operator can be applied. That is, an expression of the form

$$op_1\ \theta_1\ op_2\ \theta_2\ op_3\ \theta_3\ op_4$$

where θ_i are dyadic operators such that

$$L(\theta_1) \geqslant L(\theta_2)$$

and

$$L(\theta_3) > L(\theta_2)$$

where $L(\theta_i)$ is the hierarchical level of operator θ_i, and op_i are operands. In such a situation the subexpressions

$$op_1\ \theta_1\ op_2 \quad \text{and} \quad op_3\ \theta_3\ op_4$$

must be evaluated and their results stored before the operation θ_2 can be applied.

Such subexpression relationships can be typified by the graph shown in Figure 6.15.

Examination of this graph will reveal that in order to require that the intermediate results of evaluating (or compiling) each subexpression be stored, the following conditions must hold:

1. For all i, $h_i \geqslant 0$ where h_i is the height of the peak above the forcing operator; and

2. For all i, $k_i \geqslant 1$, where k_i is the difference in level between two adjacent operators in the subsequent state.

That is, after evaluation (or compilation) of the subexpressions, any hierarchical graph which contains a plateau of more than two operators (that is, there is some k_i equal to 0) or a valley (some negative k_i) will force compilation of all operators on the same level or uphill from the rightmost operator. In these cases no storage or temporary locations will be required, except possibly for the incorrect ordering of the operands. This latter case can be removed by the existence of reverse operations, as we shall see later.

Thus to return to the problem of expression manipulation to develop optimized (reduced) expressions with respect to storage instruc-

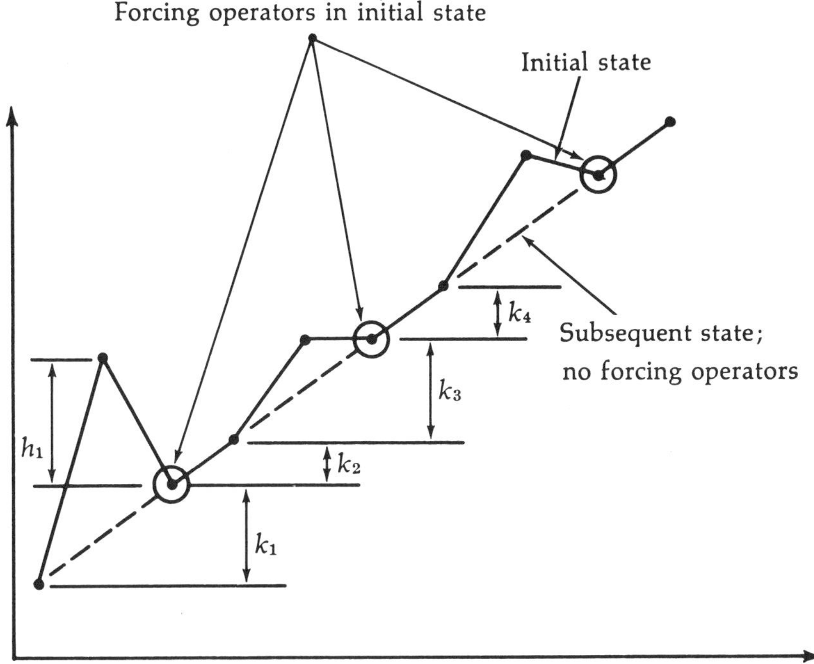

FIGURE 6.15 Hierarchical graph for an expression with isolated subexpressions.

tions and locations, it will be advantageous to remove isolated peaks in the hierarchical graphs.

Two of the most commonly occurring causes of isolated peaks in hierarchical graphs are unary operators and function references. In the normal hierarchical ordering both of these types of operators are to be evaluated (compiled) in preference to most other operators. Similarly the location of an element of an array, as defined in a subscripted variable reference, can be regarded as a function reference and therefore creates a peak. In the case of functions there is little control that the programmer or the implementer has over the results and hence little potential optimization that can be performed. On the other hand, the effects of unary operations are well defined and with the possibility of combining operations over some expression there is a possibility of operator reduction. The expression $\pi + (-\rho)$, for example, can be reduced to $\pi - \rho$ where π and ρ are any general operands, including subexpressions. Although manipulation of expressions is possible in their "raw" form, manipulation can be enhanced considerably by the use of the Reverse Polish form of the expression. In the latter form no parentheses are present and the operators which apply to a set of operands are often juxtaposed in the representation. In the case of juxtaposed operators, certain simplifying manipulations can be performed over the expression without ever considering the operands. For example, the two operator sequence ~ + can *always* be transformed to − irrespective of its placement in the postfix form of the expression. That is, the unary minus (~) can always be moved into additive expressions to form the subtractive expression. Moreover, the Postfix Polish form gives an indication of the order of performing the operations (left to right). Hence the movement of a unary minus (or any higher ordered operator) to the right has the effect of delaying its application as well as increasing the possibility of its combination with another operator to reduce the number of operations. The following table shows those operators in Reverse Polish notations which can always be replaced by other operator sequences irrespective of their location in the notational form and which either reduce the number of operators or move the unary minus to the right.

	Original expression	*Modified expression*
1.	$\pi + (-\rho)$	$\pi - \rho$
	$\pi\rho^{\sim} +$	$\pi\rho-$
2.	$\pi - (-\rho)$	$\pi + \rho$
	$\pi\rho^{\sim} -$	$\pi\rho+$
3.	$\pi * (-\rho)$	$-(\pi * \rho)$
	$\pi\rho^{\sim} *$	$\pi\rho*^{\sim}$
4.	$\pi / (-\rho)$	$-(\pi / \rho)$
	$\pi\rho^{\sim} /$	$\pi\rho/^{\sim}$
5.	$\pi * \rho \uparrow (-\sigma)$	$\pi / (\rho \uparrow \sigma)$
	$\pi\rho\sigma^{\sim} \uparrow *$	$\pi\rho\sigma\uparrow/$
6.	$\pi / (\rho \uparrow (-\sigma))$	$\pi * \rho \uparrow \sigma$
	$\pi\rho\sigma^{\sim} \uparrow /$	$\pi\rho\sigma\uparrow*$
7.	$-(-\rho)$	ρ
	$\rho^{\sim\sim}$	ρ

Using these transformations it is possible that the unary minus can be moved through a string until either it disappears by its combination with some other operator or until it reaches the right hand end of the operator sequence. In every case above (transformations 1 through 7) the number of operators is either reduced or the unary minus is moved right. This movement is consistent with our avowed intention to so modify the string so that its graph of hierarchical values is "downhill" (in a left to right sense) rather than "uphill" and that isolated peaks are eliminated.

Outside of simple operator sequences, there also exist transformations which encompass the operands. The identification of these operator/operand patterns is much more difficult to establish in either the usual notation or in Polish form. However, where a unary operator has been moved to its rightmost position in an operator sequence of a Polish representation of the expression, no further simplifications are possible without the involvement of the operands, and in particular, the recognition of the scope of the operands. For example, the string $\pi^{\sim}\rho-$ (in Reverse Polish notation) can be transformed into $\pi\rho+^{\sim}$ which patently satisfies our stated goals. However, the recognition of the operands π and ρ may not be quite so straightforward.

In the previous cases considered, the transformations were possible within any operator sequence, irrespective of the operands. However, in this case identification of the operands is necessary in order to determine that the operators are in the correct relationship with each other. That is, in the case above the unary minus *must* be to the immediate left of the operand associated with the subtraction symbol. In fact, the operand π is not an integral part of the algorithm of transformation in the above case, but where the transformation also includes the movement or transformation of the operands, the identification of π is necessary. The transformations possible over operands include the following cases:

	Original expression			*Modified expression*
8.	$-\pi-\rho$			$-(\pi+\rho)$
	$\pi^{\sim}\rho\,-$			$\pi\rho+^{\sim}$
9.	$-\pi+\rho$	or	$-(\pi-\rho)$	$\rho-\pi$
	$\pi^{\sim}\rho+$	or	$\pi\rho-^{\sim}$	$\rho\pi-$
10.	$-\pi*\rho$			$-(\pi*\rho)$
	$\pi^{\sim}\rho\,*$			$\pi\rho*^{\sim}$
11.	$-\pi\,/\,\rho$			$-(\pi\,/\,\rho)$
	$\pi^{\sim}\rho\,/$			$\pi\rho\,/^{\sim}$

The recognition of the scope of an operator can be determined only by having a knowledge of the number of operands required. If the symbol immediately to the left of an operator is an identifier, then that identifier is one of its operands. If the left symbol is not an identifier, but rather is an operator, then that operator spans the operand of the first operator and the process must be repeated until all operands have been identified. Conversely, given that a unary minus is the rightmost operator in an operator sequence which is not the rightmost sequence in the string, the "next" operator can be identified by a left-to-right count of identifiers commencing at the symbol to the right of the unary minus and continuing until an operator is located. This count can then be matched with the operator requirements for operands until the "next" operator is located. There are two situations to be taken into account within this algorithm: the leftmost operator in any operator sequence takes its normal number of operands whereas all others will require one less than their usual quota, and the matching of operands with a partial set of operators does not necessarily mean that the matching is complete since a further unary operator requires zero additional operands!

Problem

6.6 Write a program that will scan a Reverse Polish string representation of an expression and locate the "next" operator relative to the rightmost operator in each operator sequence. For example, the "next" operators are indicated in the following strings:

$$abc+d-*\sim/$$

$$a\sim bcd+ef/-$$

Consider the usual form expression

$$((-b)*(-a))$$

that is, $b^{\sim}a^{\sim}*$ in Reverse Polish notation. From production 3, page 292, the unary minus in the pair of operators farthest to the right may be interchanged with the multiplication operator; that is, the string becomes $b^{\sim}a*^{\sim}$. If braces are added for clarity to identify the operands, it may be seen that the first four characters in the string are similar to the starting formula in transformation 10.

$$\{b^{\sim}a*\}^{\sim}$$

and thus may be manipulated to the string

$$\{ba*^{\sim}\}^{\sim}$$

When the braces are removed, the expression is similar to the starting formula of production 7, where the two unary minus operations cancel. Thus the resultant string is $ba*$, or in normal form $b*a$.
Consider the expression

$$-d-a+b*(-c)$$

that is, in Reverse Polish,

$$d^{\sim}a-bc^{\sim}*+$$

In the following manipulation, the underscored operators have been either manipulated or generated in a transformation.
From transformation 3:

$$d{\sim}a{-}bc\underline{*{\sim}}+$$

From transformation 1:

$$d{\sim}a{-}bc*\underline{-}$$

Let us now bracket the groups for clarity:

$$\{d{\sim}a-\}\{bc*\}-$$

From transformation 8:

$$\{da\underline{+\}{\sim}}\{bc*\}-$$

Again transformation 8:

$$\{da+bc*\}\underline{+{\sim}}$$

At this point no more unary minus operators remain inside, and the string may be converted back to the usual form:

$$-(d + a + b * c)$$

This transformation contains one less operator and will require the intermediate storage of one less item if advantage of communtativity is not taken in the evaluation or compilation of the original expression.

At the next level of complexity in our quest for converting the graphical representation of the operator hierarchy of an expression into a "downhill" graph will be the use of commutativity to interchange operators. For example, $\pi\rho\sigma{*}{+}$ can be converted to the form $\rho\sigma{*}\pi{+}$ In general where π is a simple identifier or a constant, this transformation will not affect the efficiency of the expression evaluation, but where π is another expression there is a possibility that some storage can be saved. That is, storage can be saved by both the lack of need for intermediate storage and the absence of a store instruction. Thus there exist three transformations associated with the addition operator:

12.	$\pi + \rho * \sigma$	$\rho * \sigma + \pi$
	$\pi\rho\sigma * +$	$\rho\sigma * \pi +$
13.	$\pi + \rho \;/\; \sigma$	$\rho \;/\; \sigma + \pi$
	$\pi\rho\sigma/ +$	$\rho\sigma/\pi +$
14.	$\pi + \rho \uparrow \sigma$	$\rho \uparrow \sigma + \pi$
	$\pi\rho\sigma\uparrow +$	$\rho\sigma\uparrow\pi +$

Now obviously there does not exist a comparable set of transformations which are associated with the subtraction operation, since the latter operation is not commutative. However, the transformation of subtraction into addition and negation (unary minus) can help to solve this problem. However, it is important to note that this latter transformation introduces an additional operator which, if optimization is to be effective, must be cancelled out later. As in the case of addition, there exists a transformation which is based on the commutativity of the multiplication operator:

15. $\pi * \rho \uparrow \sigma$ $\qquad$ $\rho \uparrow \sigma * \pi$

$\pi\rho\sigma\uparrow *$ $\qquad$ $\rho\sigma\uparrow\pi *$

Similarly, the transformation of division into unary inversion and multiplication ($\pi\rho/$ transforms into $\pi\rho\div *$, where $\div$ signifies inversion) can lead to other transformation possibilities which can further lead to optimized evaluation.

This process of inserting unary operations in place of noncommutative operations is discussed by Rohl and Linn.[4] In their process of optimization they also include the reverse operators for subtraction and division in order to allow for the ordering of operands and a store negative instruction in the target language.

It is important to note that such transformations as discussed here and by Rohl and Linn can have adverse effects on the results of arithmetic operations causing a loss of precision not anticipated by the programmer. Many numerical analysts will carefully parenthesize expressions in the hope that this will force a special ordering of the evaluation of the expression. Any changes to this order might not be satisfactory to the programmer. Further a knowledge of implementation procedures and the target language can allow a clever (?) programmer to code procedures which otherwise would not be possible. Many of these require a strict adherence to the order of evaluation specified in the text expression. In some simple cases, even a standard (that is, machine-independent) procedure can be destroyed by optimization where "bit diddling" is involved.

One further advantage that can be attained by operand interchange is the possibility of removing constant expressions. That is, expressions (or subexpressions) in which the operands are constants and thus can be evaluated at compile time. Again if constants can be moved in one direction during the scanning process (that is, to the right in a left to right scan) there is a possibility that the subexpres-

4. J. S. Rohl, and J. A. Linn, "A note on compiling arithmetic expressions," *The Computer Journal*, vol. 15, no. 1 (Feb. 1972), p. 13.

sions can be evaluated. For example, the expression (in its normal form): **2. + X + 3.** should be converted into **X + 5.**. However, the expression **(I/2)*2 − I** should not be reduced to **0** in any FORTRAN compiler! Most beginning programmers are taught to utilize the facilities of the language as defined in the standards to perform their tasks, and thus the determination of evenness is exemplified by the FORTRAN statement

```
19 IF((I/2)*2.NE.I)GO TO 23
```

As in the case above, it would appear that **(I/2)*2** is always equal to **I** and thus the statement is equivalent to the null statement and need not be compiled except as needed for statement number identification. This problem can be overcome if the true (explicit) meaning of the integer division (*i/*) routine is included in the expression; that is, after division, the integer part of the result is passed on to the next operation. Thus **(I/2)*2** should be expanded to **INT(I** *i/* **2) * 2** and since we have included no transformations over functions, the simplification process would be halted.

A second class of optimization procedures can be introduced which, instead of manipulating the expression into some desirable form, replace certain operations by simpler (presumably faster) operations. For example, if we can recognize the string of the form

<integer constant> * *<variable>*

it might be possible to replace this by a sequence of the form

$<variable>\{+ <variable>\}_1^n$

where n is the value represented by the string conforming to the syntactic component *<integer constant>* minus one. Under certain circumstances this transformation may be advantageous whilst in others it could be decidedly nonoptimizing. For example, in most machines where the multiplication is performed by hardware, the time ratio between the execution of an addition and that of a multiplication is rarely greater than 3. That is, the time to multiply two numeric representations of any magnitude is no more than three times the time to add the same representations. Consequently we may conclude that for representations of two (2) it is faster to perform addition rather than multiplication and no additional storage space is required.

From the author's experience (but not explicitly reported by Knuth[5]) the most common form of the multiplication/constant/vari-

5. D. E. Knuth, "An Empirical Study of FORTRAN Programs," *Software—Practice and Experience*, Vol. 1, 1971, pp. 105–133. London, UK.

able triplet is that in which the constant is a representation of two (2). Thus a modification of such triplets into the corresponding additive triplet can potentially save some execution time.

Similarly, experiments with the time for the evaluation of integer involution show that under certain circumstances a modification of involution to repeated multiplication can save execution time. Some compilers already distinguish between the three potential forms of involution in FORTRAN:

1. *<real>* ** *<real>*
2. *<real>* ** *<integer>*
3. *<integer>* ** *<integer>*

by evaluating case 1 by use of the exponential and logarithm routines ($a^b = e^{b \ln a}$) and using repeated multiplication for the other two cases. Experiments conducted by the author on the generated code from FORTRAN compilers (provided by the manufacturers) for the Control Data 3600 and the IBM 1620 showed that the use of exponentiation and logarithmic routines was time equivalent to approximately 15 multiplication operations (with hardware multiplication in the IBM 1620) for the cases where the operand to be raised to the power was of the real mode. Obviously in the case of an integer operand the timing was much greater since the operand first had to be converted to real mode, the result had to be converted back to integer mode and in any case, integer multiplication is approximately twice as fast as floating point multiplication. This ratio was of the order of 60 and thus it was concluded that the form *<integer>* ** *<integer>* should always be converted into its repeated multiplication form or at least a routine should be provided to perform integer involution by repeated multiplication, the latter case requiring no textural modifications. In the other two cases where the power (second operand) is a constant and is either (in case 2) an integer or can be converted to an integer without loss of information (case 1 where the real constant contains no fractional part) and where the values represented are less than 15, the modification of the expression by replacing involution by repeated multiplication can have potential time-saving qualities. On the other hand, it is doubtful whether this procedure will conserve on space, unless there are no involution triplets anywhere in the program which will require the use of the exponential/logarithm routine. That is, if the involution is to be replaced by in-line repeated multiplications instead of a linkage to a routine, space will be conserved only if the routine is not present in the system. From this we might conclude that optimization of involution both from the point of view of speed of evaluation and storage is best accomplished by a run-time routine which tests the value of the power and determines which method to use for evaluation. This then is machine dependent optimization, outside of our scope at this point.

In his paper on the characteristics of FORTRAN programs, Knuth[6] reported instances where mode conversions which could have been performed at compile time (but were not) took considerable time within a loop. For example, in one of his test cases a loop contained the statement **X = 0** where the identifier **X** had not been included in any **TYPE** statement and therefore by implication was of real mode. In the unoptimized form, this statement required the conversion of the constant **0** into its real form, a task which took approximately 20% of the total time in the loop! If the programmer had written **X = 0.**, he could have saved this time, but in any case a compile-time modification of the constant **0** into its real mode form would have saved considerable time. Similarly in many statements the commonly used constant **2** is often not written in the correct mode and thus conversion is necessary at some stage of the compile/execution sequence. It might as well be the compile time. One compiler known to the author which does not permit mixed mode expressions in its FORTRAN assignments statements, issues an error message on recognizing constants of the wrong mode, irrespective of the feasibility of performing a compile time conversion. (For the sake of a decimal point, the program was lost!) In certain circumstances this lack of compiler ability may be both forgiveable and useful; that is, in an educational environment where hand coding excellence is to be preferred to the "let the machine do it" syndrome.

OPTIMIZATION BY LOOP EXPANSION

Looking forward to the chapter related to control statements and their compilation, we see that the amount of code required to implement a **DO** loop (in FORTRAN) or a **FOR** loop (in BASIC or one of the forms in ALGOL) is not inconsequential. Further much of the code which is generated from the loop descriptors (**DO-CONTINUE** or **FOR-NEXT**) must be executed on each pass through the loop thereby using some "overhead" time. As in the case of constant subexpressions which can be evaluated at compile time, so constant size loops can be expanded so as to eliminate the overhead. In many cases programmers will utilize loops to save on typing or key punching rather than to use the potential power of the commands. For example, the

6. *Ibid.*

zeroing out of an array is most easily written as a loop:

```
FOR I = 1 TO 25
A(I) = 0
NEXT I
```

Obviously this loop can be "unrolled" to the sequence of statements:

```
A(1) = 0
A(2) = 0
...
...
A(24) = 0
A(25) = 0
```

However it can be seen that the amount of code generated (that is, the static code) is far greater for the expanded case than for the original set of statements, though the dynamic code (that is, the sequence of instructions executed) is far less. At the instant of implementation, the systems programmer must make the decision as to which is more precious: space or time. This example also shows another example of potential optimization that can be achieved in the original text. If left to be compiled as individual statements, each of the statements of the form A(I) = 0 would compile to a sequence of the form[7]

```
ENA  A
INA  I
STA  * + 2
ENA  0
STO  *—*
```

Now given the presence of index registers in the target machine another implementation might be

```
ENR  A,i
INR  I,i
ENA  0
STO  0,i
```

This latter form of implementation has the advantage that the accumulator is not used for the indexing of the array element and thus it will be possible to eliminate the instruction to enter the value zero into the accumulator in the code for every sequence. Further if the array is referenced in its storage order then there is no need for the

7. See Appendix B for a description of the instructions.

initial entry of the address of the array base address into the register in each group and instead of incrementing the register by the value of I, the incrementation can be by unity:

```
ENA  0
ENR  Aj
INR  1,j
STO  0,j
INR  1,j
STO  0,j
...
...
```

This sequence is roughly equivalent to the source text statement:

A(25) = A(24) = A(23) = · · · =A(2) = A(1) = 0

which is a better form of the unrolling of the original loop. Again, Knuth noted that 39% of the DO loops (in FORTRAN) examined contained only a single statement and that 95% of the loops had an increment of unity. Combining these statistics with the observation that 68% of the assignments statements were of the simple form A = B where no arithmetic operations were involved, it is contended that the optimization of the above seemingly "special" case is worthwhile. A statistic not given by Knuth but which would seem to be correct is that within loops, the loop index is used primarily as the subscript of array variables.

RECOGNITION OF COMMON SUBEXPRESSIONS

The attainment of partial optimization by the recognition and elimination of common subexpressions within a statement or block of statements, has been one of the most researched (or at least written about) topics in this area. As in the simplification of algebraic expressions where the factoring of terms is one means of compression, so the recognition of subexpressions should lead to reduced code generation sets. Whilst this is a noble end to desire to attain, there also exist situations where common subexpression recognition is a highly useful aid in order that the meaning of the statement as compiled agree with the language definition.

The problem of side effects in programming languages has been one of the more serious bugs in the use of the product of language designers. Some of these side effects have been introduced into the languages as the result of implementations where the language specifications were insufficient and the implementer has chosen an easy (and many times efficient) means of accomplishing the compilation of the statements. This lack of "purity" and the accompanying side effects can result in two compiler-generated codes which when executed do not develop the same results *on the same computer*. In particular the impurity of FORTRAN functions is an example of this problem.

The American National Standard on FORTRAN permits the use of the arguments in a function reference as value returning elements and further permits the unrestricted use of elements in **COMMON** for the same purpose. Besides providing the language with a **SUBROUTINE** in which *all* parameter passing is accomplished through the argument list and **COMMON**, the standard provides an extension under the misnomer of **FUNCTION** which also adds the passage of a value through a system defined register (usually the accumulator). In fact it is only in the latter extension that a FORTRAN **FUNCTION** differs from a **SUBROUTINE**. This means that **FUNCTION** side effects can (if undetected) alter the meaning of statements. Further such alterations are usually beyond the understanding or expectations of the programmers who use the language and thus the compiler must protect the unwary (caveat emptor).

Let us consider the simple FORTRAN expression

$$\mathsf{F(A) + F(A)}$$

where **F** is a user-defined function and **A** is a simple real variable. Now it should be expected (and is required by the standard) that the value of this expression is the same as would be obtained if the statement containing the expression were to be preceded by the statement (say) **X = F(A)** and then the expression is modified to **X + X**. In the latter case there exists only one activation of the function evaluation routine instead of two activations, a situation which should not cause any difference in meaning to the expression. However, most compilers of FORTRAN programs will not give the same results for these two cases, due to their lack of recognition of the side effect problem. As a concrete example of the potential problem, let us define a FORTRAN **FUNCTION F** in which the value of the two cases will differ:

```
FUNCTION F(B)
...
F = ...
B = ...
...
END
```

In this example, provided that the assignment statement involving the parameter B does not simply assign the value of B to B, but instead makes some modification to the value of the parameter B, then the expression F(A) + F(A) does not equal X + X where X = F(A). Another case, which is not specifically addressed by the standard and yet which falls into our classification of common subexpressions is the extended assignment of the form

A(I) = I = K + 2

which had been preceded by the assignment (say) I = K. Again some FORTRAN compilers, during a left-to-right scan, will compute the location of the array element A(I) before evaluating the expression K + 2 or assigning any value to the variable I. Similarly, for the type of FUNCTION described above, the expression

A + F(A)

can have two meanings depending on the order of evaluation!

These considerations immediately lead to a conclusion not directly related to optimization but which is part of the process of common subexpression recognition: the assignment of values to their storage locations must take place, not as the values are available, but instead all together at the termination of the execution cycle for that statement. Thus a statement can be regarded as a program block with activation and deactivation processes, local storage and local variables. Given this style of organization we may see that temporary storage locations exist only within this local environment, and can be regarded as local variables when their contents are the result of the evaluation of a common subexpression. A statement such as G = F(A) + F(A) can thus be modified to

G = f + (f = F(A))

where f is a local variable or name of a temporary storage location. The local environment must be composed of three parts: referenced COMMON elements; referenced non-COMMON elements; and temporary or local variable storage.

Where the statement being compiled (and subsequently executed) does not contain any language element which is capable of inducing side effects (such as FORTRAN FUNCTIONs), then the local environment can be reduced to merely the temporary storage system, and all references within the body of the code generated from the original text can be direct references to the storage system of the encompassing block or subprogram.

The process for recognizing common subexpressions can take one of two basic forms: a pattern recognition process operating over the symbolic form of the statements or a pseudoevaluation scheme operating over the evaluation sequence of the statement. The former scheme has been paid some attention in the area of symbol manipulation processing, especially in relation to algebraic languages such as FORMAC. The process which we shall describe here is a combination of the two.

Examining statements in terms of their symbolic representations is comparatively simple, provided that the number of symbols to be compared is small. That is, given two simple subexpressions A + B and C + D, it is simple to recognize that they are not common, whereas the subexpression A + B is common to one of them. However, a strictly symbolic recognition process would fail if it attempted to match A + B and B + A unless some additional information on commutative operators were also provided. On the other hand, if we were to look at the result of the evaluation of A + B and B + A we would expect to get the same result and thus recognize the equivalence of the two subexpressions.

As in the majority of subexpression recognition systems, the one described here operates over a set of triplets which can be developed from an arithmetic expression. By extension, this same technique can operate over machine code where one of the operands in the triplets is the accumulator. For the time being we shall consider that an expression can be reduced to triplets where the three components are the operator and the two operands. In the case of unary operators, one of the operands will be considered to be null. In the case of functions, the same null operand will be introduced, the remaining operand being considered to be composed of a list of operands. In the production of triplets, certain operands will be dependent on the results of previous triplets evaluations; these we will indicate through parenthesized numbers which will correspond to the triplet which developed that result. This form of representation is merely a two dimensional form of the fully parenthesized or Polish notation, and thus is totally attainable with the knowledge presented earlier in this chapter. For example the expression (in normal form)

$$x = a + b \; / \; c$$

has the Polish form

$$xabc/+=$$

and the triplet form

1. $b\ c\ /$
2. $a\ (1) +$
3. $x\ (2) =$

Similarly the expression

$$x = (a + b)\ /\ (c \uparrow d)$$

has the equivalent Polish form

$$xab{+}cd \uparrow /{=}$$

and the triplet form

1. $a\ b +$
2. $c\ d \uparrow$
3. $(1)(2)/$
4. $x\ (3) =$

The process of recognition, other than the methods of total comparison of every triplet with every other triplet, requires some factor which will speed up recognition and enhance the identification processes. Gries[8] has suggested a dependency number system in which the dependency of each triplet is determined; where two triplets have the same dependency number, there exists a possibility that they are attached to common subexpressions. This method is straightforward but requires the computation of a number based on the comparison of other numbers. The method presented here is based on the direct computation of a dependency number and has the advantage that no comparisons are necessary and commutated operands in triplets are recognized; thus ab+ and ba+ are assigned the same dependency number. Unfortunately so are triplets in which the operands cannot be commutated. Given a set of triplets for a single expression, containing no assignment operator except as the operator in the last triplet, the process of recognition proceeds as follows:

1. Establish a symbol table for all the variables in the triplets and assign a unique prime number to each variable; the prime numbers should be assigned in sequence above 23. Also provide space for each triplet in the table but assign no prime numbers yet.

2. For all triplets in the set in which the values of the operands are known (initially for only those in which both operands are variables), mark the triplet as "ready."

3. Compute the dependency number of each triplet which is marked

8. D. Gries, *Compiler Construction for Digital Computers* (New York: John Wiley, 1971).

"ready"; the dependency number is the product of the prime numbers assigned to the operands and to the operator. The prime numbers assigned to the operators are

=	3
+	5
−	7
*	11
/	13
~	17
↑	19
F	23 (functions)

In the case of the unary negation operator, the value assigned to the null operand is 1. In the case of functions the individually assigned values of the arguments are contained in the product.

4. Scan the "ready" triplets. Where there exist two or more with the same dependency number, these two then are candidates for more detailed comparison. Except for functions where the actual functions are discriminated in the development of dependency numbers, the only differences that can occur in two triplets with the same dependency numbers will be the ordering of operands. Only in the cases of subtraction (−), division (/) and involution (↑) is this to be checked further.

5. For each set of common triplets, delete all except the first and replace all referencing operands by the number of the sole remaining triplet. Mark all "ready" triplets as "done" and assign new prime numbers to each of the entries in the symbol table corresponding to the triplets just marked.

6. If all the triplets are marked "done" skip to step 7. Otherwise, regard all triplets that have been assigned a prime number as variables and return to step 2.

7. Having eliminated common subexpressions it is now necessary to determine those subexpressions whose values have to be saved for reuse later. A scan through the set of triplets remaining will indicate that where the referenced triplet is not that immediately preceding, then the result of the referenced triplet must be saved, and thus "saving" triplets should be inserted immediately following the referenced triplets. (This process was delayed until the end of the algorithm so as to eliminate unnecessary store operations that would have been inserted if this process were to be followed in step 5, where the recognized subexpressions are portions of larger common subexpressions.)

This algorithm of common subexpression elimination is also shown as a flow chart in Figure 6.16.

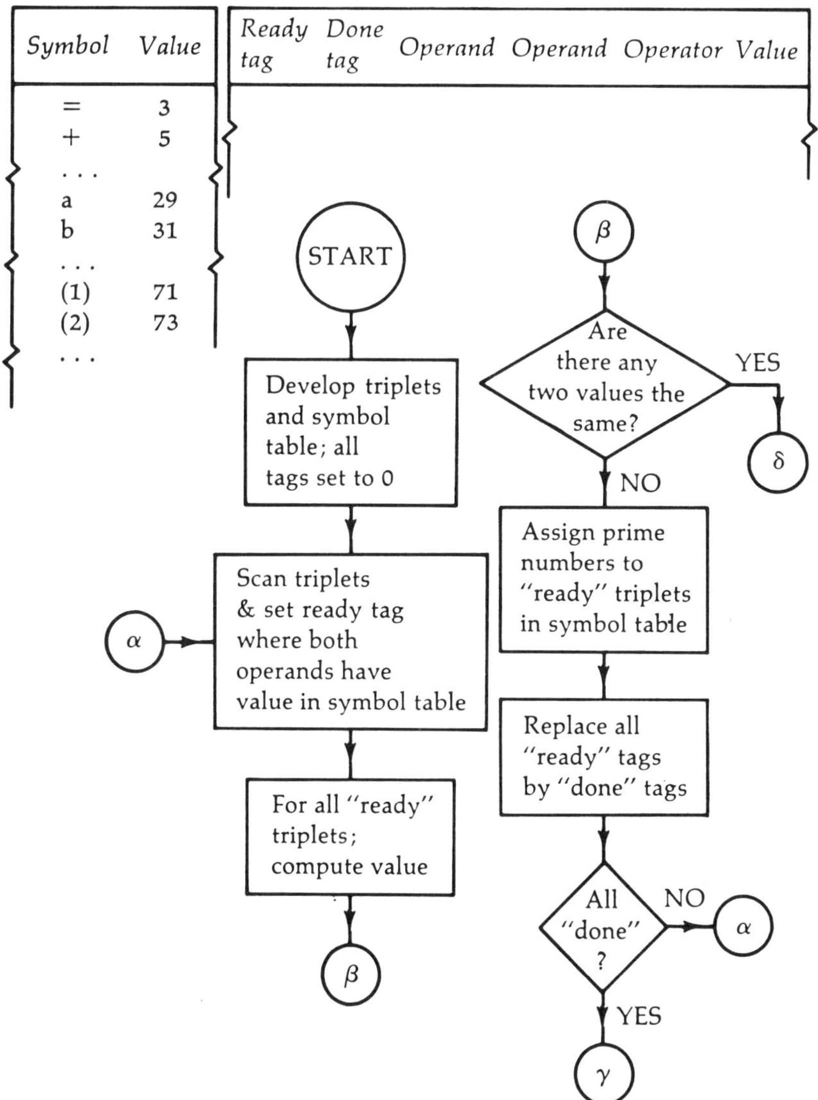

FIGURE 6.16 Algorithm for the recognition and elimination of common subexpressions.

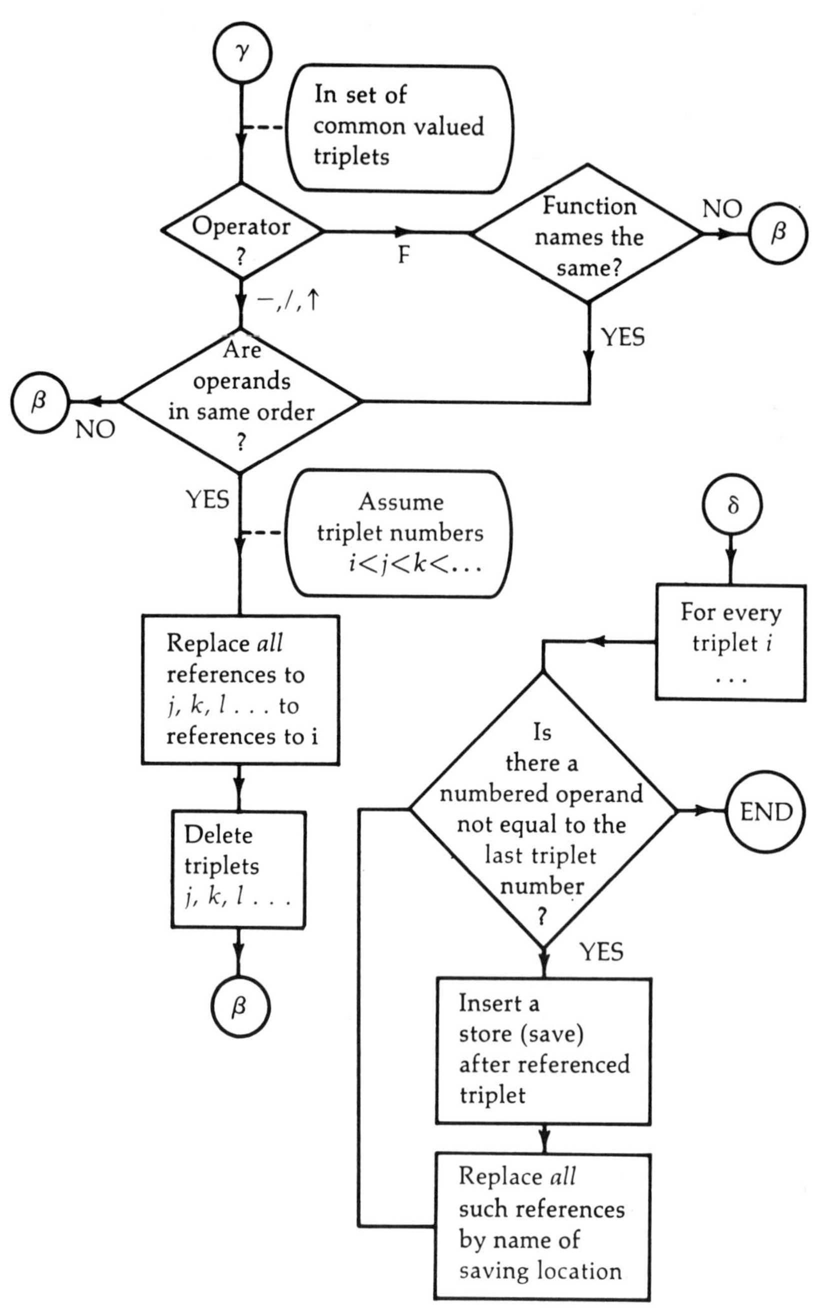

FIGURE 6.16 (Continued)

Problem

6.7 Extend the process of common subexpression elimination to include the case where the assignment operation may occur in any position in the expression, such as in the APL statement

$$(A + B) + (A \leftarrow (A + B))$$

in which the two subexpressions (A + B) are not common.

The success of this and other subexpression-elimination routines which depend on the existence of triplets is in large part a function of the triplet producing system. In particular, expressions may contain common subexpressions which are unrecognizable in their triplet form. For example consider the expression

$$A + B + A + B$$

Following our normal procedures for parenthesizing to produce

$$(((A + B) + A) + B)$$

and subsequently to produce the triplet set

1.	A B +
2.	(1) A +
3.	(2) B +

it is obvious that no two triplets are common to the set, and hence we should conclude that no common subexpressions exist. However, the expression (A + B) + (A + B) would be converted into the triplet set

1.	A B +
2.	A B +
3.	(1) (2) +

which would be recognized to contain common subexpressions.

GLOBAL SUBEXPRESSION ELIMINATION

In the previous discussions we have limited ourselves to the elimination of common subexpressions in single higher level language expressions and by inference (Problem 6.2) to sequences of statements and to "straight-line" code. Provided that such improvements in the source language can be made within heavily utilized sections of the program, there can be some savings which accrue from this local optimization process. However, it is obvious that the most substantial savings can be achieved by examining the overall program and in particular heavily-used portions of that program. As pointed out by Knuth[9] in one example, the movement of a mode conversion from within a loop to a single execution outside could have saved about 20% of the time spent in that loop at execution time. Savings of this magnitude can be significant, whereas the 1% or 2% picked up by local optimization may not be worth the additional cost of compile time execution. At this time research is continuing on the task of global optimization schemes and thus we shall refrain from "jumping the gun" here until practical techniques have been developed. The reader should be aware of the several papers presented at the Symposium on Compiler Optimization at the University of Illinois in 1970.[10]

9. Ibid.

10. *Proc. of a Symp. on Compiler Optimization*, SIGPLAN Notices, vol. 5, no. 7 (New York: ACM, July 1970).

7
The ASCAN Generator

The previous chapter discussed the techniques and algorithms for the generation of Reverse Polish strings from more normal algebraic statements. In this chapter this concept will be extended to produce a set of machine instructions. This discussion will be based on those instructions already defined for an imaginary machine, together with new instructions which will be added to the repertoire as needed. We shall not discriminate between the various modes of execution (that is, real, integer, etc.) since these have no part in the general algorithm and are either machine or language dependent. For the moment, let us review the arithmetic instructions and their semantics:[1]

Instruction		*Meaning*
LDA	a,i	$C(a+C(i)) \rightarrow ACC$
STO	a,i	$C(ACC) \rightarrow a + C(i)$
ADD	a,i	$C(ACC) + C(a + C(i)) \rightarrow ACC$
SUB	a,i	$C(ACC) - C(a + C(i)) \rightarrow ACC$
MUL	a,i	$C(ACC) \times C(a + C(i)) \rightarrow ACC$
DIV	a,i	$C(ACC) \mathbin{/} C(a + C(i)) \rightarrow ACC$
ENA	a,i	$a + C(i) \rightarrow ACC$
INA	a,i	$C(ACC) + (a + C(i)) \rightarrow ACC$
RVS		$-C(ACC) \rightarrow ACC$

1. These descriptions do not take into account the possibility of indirect addressing. For more concise details see Appendix B.

where the notation C(x) is taken to mean the contents of x. In particular, the element a is an address or a numeric representation (in the case of **ENA** and **INA**) and where i is the designator of an index register. The accumulator is signified by **ACC**. The general semantics of a meaning is that the value defined on the left of the arrow (→) is to be assigned to the location specified on the right. Thus **STO** takes the contents of the accumulator (C(ACC)) and assigns them to the location whose address is a + C(i).

The conversion from normal algebraic notation to Reverse Polish notation is unhampered by the need to convert the symbolism of the string. That is, the operands and operators have the same meaning in a normal algebraic string as in a Reverse Polish string. However, when one converts to machine instructions, the symbolism is different (for example, + becomes the mnemonic **ADD**), and more than a single string is created. In general, the conversion of a single set of operands and operator in the Reverse Polish notation to a set of machine instructions may be represented by the production

$<\mathit{operand}_1><\mathit{operand}_2><\mathit{operator}>$	→	LDA	$<\mathit{operand}_1>$
		$<\mathit{op}>$	$<\mathit{operand}_2>$
		STO	$<\mathit{temp}>$

where the <*op*> in the resultant set of strings is dependent on the <*operator*> in the source string. In particular, the following correspondences will be in effect:

Input string operator	*Output string operator*
+	ADD
−	SUB
*	MUL
/	DIV

In the particular case of the replacement sign, the production strings are

$<\mathit{operand}_1><\mathit{operand}_2> =$	→	LDA	$<\mathit{operand}_2>$
		STO	$<\mathit{operand}_1>$

In these productions, <*temp*> refers to an unbounded set of memory addresses which are free of other uses. It is assumed that once an element has been used in this set it is no longer available for use; that is, it is no longer free.

In those cases where the operand is a numeric representation, two basic steps can be taken. As a first transformation, the numeric representation may be allocated a memory location which we shall signify by **L(n)** (location of the numeric representation.) The transformations listed above can then be utilized exactly. However, if the numeric representation is both an integer and of such a value as can be represented in the address field of an instruction, and the operand is related to either a **LDA** or an **ADD**, then two further transformations are possible:

```
        LDA   L(n)  →  ENA   =n
and     ADD   L(n)  →  INA   =n
```

In this notation we include the notation "=" to signify a numeric representation as contrasted with an address. This is not necessary from the point of view of the assembler since addresses and numeric representations are assembled synonomously†. However this notation helps us recognize this special case. Further in all the above transformation rules the use of the index register is omitted. It may be anticipated that the reference to the register is to be provided by some external decision making system not controllable by the compiler. For example, the host system may prescribe that (say) index register 6 be a base register used to locate relocated code. In those instructions where the address field refers to an address (as contrasted with the immediate style instructions **ENA** and **INA**) the index register reference 6 must be added to the instruction.

FROM POLISH NOTATION TO MACHINE CODE

Let us review the rules for converting Reverse Polish notation to normal notation form:

1. Scan from left to right to locate the first operator.

2. The two preceding operands are then the operands of that operator.

3. Exchange the positions of the operand immediately to the left of the operator and the operator, at the same time enclosing the operands and the operator in parentheses. For all further processing this parenthesized group is regarded as an operand or, when enclosed in further parentheses, as part of an operand.

4. If the last parentheses added comprise a pair that encompasses the whole string, then the process is complete. If not, then continue to scan to the right until another operator is located, and return to step 2.

†In relocatable code, "=" can indicate "do not modify."

This same process can be used to generate a set of machine instructions if step 3 is changed to the following:

3. Use the production (on page 312) to generate instructions appropriate to the operands and operator. Replace the three elements of the input string by the name of the temporary storage location.

Using this new set of rules, let us consider the input string

$$xabc/*d+=$$

At the first scan, the located operator is / which has the operands b and c. Thus using the production rule appropriate to /, we shall generate the instructions

```
LDA  b
DIV  c
STO  τ1
```

where τ_1 is a free element from the set <*temp*>. The string then is reduced to $xa\tau_1*d+=$. Continuing to scan to the right, the next operator is * and its operands are a and τ_1; hence the generated instructions are

```
LDA  a
MUL  τ1
STO  τ2
```

and the string is reduced to $x\tau_2d+=$. Further applications of the rules of generation will produce the instructions:

```
LDA  τ2
ADD  d
STO  τ3
LDA  τ3
STO  x
```

It is obvious that in the total set of generated instructions there are, in certain instances, back to back store and load instructions that reference the same operand. That is, a result is stored in a temporary location by the use of one production and is brought back immediately by the next production. Further, in those cases where the operator is commutative, a temporary storage location can be saved by reversing the positions of the operands. However, although these deficiencies may be recognized at this time, we shall postpone detailed consideration of them until a later section.

FROM ALGEBRAIC NOTATION TO MACHINE CODE

Machine instructions may be generated from the normal algebraic string if the algorithm above is preceded by the instructions describing conversion from normal form through parenthesized form to Reverse Polish notation. This technique, which combines the considerations of the previous chapter together with the above algorithm, may be described as follows:

1. Assign hierarchy levels to each operator taking into account the step increases and decreases when a parenthesis is encountered.

2. Starting from the left-hand end of the statement, locate the operator such that $\mathsf{V}(\mathsf{op}_n) \geqslant \mathsf{V}(\mathsf{op}_{n+1})$.

3. The operands immediately to the left and right of this operator are the operands pertinent to the chosen operator.

4. (Note that at this point in the algorithm to convert to Reverse Polish notation we would have interchanged the right-hand operand and the operator and enclosed the two operands and the operator in braces. In this algorithm we merely rewrite the productions.) Using the following productions, generate the appropriate instructions:

$$\begin{array}{lcll} <operand_1><operator><operand_2> & \rightarrow & \mathsf{LDA} & <operand_1> \\ & & <op> & <operand_2> \\ & & \mathsf{STO} & <temp> \end{array}$$

except where the operator is the replacement sign in which case the production rule is

$$\begin{array}{lcll} <operand_1> = <operand_2> & \rightarrow & \mathsf{LDA} & <operand_2> \\ & & \mathsf{STO} & <operand_1> \end{array}$$

and where the additional transformation productions for numeric operands are still applicable.

5. Replace the operator and its operands by the name of the temporary location in which the result is being stored.

6. If the operator that forced the compilation of the instructions pertinent to op_n is the end of the statement ($\dashv$), return to step 2, unless the statement is now null, which indicates that the compilation (or generation) is complete.

7. If the forcing operator is not the end of the statement, check op_{n-1} for the possibility that the forcing operator will also force the compilation of this operator. That is, set the pointer to the operator

previous to the one just compiled and return to step 2 without returning the pointer to the left-hand end of the statement.

Let us consider an input string in normal form which is to be compiled by this set of instructions. In the following discussion, the symbols

$$\underset{\mathsf{C}}{\uparrow} \text{ and } \underset{\mathsf{H}}{\uparrow}$$

are used to indicate the operators that are currently (C) being investigated and that which is in hand (H) as a possible forcing operator. Given

$$\begin{array}{cccccccccccc} \vdash & x & = & a & * & b & / & c & + & d & \dashv \\ 0 & & 1 & & 3 & & 3 & & 2 & & 0 \end{array}$$

the first scan will place the current operator pointer under the * symbol while that in hand will be the division operator. That is,

$$\begin{array}{ccccccccccc} \vdash & x & = & a & * & b & / & c & + & d & \dashv \\ & & & & \uparrow & & \uparrow \\ & & & & \mathsf{C} & & \mathsf{H} \end{array}$$

At this point, the compilation of the multiply operator and its operands is forced, thus producing the instructions

```
LDA  a
MUL  b
STO  τ1
```

and the string is reduced to

$$\begin{array}{ccccccccc} \vdash & x & = & \tau_1 & / & c & + & d & \dashv \\ & & \uparrow & & \uparrow \\ & & \mathsf{C} & & \mathsf{H} \end{array}$$

which shows that the in hand pointer remains in position and the current operator pointer moves to the left. At this point, the hierarchical level of the in hand operator does not force the compilation relevant to the current operator, and so we will scan to the right, until the following situation exists:

$$\begin{array}{ccccccccc} \vdash & x & = & \tau_1 & / & c & + & d & \dashv \\ & & & & \uparrow & & \uparrow \\ & & & & \mathsf{C} & & \mathsf{H} \end{array}$$

The divide operator is now forced to be compiled, and because of the reduction of the string, its operands are still immediately adjacent to the operator. Thus the instructions

```
LDA   τ1
DIV   c
STO   τ2
```

are generated, and the string is reduced to

$$\vdash x = \tau_2 + d \dashv$$
$$\begin{array}{cc} \uparrow & \uparrow \\ \text{C} & \text{H} \end{array}$$

which does not cause the compilation of the replacement operator. At the next shift of the pointers, the addition is forced:

```
LDA   τ2
ADD   d
STO   τ3
```

The string is then reduced to

$$\vdash x = \tau_3 \dashv$$
$$\begin{array}{cc} \uparrow & \uparrow \\ \text{C} & \text{H} \end{array}$$

at which point the replacement operator is compiled:

```
LDA   τ3
STO   x
```

and the string is reduced to

$$\vdash \quad \dashv$$

which is obviously empty, thereby signifying that the compilation is complete.

This discussion does not include provisions for the compilation of either the involution operator or the unary minus. The former has been omitted because most computers do not include a single instruction for the computation of an involute. For the purposes of discussion, let us assume that there exists, at least in the assembly language, an instruction of the form

```
EXP   a,i
```

which means

$$\text{C(ACC)}^{\text{C}(a + \text{C}(i))} \rightarrow \text{ACC}$$

This instruction may in fact in a macroassembler system assemble to a set of instructions linking to a routine that will execute this operation. The unary minus is a special case of a function that requires a single argument but does not necessarily compile as a linkage to a routine to compute the function. For the purposes of this text, assume that the computer contains an instruction to reverse the sign of the accumulator. This instruction will not require an operand explicitly since it is implied that the operand is the accumulator. Thus the production for unary minus will be

~*<operand>* → LDA *<operand>*
RVS
STO *<temp>*

In some computers which utilize complement representation for negative numbers, the RVS operation may be replaced by a complement (CMP) followed by an increment by unity (INA = 1).

THE FIRST PASS AT OPTIMIZATION

Let us now return to the problem of using temporary accumulators and the redundancy of store and load instructions that use the same operand in sequence. The accumulator may be regarded as a temporary storage location until its use is precluded by the necessity to store more than one intermediate result or until its position as an operand in the reduced string will not permit the compilation of the instructions as defined above. In other words, so long as the accumulator is the first operand of a binary operator or the only operand of a function, a temporary storage location is not needed. Further instructions in the above productions either to load into or store out of the accumulator will be omitted except in the case of the replacement operator, or when the accumulator is empty (effectively).

Consider the following input string:

$$\begin{array}{cccccccccccc} \vdash & x & = & a & * & b & + & c & * & d & \dashv \\ 0 & & 1 & & 3 & & 2 & & 3 & & 0 \end{array}$$

During the first scan from left to right, when the first compilation is forced, the pointers are set to the following positions:

$$\begin{array}{ccccccccccc} \vdash & x & = & a & * & b & + & c & * & d & \dashv \\ & & & & \uparrow & & \uparrow & & & & \\ & & & & \text{C} & & \text{H} & & & & \end{array}$$

Under these conditions the coding

LDA *a*
MUL *b*

is generated; the result is stored in the accumulator, and the store instruction to a temporary location is not output. The reduced string becomes

```
⊢ x = ACC + c * d ⊣
  ↑       ↑
  C       H
```

In this situation, the coding does not have to be generated for the replacement sign, and thus the scan from left to right is continued. However, the movement of the pointers does not immediately cause the compilation of the operator with which the accumulator is associated. In fact, the next operator to be forced into a compilation is the succeeding multiply operator. Therefore since this does not involve the result that was saved in the accumulator, the result must be saved in a temporary location to allow the use of the accumulator in the next unassociated production.

Thus we may state the following rule: If the in hand pointer is moved and the previous in hand operator does not become the operator for the next production, the result of any previous calculation must be stored temporarily and that storage location must be substituted for the accumulator in the reduced input string.

In the examples which follow we shall tabulate the sequential actions of compilation, showing in the left hand column the string from the source program text and the decisions which were made regarding that string, whilst in the right-hand column the generated code is displayed.

Consider the example:

$$x = \sim a * b + c$$

The reduced string and decisions	*Generated instructions*

⊢ x = ~a * b + c ⊣
0   1 5 3   2   0
      ↑ ↑
      C H
	LDA *a* C(*a*) → ACC
	RVS −C(ACC) → ACC

⊢ x = ACC * b + c ⊣
   ↑   ↑
   C H	

V(=) ⩽ V(*); move right.	

⊢ x =ACC * b + c ⊣
           ↑   ↑
           C H	

The previous in hand operator is now to be compiled, and the ACC is the left-hand operand; thus no temporary storage is needed.	MUL	b	$C(ACC) * C(b) \rightarrow ACC$

$\vdash x = ACC + c \dashv$
(C under =, H under +)

$V(=) \leqslant V(+)$; move right.

$\vdash x = ACC + c \dashv$
(C under +, H under $\dashv$)

The previous in hand operator is now to be forced; no temporary storage is needed.	ADD	c	$C(ACC) + C(c) \rightarrow ACC$

$\vdash x = ACC \dashv$
(C under =, H under $\dashv$)

At this point, the in hand operator is not the next operator to be compiled. However, the replacement operator is to be forced and the accumulator is in the correct relationship with the operator and is to compile normally.	STO	x	$C(ACC) \rightarrow x$

$\vdash \quad \dashv$

The string is now empty; hence the compilation is complete.

Now consider the string

$$x = a + b \,/\, c \uparrow d - e$$

The reduced string and decisions	*Generated instructions*		
$\vdash x = a + b \,/\, c \uparrow d - e \dashv$ 0 1 2 3 4 2 0 (C under $\uparrow$, H under $-$)	LDA EXP	c d	$C(c) \rightarrow ACC$ $C(ACC) \uparrow C(d) \rightarrow ACC$
$\vdash x = a + b \,/\, ACC - e \dashv$ (C under /, H under $-$)			

Immediately after the compilation of the operator of involution, the pointers are set as shown above. In this situation, the in hand operator did not become that to be compiled next. Further, although the forced operator (/) does have the accumulator as one of its operands, it is the divisor that is in the accumulator and not the dividend. Hence the contents of the accumulator must be stored temporarily.

STO τ_1 Store C(ACC) temporarily

$$\vdash x = a + b \,/\, \tau_1 - e \dashv$$

```
            ↑   ↑
            C   H
```

Having stored the contents of the accumulator, we are effectively compiling a new statement. Thus the first operation will be that of loading the accumulator.

LDA b $C(b) \to ACC$
DIV τ_1 $C(ACC) / C(\tau_1) \to ACC$

$$\vdash x = a + ACC - e \dashv$$

```
        ↑      ↑
        C      H
```

Once again the forced operator is not that which was in hand, and therefore the contents of the accumulator must be saved.

STO τ_2 Store C(ACC) temporarily

$$\vdash x = a + \tau_2 - e \dashv$$

```
        ↑   ↑
        C   H
```

LDA a $C(a) \to ACC$
ADD τ_2 $C(ACC) + C(\tau_2) \to ACC$

$$\vdash x = ACC - e \dashv$$

```
    ↑      ↑
    C      H
```

After the generation of the instructions pertinent to the addition operator, the pointers are set as shown above, and since the V(=) is less than V(−), then the previous operator is not forced. A single shift left of the pointers will indicate that the in hand operator becomes that to be compiled. Thus no temporary storage location is needed.

SUB e C(ACC) − C(e) → ACC

$\vdash x =$ ACC $\dashv$

↑ ↑

C H

In the above situation, the in hand operator has not become that to be forced; however, the operator being forced is the replacement sign, with the accumulator in the correct relationship.

STO x C(ACC) → x

$\vdash$ $\dashv$

↑ ↑

C H

Compilation is complete.

In the latter example, two instructions and a storage location could have been saved if it had been recognized that an add operation is commutative, for although the accumulator was not in the correct relationship to the operator with respect to our rules of productions, the add operation could have been generated by the first operand. In general, the commutative operations are particular cases which are in a minority among the total number of operators. However, a survey of operations executed will show that these two operations (+ and *) are most frequently used. Thus it would be advantageous to arrange the productions to produce efficient codings of these operations. With respect to the subtraction operation, if, instead of the in hand operator, the operator immediately to the left of the last forced operator is the one to be compiled, the sequence of instructions RVS and ADD may be used to simulate the subtraction without the use of a temporary storage location. For example,

$$x = a - b * c$$

The reduced string and decisions	*Generated instructions*		
$\vdash x = a - b * c \dashv$			
0 1 2 3 0			
↑ ↑			
C H	LDA	b	$C(b) \to ACC$
	MUL	c	$C(ACC) * C(c) \to ACC$
$\vdash x = a -$ ACC $\dashv$			
↑ ↑			
C H			
At this point the contents of the accumulator are to be subtracted from the value of the variable a.	RVS		$-C(ACC) \to ACC$
	ADD	a	$C(ACC) + C(a) \to ACC$
$\vdash x =$ ACC $\dashv$			
↑ ↑			
C H			
	STO	x	$C(ACC) \to x$
$\vdash$ $\dashv$			
↑ ↑			
C H			

Compilation is complete.

This saving in instructions and storage cannot be extended to the other noncommutative operators / and ↑. However, there can be an overall saving within a program if reverse divide and reverse involution are performed by a subroutine. That is, if the subroutine will save the contents of the accumulator in a private (local) storage area, the first operand can be placed in the accumulator and the operation performed in the normal manner; the only instructions needed in the program proper are the linkage.

Suppose n instructions are required to link from the main line program to the subroutine which itself consists of m instructions, whereas using in line coding p instructions would be required; then if $p > n$ and the operation is repeated in the total program more than $m/(p-n)$ times, there is a saving in instructions but not necessarily in time. The compiler writer, knowing the environment in which the system is to be used, must determine whether it is more important to save memory space or execution time. For the sake of the present discussion, consider two macro-instructions:

RDIV	$a,i/+\mathrm{C}(i)$	$\mathrm{C}(a)/\mathrm{C(ACC)} \rightarrow \mathrm{ACC}$
REXP	$a,i/+\mathrm{C}(i)$	$\mathrm{C}(a)\uparrow\mathrm{C(ACC)} \rightarrow \mathrm{ACC}$

For example,

$$x = a - b \;/\; c \uparrow (e - f)$$

```
        Reduced string                      Generated instructions
--------------------------------------------------------------------
⊢ x = a − b / c ↑ e − f ⊣
0   1   2   3 4  12  0
                 ↑   ↑
                 C   H                      LDA    e
                                            SUB    f
⊢ x = a − b / c ↑ ACC ⊣
                ↑     ↑
                C     H
                                            REXP   c
⊢ x = a − b / ACC ⊣
            ↑     ↑
            C     H
                                            RDIV   b
⊢ x = a − ACC ⊣
        ↑     ↑
        C     H
                                            RVS
                                            ADD    a
⊢ x = ACC ⊣
    ↑     ↑
    C     H
                                            STO    x
⊢   ⊣
↑   ↑
C   H
```

Compilation is complete.

Problem

7.1 Show the successive steps of analysis to code the following arithmetic statements:

(a) $x = (-b + (b * b - f * a * c) \uparrow h) / (t * a)$
(b) $y = (-a * b + c) \uparrow (-(d - e))$
(c) $z = -d - a + b / (c * e - f / g)$
(d) $v = (a + b) - (c + d)$
(e) $n = -a \uparrow b / (-(a \uparrow b))$

FURTHER IMPROVEMENTS

In normal practice, the hierarchy of operators places a unary minus at a higher level than all other operators; thus expressions such as $a * -b$ and $a \uparrow -b$ are parenthesized so that the sign of the second operand is always reversed before the operation to its left is executed. However, this also implies the following translations:

$$-a * b \quad \rightarrow \quad ((-a) * b)$$
$$-a \uparrow b \quad \rightarrow \quad ((-a) \uparrow b)$$

The latter is a possible meaning, but, in general, if b is a mixed number (integer + fraction), the result of $((-a) \uparrow b)$ is undefined. Therefore let us define $-a \uparrow b$ as meaning $-(a \uparrow b)$. While $-(a * b)$ can be accepted as a meaning for $-a * b$, $-a + b$ cannot be translated as $-(a + b)$. Thus if the unary minus is placed between +, − and *,/ the resultant meaning will be as desired. However, this meaning creates some ambiguity as to the possibility of the occurrence of two operators without separating operands. To overcome this problem, let us insist that no two operators may be placed in sequence except when the replacement sign and unary minus occur in juxtaposition. Thus the hierarchical table is revised to the sequence

0	$\vdash \quad \dashv$
1	$=$
2	$+ \quad -$ (dyadic)
3	$-$ (monadic or unary)
4	$* \quad /$
5	$\uparrow$

with the adjustments of +10 and (and −10 for).

If the reverse operations for subtraction, division and involution are regarded as the normal operations, as opposed to the regular forward operations, some time can be saved in the compiler by reducing the amount of scanning necessary in the majority of cases. Examination of a operator level graph (as shown in Figure 6.15) reveals that in many cases the compilation of the code relative to one operator is followed by the compilation of the code for its left neighbor. In this circumstance the order in which operands are available is more suited to the compilation of code containing reversed operand instructions instead of the regular forward instructions. Consider the input string

$$x = a - b.$$

Reduced string	*Generated instructions*
$\vdash x = a - b \dashv$	
0 1 2 0	
↑ ↑	
C H	LDA b
	RVS
	ADD a
$\vdash x =$ ACC $\dashv$	
↑ ↑	
C H	STO x

In this particular production sequence, a two instruction sequence, not a true reverse subtract operation, has been introduced. Another technique of simulation for the reverse subtract is:

SUB a	C(ACC) − C(a) → ACC
RVS	−C(ACC) → ACC

Let us consider the previous example:

Reduced string	*Generated instructions*
$\vdash x = a - b \dashv$	
0 1 2 0	
↑ ↑	
C H	LDA b
	SUB a
	RVS
$\vdash x =$ ACC $\dashv$	
↑ ↑	
C H	STO x

If the expression being compiled had been

$$x = -(a - b)$$

the instructions generated would have been as follows:

Reduced string	*Generated instructions*
$\vdash x = -\ (a - b) \dashv$ 0 1 3 12 0 ↑ ↑ C H	LDA *b* SUB *a* RVS
$\vdash x = -$ ACC $\dashv$ ↑ ↑ C H	RVS
$\vdash x =$ ACC $\dashv$ ↑ ↑ C H	STO *x*

In this case, the accumulator is reversed in sign in two successive instructions, each canceling the effect of the other and therefore being redundant. This effect was discussed in Chapter 6 with respect to moving reverse sign operations (unary minuses) through an expression in order to find a canceling operation. During compilation, the order in which instructions are generated is controlled somewhat by the various hierarchical levels of the operators, and thus complete analysis of the expression, as was performed in Chapter 6, is not necessarily economical. However, if the instructions are ordered so that the reverse sign operation is the last to be generated in a production, then there is a chance of either canceling it with a subsequent reverse sign operation or combining it with another operator. The algorithm of generation should take note of the generation of a reverse sign operation and check to see if the next instruction is also a reverse sign. If this is the case, then both the generated instructions may be canceled before they are passed into the object code. Further, if the operator to be generated next is either an ADD or SUB and the accumulator is the right-hand operand, then these operations may be converted to their converse operation without affecting the true representation of the expression. Consider the following examples.

Reduced string	Generated string: Without reversal	Generated string: With reversal
$\vdash x = a - (b - c) \dashv$		
0 1 2 12 0		
↑ ↑		
C H	LDA c	LDA c
	SUB b	SUB b
	RVS	
$\vdash x = a - \text{ACC} \dashv$		
↑ ↑		
C H	SUB a	
	RVS	ADD a
$\vdash x = \text{ACC} \dashv$		
↑ ↑		
C H	STO x	STO x
$\vdash x = a + (b - c) \dashv$		
0 1 2 12 0		
↑ ↑		
C H	LDA c	LDA c
	SUB b	SUB b
	RVS	
$\vdash x = a + \text{ACC} \dashv$		
↑ ↑		
C H	ADD a	SUB a
		RVS
$\vdash x = \text{ACC} \dashv$		
↑ ↑		
C H	STO x	STO x

These transformations can be expressed in terms of productions over the pairs of instructions:

$$\left.\begin{array}{ll}\text{RVS} & \\ \text{ADD} & x\end{array}\right\} \rightarrow \left\{\begin{array}{ll}\text{SUB} & x \\ \text{RVS} & \end{array}\right.$$

which is equivalent to the transformation

$$-\text{ACC} + x \quad \rightarrow \quad -(\text{ACC} - x)$$

and

$$\left.\begin{array}{ll}\text{SUB} & x \\ \text{RVS} & \end{array}\right\} \rightarrow \left\{\begin{array}{ll}\text{ADD} & x \\ \text{RVS} & \end{array}\right.$$

which is equivalent to

$$-\text{ACC} - x \quad \rightarrow \quad -(\text{ACC} + x)$$

Obviously, one important transformation is

$$\left.\begin{array}{l}\text{RVS}\\ \text{RVS}\end{array}\right\} \rightarrow \quad \text{(null)}$$

which is equivalent to

$$-(-\text{ACC}) \quad \rightarrow \quad \text{ACC}$$

The instructions generated in the first example show that there is a saving of two instructions when reversal is taken into account, whereas in the second example, there is no saving. The strings generated with reversal show that when the reverse sign instruction is kept back until the next productions are generated, the reversal of the ADD or SUB instructions can save instructions and, if not, will not be detrimental to the program. It is better to save instructions occasionally, than to allow the generation of uneconomical sets of instructions.

In each of the above examples, the in hand operator has forced the compilation of the left-hand operator. When a move to the right is needed, the production rules are different, since in this case the accumulator is the left-hand operand and the normal mode of operations is possible. For example, the input string $x = a - b - c$ produces the instructions

```
LDA  b
SUB  a
RVS
SUB  c
STO  x
```

However, if the subsequent subtract had been converted to an add while the reverse sign was maintained on the outside of the grouping, the same number of instructions would have accrued. That is,

$$(x{=}a{-}b{-}c) \equiv (x{=}{-}(b{-}a){-}c) \equiv (x{=}{-}((b{-}a){+}c))$$

the latter generating the coding

```
LDA  b
SUB  a
ADD  c
RVS
STO  x
```

This allowance in the algorithm does not show any increase in the object coding, but the movement of the unary minus (reverse sign operation) to the outside of the expressions and subexpressions increases the possibility of the unary minus being canceled.

If a unary minus is located or brought to the outside of a group and the next operator is either a * or a / without an intermediate store in a temporary location, the unary minus may be carried further. However, if the next operator is the involution operator, the **RVS** must be executed independently of the direction of the scan. That is, the following transformations are applicable:

$$\left.\begin{array}{ll}\textsf{RVS} & \\ \textsf{MUL} & x\end{array}\right\} \rightarrow \left\{\begin{array}{ll}\textsf{MUL} & x \\ \textsf{RVS} & \end{array}\right.$$

and

$$\left.\begin{array}{ll}\textsf{RVS} & \\ \textsf{DIV} & x\end{array}\right\} \rightarrow \left\{\begin{array}{ll}\textsf{DIV} & x \\ \textsf{RVS} & \end{array}\right.$$

as well as

$$\left.\begin{array}{ll}\textsf{RVS} & \\ \textsf{RDIV} & x\end{array}\right\} \rightarrow \left\{\begin{array}{ll}\textsf{RDIV} & x \\ \textsf{RVS} & \end{array}\right.$$

Consider the following example:

x = ~ a * (~ b)

Reduced string	*Generated string*
⊢ *x* = ~ *a* * (~ *b*) ⊣ 0 1 3 4 13 0 ↑ ↑ C H	LDA *b*
The actual code generated included a **RVS** but this is being held in case it interacts with other instructions.	
⊢ *x* = ~ *a* * ACC ⊣ 0 1 3 4 0 ↑ ↑ C H	MUL *a*
The generated instruction **MUL** allows the **RVS** instruction to pass through.	

$\vdash x = \sim$ ACC $\dashv$
0 1 3 0
↑ ↑
C H (null)

The compilation of this string with the pointers in this position causes the generation of a RVS instruction. However, this instruction reacts with the RVS which has been held back, so that the generated code is null.

$\vdash$ x = ACC $\dashv$
0 1 0
↑ ↑
C H STO x

$\vdash$ $\dashv$

Compilation is complete.

Problem

7.2 Generate the coding for the following expressions, indicating the process of production step by step.

(a) $-\left[\frac{a}{-b} + (-c)\right]$

(b) $(-ab + c)^{-(d-e)}$

(c) $-(a-(c*(-b/(d^{-k}))))$

A TABULAR METHOD OF ANALYSIS

Within a computer, it is not economical to analyze an arithmetic expression in its algebraic linearized form. It is particularly inconvenient to keep moving about an expression and replacing groups by a notation which indicates that the result is either in the accumulator or in temporary storage. Further, as the expression is analyzed, it becomes vacuous, and time is wasted if the compiler must scan blanks in the statement and blocks that have already been scanned, or must condense the statement.

To avoid these problems, let us scan the statement left to right and place the operands in a table of encountered addresses (**TEA**) and the operators in a table of encountered operators (**TEO**). The table of encountered operators will also include a listing of the hierarchical levels for each operator; a fourth entry in the table (although not implemented as a table but instead as a single cell) is the in hand operator and its hierarchical level. Even before each statement is examined, the left-hand end delimiter (⊢) is placed in **TEO**, and when the end is located,[2] the right-hand end delimiter (⊣) is generated. As the scan is conducted, each new operator encountered (except the end delimiter to the left of the statement) is placed in the "in-hand" bin. If the new operator is of a lower level or equal level to the operator last placed in **TEO**, then the last two operands are used and the last operator placed in **TEO** is used in the production that generates the required code. These operands and operator are removed from their respective table, and a new operand is placed in **TEA**, indicating that the result is in the accumulator. The "in-hand" operator is then compared to the (new) last operator in **TEO**. If this operator is still of a higher hierarchical value than that in hand, this operator is also forced into the compilation sequence. If not, the scan is continued to the right, and the in-hand operator and operand are placed in **TEO** and **TEA**, respectively. However, if two operands[3] are added to **TEA** before another compilation is forced, then the previous result (now residing in the accumulator) must be stored in a temporary storage location, and that location must be recorded in the correct position in **TEA**. Consider the input string

$$x = a - b * c$$

TEA	*TEO*	*Level*	*In hand*
x	⊢	0	
a	=	1	
b	−	2	
c	*	3	⊣(0)

At this point in the construction of the table, V(⊣) ⩽ V(*) and the accumulator does not contain anything. Hence, the last entry in **TEA** is

2. The ease with which the end of an arithmetic expression is located depends on the statement in which it is embedded. For example, if the statement under consideration is an assignment statement, then the end of the expression is also the end of the statement. In other types of statement (for example, the **IF** statement) the decision-making machinery for recognizing the end of the expression may be more complex.

3. For the time being, only dyadic operators are being considered.

placed in the accumulator and the entry removed from TEA:

LDA *c*

The last operator in TEO is *, and its operand is *b*:

MUL *b*

The last two entries are removed from TEA and TEO, respectively, and the table reduces to:

TEA	*TEO*	*Level*	*In hand*
x	⊢	0	
a	=	1	
	−	3	⊣(0)

At this point, V(⊣) is still less than V(last entry in TEO), so we are, in effect, scanning left. The accumulator is presently in use so it does not have to be loaded. Thus the last operator and operand are the relevant items for the construction of the next instruction:

SUB *a*

The next instruction to be generated should be the RVS, which will be held in reserve until the items relevant to the last instruction generated are removed from the tables. The reduced table now shows that the replacement sign is the last entry in TEO, and the in hand operator is still the right-hand end delimiter. Since no more items are to be added to the table and the in hand operator is forcing the compilation of the instructions pertinent to the replacement sign, the RVS instruction will not have the opportunity to interact with any other instructions. Thus it may be placed into the object code. The table is now:

TEA	*TEO*	*Level*	*In hand*
x	⊢	0	
	=	1	⊣(0)

and since V(in-hand operator) is still less than V(last entry in TEO), the instruction

STO *x*

is forced. The TEA table is now empty, and TEO contains only the left-hand delimiter which is to be matched with the right-hand delimiter in the in hand column. Thus the compilation is complete.

Now let us consider the expression

$$x = a * b + c * d$$

Scanning from left to right, the tables are built up until the following situation exists:

TEA	TEO	*Level*	*In hand*
x	⊢	0	
a	=	1	
b	*	3	+(2)

At this point, V(in-hand operator) is less than V(*), and the accumulator is empty since no coding has been produced previously. Hence the generator produces the following instructions:

```
LDA  b
MUL  a
```

and the tables reduce to:

TEA	TEO	*Level*	*In hand*
x	⊢	0	
	=	1	+(2)

But, V(in-hand operator) is not less than or equal to V(TEO operator), and so the ACC must be added to the TEA and the scan continued.

TEA	TEO	*Level*	*In hand*
x	⊢	0	
ACC	=	1	
c	+	2	*(3)

At this point, the in-hand operator of the last production is not forced into the compilation cycle by the new in hand operator. Therefore the contents of the accumulator must be stored in a temporary storage location and the TEA updated to reflect this storage. The instruction produced is

STO τ_1

Scanning of the input statement is continued and the table is constructed to the point, shown below, where the level value of the in hand operator forces the next compilation:

TEA	*TEO*	*Level*	*In hand*
x	$\vdash$	0	
τ_1	$=$	1	
c	$+$	2	
d	$*$	3	$\dashv$

Now the accumulator may be considered empty since the last computed result has been placed in temporary storage. Thus the generated instructions are

LDA d
MUL c

After the last operator and its operands are removed from the tables, the level value of the in hand operator is still less than that of the last entry in TEO, thus forcing the compilation of this operator:

ADD τ_1

Since the end delimiter always has a level value less than every other operator, except the left-hand delimiter, all operators will be forced into the compilation cycle. In this case, only one other operator exists in the TEO besides the left-hand delimiter, that is, the replacement sign. This causes production of the instruction

STO x

after which the tables are empty and the compilation is complete.

Let us now consider an example involving a reversal of an operation caused by the interaction of a unary minus (or RVS). The input string $x = a - (b - c)$ contains parentheses that will be discarded during the scan and will not be placed in TEO. However, when the left parenthesis is encountered, all levels of hierarchy are incremented by 10, and when the closing parenthesis is recognized, the levels are reduced by 10. If at any point the levels become negative, then there are additional closing parentheses that appear before their matching opening parentheses, and an invalid statement is in the input area. Similarly, if the level of the end delimiter is not zero after a series of hierarchical incrementations and decrementations, then unmatched parentheses exist in the input string.

For the above string, the table is constructed to the point where the end delimiter is the in hand operator.

TEA	*TEO*	*Level*	*In hand*
x	⊢	0	
a	=	1	
b	−	2	
c	−	12	⊣(0)

Since no instructions have been generated up to this point, the accumulator is not in use, and hence the first instruction must be to load the accumulator with the last entry in **TEA**.

LDA c
SUB b

The **RVS** instruction is held in reserve; the tables are reduced by the operands and the operator used in the last production. The last entry in **TEO** is now −, which is to be forced by the in hand operator. In effect, the scan is proceeding to the left across the input string; therefore the unary minus (**RVS**) will interact with this operator and convert it to an **ADD** operator, and the **RVS** instruction which is being held in reserve will be discarded. The table is thus reduced and modified to

TEA	*TEO*	*Level*	*In hand*
x	⊢	0	
a	=	1	
	+	2	⊣(0)

The in-hand operator, which is the end delimiter, will now force the compilation of the instructions relevant to the last entry in **TEO**, and since the accumulator is still in use, no temporary storage is required. The instruction generated is **ADD** a. Finally, the in hand operator forces the compilation of the replacement operator, **STO** x.

Now, consider the string $x = a - b - c$.

TEA	*TEO*	*Level*	*In hand*
x	⊢	0	
a	=	1	
b	−	2	−(2)

At this point, the accumulator is not in use, and compilation of the operator, −, is being forced by an operator of the same level.

LDA *b*
SUB *a*

After the operands and the operator have been removed from the tables (and an **RVS** is pending), the current operator (that is, the item in **TEO** that is now unmasked) will not be forced by the in hand operator and thus the table must be constructed further until the next forced operator is discovered. The pending **RVS** operation is equivalent to a unary minus that is operating on the accumulator and will be placed in the **TEO**. Normally, this should be forced into compilation except under one condition: if the next operand (which is currently in hand) is to be forced at the next stage. If the next operand is not to be forced then this operation must be forced. In this example, the in hand operator is the next to be forced and will be converted to +. Thus before the next stage of compilation, the tables are as follows:

TEA	*TEO*	*Level*	*In hand*
x	⊢	0	
ACC	=	1	
c	[~	3]	
	+	2	⊣(0)

In effect,

$$\sim\text{ACC} - c$$

has been converted to the equivalent form ~(ACC + c). If the next operator had not been forced, then the reverse sign operation would have had to have been compiled into the object coding. However, if for any reason, the next operator had been either a multiply or divide, the reverse sign could have remained in the table. In the above case, the compiled instructions are, successively:

ADD *c*
RVS
STO *x*

Problem

7.3 Using the tabular method of compilation, generate the instructions for the following input strings:

(a) $x = {\sim}a - b - c - d$

(b) $x = {\sim}(a-b) + (c - d)$

(c) $x = \dfrac{{\sim}a}{cb} - e$

(d) $x = \dfrac{{\sim}b + \sqrt{b^2 - 4ac}}{2a}$

(e) $y = (x_i + x_{i+1})/z_{n-2}$

(f) $y = \cos(x)$

FUNCTIONS IN EXPRESSIONS

When the symbol table reports back to ASCAN that it has encountered a function, the compiled code to be generated will depend on the type of function being referenced, that is, library function or user defined, and the methodology of linkage. If one could be assured that every function had only one argument (even if that argument were an expression) then that argument could be regarded as the right hand side of an assignment statement, the result being placed in the accumulator. Thus the linkage to the subroutine which implements the function could be simply a MARK PLACE AND TRANSFER (MPT) and the subprogram could return control through the use of a BRANCH BACK (BB), the result being placed in the accumulator also.

However such assurance can not be given except in the case of some elementary library functions. In particular, some functions can have a varying number of arguments. It is important to note that functions have the property that their output consists of a single value whose location is not directly associated with any variable in the program, except by the use of an assignment operation. Thus there is no need to provide a facility for the function to alter the values of any of the input arguments. That is, the method of argument passing (see Chapter 10 for a complete discussion of the various techniques) is by the passage of values. However, the method of passing arguments by address generalizes sufficiently to provide an easier means of argument passing. That is, rather than preparing exotic code in order to place the argument values into a prearranged set of locations known to the subprogram which implements the function, it is easier to have the compiler place addresses into locations at compile time and then have the expression evaluation routines (which may in fact be in line with the code) place their results into the specified addresses.

This method is applicable equally to FORTRAN style **SUBROUTINE** linkages. The compilation system is to scan the argument list and to compile the code necessary to evaluate each argument. The result of this evaluation is then placed in a temporary location if any computations were necessary to achieve the evaluation. If no operations were necessary then the actual address of the value can be used. This list of temporary locations and actual addresses then becomes the list which is to be transmitted to the subprogram. In order to allow for a varying number of arguments, the last element in the list is succeeded by a word containing a recognizable terminating mark, indicated here by "≠."

The operation of linkage to the subprogram is to pass the address of the first element in the address list to the subprogram which is responsible for picking up the actual arguments.

In the previous discussions, linkages to system provided routines were assembled by means of a two-instruction sequence:

```
ENA     *+2
B       SUB
```

where **SUB** was the name of the routine to be entered. In the case of functions and subprograms, and in particular for user defined routines, the compiler may not be able to ascertain a real address to use for the object of the branch instruction. The problem is similar to that in a one pass system where a forward reference is made to a statement identifier. However, in this case the compiler is incapable of providing the mechanism for generating these addresses; this task has to be left to the loader. To provide a linkage mechanism which can be bound at compile time, the system may provide a transfer vector at a fixed (or least known) location in the object time memory system, each element of which corresponds to one of the referenceable subprograms. This system is used equally for both user defined and library functions and subroutines. The first n elements of the vector correspond to the n system provided library functions; the remainder of the vector is available for user defined functions and subroutines. The position in the transfer vector of the linkage address for each function or subroutine is stored in the symbol table.

Let us introduce the following commands for use in our discussion:

1. **MPT**, *m*ark *p*lace and *t*ransfer. The execution of this instruction causes the program counter (**PC**) of the machine to be set to the contents of the address portion of the **MPT** instruction (modified if neces-

sary by the contents of a specified index register), and a return address (the original contents of the program counter plus one) to be placed in a special return address register (**RAR**).

$$\text{MPT} \quad a,i \qquad \text{C(PC)} + 1 \rightarrow \text{RAR}$$
$$a + \text{C}(i) \quad \rightarrow \text{PC}$$

2. **BB**, *b*ranch *b*ack. This instruction causes the current contents of the program counter to be replaced by the contents of the return address register. Thus the next instruction to be executed is that immediately following the last **MPT** instruction (unless the contents have been modified by the programmer.)

BB (address portion not used) C(RAR) → PC

The following two declarations are used by the assembler:

3. **DA**, *d*efine *a*ddress. This pseudo-instruction causes the assembler to place the specified address in the next available location in memory.

4. **DC**, *d*efine *c*onstant. This instruction causes the assembler to supply a one-word location at the next available memory location and to store into that location the internal representation of the argument which follows the code **DC**. It is assumed here that some syntactic mechanism is provided to instruct the assembler as to which mode of constant is to be formed. Very simply this syntactic mechanism could be the same as provided in FORTRAN: a digit string which does not contain a decimal point is assumed to be an integer, otherwise the internal representation is to be floating point. In some of our generated code here, the notation **L**(n) will be used in the address portion of an instruction. This indicates that the location of the constant n is to be inserted here. It is a comparatively simple task for the assembler to provide corresponding define constant declarations for these notations.

Let us now consider the linkage to be generated when an arithmetic expression evaluator encounters a reference to a function. For the purposes of example, consider the reference

GET(A,B+C,E/D,F)

where the number of arguments in the list is unlimited. Each argument must be considered primarily as an expression and the result stored in a temporary storage location if any arithmetic operators are included in the expression. In this situation, the delimiting commas and the closing parenthesis are to be considered as expression end delimiters. The above expression would be compiled to the set of instructions:

```
LDA   C
ADD   B
STO   τ1
LDA   D
RDIV  E
STO   τ2
MPT   GET
DA    A
DA    τ1
DA    τ2
DA    F
DC    ≠
```

where **GET** is a reference to the first instruction of the function **GET**. Depending on the manner in which the system is to accomplish the transfer of control between a calling program and the (possibly) relocatable routine, the value of the address provided as the assembly code of the operand **GET** could be an indirect address through a transfer vector or a direct address to the first instruction of the routine.

This linkage code assumes that the called routine has access to the return address register (**RAR**) and has the ability to both obtain that address and to update it. In this type of linkage, the address carried into the routine by the **MPT** instruction is actually used as the address of the first element of the list of argument values (or pointers thereto), it being the responsibility of the routine to determine the return address for the **BB** instruction from the location of the "stopper" in the list.

If the return address register (**RAR**) is not accessible, then an alternative form of linking instruction, or set of instructions, is necessary. For example, the PDP-8 series of machines have an instruction **JMS** (*Jump* to *Subprogram*) which uses a pseudo-return address register, which is actually the first location in the routine being called, the actual transfer of control being performed to the second word in the routine. No explicit branch back command is included since a simple indirect branch to the first word of the routine accomplishes the same action. Utilizing this command (**JMS**) the routine **GET** would be expected to access the arguments through this given address and to reset the address for return to the calling routine.

If neither style of subprogram linkage is provided then the simulation of the **JMS** instruction through the sequence

```
ENA   *+3
STA   GET
B     GET+1
```

will accomplish the same result.

When an argument is a constant, the address of that constant should not be communicated to the subprogram as a precaution against its value being altered in the subprogram. For example, if the parameter list of a subprogram contains a parameter that is to be used as both an output and an input parameter, it would be unfortunate if, by an error in programming, the value of the constant were changed. Storing the value of the constant in a temporary storage location instead of giving a direct reference to the actual location of the constant will prevent this possibility.

When a function reference is noted in the input string, the generator must take special actions in order to regard that reference as a single value. In particular, it may not be necessary to compile the linkage instructions to the function immediately. The entry in TEO may then be the pseudo-operator F, standing for "function," together with a pointer to the name of the function, which has been placed in TEA. The function name may then be regarded as a "placeholder" for the operand which will be the value of the function after evaluation. The key to the evaluation of the function will be the entry in TEO of the pseudo-operator F.

In the processing of expressions, the recognition of a function reference is "triggered" by the recognition of the syntactic string <*name*> which will initiate a look-up operation over SYMTAB to determine the type of reference being made. Provided that compilation is being performed over a valid program, SYMTAB can return one of only two possible responses: function reference or array element reference. Let us assume that SYMTAB returns a symbolic reply, F or A, meaning *f*unction or *a*rray. The ASCAN generator should then enter this reply into the next available location in the TEO list, add the function (or array) name to TEA, attach a pointer to this TEA entry, increment the bias by 10 for the recognition of the opening left parenthesis, and then continue to scan the statement. At this point we have taken similar actions irrespective of whether SYMTAB reported back to the recognition of either a function or array element reference. In the table of hierarchies of operators, we shall place functions (and subscripting calculations) in such a position as to precede execution of all other operators, that is, according to the table on page 325, level 6.

However, prior to the evaluation of a function (or the identification of an element of an array through subscripting calculations) it is necessary to evaluate the arguments of the function reference.

Each argument expression in a function reference (or subscript expression in an array element reference) is independent of the remainder of the expression in which it is enclosed and each must be evaluated independently. Normally, we have assumed that the right-hand end delimiter of an expression forces all compilation necessary, but in this case it is necessary to have a special delimiter for this enclosed expression. This type of delimiter is provided in the language by the separators between arguments (or subscripts). In FORTRAN this is the symbol "," which we shall regard as a special end delimiter and operator.

Within each list of arguments (or subscripts) it is necessary that the separator force the compilation of code relevant to the expression which it delimits to the left (assuming a left to right scan) without necessarily forcing the evaluation of the function (or array element subscripting) itself. Thus the hierarchical place of the separator should be such as to force all other operators. However, it must be recognized that a separator only occurs in expressions when surrounded by parentheses (see page 119) and thus is affected by the current bias value. This bias was itself incremented by the opening left parenthesis of the list of expressions, and thus the minimum effective value of the level of a separator is the value of the bias. If a separator is given the same hierarchial value of the expression delimiters (⊢ and ⊣), then within an expression list all operators of higher hierarchical value will be forced into compilation without affecting the compilation of the function (or subscripting operation).

The forcing of compilation of operators by a separator works only for those expressions which lie to the left (in a left-to-right scan) of the separator. It is common practice not to include a separator after the last expression in the list, the termination of the list being signified by the closing (right) parenthesis. It would be possible to arrange for the **ASCAN** routine to match up parenthesis pairs so that the closing right parenthesis of a function (or array element) reference could be identified. This would set this particular type of use of a closing parenthesis off from that of the use of parentheses for affecting the normal hierarchy of expressions. Let us regard this process as introducing just one more exception to the rules and thus attempt to solve the problem without a special action. Normally the recognition of a closing right parenthesis does not affect the construction of the scanning tables but merely affects the current value of the bias. If this same procedure were to be followed in the case of a function (or array element) reference, then *any* operator outside and to the right of the reference will force the compilation of the last expression in the list.

The conditions under which an operand must be transferred to a temporary storage location within the evaluation of the list of arguments of a function reference (or subscript expressions in an array element reference) differ from those defined for the "normal" expression. Since the linkage to a routine is accomplished by a list of argument addresses, no arguments are passed through the use of the accumulator. Thus when the compilation of a function reference is being performed, the existence of any argument in the accumulator must be remedied by a store into a temporary storage location. However, it is obvious that whenever a separator is forcing the compilation of an expression, the result must be placed in a temporary storage location, irrespective of any other subsequent compilation steps. Further, since a separator is not a true operator, but merely a forcing operator, it is never to be placed into the **TEO** list of the scanning table. When the separator no longer forces compilation, (that is, its current hierarchical level is not less than or equal to that of the last entry in **TEO**), the contents of the accumulator should be stored in the next available temporary storage location, the separator removed from the in-hand register, and scanning continued as normally. Again, the absence of a separator after the list will not trigger this latter action and thus clean up of the storage of the last argument of the list must be undertaken by the generator of the **F** (or **A**) operator.

Consider the following examples of scanning, analysis and code generation. First,

$$\vdash \mathbf{A = B + BL(X)/C} \dashv$$

The organization of the scanning table proceeds normally until the following condition is achieved:

TEA	*TEO*	*Level*	*In hand*
A	⊢	0	
B	=	1	
ptr → **BL**	+	2	
X	**F**	6	/(3)

At this point the table shows that the **SYMTAB** routine returned the code "**F**" in response to the inquiry regarding the status of the name string **BL** and that the scanning routine added a pointer to that name in **TEA**. At this point in the scan, the operator "/" is forcing the compilation of the operator "**F**." The general form of code generated by the compilation of the function reference is to be

```
MPT  funct
DA   arg1
DA   arg2
...
DC   ≠
```

where *funct* is the address (possibly indirect) of the entry point to the function subprogram, and the arg_i are the addresses of the arguments of the function reference.

Examining the present contents of **TEA** it will be noted that the last entry to which there is a pointer and all succeeding entries match exactly with the operands of the instructions to be generated. That is, the code to be generated by the compilation of the operand "**F**" will be

```
MPT  BL
DA   X
DC   ≠
```

Assuming that each subprogram of the function type returns the value of the function through the accumulator, then the tables will be reduced to

TEA	*TEO*	*Level*	*In hand*
A	⊢	0	
B	=	1	
ACC	+	2	/(3)

and since the operator "/" does not force further compilation, scanning can continue to the right and the remainder of the statement scanned and eventually compiled.

To show that the presence of two functions (with their associated pointers) does not affect the procedures and that there is no ambiguity in deciding which pointer to use, consider the example:

$$\vdash A = B + B1(B2(X))/C \dashv$$

where both **B1** and **B2** have been identified as functions, possibly by their absence from the **DIMENSION** statement of the program. Scanning from the left as usual, the tables develop to the state

TEA	*TEO*	*Level*	*In hand*
A	⊢	0	
B	=	1	
ptr → B1	+	2	
ptr → B2	F	6	
X	F	16	/(3)

at which point the compilation of the code related to the operator "F" is being forced. By the same scheme as utilized in the previous example, the operands up to and including that indicated by the *last* pointer are mapped into the skeleton code;

```
MPT  B2
DA   X
DC   ≠
```

and the tables are reduced to

TEA	*TEO*	*Level*	*In hand*
A	⊢	0	
B	=	1	
ptr → B1	+	2	
ACC	F	6	/(3)

At this point, the operator "F" is being forced. However, one of the arguments of the function, as identified by those elements of TEA "below" the entry identified by the last pointer, is in the accumulator (ACC) and must be placed in temporary storage before the code related to the function linkage is generated. Thus the code generated by the compilation of the function will be

```
STO  τ1
MPT  B1
DA   τ1
DC   ≠
```

and the table is reduced to

TEA	*TEO*	*Level*	*In hand*
A	⊢	0	
B	=	1	
ACC	+	2	/(3)

after which, compilation continues normally.

The compilation of expression which are arguments of a function is exemplified in the following case;

$$\vdash \text{A} = \text{CB}(\text{X} + \text{Y}) - \text{D} \dashv$$

The scanning table develops to the point

	TEA	*TEO*	*Level*	*In hand*
	A	⊢	0	
ptr →	CB	=	1	
	X	F	6	
	Y	+	12	−(2)

The operator "−" now forces compilation related to the operator "+," generating the code sequence

```
LDA  Y
ADD  X
```

and the table is reduced to

	TEA	*TEO*	*Level*	*In hand*
	A	⊢	0	
ptr →	CB	=	1	
	ACC	F	6	−(2)

At this point, the operator "F" is forced, but one of the arguments is in the accumulator. Temporarily storing this value, the code generated will be

```
STO  τ1
MPT  CB
DA   τ1
DC   ≠
```

Let us now consider the case of multiple arguments with the example

$$\vdash \text{A} = \text{FUNCT}(\text{X} + \text{Y},\text{P}/2.) \dashv$$

Using the same procedures as before, the scanning table develops until the following state is achieved;

	TEA	*TEO*	*Level*	*In hand*
	A	⊢	0	
ptr →	FUNCT	=	1	
	X	F	6	
	Y	+	12	,(10)

The operator "," now forces the compilation of the "+" operator, thus generating the code

```
LDA  Y
ADD  X
```

and reducing the scanning table to

	TEA	TEO	*Level*	*In hand*
	A	⊢	0	
ptr →	FUNCT	=	1	
	ACC	F	6	,(10)

At this point the operator "," forces no further compilation and thus the value of the expression must be stored temporarily,

```
STO  τ1
```

updating the scanning table to

	TEA	TEO	*Level*	*In hand*
	A	⊢	0	
ptr →	FUNCT	=	1	
	τ_1	F	6	

where the operator "," has been discarded. Continuing the scanning process, the next argument expression is scanned and the table is formed to the point

	TEA	TEO	*Level*	*In hand*
	A	⊢	0	
ptr →	FUNCT	=	1	
	τ_1	F	6	
	P	/	13	
	C(2.)			⊣(0)

where C(2.) is the storage location of the constant 2. Compilation of the expression P/2. is now forced

```
LDA   C(2.)
RDIV  P
```

and the table is reduced to

	TEA	TEO	*Level*	*In hand*
	A	⊢	0	
ptr →	FUNCT	=	1	
	τ_1	F	6	
	ACC			⊣(0)

the operator "F" being forced into the compilation process by the in hand operator. Before compiling the linkage code to the function, it is observed that one of the arguments is in the accumulator and must be stored in a temporary location, say location τ_2. Thus the generator will produce the code

```
STO  τ2
MPT  FUNCT
DA   τ1
DA   τ2
DC   ≠
```

and the table will be reduced to

TEA	TEO	*Level*	*In hand*
A	⊢	0	
ACC	=	1	⊣(0)

It may be deduced from the foregoing scanning and compilation procedures that the need to store a value into a temporary location can be recognized by examining only the *last* (the very last) entry in TEA. That is, since we have included a temporary storage action in the generator related to the forcing operator, there exists a possibility of only the rightmost (last scanned) argument being retained in the accumulator, since no special discriminator was included to distinguish the closing right parenthesis of a function argument list from that of a hierarchial arithmetic expression group, and no special element was added to the generator related to storing the contents of the accumulator before compiling the function linkage.

TO COMPILE OR NOT?

The solution to the problem of when to evaluate a function or determine the address of an element of an array can affect the efficiency of the resultant object code. In the scanning system utilizing the tables which we considered previously, the pseudo-operator "F" was given the hierarchial level 6, thus forcing the compilation of the linkage code prior to the compilation of code relevant to other operators. On this basis, the result of the evaluation of a function reference or the determination of the location of an array element may have to be stored temporarily while other operations are performed. For example,

$$\vdash \mathrm{A} = \mathrm{F}(\mathrm{X},\mathrm{Y},\mathrm{Z}) + \mathrm{B} * \mathrm{C} \dashv$$

would be compiled into the instruction sequence

```
MPT  F
DA   X
DA   Y
DA   Z
DC   ≠
STO  τ1
LDA  C
MUL  B
ADD  τ1
STO  A
```

On the other hand, if some technique could be developed which would regard a function reference as a simple variable until its value is essential to the continued evaluation of the expression, the code sequence generated would be

```
LDA  C
MUL  B
STO  τ1
MPT  F
DA   X
DA   Y
DA   Z
DC   ≠
ADD  τ1
STO  A
```

This sequence contains *exactly* the same number of executable instructions as that in which the function was evaluated at the instant it was recognized by the compiler. No advantage has been gained by the inclusion of (yet undefined) delaying code in the compiler so as to require evaluation of the function only when absolutely necessary. Similarly, inclusion of array element references in an expression would require separate evaluation procedures apart from the expression in which they are embedded thus requiring the use of temporary storage locations and the associated store and load instructions.

We shall consider this problem further in relation to the compilation of the code necessary to generate the location of an array element.

SUBSCRIPTED VARIABLES[4]

Before considering the actual inclusion of subscripted variables in an arithmetic statement which is to be compiled, two points should be noted:

1. Subscripted variables are not peculiar in an arithmetic statement. They play the same part as any simple variable. In other words, subscripted variables vary from simple variables in their notation but not in their use.

2. The computation required to locate the address of a subscripted variable (or in purer mathematical terms, to locate the element of an array), is dependent on the dimensions of the whole array in which the element is located.

When a **DIMENSION** statement is located in a program, not only is space reserved for that array but also information is generated which aids the compilation of instructions to generate the address of the particular element under consideration. As a review of this procedure (described in Chapter 5), consider a two-dimensioned array specified in the statement:

DIMENSION A(5,3)

and a reference in an executable statement to the element A(2,2). At the time the storage for A is set up in **SYMTAB**, the address of the base of A (that is, the fictitious element A(0,0)) is computed and is available to the compiler at the time when the instructions to locate the particular element are generated. The location of A(2,2) may be computed from the expression

Address(A(2,2)) = Address(Base of A) − (2*5 + 2)

4. In this discussion, it is assumed that the object time memory layout is such that all data are stored in high order memory, with elements of arrays placed in descending locations. Such a practice has not been followed in IBM System/360, where arrays are stored in ascending storage locations. See IBM form No. C28-6515-4, IBM System/360, FORTRAN IV Language.

Further, the formulas must be amended when either the data being referenced are stored in multiple word blocks (for double precision or complex data) or the computer on which the compiler is being implemented is character rather than word oriented.

In general, if one is presented with a **DIMENSION** statement containing the specification

$$\text{DIMENSION A}(d_1, d_2, d_3, \cdots d_N)$$

and wishes to refer to any element

$$\text{A}(s_1, s_2, s_3, \cdots s_N)$$

then one must evaluate the expression

$$\text{Address(A(1,1,1,} \cdots 1)) - (s_1 - 1) - d_1 (s_2 - 1) - d_1 d_2 (s_3 - 1) - d_1 d_2 d_3 (s_4 - 1) - \cdots - d_1 d_2 d_3 \cdots d_{N-1} (s_N - 1)$$

That is,

$$\text{Address(A}(s_1, s_2, s_3, \cdots s_N)) = \text{Address(A(1,1,1,} \cdots 1)) - \sum_{i=1}^{N} \{\prod_{k=0}^{i-1} d_k\}(s_i - 1)$$

where it is assumed that $d_0 = 1$. Since the coefficients of the product will be required each time a subscripted variable address is to be calculated, one should calculate this product when the **DIMENSION** statement is encountered, rather than leave it for the individual generators to calculate.

If $\quad p_i = \prod_{k=0}^{i-1} d_k \quad$ and $\quad p_1 = 1$

then $\quad p_{i+1} = d_i p_i, \quad$ for $\quad 1 < i \leqslant (N-1)$

and hence

$$\text{Address of element} = \text{Address(A(1,1,1,} \cdots 1)) - \sum_{i=1}^{N} p_i (s_i - 1)$$

That is,

$$\text{Address of element} = \text{Address(A(1,1,1,} \cdots 1)) + \sum_{i=1}^{N} p_i - \sum_{i=1}^{N} p_i s_i$$

Now since the terms

$$\text{Address(A(1,1,1,} \cdots 1)) \qquad \text{and} \qquad \sum_{i=1}^{N} p_i$$

are constants, they may be combined into a single constant term which is computable at the time that the **DIMENSION** statement is under cosideration. This is the constant that was referred to as the **BASE** of the array in Chapter 5. In fact, the address of the **BASE** of an array is also the address of the fictitious element **A(0,0,0, . . . ,0)**.

The algorithm for determining the address of the array element may be incorporated into a single subprogram which is "called" when the subscripting calculations are to be executed. Conversely, subscripting calculations may be compiled in-line with the code for the evaluation of the expression in which the array element reference is contained. Since an array element reference has the same syntactic form as function reference, let us primarily consider the compilation of linkages to a subscripting subprogram. We shall assume that this subprogram has been written to the same specifications as were imposed on the function subprograms considered in the last section:

1. Linkage is of the skeletal form

```
MPT  SUBSCR
DA   arg1
DA   arg2
...
...
DC   ≠
```

2. It is the responsibility of the subprogram to access the arguments provided,

3. The resulting address is returned to the calling program through the accumulator.

Let us follow the same procedures as were established for the compilation of a function reference, to the point at which subscripting function operator is forced into the compilation process. Consider

$$\vdash A = B + C(I+3,J) \dashv$$

As previously, recognizing the left parenthesis as a bias-incremental operator and the comma as a terminating operator with the same hierarchical value as the statement delimiter, the tables are built to the point

	TEA	TEO	*Level*	*In hand*
	A	⊢	0	
	B	=	1	
ptr →	C	+	2	
	I	A	6	
	3	+	12	,(10)

where the operator "A" is provided by the **SYMTAB** routine. At this point, the operator "," forces the compilation of the subscript expression I+3 as the sequence

```
ENA   3
ADD   I
STO   τ1
```

where the storage of the result into a temporary location is a standard part of the generation process associated with the operator "," and the table is reduced to

	TEA	TEO	*Level*	*In hand*
	A	⊢	0	
	B	=	1	
ptr →	C	+	2	
	τ_1	A	6	

Continuing the scanning process, the operand J is added to **TEA** and the closing operator ⊣ becomes the "in hand" operator and the subscripting operator "A" is forced into the compilation process. The subscripting routine (be it in line or a subprogram) requires, as its arguments, not only the values of the subscripts but also the products of the dimensions p_i and the address of the fictitious element C(0,0,0, . . . ,0). It is assumed that this information is available as a stream of addresses in the symbol table which is accessible to the code generator through the entry in **TEA** which is indicated by the pointer. Let us assume that this list is in the order:

Base address
p_1
p_2
. . .
. . .
p_N

Now it is not this list which is to be transmitted to the subscripting routine but rather, the addresses of these values. Thus, it is necessary that this list be placed in the object time data table. Obviously, if an array is declared in the program there is an excellent possibility that this list will be needed in the program and thus the compiler can arrange to have the list placed in the object time data table at the instant of recognizing the declaration rather than waiting for an element reference.

In the following code sequences, we shall assume that p_i refers to the address of the constant p_i and **BASE** to the location of the address of the base element of the array. This list of addresses takes the place of the entry in **TEA** indicated by the pointer. Thus the generation of code related to the pseudo-operator "A" can produce the sequence

```
MPT  SUBSCR
DA   BASE
DA   p1
DA   p2
...
...
DC   ≠
DA   s1
DA   s2
...
...
DC   ≠
```

where the s_i are the subscript value locations. Two "stoppers" are necessary in this sequence since the number of dimensions (or subscripts) is not included in the argument list, the first "stopper" acting as a separator between the dimension products and the subscripts. This scheme has the advantage that the mapping from the list of addresses of dimension products and the list of subscripts is a linear sequential system. However, this organization requires that the subprogram "take in" at least all the dimension products before any calculation can be performed in the process of evaluating the array element address. This may place an almost intolerable burden on the subprogram.

Thus a little more work in the compiler can save object-time work space and possibly time. By interleaving the dimension products and the subscripts, it would be possible for the subprogram to evaluate the location of the array element using only one local storage location for an argument and one temporary storage location for the partial result. That is, the sequence

```
MPT  SUBSCR
DA   BASE
DA   p1
DA   s1
DA   p2
DA   s2
...
...
DA   pN
DA   sN
DC   ≠
```

Thus in the example above, if the corresponding **DIMENSION** statement specified the dimensions of the array **C** as **(5,2)**, then the sequence

```
MPT  SUBSCR
DA   BASE of C
DA   constant(1)
DA   τ1
DA   constant(5)
DA   J
DC   ≠
```

would be generated as the code for the evaluation of the address of the element **C(I+3,J)**.

At this point in the compilation process, the address (or location) of the array element has been computed and is, presumably, in the accumulator. In the process demonstrated, the contents of the **TEA** are utilized as addresses since the assembler of the generated code will replace operand symbols by addresses. However, in the case of an array element this address is not computed until object time and thus is not available to the assembler of the generated code. Hence, following the generation of the code for linkage to the subscripting subprogram (**SUBSCR**) the generator related to the pseudo-operator "**A**" must add the instruction

STO τ_n

and then the **TEA** be updated to include the indirect reference to this location. This we will signify by $-\tau_n$. Thus after the compilation of the code for the pseudo-operator "**A**" in the example under consideration, the tables are reduced to

TEA	TEO	*Level*	*In hand*
A	⊢	0	
B	=	1	
$-\tau_n$	+	2	⊣(0)

From this table, the following code will be generated:

```
LDA  −τn
ADD  B
STO  A
```

It would be possible for the subscripting routine (**SUBSCR**) to return the value contained in the array element location. However, it would be inefficient to provide two subscripting routines; one to provide the value currently assigned to the array element and one to provide the address of the array element. Further the necessity to distinguish between the two routines would add an additional burden on the compiler and require additional object time storage. Thus as far as the compiler is concerned the recognition of an array element reference in any statement leads to the same generator routine.

The use of a subprogram to perform the subscript calculations necessary to determine the address of an array element reference, can add additional features to the object time program which otherwise would be very expensive to provide. For example, the subprogram can provide checks on the values of subscripts and the inclusion in the domain of the array of the generated address. Although such checks are not usually provided in FORTRAN systems since the interaction between **DIMENSION**, **COMMON** and **EQUIVALENCE** will permit subscripting out of the specified ranges, other languages specifically prohibit such actions. For example, the declaration pair

```
DIMENSION A(1),I(10)
EQUIVALENCE(A(1),I(1))
```

provides a means by which the elements of a 10 element array can be referenced either as real mode or integer mode elements, provided that references to fictitious elements (the element A(2) through A(10) of A) are permitted.

As another example, consider the case where a table is to be established (for look-up during the program) which has keys which range from −5 to +5 in steps of 1 (that is, 11 elements). In ALGOL we could describe this array by the specification

array A[2,−5:5]

However, in FORTRAN it would be necessary to declare a pair of arrays and their equivalence so that a similar structure is created;

```
DIMENSION DUMMY(2,11),A(2,1)
EQUIVALENCE (DUMMY(1,7),A(1,1))
```

which results in the following mapping between the two arrays:

DUMMY(1, 1)		A(1,−5)
(2, 1)		(2,−5)
(1, 2)		(1,−4)
(2, 2)		(2,−4)
(1, 3)		(1,−3)
(2, 3)		(2,−3)
(1, 4)		(1,−2)
(2, 4)		(2,−2)
(1, 5)		(1,−1)
(2, 5)		(2,−1)
(1, 6)		(1, 0)
(2, 6)		(2, 0)
(1, 7)	⟷	(1, 1)
(2, 7)		(2, 1)
(1, 8)		(1, 2)
(2, 8)		(2, 2)
(1, 9)		(1, 3)
(2, 9)		(2, 3)
(1,10)		(1, 4)
(2,10)		(2, 4)
(1,11)		(1, 5)
(2,11)		(2, 5)

In BASIC, such aberrations are not permitted, since the language is much more restrictive due to its intended educational use. In running a BASIC program it would be expected that the programmer be informed that an error has occurred if (1) the subscript is out of the specified range, or (2) the address generated is not the specified range. If condition 1 is the key to error analysis, then obviously condition 2 is also satisfied when condition 1 is satisfied, but a situation can arise when condition 1 would result in an error message whilst condition 2 would not. That is, it is possible for there to exist a value of s_i outside the range 0 to d_i (assuming 0-based indexing) while the value of the expression

$$\sum_{i=1}^{N} \{\prod_{k=0}^{i-1} d_k\} \ (s_i - 1)$$

is inside the range 0 to $d_1 d_2 d_3 \cdots d_N$

The inclusion of these tests in line with the coding for the evaluation of the expression in which it is embedded would be very expensive in storage space.

Similarly, in the case of the implementation of a language system in which dynamic storage of arrays is permitted such that elements are added to an array as needed (for example, in APL), it is necessary that subscripting be performed by a subprogram, so that the need for additional storage may be recognized and provided for the available storage space.

Let us now consider the case where subscript calculations are to be performed in line rather than by a subprogram. So far, we have attempted to reduce the number of special cases to be recognized in an analyzer to a minimum. The opening parenthesis of a function or array element reference does not play the same part in an expression as an unattached parenthesis which is influencing the hierarchial level of the enclosed operators. However, we have chosen to take the same action within the compiler for an unattached parenthesis as for one associated with either a function or array element reference. Syntactically, the closing right parenthesis of a group should have the effect of forcing the compilation of the function or subscripting routine linkage. However, we treated this special parenthesis only as having an influence on the bias of the hierarchial level, a successor operator acting as the forcing operator. In regarding a subscript expression list as the argument list of the subscripting routine, the computation of the address of an array element reference differed only very slightly from the computation of the value of a function reference. When it is deemed necessary to compile subscripting calculations in line, it is necessary to ascribe a special meaning to the pseudo-operator of the comma.

Let us assume that the dimension products are stored in their negative form so that the calculation

$$\textbf{Base address} - \sum_{i=1}^{N} p_i \, s_i$$

can be performed without the necessity to use the operations of subtract or reverse sign. Let us assume further that **SYMTAB** provides pointers (addresses) to the object time storage location of the base address of the array and to the dimension products. When **SYMTAB** reports that the <*name*> accretion refers to an array, the code

```
ENA  BASE
STO  τ1
```

may be generated and then the entry in **TEA** is set to τ_1 whilst the entry in **TEO** is **A**. That is, in the previous example, the tables would be developed to the point

	TEA	TEO	*Level*	*In hand*
	A	⊢	0	
	B	=	1	
ptr →	C	+	2	
	I	A	6	
	3	+	12	,(10)

when the first operator is to be forced into compilation, although the code for transferring the base address to temporary storage was generated when the pseudo-operator "A" was recognized. As usual, the comma will generate code for the computation of the value of the subscript. In the case of a function reference the last action generated by the comma would be to store this partial result in a temporary storage location. However, for in line coding this is not necessary. Instead, the value of the subscript is to be multiplied by the corresponding dimension product and that result added to the contents of the temporary storage location. Thus the compilation of the code for the operator "+" is the sequence

```
ENA 3
ADD I
```

and then, because the operator "," is about to disappear and is facing the pseudo-operator "A" (instead of "F"), the code

MUL p_1

where the dimension multiplier p_1 is chosen from the symbol table by a special register, set up at the time that the array reference was recognized, which points to the next multiplier, and which after generation of the above MUL instruction should be incremented to point to the next element in the list. Depending on the type of system, the determination that the proper number of subscripts has been supplied can be performed at this point in the algorithm of generation. That is, if the end of the multiplier list is identified by a "stopper," then an attempt to use this value will indicate that too many subscripts have been provided, and the lack of a pointer to the stopper when the last subscript has been compiled will indicate that too few subscripts were provided.

After multiplying the subscript value by the dimension constant, the generated value must be added to the base address to develop the address of the array element:

ADD τ_1
STO τ_1

which instruction pair is also to be generated by the comma. The operand τ_1 was the last (and always will be) address in **TEA**.

This address is also to be retained in the **TEA** after which the comma is deleted from the in hand register and the scanning continues. When the right hand end delimiter forces the compilation of the pseudo-operator "A," the table is in the state:

	TEA	TEO	*Level*	*In hand*
	A	⊢	0	
	B	=	1	
ptr →	C	+	2	
	τ_1	A	6	⊣(0)
	J			

The generator of the operator "A" acts as a comma initially, generating the code for the evaluation of the last portion of the address of the array element:

LDA J
MUL p_2
ADD τ_1
STO τ_1

However, the process after this generation differs from that of the comma. The address of the location of the address of the array element is now to be placed in the **TEA** but in an indirect form. Thus the tables reduce to

TEA	TEO	*Level*	*In hand*
A	⊢	0	
B	=	1	
$-\tau_1$	+	2	⊣(0)

The remaining elements of the tables generate the code sequence

LDA $-\tau_1$
ADD B
STO A

This method of generation does not take advantage of the availability of index registers in the target computer. If code is to be generated to take advantage of index registers, then the algorithm of generation must be amended. The address which is to be influenced by the index register is the base address of the array. When the **SYMTAB** routine reports back that the string has been recognized as an array element reference, the **TEA** should be set to contain the base of the array, influenced by the chosen index register. At the same instant the next available temporary storage location should be preset to the value zero.

Thus at the point that the scanning pointer to the input string has advanced to the first character of the first subscript expression, the tables have been developed to the state

	TEA	TEO	*Level*	*In hand*
	A	⊢	0	
	B	=	1	
ptr →	C,2	+	2	
		A	6	

where the chosen index register is 2, and it is assumed that a reference to **C** by the assembler will result in the substitution of the base address of the array **C**, and the code generated so far is:

```
ENA  =0
STO  τ1
```

The generation of code relative to the pseudo-operator "," is the same in this algorithm as in the case previously considered, that is, when the comma forces no further operators and the operator exposed in **TEO** is "A," generate the sequence

```
LDA  si
MUL  pi
ADD  τ1
STO  τ1
```

Further when the pseudo-operator "A" is forced, then the same code as for the comma is generated with the exception that instead of storing the result back into the temporary storage location, the result should be placed in the index register, that is,

```
LDA   s_N
MUL   p_N
ADD   τ1
LDR   ACC,2
```

LDR stands for "load register." Following this generation, the pseudo-operator "A" is removed from **TEO** and scanning of the input string continues.

In the compilation of any general expression, the problem of deciding when to compute the addresses of references to elements of an array cannot be solved, either simply or uniquely. Whenever a subscript evaluation is required, the existing contents of the accumulator must be stored. Consequently, it is not always efficient to attempt to evaluate subscript expressions within the computation of the value of the containing expression. For example, the expression:

A(I,J) = B(I,K+3)*C(L) + A(I,J−1)

would compile, without subscript evaluation, to the sequence:

```
LDA   C(L)
MUL   B(I,K+3)
ADD   A(I,J−1)
STO   A(I,J)
```

Suppose that the arrays mentioned above are described in the statement:

DIMENSION A(5,3), B(10,2), C(25)

then by the process described here, where subscript calculations are placed in the code sequence where they fall according to the hierarchical rules established, then the code sequence generated would be:

```
ENA   0
STO   τ1
LDA   I
MUL   Constant(−1)
ADD   τ1
STO   τ1
LDA   J
MUL   Constant(−5)
ADD   τ1
LDR   ACC,1
ENA   0
STO   τ2
```

```
LDA  I
MUL  Constant(−1)
ADD  τ2
STO  τ2
ENA  3
ADD  K
MUL  Constant(−10)
ADD  τ2
LDR  ACC,2
ENA  0
STO  τ3
LDA  L
MUL  Constant(−1)
ADD  τ3
LDR  ACC,3
LDA  C,3
MUL  B,2
STO  τ4
ENA  0
STO  τ5
LDA  I
MUL  Constant(−1)
ADD  τ5
STO  τ5
ENA  1
SUB  J
RVS
MUL  Constant(−5)
ADD  τ5
LDR  ACC,4
LDA  A,4
ADD  τ4
STO  A,1
```

Apart from the computation of the adjustment to the base address for each array element reference, this sequence differs from the sequence above by only two instructions—the **STO** τ_4 which is forced into the sequence after the calculation of the term

B(I,K+3) * C(L)

since it is necessary to compute the location of A(I,J−1) before the next operation can be performed, and its corresponding load.

On the other hand, if all subscript calculations had been performed before the code for the evaluation of the expression had been generated, these extra instructions would be saved. The code sequence above does not take into account any saving on the use of either temporary storage locations or index registers. In fact, this code could have been developed using only two temporary storage locations and three index registers. However, if all subscripting had been evaluated prior to the evaluation of the basic expression then four index registers would have been required (one for each array element reference) and one temporary storage location.

The use of index registers for adjusting base addresses of arrays in order to locate a single element within the array is satisfactory until the computer runs out of index registers. At worst, when one has an expression containing no parenthesized expressions (apart from those defining subscripts) and subscript adjustments are saved until all subscripts have been evaluated, five index registers, at the most, will be required. That is, the worst case would be an expression of the form:

$$\underset{1}{A_i} = \underset{2}{B_j} + C_k * \underset{4}{D_l} \uparrow \underset{5}{E_m}$$

where, according to the forcing techniques of the above system, all adjusted addresses are computed before the total "main line" expression is evaluated. However, when parentheses are included it is possible for an unlimited number of registers to be required. For example, the expression

$$A_i = B_j + (C_k + (D_l + (E_m + (F_n + (\cdots$$

would be prepared in the tables in such a manner that each subscript would be evaluated as it occurred with the associated operator being forced and thus denying the use of that index register for other purposes.

For a complete description of the efficient use of index registers and the use of a limited number of registers in the compilation algorithm, see Horwitz et al.[5]

Besides the concern for the efficient use of index registers related to the compilation of array element references, a certain amount of improvement of code can be achieved by evaluating the addresses of array elements with constant subscripts at compile time rather than at execution time. Similarly, the adjustment of the base address by the

5. L. P. Horwitz et al., "Index Register Allocation," *Jour. ACM*, vol. 13, no. 1 (Jan. 1966): 43–61.

constant *part* of a subscript may save some operations, at the cost of compile-time recognition and manipulation procedures.

If the subscript expressions are restricted to the standard form, that is,

*<integer constant>***<integer variable>*{+|−}*<integer constant>*

then all the computations required to compute the address of any element may be performed with the use of only one temporary storage location. In particular, if the computer being used at object time has index registers, the result of the computation of

$$-\sum_{i=1}^{N} p_i$$

may be placed in an available index register, and then the instruction that references that particular element will have the operand address of the base of the array that is influenced by that index register.

In general, a subscript, irrespective of its form, that is standard (c*v±k) or nonstandard (any expression that results in an integer value), may be broken down to the form:

<variable expression> ± *<constant expression>*

where the *<variable expression>* contains not only variables but also any associated multipliers or divisors that are constants. That is, the subscript

(3*I + 32/J)*4 + 32

contains the *<variable expression>*

(3*I + 32/J)*4

and the *<constant expression>* +32.

If all subscripts are broken down in this manner, the address of a subscripted variable may be computed from

$$\text{Address(base of array)} - \sum_{i=1}^{N} p_i\, c_i - \sum_{i=1}^{N} p_i\, v_i$$

where c_i is the *<constant expression>* of the subscript s_i, and v_i is the *<variable expression>* of the subscript s_i. At compile time, in the subscript evaluation generator, the base of the array may be further adjusted by the term

$$-\sum_{i=1}^{N} p_i\, c_i$$

thus saving valuable execution time.

If one considers only standard subscripts, it can be seen that the first subscript may easily be separated into its two parts: The instructions to compute the <*variable expression*> may be placed into the object time coding, and the value of the <*constant expression*> then may be evaluated and the result applied to the base address of the array to produce an adjusted base for modification at object time. If this first subscript is also the only subscript needed to refer to an element of the array, instructions to store the resultant element address in a chosen index register may be generated. In fact, this set of instructions will be generated whenever a closing parenthesis of a subscripting set is encountered. On locating any delimiting comma or the closing parenthesis, instructions to multiply the value of the variable portion of the subscript by the p_i value must be generated. To enable the performance of this operation, the constants p_1 to p_N must be stored in the object time data table. At the same time, the value of the constant portion of the subscript must be applied, along with the associated multiplying factor, to the adjusted base.

TEMPORARY STORAGE LOCATIONS

The provision of temporary storage locations is truly the task of the symbol table routines but since such provisions are needed by the ASCAN generator, the problem will be considered here. Firstly, the question of how many temporary locations to reserve cannot be answered definitively. Some programs never need a temporary storage location, whereas others need a comparatively large number, especially when such locations are used in the subscripting calculations. Secondly, the compiler implementer must decide whether temporary locations are to be provided from a previously reserved array or from randomly chosen words. Thirdly, the implementer must decide whether or not it is necessary to preserve memory and thus to reuse temporary storage locations as they become free—that is, whether within a single statement a single storage location should be used wherever possible.

Since one cannot determine the exact (or maximum) number of storage locations that will be needed in a program, implementers, who constantly strive for maximum available storage for the person who uses the system, prefer not to set aside a specific section of available memory for temporary storage locations. To reserve memory just in case it has a use seems pointless. Thus the technique of selecting temporary storage locations from an array is discarded in favor of selection of storage as and when it is needed. Further, since FORTRAN and most other algebraic languages consist of a system of discrete statements, as a minimum requirement, temporary storage locations may be recovered before the execution of each statement.

Let us propose the following technique. If a routine requests a temporary storage location, a new location should be chosen by the symbol table routine as if the request were for the storage of a regular variable or constant. However, at the same time, the **SYMTAB** routine should record this reserval in a special table and note that this location is in use. In the event that there have been previous requests, during the current compilation, for temporary storage locations, this table can be checked for any that are not in use; if available, a previously used location is preferable to the reserval of another memory word.

Once a temporary storage location has been allocated in a single compilation, it should be reserved for the whole program and reused whenever possible. Thus all temporary locations are "freed" when the compilation of a single statement is completed. However, **ASCAN** should also report the freeing of a temporary location during a scan if space is to be conserved. Thus the same location may be used more than once in a single statement.

By fixing the **SYMTAB** location of the first entry referring to a temporary location, a linked list may be formed for sequential scanning whenever a location is needed or is being freed. If the **SYMTAB** routine provides the compile time address of the temporary storage location data to the requesting routine, a storage area may be freed without a sequential scan of the whole threaded list. The **SYMTAB** entry may take the form:

Tag	*Object time address*	*Compile time forward link*	*In use tag*

The use of temporary storage locations within a subprogram must not conflict with the storage locations being used in the calling program. That is, since a **CALL** statement may include expressions that involve the use of a temporary storage location for the transference of the value, the subprogram must not, at any point, use these same locations. If all temporary locations are regenerated when compilation of each new statement begins, then the maximum number of temporary accumulators in use by a **CALL** statement is equal to the number of arguments. Thus if the calling program has used n temporary storage locations, numbered, for example, from 1 to n and the called subprogram requires k arguments, then (provided $k < n$) the subprogram should not use temporary storage locations 1 to k, but those from $k+1$ to n will be available. If the number of temporary storage locations used by the calling program is less than the number of parameters of the subprogram, then a complete new set of locations will be required.

Problem

7.4 Write a FORTRAN program that will compute the numerical value of numerical expressions that contain no parentheses. Each expression will be punched into a data card in the **FORMAT(8(A1,F8.3))** where the first alphabetic field may be only a unary operator or a blank. All other alphabetic fields will be binary operators or blank. However, a blank binary operator is to be considered as an end code. No data will be punched in cols. 73–80. Such a data card might take the form

```
+ΔΔΔ5.000*ΔΔ20.000+0003.715/0000.001
↑
Col. 1
```

where Δ signifies a blank column. Since only one column is allocated to an operator and the up arrow is not a standard element of a key punch, the involution operator (**) will be replaced by the alphabetic character **E**. The program should output the result in the **FORMAT(8(A1,F8.3),1H=,E16.8)** where the input string is duplicated into the first 72 columns. The program should check for division by zero and other execution errors within its control such as raising a negative value to a fractional power. Note that due to the **FORMAT** chosen, each piece of data may contain its sign, so that the input string

```
--0012.000E-1271.972*-1736.000
```

is valid.

8
Control Statements

Within most programming languages there exists an implicit execution order of statements corresponding to the physical ordering of the statements. Superimposed on this is the set of explicit instructions which either define a new starting point for a sequential order of execution, describe a new sequence to be inserted at this point, or delimit a sequence of instructions which are to be executed a number of times under some set of controls. Specifically we may refer to these classes of instructions as **branching, subprogram reference,** and **loop control**. Essentially, the latter two forms of sequence control can be implemented by the use of simple branching instructions combined with "regular" instructions which operate over the data elements rather than the program instructions. That is, if we accept that the fundamental branching instruction is of the form

if <*relational expression*> **then** <*statement*> **else** <*statement*>

where a <*statement*> may include a simple unconditional branch (**go to** <*label*>) then both subprogram references (with all the intricacies of parameter passing which we will consider in detail later) and loop control can be simulated. In fact, the code compiled from higher-level language elements such as subprogram reference and loop control, where the target language does not include specifically designed instructions for those purposes, must be a simulation of these language elements rather than their mere translation.

Based on these concepts we shall omit detailed discussion of the compilation of subprogram references (including parameter passing) until Chapter 10. However, we shall assume that linkages to run-time routines are achieved by the use of one of the various address passing schemes (MPT, JMS or ENA/B) outlined in Chapter 7.

STATEMENT IDENTIFIERS

Since the compilation of control statements is heavily dependent on the acquisition of data from the symbol table with respect to the identifiers associated with statements (occasionally referred to as *labels*), let us review the various alternatives available to the implementer for the acquisition and maintenance of data relevant to statement identifiers. Further, since the severest case will be found in the implementation of one-pass systems, all others being somewhat simpler to handle, let us examine closely the one-pass implementation schemes. For the purposes of this discussion however, we shall limit ourselves to FORTRAN-like languages where there is no question of the environment or scope of a label, except in the case of ASSIGN (and consequently in assigned GO TO) within subprograms. The scope of labels in block-structured environments will be discussed later.

On encountering a statement identifier as the prefix to a statement, and hence being in the position to relate the identifier and its statement which may be considered to be statement identifier definition, the symbol table entry corresponding to the label will be constructed so as to contain:

1. a statement identifier tag (to distinguish the entry);
2. a representation of the identifier;
3. the object time address of the first instruction compiled from the associated statement; and
4. a tag to indicate that the statement has been encountered; that is, that (3) contains the actual address of the first instruction in the compiled version of the statement.

Where the first reference to a statement identifier occurs in a statement which physically precedes the statement in which the identifier is defined, then the symbol table entry can be partially created. That is, elements 1 and 2 can be constructed permanently but the data for elements 3 and 4 are not available. In a one-pass system, where such a reference almost certainly implies that a jump or branch instruction is to be compiled immediately, it will be necessary to allocate a location through which the branch can be made indirectly. Thus element 3 of the symbol table entry will contain the address of the cell which will contain the actual address of the first word compiled from the referenced statement. To indicate this alternative entry, element 4 is set to indicate that element 3 contains an indirect address.

At the time that the actual statement which defines the statement identifier is encountered, element 4 should be examined; if (4) contains a direct address tag, then the statement identifier is doubly defined and thus an appropriate error message should be issued. If there is no symbol table entry corresponding to the statement identifier then this is obviously the first occurrence or reference to the label and hence the symbol entry must be created. On the other hand, if there exists a symbol table entry in which element 4 is set to the indirect address tag value, then provision must be made for the loader to insert the actual first instruction address of the compiled statement into the reserved location whose address is stored in element 3. At the same time, the first instruction address can be inserted into element 3 and element 4 updated accordingly.

It is important to make it clear at this point that there is no semantic difference between a statement identifier which has the same syntax as an integer and one which is syntactically identical with a variable. However, it is equally important to clearly distinguish between a statement identifier and an identifier (variable) which may take a statement identifier as a value. That is, for example a system must be able to distinguish between **go to** L3 where L3 is a statement identifier and **go to** L3 where L3 is an identifier whose currently associated value is the statement identifier (say) L3! Similarly, a system should be able to determine the semantic meaning of

```
H :=   3
go to  H
```

in a language which permits numeric statement identifiers (such as in a conversational system where the system provides line numbers) as contrasted with

```
H :=   L3
go to  H
```

in a language in which labels are alphanumeric. Most of these situations occur because of a lack of control in language development which has caused ambiguities, or potential ambiguities which are resolved by context free syntactic constructions. For example, if an analyzer is to distinguish between H := 3 where 3 is a statement identifier and H := 3 where 3 is an integer numeric representation, some clue as to the intent must be provided in the language for use by the programmer. In such a case, either an entirely separate statement is provided (as in FORTRAN by the use of the ASSIGN statement) or a tag is added to clearly identify the type of the element; such as H := **label**(3). We shall assume here that the language specifications are sufficient to distinguish between these various alternatives.

Further, for the purposes of discussion here we shall omit discussion of the scope of labels (as in block structured environments), the problems of locating a referenced label being equivalent to the problems of locating a referenced identifier. The latter topic will be discussed in some detail in Chapter 10.

UNCONDITIONAL BRANCHES

Let us now consider the compilation of the unconditional or assigned GO TO statements. That is, the statements

<GO TO statement> :=

GO TO $\{$*<statement number>*|*<variable>*$\}_1^1$

In a backward reference in a one-pass compiler, the form of the compiled instruction depends on the previous encounter of the statement number. In this case, the instruction may be compiled as[1]

B Address(n)

where Address(n) is the actual object time address of the first instruction compiled from the statement labelled n.

Where the reference is forward, we may compile

B −Data(n)

where Data(n) is the address of the object time data word that contains the actual address of the statement labeled n, and the minus sign preceding the address portion of the symbolic instruction indicates indirect addressing.

Alternatively, in a forward reference the compiled instruction in a one-pass system may be left blank (or filled with any arbitrary address) and then be overlaid with the actual address by the loader

1. B is the mnemonic for BRANCH or unconditional JUMP.

routine. To accomplish this, it would be necessary to append a list of addresses of incomplete instructions to the preliminary entry in the symbol table containing the data on the statement number. The acceptability of such a procedure depends on considerations of available memory at compile time, a specialized loader and extra loading time, or simply the extra cost of implementation.

In the case of the assigned GO TO statement, the instruction must always be compiled as an indirect branch, since the address can never be determined at compile time; hence GO TO α compiles to

B −Data(α)

where Data(α) is the object time address of the variable α.

While considering the assigned GO TO statement, let us consider the ASSIGN statement. The general form is

<ASSIGN statement> :=
ASSIGN*<statement number>*TO*<simple integer variable>*

Where the referenced statement has already been encountered, we may compile

```
ENA  Address(n)
STO  i
```

where Address(n) is the object time address of the first word in the referenced statement. In the case of a forward reference we must use a data table reserved word, which will be filled with the address of the referenced statement at load time, to compile:

```
LDA  Data(n)
STO  i
```

An interesting situation may occur in systems that permit the assigned GO TO statement and have subprogram capabilities. If a statement number has been assigned to an integer variable, then that variable may be used as an argument in a FORTRAN subprogram CALL. Hence, within the subprogram an assigned GO TO statement that uses that variable can cause control to be returned to the calling program without a RETURN statement or necessarily executing the statement immediately following the CALL statement.

For example, consider the following program:

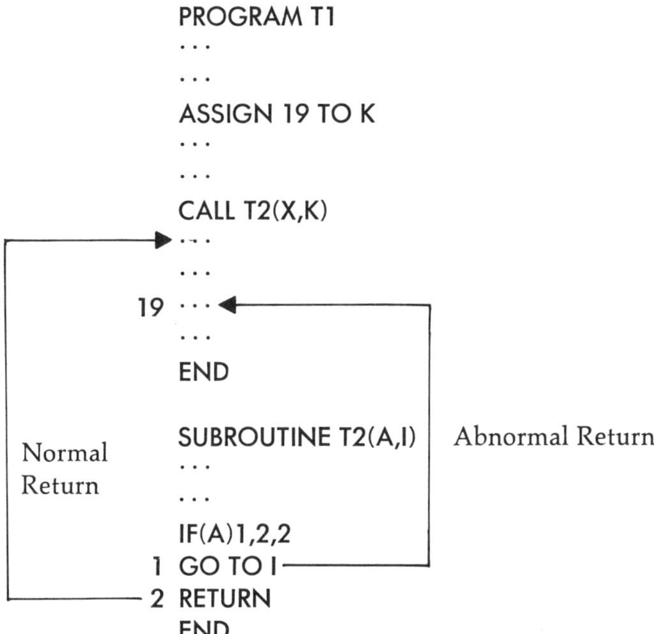

PROGRAM T1
. . .
. . .
ASSIGN 19 TO K
. . .
. . .
CALL T2(X,K)
. . .
. . .
19 . . .
. . .
END
SUBROUTINE T2(A,I)
. . .
. . .
IF(A)1,2,2
1 GO TO I
2 RETURN
END
Normal Return
Abnormal Return

While one may argue that this is an invalid use of an assigned GO TO statement and a CALL statement, there is no specific rule prohibiting the use of a formal parameter in the assigned GO TO statement.

As will be discussed later, formal parameters have no private (local) existence since they take values from the CALL arguments. Thus, the variable I will contain the address of the argument K (in this case), and K will contain the address of the statement labeled 19. Now in the calling program we may compile

B −K

for the FORTRAN instruction GO TO K, but to compile

B −I

in the subprogram would lead to an error since I contains not −K but the address of K itself. Thus if the variable in an assigned GO TO statement is a formal parameter, we must compile the set of instructions

LDA −I Contents of −I to ACC, i.e., contents of K to ACC, i.e., address of 19 to ACC.

STA *+1 Store contents of ACC in next instruction; i.e., put address of statement numbered 19 in the next instruction.[2]

B *-* Branch to address to be filled in.

With this scheme, the statement address may be transmitted through many levels of subprogram provided that all references to formal parameters in a subprogram are addressed indirectly. Thus, the following program would execute correctly with cascading indirect addressing:

```
   PROGRAM T1
   ...
   ...
   ASSIGN 19 TO K
   ...
   CALL T2(A,K)
   ...
   ...
19 ...
   ...
   END
   SUBROUTINE T2(X,I)
   ...
   CALL T3(X,I)
   ...
   RETURN
   END
   SUBROUTINO T3(Y,J)
   ...
   ...
   CALL T4(Y,J)
   ...
   RETURN
   END
   SUBROUTINE T4(Z,K)
   ...
   ...
   GO TO K
   ...
   RETURN
   END
```

2. The "*" symbol stands for the address of *this* instruction; STA stands for "store address."

The statement **CALL T2** in the main program will place the address of **K** into the space reserved for the formal parameter **I**. **CALL T3** in subroutine **T2** will transfer **−I** to **J** since all references to formal parameters in a subprogram are referenced indirectly. **CALL T4** will transfer **−J** to **K**. Then the compiled instruction **LDA −K** in subprogram **T4** will chain through three levels of indirect addressing to pick up the address of the variable **K** in the main program and hence place the address of statement numbered **19** in the accumulator. This address will then be stored in the branch instruction.

In computers without cascading indirect addressing, only one level of assigned **GO TO** may be permitted in a subprogram, and with this restriction, *all* assigned **GO TO** statements using formal parameters should be rejected. This "remote" transfer of control is possible in FORTRAN as a result of the peculiarities of implementation. That is, parameter passing is accomplished by the use of addresses rather than values or names (Chapter 10) and the storage is statically allocatable at compile time. By these means the extensions outlined above can be achieved inexpensively. As a result of the simplistic subprogramming facilities provided in FORTRAN with statically determinate storage allocation, the subprogram activation and deactivation routines are nonexistent. Hence the movement from one environment to another (such as from within a subprogram back to the calling program) is achieved by a simple transfer of control.

Conversely in any implementation which entails dynamic storage allocation combined with subprogram activation would require that the appropriate deactivation routine be followed before leaving the subprogram and the corresponding reactivation routine be reentered before entering the calling routine. Even in FORTRAN or BASIC however, there exists a similarity here which will be examined closely in the next section; that is, the entry into and exit from statement groups which are under loop control such as **DO** or **FOR** blocks.

FORTRAN COMPUTED GO TO OR BASIC ON STATEMENTS

The development of the multi-way branch started with the FORTRAN style "computed **GO TO**" and has since been extended somewhat to the BASIC style in which the selection of a statement identifier is defined by an expression rather a simple integer variable. The discussion here shows how this can be extended further without excessive cost if **ASSIGN** has been implemented. Let us develop these concepts step by step.

The American National Standard FORTRAN (1966 version) of the computed **GO TO** has the syntactic form:

<*computed GO TO statement*> := **GO TO**(<*statement number*> {,<*statement number*>}$_0^\infty$), <*integer variable*>

In its standard form, this may be compiled to the instructions:

```
ENA   *+3      Address of branch to ACC
ADD   I        Add contents of I
STA   *+1      Store in branch instruction
B     -*-*     Branch indirectly³
```

This set is to be followed by a list of addresses of the statement numbers, modified to indirect addresses, if necessary, for forward references.

Such a compilation does not protect the user from attempting to use a value of the index that is zero, negative or greater than the number of items in the parenthesized list. This would be an object time error, and thus any instructions to check this value must be included in the target code.

The 1966 FORTRAN standard did not specify any course of action to be followed in the event that the computed **GO TO** was executed with an index outside of the range of values implied by the size of the statement number list. The American National specification (Sec. 7.1.2.1.3) is as follows:

> *Computed* **GO TO** *statement*. A computed **GO TO** statement is of the form:
>
> **GO TO**($k_1,k_2, \ldots, k_n$),i
>
> where the k's are statement labels and i is an integer variable reference. . . . Execution of this statement causes the statement identified by the statement label k_j to be executed next, where j is the value of i at the time of execution. This statement is defined only for values such that $1 \leqslant j \leqslant n$.

This statement left the implementers in a dilemma; although specifically instructed as to the actions to be taken in the defined range, no precise instructions were given for actions to be taken in the undefined range. In fact, most implementers assumed that the phrase ". . . is defined only . . ." referred to the standard and not to their implementation. Thus most compilers, or in fact, most object-time routines,

3. It is assumed that the indirect addressing bit is not destroyed by the **STA** instruction.

provide for the contingency of a value of the index outside the range. For example, the FORTRAN 3600 specifies that for the purpose of execution, a value of the index greater than the number of items in the list is taken to have a value equal to the limit. That is, if $j > n$, the next statement to be executed will be that labeled k_n. On the other hand, other systems use modular arithmetic to pick out the appropriate statement number based on the limit. That is, j is taken to have the value $j - n(\text{int}(j/n))$ where int is the integer function of the argument.

Such routines take considerable storage and cannot be stored (or compiled) efficiently in line when several computed GO TO statements are anticipated in a program. Using a special routine within the system, we may compile the following:

```
ENA   *+2
B     COMGO
      Address(i)
      n
      Address(k1)
      Address(k2)
      ...
      ...
      Address(kn)
```

where COMGO is the entry address to a routine that checks the value of the index against the limit (provided by the compiler in the appended list), corrects the value if necessary and then picks out the correct statement number address from the list. Since the accumulator contains the address of the list on entry to this routine, the list may be accessed from the routine easily. Similarly, knowing both the location and the size of the list, the compiler will have no problems in providing the correct starting location for the next set of instructions.

Another alternative to this problem of implementing the computed GO TO for index values outside of the specified range is proposed in the 1975 proposed FORTRAN standard. In this case, the standard specifies that if the value of the index is outside the range (and thus includes zero and negative values) the following statement is to be executed.

In this case the COMGO routine, after checking the value of the index against the range (the value of n in the argument list) will return control to the instruction at location immediately following the location containing the address of the statement labelled k_n. Under these circumstances the COMGO routine could be coded as follows:

```
*Accumulator contains address of first argument
COMGO   STO   VALUE    Store location of index value
        INA   =1       Increment argument list pointer
        STO   N        Store location of list size (n)
        INA   =1       Increment argument list pointer
        STO   LIST     Store location of list of addresses
        LDA   -VALUE   Fetch index value
        BP    CHKUPR
*If test fails, value is zero or negative
GETOUT  LDA   -N       Fetch list size
        ADD   LIST     Add address of first element in list of
*                      addresses
        STA   *+1      Set up exit
        B     *-*      Exit to mainline program
*Check for value of index greater than range
CHKUPR  SUB   -N       Subtract range size
        BP    GETOUT   Exit if out of range
*If test fails, value is in range
        LDA   -VALUE   Fetch index value
        ADD   LIST     Add address of address list
        STA   *+1      Set up for branch
        LDA   *-*      Remove indirection
        STA   *+1
        B     *-*      Exit through address list
```

Before extending the computed GO TO to the BASIC form in which the index may be replaced by an expression (which is also now permitted in the 1975 proposed FORTRAN standard) let us consider the implementation of some features which do not cause the compiler writer any major problems and do not detract from the available space at object time or speed of execution. For example, if one is prepared to implement the assigned GO TO statement using a simple integer variable, then there is little difficulty in extending the power of this statement to include subscripted variables. As will be shown later, the compilation of a subscripted variable reference is merely the use of the algorithm to generate the address of the variable. Thus if reference is made to the arithmetic scanning routine to pick out the address of the variable instead of simply referring to the symbol table routine, statements such as

```
ASSIGN 103 TO L(3*I+5)
...
...
GO TO L(J)
```

are compilable and executable. However, in a single accumulator machine, care must be taken to ensure that the computations to determine the address of the element in the array do not conflict with the load and transfer instructions necessary to place the address of the statement number in the branch instructions. Thus the simple pair of symbolic instructions

```
ENA  Address(n)
STO  i
```

for the compilation of the ASSIGN statement must be preceded by those necessary for the determination of the element address. The above ASSIGN statement might be compiled to:

Compute address of L(3*I+5)	ENA	=3	Enter literal 3 into the ACC.
	MUL	I	ACC*I to ACC.
	INA	=5	Increment the ACC by literal 5.
	RVS		Reverse the sign of the ACC.
	INA	Address(L(0))	ACC+base of array L to ACC.
Save result →	STA	*+2	
Compile ASSIGN	ENA	Address(103)	Address of first word of reference statement to ACC.
	STO	*−*	Store ACC in location to be provided

If the arithmetic expression routine provides information regarding its actions to the calling routine, then the calling routine can compile in one of two manners. If the arithmetic expression routine provides the current address of the result of the compilation as it would appear at object time, then the calling routine is able to determine whether in line instructions have been compiled. For example, if the second element of the ASSIGN statement is a simple variable, the arithmetic expression routine has done no work past that of determining the address of that variable; thus the called routine will report that the address of the result is that address. On the other hand, if the arithmetic expression routine is forced to compile in line instructions the address of the result will be placed in the accumulator. On the basis of these reports, the computer will compile

```
STA   *+2
ENA   Address(n)
STO   *-*
```

for the case when the called routine reports that the result will be placed in the accumulator at run time, or

```
ENA   Address(n)
STO   i
```

when the result is available at compile time.

Similarly, if variables are allowed in a GO TO statement, then it is feasible to use the same process in connection with the computed GO TO statement such that the following statement would be valid:

```
GO TO(I, 1, 17, J ( K ) , 99 ),L
```

where both I and J(K) have appeared on the right-hand side of a previously executed ASSIGN statement. Once again, however, the order of processing in the compiler must be revised. For example, when the list contains only statement numbers and simple variables, the list appended to the instructions that link to the COMGO routine will contain either the actual address of the statement referenced provided that the statement has already been encountered or an indirect address to a forward reference or to a variable reference. When subscripted variables are included in the list, the one for one ordering of the object time list will be disturbed by the presence of instructions to compute the actual location of that element. Thus we may propose to perform all these subscripting instructions before entering the COMGO routine, placing the appropriate addresses into the appended list. However, this technique would mean that prior to each and every execution of the computed GO TO all subscripting computations would be executed *whether or not that reference were used.* This could seriously slow down the execution of this type of statement.

Alternatively, since it may be recognized that this computed GO TO statement causes a complete break in the sequence of execution of the program, it would not affect the operation materially if an extra routine were slipped in between a branch from the GO TO statement routine and a branch to the final destination. Thus if the appended list contains the addresses of the first instructions in routines to compute the address of elements in arrays, instead of addresses of the next instruction in the program (direct or indirect), the computation of the location of the element in the named array need only be performed when necessary. Consider the GO TO statement:

GO TO (13, K, 7, J(I), M(N)), L

which would be compiled to the sequence:

```
       ENA   *+2                   Address of list to ACC
       B     COMGO                 Jump to COMGO routine
             Address(L)
             =5
             Address(13)
             -Address(K)
             Address(7)
             Address(LINK1)        Address of subscripting routine
             Address(LINK2)        Address of subscripting routine
LINK1  LDA   I                     Compute address of J(I)
       RVS
       INA   Address(Base of J)
       STA   *+1                   Store address
       B     -*-*                  Branch indirectly
LINK2  LDA   N                     Compute address of M(N)
       RVS
       INA   Address(Base of M)
       STA   *+1                   Store address
       B     -*-*                  Branch indirectly
```

Since the index of a computed GO TO merely provides a source of data, this extension can be carried further with any integer expression in place of the index such as:

GO TO (I, 1, 17, J(K), 99), I1+(J3**2)/3

This expression may be computed in the place of an index before entry to the COMGO routine, and the location of the result may be placed into the appropriate word location in the appended list. That is, the result of this calculation must be placed into temporary storage if arithmetic operations are involved in the computation; if the index is merely a subscripted variable with a variable subscript, the address of that element may be placed directly into the list. Thus the index

I+J*3

would compile to the instructions

```
LDA   J              J to ACC
MUL   Address (3)    ACC*3 to ACC
ADD   I              ACC+1 to ACC
STO   TEMP           ACC to temporary location
```

The appended list would then contain the address of the temporary location provided by the compiler. On the other hand, if the index is a subscripted variable with a variable subscript, the subscripting computations must be performed before entry to COMGO and the address of the element put into the list at object time. That is, an index of I(J) could cause the compilation of the following instructions

```
LDA   J                        J to ACC
RVS                            Reverse sign of ACC
ADD   Address(Base of I)
STA   *+3                      Store address in list
```

However, the special precautions taken to recognize this latter condition may not worthy of their place in the compiler if they take excessive space. Thus the regular code output by the expression analyzer may be utilized in place of the special code above. In this case this wastes one instruction which is inserted to fetch the value of the subscripted variable into the accumulator.

```
LDA   J                        Subscript to ACC
RVS
ADD   Address(Base of I)
STA   *+1
LDA   *-*                      Fetch contents of I(J)
STO   TEMP                     Store result
```

Indices that are simple variables or subscripted variables with constant subscripts may be compiled with no extra instructions and with the actual address of the index in the appended list.

Irrespective of these extensions to the computed GO TO statement, the overall power of the statement is somewhat diminished when the extension to the assigned GO TO statement to include subscripted variables is permitted. That is, for example:

```
GO TO (1,2,3),I(J)
```

is equivalent to:

```
ASSIGN 1 TO I(1)
...
ASSIGN 2 TO I(2)
...
ASSIGN 3 TO I(3)
...
GO TO I(J)
```

where the value of J is specified somewhere. This form has the advantage that the programmer has the option of modifying the labels associated with each element of the array I at run time.

IF STATEMENTS

The further logical extension of program control from the original basis of unconditional branching through the computed GO TO (or BASIC ON) is the generalized IF statement which has the form

if *<relational statement>* **then** *<statement>* **else** *<statement>*

and has the general meaning:

> **if** the result of evaluating the relational expression is true,
> **then** execute the first statement, (otherwise)
> **else** execute the second statement.

This style of statement exists in ALGOL and some other languages, but FORTRAN chose the implementation of several differing styles, each of which is a special case. These are the arithmetic IF, the single- and two-exit logical IF, and the conditional statement.

The arithmetic IF *statement.*[4]
FORTRAN syntax:

IF(*<expression>*)*<statement number>*$_1$,*<statement number>*$_2$,
<statement number>$_3$

Equivalent ALGOL-style syntax:
if *<expression>* $<$ 0 **then go to** *<statement number>*$_1$ **else**
if *<expression>* $=$ 0 **then go to** *<statement number>*$_2$ **else**
go to *<statement number>*$_3$

Assuming that the expression scanner is sufficient to compile the code relevant to both arithmetic and logical expressions (see Chapter 7), and that scanner returns to the calling routine an indication of the mode of the result (that is, arithmetic or logical), then a source level transformation of the FORTRAN arithmetic IF statement into an ALGOL form can lead to a generalized compilation schema for conditional transfer of control statements. For example, let us consider the transformations that are necessary for the three other FORTRAN-style IF statements.

The two-exit logical IF *statement:*

FORTRAN syntax:

4. The subscripts used here are for the purpose of identification in the equivalent form rather than for the purpose of statement generation.

IF(<*logical expression*>) <*statement number*>$_1$,
<*statement number*>$_2$

Equivalent ALGOL-style syntax:

if <*logical expression*> **then go to** <*statement number*>$_1$ **else go to** <*statement number*>$_2$

The single-exit logical **IF** *statement:*

FORTRAN syntax:

IF(<*logical expression*>) <*statement number*>

Equivalent ALGOL-style syntax:

if <*logical expression*> **then go to** <*statement number*> **else** <*null statement*>

where <*null statement*> indicates a "do nothing" instruction which has been inserted both to maintain a standard **if** statement format and to obviate the problem of a "dangling **else**."[5]

The conditional statement.

This form of FORTRAN **IF** statement is truly the generalized form of the single-exit logical **IF** statement. By replacing the single statement number by a **GO TO** statement, to which it is equivalent, the single-exit logical **IF** statement can be seen to be a special case of the conditional statement.

FORTRAN syntax:

IF(<*logical expression*>) <*statement*>

Equivalent ALGOL-style syntax:

if <*logical expression*> **then** <*statement*> **else** <*null statement*>

Compilation of the generalized form.

The generalized form of the **if** statement can be compiled according to a common template which corresponds to the flowchart shown in Figure 8.1 In most implementations the logical truth values are represented by the pair {0, not 0} corresponding to {False, True} although defined logical mode variables will contain binary values {0,1} only. By this means logical expressions can be formed by forming the result of an arithmetic expression and then comparing that result with

5. For a discussion of the "dangling **else**" problem see P. W. Abrahams, "A Final Solution to the Dangling **else** of ALGOL 60 and Related Languages," *Comm. ACM*, vol. 9, no. 9 (September 1966).

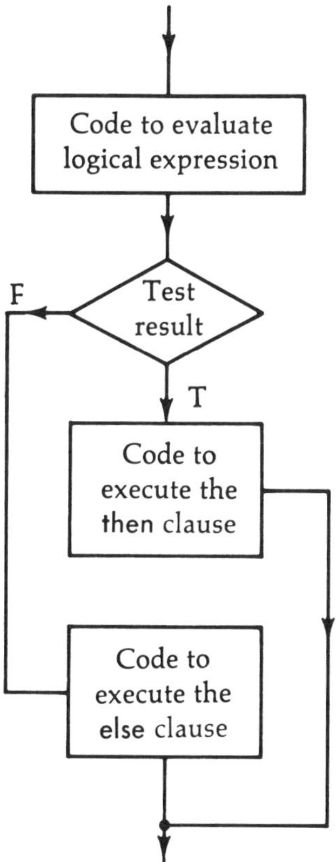

FIGURE 8.1 Template for compiled code for an **if** statement.

zero. Thus the only necessary testing instruction required is the branch on zero accumulator, BZ, although it may be more convenient in some circumstances to use the complementary instruction, branch on nonzero accumulator, BNZ. Using this domain of logical truth values, IF statements of the form IF(A)GO TO 34 are valid even when the variable A has not been defined to be a logical variable. The result would be equivalent to testing the contents associated with A with zero and then transferring control to the statement identified by the number 34 if the value is not zero.

There exists one problem which should be considered at this point with respect to the compilation of **if** statements. That is, the object of the branch after the test which will select the **else** clause and the object of the branch succeeding the execution of the **then** clause are forward references which must be compiled indirectly through address cells in a one-pass compilation system. In neither of these cases is there a user-defined language element (such as a statement identifier) associated with the address cells and thus the compiler will be required to invent unique entries into the symbol table to locate these cells.

Some implementations of conditional transfer of control statements specifically omit from the list of valid statements that can occur in **then** or **else** clauses other conditional transfer statements. One reason for this was the "dangling **else**" problem. This was caused through the provision that when the **else** clause was the null statement (a "do nothing"), the whole **else** clause could be omitted. This then resulted in an ambiguity in the analysis of **if** statements in which the **then** clause was another **if** statement and the **else** clause (of the outer **if**) was omitted. For example, the condensation of the compound statement

if a=b **then if** b=c **then** r:=1 **else** r:=0 **else** (do nothing)

into

if a=b **then if** b=c **then** r:=1 **else** r:=0

results in an ambiguous statement since it is impossible to determine to which **if** the **else** clause belongs. Further the embedment of an **if** statement within an **if** statement will appear to require the code generator for the **if** statement to be recursively entered, or at least to be re-entrant. However, it may be seen that these two problems can be overcome very simply. Firstly require that all **else** clauses be associated with the last **if** statement, effectively adding sufficient **else** (do nothing) clauses to the right end of the statement to match the number of **if** statements. Secondly, the reentrant compilation problem can be overcome by generating all code relevant to each **if** statement prior to entering the code generation routines for the embedded **then** and **else** clauses. This is equivalent to proposing that **if** statements be unraveled to form three separate statements corresponding to the template shown in Figure 8.1. Thus the general statement

if <*logical expression*> **then** <*statement*>$_1$ **else** <*statement*>$_2$

is unraveled into the sequence

if <*logical expression*> **then go to** <*label*>$_1$ **else go to** <*label*>$_2$;
<*label*>$_1$: <*statement*>$_1$; **go to** <*exit*>;
<*label*>$_2$: <*statement*>$_2$;
<*exit*> : · · ·

In this manner it is obvious that there is no need to limit the user of the implementation to the use of **if** statements that do not incorporate other **if** statements.

As with most generalizations, the code generated is not necessarily the best that could be generated if the advantages of the particular statement were to be taken into account. For these reasons let us now examine the various forms of FORTRAN IF statement in detail and develop specialized code sequences for each.

FORTRAN IF statements

In the standard IF statements, the difference between those statements that reference statement numbers in the equivalent part to either the **then** or **else** clause, and those that contain the actual statement to be executed if the result of the expression is true, may be recognized easily by examination of the first character following the closing parenthesis. Only when an actual FORTRAN statement body is defined is the next character alphabetic. In fact, an examination of the possible statement bodies in the FORTRAN language reveals that the next character must be alphabetic in this case.

Once the latter type of IF statement has been recognized, there are several distinct steps to be undertaken:

1. On the basis that the result of the execution of the logical expression is residing in the accumulator and that a zero value indicates falsehood and unity represents truth, compile the single instruction

```
BZ      *-*
```

The address of this instruction is left blank since the location of the next instruction to be executed is not known at this juncture. This instruction when executed at object time will cause control to branch around the set of instructions that will be compiled from the FORTRAN body when the result of the execution of the logical expression is false. Also, the address of the above instruction is stored for future reference.

2. Compile the code relative to the statement body.

3. After compiling the statement body, insert the address of the next instruction, which is now known, into the **BZ** instruction by referencing the address that was stored by step 1. If the compiler is a load and go system, this insertion is simple; but when the object code is transmitted to some external device, the loader must overlay this address correctly, and it must be assured that the instruction is loaded

before the address portion is overlaid. In a multipass system, the address portion of the **BZ** instruction may be filled in with a symbolic address and that address be used to label the instruction of the next statement.

In contrast to compilation of the **GO TO** where it is proposed that an indirect branch to a data word be used when the statement number has not been encountered, *backtracking* is more feasible in the case of an **IF** statement since it is known that the only instruction to be overlaid is the **BZ** instruction. Further, this process of backtracking to fill in the address is within the same generator, whereas in the case of the **GO TO**, backtracking must be accomplished by the routine that recognizes statement numbers in the label position of the FORTRAN instruction.

The process of compiling the branches to other types of **IF** statement may be combined into a single scanner and checker. Given a three element list such as a_1, a_2 and a_3, the following algorithm will suffice:

1. Extract the first number and store its address (from **SYMTAB**) in the word a_1.

2. If the delimiting character following the extraction of the first number is the end of the statement, then the **IF** statement is of the type

IF(<*logical expression*>)<*statement number*>

and may be compiled as simply

BNZ (a_1)

where (a_1) is the address of the referenced statement. Following this compilation, the **IF** generator may be exited.

3. Extract the second number and store in a_2.

4. If the delimiter to the second number is the end of the statement, the class of **IF** statement is that of

IF(<*logical expression*>)<*statement number*>,
<*statement number*>

where the next statement to be executed if the result of the execution of the logical expression is true is that referred to first in the list of exits and if false, the next statement is that labeled lastly. With the data stored in a_1 and a_2 this **IF** statement may be compiled in one of two manners, either

	BZ	(a_2)	If false, branch to second statement reference.
	B	(a_1)	If true, jump to first reference.
or	BNZ	(a_1)	If true, branch to first statement number.
	B	(a_2)	If false, go to second reference.

5. Extract the third statement number and store in a_3.

6. By default, the **IF** statement must be of the class of arithmetic **IF** statements, that is,

IF(<*arithmetic expression*>)<*statement number*>
{,<*statement number*>}$_2^2$

where the statement numbers refer to the exits corresponding to the results which are negative, zero and positive, respectively. By using the data stored in the elements a_1, a_2 and a_3, the following instructions may be compiled:

BZ	(a_2)	Branch on zero accumulator to address contained in a_2.
BN	(a_1)	Branch if accumulator is negative to address contained in a_1.
B	(a_3)	Branch to address contained in a_3. As a result of the previous branches this instruction is effectively a branch on a positive accumulator.

Note that since the statement numbers were originally contained in the a elements, these elements may be replaced before compilation by the actual or indirect addresses of the referenced statements. Thus in the above instructions the elements have been enclosed in parentheses to show that the addresses are to be obtained from the elements a at compile time.

The seemingly peculiar disarrangement of these branch statements is chosen to overcome the peculiarity of some computers that give a sign to zero values. This occurs because in some machines the sign of the original accumulator value is retained when the result of a single operation is zero. Similarly, the second instruction is for a negative condition since, in some computers, the speed of execution of a test for a negative value is faster than that of the other tests. The order of the tests may, therefore, be machine dependent though in theory there is no particular significance to the order described above.

Let us now discuss the possibility of allowing *statement identifier variables* in **IF** statements. In standard **IF** statements, the distinction between those statements containing statement numbers and those containing a statement body after the closing parenthesis may be made by examining the first character following the parenthesis. However, if statement identifier variables are allowed, this test is not valid. Compared to variables used as a data source, such as in the index to a computed GO TO statement, which can easily be replaced by a complete expression, a statement identifier variable is merely the source of an address to which a reference may be made and, therefore, cannot be replaced or influenced by an expression. Thus the statement identifier variable is similar to the variable that occurs on the left-hand side of an arithmetic assignment statement. If the routine that scans arithmetic expressions were divided into two parts, these would be:

1. The right-hand side scanner, which compiles instructions to execute the specified operations which will leave the result (a value) in the accumulator.

2. The left-hand side scanner, which compiles subscripting, if necessary, and provides the address of the variable. In an arithmetic assignment statement, it is into this address that the result of executing the right-hand side is to be placed.

Hence, the left-hand side scanner will check for the presence of any operator and "complain" if necessary, and from the result of the scanner, one may determine the difference between the two main types of IF statement. In particular, the scanner will probably believe that a statement number is an integer constant, which is not a valid "loadable," and will thus complain. However, if the manner of complaining is not the output of an actual error message, this task being left to the calling generator, then this special routine will enable the IF generator to scan across to the first delimiter. If this delimiter is a comma or the end of the statement, then the IF statement is the type that contains statement numbers (in the standard form), whereas if the delimiter is not one of this type, further scanning is necessary. This task may be taken over by the SIEVE routine and the statement handled as a normal logical IF statement with an embedded statement body. Some statement bodies, unfortunately, may be taken for variables, and thus exact specifications must be laid down with regard to the inclusion of special delimiting characters. For example, the exclusion of the spaces between the elements of the standard GO TO statement, such as

```
GOTO100
```

could cause confusion. However, if we insist that the blanks be included, then the left-hand scanner will light upon the blank as the delimiter. Similarly, an input statement without a blank between the keyword and the statement number or logical unit specifications could be scanned in either of two ways: the input statement could be taken for either a list of simple variables or a subscripted variable. For example, consider the scanning of the following statements:

```
IF(PASS.EQ.1)READ1,A
```

and

```
IF(IT.EQ.THAT)READ(12,61)A
```

If the embedded blanks are not included as part of the language, then the only alternative to obtain a correct scan would be to reserve certain variable character combinations such as those beginning with the characters READ, WRITE, GO TO, etc. However, the proponents of FORTRAN have always been able to claim that the language contains no reserved words. Further, if the extension of the language is such that previously valid programs will no longer compile or execute correctly, then the extension itself must be considered invalid.

When statement identifier variables are also subscripted, the order of executing the subscripting instructions will substantially affect the efficiency of the object program. That is, as with the extended computed GO TO, it is inefficient to perform the subscripting instructions when an identifier is not to be used as the exit to the statement. Thus any compiled instructions for subscripting that the left-hand scanner generates must be saved in the computer memory before being added to the object code. That is, if the subscripting instructions are placed in line as the scanner generates them, the following arrangement might occur in the worst case (the arithmetic IF with subscripted statement identifier variables):

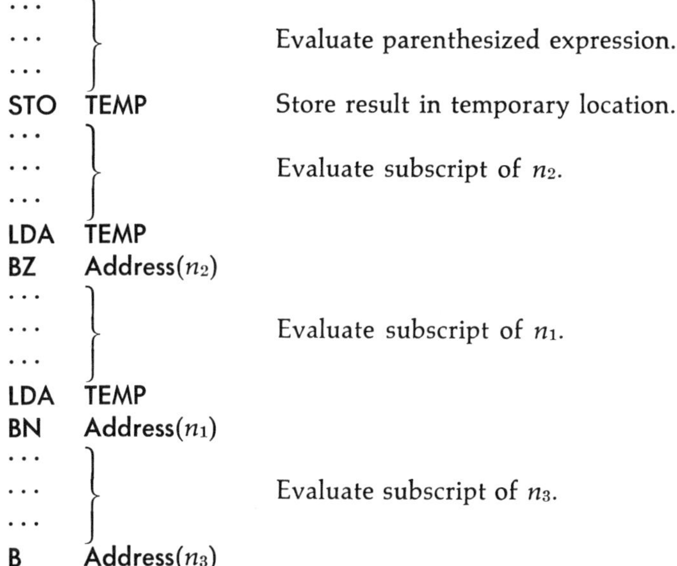

. . .
. . .
. . .
Evaluate parenthesized expression.
STO TEMP
Store result in temporary location.
. . .
. . .
. . .
Evaluate subscript of n2.
LDA TEMP
BZ Address(n2)
. . .
. . .
. . .
Evaluate subscript of n1.
LDA TEMP
BN Address(n1)
. . .
. . .
. . .
Evaluate subscript of n3.
B Address(n3)

To alleviate this excessive amount of coding as well as the execution of unnecessary instructions at object time, the subscript calculations should be executed after the test of the result of the parenthesized expression:

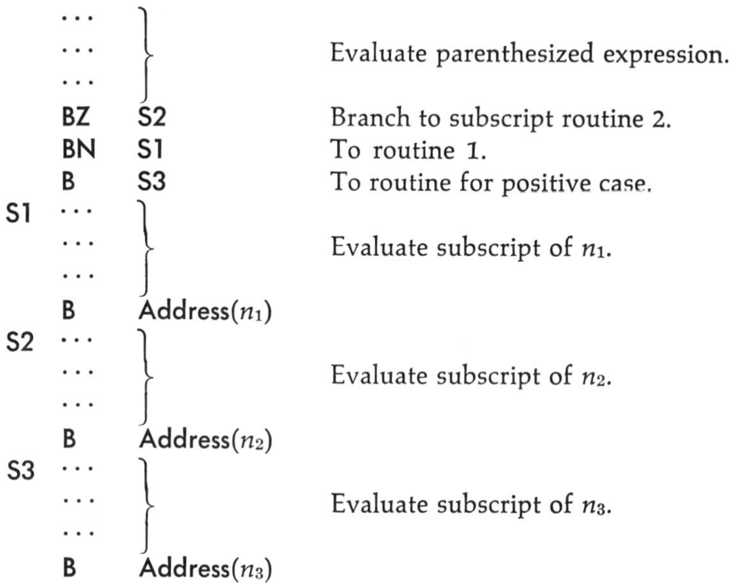

```
        ...  }
        ...  }        Evaluate parenthesized expression.
        ...  }
        BZ   S2       Branch to subscript routine 2.
        BN   S1       To routine 1.
        B    S3       To routine for positive case.
S1      ...  }
        ...  }        Evaluate subscript of n1.
        ...  }
        B    Address(n1)
S2      ...  }
        ...  }        Evaluate subscript of n2.
        ...  }
        B    Address(n2)
S3      ...  }
        ...  }        Evaluate subscript of n3.
        ...  }
        B    Address(n3)
```

Obviously, if the statement identifier variable is unsubscripted, this extra set of instructions is not necessary, and the exit may be made directly from the first set of tests.

LOOP CONTROL STATEMENTS

The need to execute repeatedly a segment of code with a given index varying during each iteration results from the provision of various mathematical shorthands that are available and frequently used. For example the sigma notation (Σ) for summation and the pi notation (π) for repeated multiplication are commonly used mathematical symbolisms for which the loop control statements in programming languages provide an implementation. However, the programming language style of loop control is far more generalized than either of the two notations above (Σ and π), and instead are likened to the verbal statement that is often used:

$$\textbf{for } i=1,2,3, \cdots$$

It is possible to eliminate loop control statements from a programming language since their effect can be emulated using other, more fundamental, instructions. This immediately provides one method of compilation; loop control statements are unraveled into the corresponding fundamental statements at the source language level. These statements can then be compiled in the normal fashion.

There exist two basic forms of loop control; the style in which the loop is controlled by an index which is constrained to a given range and whose values are specified in advance as some predetermined sequence, and the style in which some condition is specified and the loop is repeatedly executed until either the condition is met or so long as the condition is satisfied. The former of these styles has the general form

for <*index*> := <*value list*>

while the second style has the syntactic form:

do $\{$**until** | **while**$\}_1^1$<*logical expression*>

PL/I provides both of these forms as well as the variant of the former in which the value list is expressed in the form of an initial value, a limiting value and an incrementing value. This particular form was the original basis for loop control in the FORTRAN language. This form we shall consider primarily.

The DO Statement

The FORTRAN DO statement, in its standard form, is a combination of statements. In fact, the general statement

```
DO 1 I=J,K,L
```

can be implemented equally as well by the statements:

```
    I=J
S2  ...
    ...
    ...
1   I=I+L
    IF(I.GT.K)S11,S2
S11 ...
    ...
```

where the statement identifiers S2 and S11 are provided by the compiler and do not, in fact, conflict with other statement numbers in the program. In symbolic code, the above DO statement could be compiled as:

```
        LDA  J
        STO  I
NEXT    ...
        ...
        ...
ST1     LDA  I
        ADD  L
        STO  I
        SUB  K
        BN   NEXT
        BZ   NEXT
        ...
        ...
```

These three equivalent programs correspond structurally to the flow chart shown in Figure 8.2.

When the parameters of the **DO** list are integer constants, advantage should be taken of any machine instructions that use their address

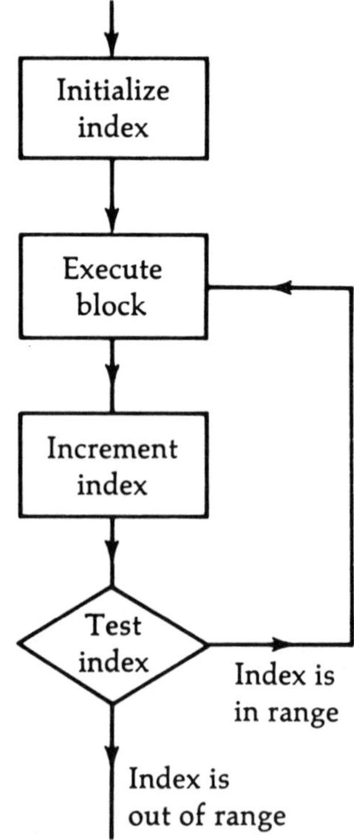

FIGURE 8.2 The semantic form of a **DO** statement.

portion as the actual data to be used in the instruction. That is, if the machine has instructions such as INA (increment accumulator) or ENA (enter accumulator) where the increment or value to be used is actually within the instruction itself, then data table storage space may be saved by using these instructions where possible. Thus the FORTRAN statement,

DO 13 N=1,K,3

may be compiled to:

```
       ENA  =1      Literal 1 to ACC
       STO  N
NEXT   ...
       ...
       ...
ST13   INA  N       N to ACC
       LDA  =3      Increment ACC by literal 3
       STO  N
       SUB  K
       BN   NEXT
       BZ   NEXT
```

When a DO statement occurs in a subprogram and any one of the parameters or the index itself is a formal parameter, indirect addressing references to the address of that formal parameter will take care of the necessary chaining (or cascading) through to the actual value of the element.

The main drawback in implementing the DO statement is the necessity to split the object coding between the beginning and the end of the range. One technique for obtaining this split is to add a set of special information to statement number entries in the symbol table.

When a DO statement is encountered, the statement number defining the last statement within the range is not yet defined. However, the statement number may already be in the symbol table as it may have been referenced in an exterior DO range. Since the address is not yet defined and cannot be referenced by any other control statement from outside the range, a special tag may be included in the symbol table entry which will define this statement number as the termination of a DO range. Emanating from this symbol table entry will be a linked list containing five entries per element:

NEXT, LIMIT, INCREMENT, INDEX and LINK

where LIMIT, INCREMENT and INDEX are the addresses of the parameters in the **DO** statement; **NEXT** is the address of the first instruction in the **DO** range after the initialization instructions; and **LINK** is the address of the next sublist (which will be undefined if this is the last sublist). That is, this is the data pertinent to the innermost **DO** range that uses this statement number up to this point in the compilation. This list and its sublists are constructed as the **DO** statements are encountered and are destroyed as the range terminating statements are recognized. In the symbol table itself there will be a pointer to this list. By inserting each new element between the symbol table and the current first entry, the linked list will simulate a stack, the first entry of the list referencing the innermost **DO** block. Thus on "unwinding" access to the appropriate **DO** statement data will be easy. This process is shown in Figure 8.3.

As originally conceived for the IBM 704, a **DO** statement was based on the control of its range by the use of an index register, which

PROGRAM BEING COMPILED

```
DO 1 I = J,K,L

DO 1 II = JJ,KK,LL

DO 1 III = JJJ,KKK,LLL

DO 1 IV = JW,KX,LY  <--
```

Statement being compiled

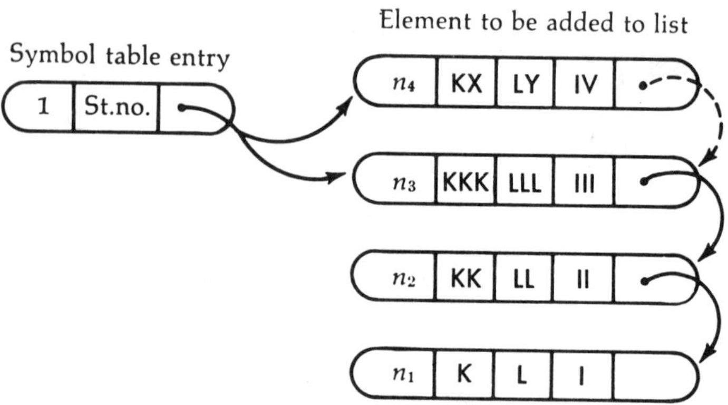

FIGURE 8.3 **DO statement data stack.**

coupled with two-register instructions, helped mold the original syntax and restrictions of the FORTRAN loop control statement. The two instructions were

AXT *i,j* and TIX *a,j,i*

which each refer to index register *j*. The AXT instruction allowed the loading of the register with the actual value *i* and was intended for the placement of an address into the register. Hence the acronym AXT was derived from the phrase ADDRESS TO INDEX — TRUE. The instruction TIX (TRANSFER ON INDEX) performed two specific operations—the testing and modification of the contents of the register. If the contents of register *j* are greater than the specified decrement value (*i*), then the contents of the register are reduced by the amount of the decrement and control is transferred to the location specified in the TIX instruction as the address *a*. Otherwise, the contents of the register are untouched and no branch is performed. It may be seen that a loop control can be constructed using the AXT instruction as the initialization phase and the TIX as the range terminator. That is, to execute a range under the control of (say) index register 3, with the value contained in the index register starting at 24 and reducing in each successive pass through the loop by 2 until the range is executed last with the index register set to 2, the following pair of instructions could be used to parenthesize the range:

```
        AXT   24,3          Initialize
NEXT    ...
        ...
        TIX   NEXT,3,2      Test, decrement and branch.
```

Using these instructions, the original DO statement was constructed, and yet it was *not* required that the indices of the loops count backwards! However, the algorithm for transforming the DO indices (initial value, limit and increment) into the values needed to establish the parameters for the index was not simple (or at least straightforward) particularly in those cases where the range was not exactly equivalent to the zero based register control instruction TIX, such as

DO 93 I = 4,16,1

or where the limit is not the exact limit to be used in executing the range, such as in the statement

DO 93 I = 4,16,5

This mode of implementation created several restrictions:

1. The depth of DO nests could not exceed the number of available index registers.

2. The index of the DO loop, *i*, for example, was not related to the variable *i* in the rest of the program, but was related to all the references to *i* within the range.[6]

3. Because of the limited availability of index registers, the same register had to be used for several unrelated loops. Hence, since the compiler could not ascertain the logical flow of the program, a DO index had to be considered undefined outside the range.

4. The index could be incremented only.

5. The range had to be traversed at least once, even if the original (initial) value of the index was greater than the limit.

6. Real variables or constants were not permitted as elements of the DO statement.

7. For obscure reasons, expressions were not permitted as elements of the parameter list; that is, the initial value, the limit and the increment.

8. Although references to the index were possible as the source of a value, no provision was made for the modification of the index value in the range. Similarly since the values computed at the initialization phase for the limit and increment were stored in the address portion of the instructions, their values could not be altered in the range.

Let us now consider these restrictions in the light of the type of implementation described in this chapter.

1. Since index registers are not utilized, the depth of a DO nest is limited only by the available space at compile time for storing the list of uncompleted DO statement elements.

2. Since, in the original implementation, the index was unrelated to a similarly named variable in the rest of the program and was, in fact, stored in a register, the initialization of the range could only be accomplished by entering the range through the DO statement. In the implementation proposed herein, the index variable and parameters *are* related to the similarly named variables in the rest of the program;

6. Strangely enough this corresponds with the ALGOL style block structure rules for the scope of identifiers. In this case only the index, *i*, is a local variable. All others are global in scope.

the programmer can cause control to enter the range abnormally provided that the work of the initialization phase is simulated.

3. By the same reasoning, which allows the overriding of the second restriction, the value of the index will be available outside the range either after a normal completion or through a branch out without normal termination.

4. If the implementation of DO loops is not dependent on index registers, then the restriction of a unidirectional indexing is not necessary except that there may be a need to redefine the meaning of a DO statement. American National Standard (1966) Basic FORTRAN (Sec. 7.1.2.8) states that:

The action succeeding execution of the DO statement is described by the following five steps:

1. The control parameter is assigned the value represented by the initial parameter. *This value must be less than or equal to the value represented by the terminal parameter.*[7]

2. . . .

3. . . . after execution of the terminal statement, the control variable . . . is *incremented* by the value represented by the associated incrementation parameter.

4. If the value of the control parameter after incrementation is *less than or equal to* the value represented by the associated terminal parameter, the action described in step 2 (executing the range) is repeated . . . If the value of the control variable is *greater than* the value represented by its associated terminal parameter, the DO is said to be satisfied and *the control variable becomes undefined.*

If these restrictive specifications were revamped slightly, a standard DO statement could execute as specified but, at the same time, allow some desirable variations.

For example, if the restriction that the initial parameter value be less than or equal to the value of the terminal parameter is removed, then the relative values of the initial and terminal parameters are irrelevant and merely define a domain of values within which the DO range is to be executed. In paragraph 3 of Sec. 7.1.2.8, a negative incrementation should be allowed. In paragraph 4, the pertinent wording might be changed to read:

7. Author's emphasis.

4. If the value of the control parameter after incrementation is within the domain of the initial and terminal parameter values, the action described in step 2 . . . If the value of the control parameter is outside the domain of the initial and terminal parameters, the **DO** is said to be satisfied.

The last statement, ". . . and *the control variable becomes undefined,*" is purposely omitted, so that if the loop is terminated normally, the control variable will have the value at which the range was not repeated.

If the direction of the incrementation of the **DO** control variable (or index) is unknown at the time of compilation, the most efficient manner of testing of the control variable after incrementation is to call upon a system routine which will test the new value against the domain. In this case, the coding generated may take the form:

```
        LDA  J            Initial value to Index.
        STO  I
NEXT    ...
        ...
        ...
        LDA  I            Increment index.
        ADD  L
        STO  I
        ENA  *+2          Address of list to ACC.
        B    UNDO
             Address(I)
             Address(K)
             Address(L)
             NEXT
```

where the **UNDO** routine collects the addresses of the elements of the **DO** statement and the branching address from the appended list that follows the statement which transferred control to the routine. This routine checks the current value of the index against the limiting value, the test being influenced by the sign of the increment. That is, if the value of the increment is positive, the test in the **UNDO** routine is *less than or equal to* the limit, whereas if the sign is negative, the test is *greater than or equal to.*

5. At object time the **DO** statement is constructed so that the control variable can only be tested after a pass through the range; thus the range must be traversed at least once. However, under the redefinition proposed above, the initial value of the control parameter is a

limit in the domain of values and hence is a valid value for a pass through the range. One may argue that if the direction of incrementation is determined at the entry to the range and is, by definition, unalterable, then the range should not be traversed if the successive incrementation would never reach the limiting value. For example,

```
DO 1 I=1, 10,-1
```

should never cause a single execution of the range since the limit can never be attained. In view of the proposed rearrangement, above, the range would be executed with I=1 but not a second time with I=0 since this value of the control variable is outside the domain of the DO statement.

This style of implementation is mandatory in other language implementations such as in both ALGOL and BASIC.

6. If the DO statement is implemented without the use of index registers, the elements do not need to be restricted to integer mode. However, the compiler must be able to examine the mode and to link to an incrementation and testing routine of the appropriate mode.

It is important to realize that due to the architecture of the host machine, and in particular the internal numeric representation system, there can be significant differences in operation between two mathematically equivalent statements of the range of the DO index. For example in a binary machine it is not necessarily true that the following two statements of index range will result in the same action at execution time:

```
DO 63 I = 1,100,1
DO 63 I = 0.01,1.00,0.01
```

Such variances should be brought to the attention of the programmer if they are permitted by the implementer.

7. Even when index registers are used, there is no reason to prohibit expression as the elements of a DO list. For example, if the arithmetic statement scan routine is again considered as two routines, the left-hand side scanner and the right-hand side scanner, then each element in the DO list may be considered to be a right-hand side (executable), while the index (or control variable) is a left-hand side variable (or loadable). In each case, when a DO statement is encountered, the expressions are evaluated and the results, if necessary, placed in temporary locations. For example,

```
DO 13 N(I+ 7)=K*J , N(3) , I+3
```

would be compiled in the form:

```
        ...  }
        ...  }                     Compute address of N(I+7).
        ...  }
        STO  TEMP1                 Store address in temporary location.
        LDA  K                     K to ACC.
        MUL  J                     ACC*J to ACC
        STO  -TEMP1                ACC to N(I+7)
        LDA  I                     I to ACC
        INA  =3                    ACC+3 to ACC
        STO  TEMP2[8]
NEXT    ...
        ...
        ...
ST13    LDA  -TEMP1                N(I+7) to ACC
        ADD  TEMP2                 ACC+(I+3) to ACC
        STO  -TEMP1                ACC to N(I+7)
        SUB  Address(N(3))         Test against limit.
        BN   NEXT
        BZ   NEXT[9]
```

In this type of implementation all the necessary auxiliary computation is performed prior to entering the DO range and therefore detracts from the main line program, not from the DO range itself. That is, the auxiliary computations are not executed each time through the range, thereby increasing the efficiency of the range. However, since these are one-time calculations, the values of the elements cannot be altered during the course of the execution of the range.

8. If the elements of the DO list are restricted to simple variables or constants and index registers are not used, there is no need to restrict the alteration of the elemental values during the execution of the range. However, if subscripted variables or expressions are permitted, and the addresses of subscripted variables and the values of expressions are computed outside the range in the initialization instructions, then these values are fixed and can only be altered by repeating the initialization computations. For example, if the implementation were to compute the expression or subscript *each* time the ele-

8. Note that at this point in the compilation the symbol table would contain a sublist appended to the entry referring to statement number 13, the elements in the sublist being the addresses

NEXT, -TEMP1, Address(N(3)), TEMP2

9. Note that for the purposes of this example, the UNDO routine was not used.

ment was mentioned within the range, then such an allowance could be made, but the execution time would increase considerably. Further, the programmer would have to realize that such variations would not be in force until the next time through the range and not immediately after the value had been altered.

Suppose that the above example (DO 13 N(I+7)=K*J , N(3) , I+3) were entered with I set to 3 and that during a traverse through the range, I was incremented by 1. Should one consider taking the control variable value from N(10) for the remainder of the range or from N(11) the value of which may already exceed the limiting value? Or since the value of the increment has been altered, should the value of the index be incremented by 1 immediately by implication of the change in incremental value or should such an alteration wait for the normal incrementation at the end of the range? These questions probably should remain unanswered until we have a better understanding of the semantics of these situations. Just because it is possible it is not necessarily an excuse for giving the programmer freedom in a poorly defined domain.

A DO with an explicit value list

An alternative to the DO statement in which the successive values of the control index are related in some arithmetic progression, is to provide an explicit listing of the values to be taken by the control index. The general form of this statement might be

for *<index>* := *<value list>*

where

$$\langle value\ list\rangle ::= \langle expression\rangle\{,\langle expression\rangle\}_0^\infty$$

Leaving aside the questions asked in the previous section regarding the binding time of the elements of the value list, let us consider the means by which the values of the index are to be successively provided to the loop. In the FORTRAN (or BASIC) style of DO, the list of values is generated in the program itself, the generation of the successor to any current index value being well defined. However, in this case there is no such well defined successor function. It will be necessary therefore to provide a list of the values and a scheme which will successively retrieve elements from that list. Let us consider the source language level equivalent programs. Obviously, the length of the list is known in advance, or at least can be derived by the compiler. If we use the variable LENGTH as the source of this data element, and assume that the elements of the list have been placed in an array named ARRAY, then an equivalent FORTRAN-style sequence of statements can be derived:

for I ::= 1,2,3,5,7,11,13,17,19

is equivalent to

```
DO nn INDEX = 1,LENGTH,1
I = ARRAY(INDEX)
```

where the identifiers INDEX, LENGTH and ARRAY are chosen so as not to conflict with any identifiers used by the programmer in the program. With this expansion, an equivalent machine language template can be constructed for this type of loop control statement.

DO . . . WHILE or UNTIL

Loop control without a varying index value is commonly used in connection with iterative numerical computations where the contents of the loop are to be executed repeatedly until some tolerance value is attained. For example in computing the sum of a convergent series, it is possible to execute a block of code until the change registered in some value associated with a variable is small. Alternatively a loop might be executed repeatedly so long as some condition holds; that is, in the above case of summing a convergent series, the loop is to be executed so long as the change is greater than a given amount. These two styles of loop control correspond to the UNTIL and the WHILE forms respectively.

The general form of this statement is

$$\textbf{do}\ \{\textbf{until} \mid \textbf{while}\}_1^1 \langle \textit{logical expression} \rangle$$

In contrast to the other forms of loop control where the value of a controlling element was computed once and for all (with the exception of the cases which we questioned but could not resolve) at the beginning of the loop, in this case it is expected that the value of the logical expression will change during the execution of the range, and thus the expression must be evaluated on each pass through the loop. That is, the implementation will correspond to the flow chart shown in Figure 8.4.

Since the logical expression must be evaluated during each pass through the loop it is important that the compiler carry out some loop optimization procedures to minimize the amount of "work done" in the loop. For example, if the logical expression contains several variables but only (say) one of them occurs on the left hand side of an

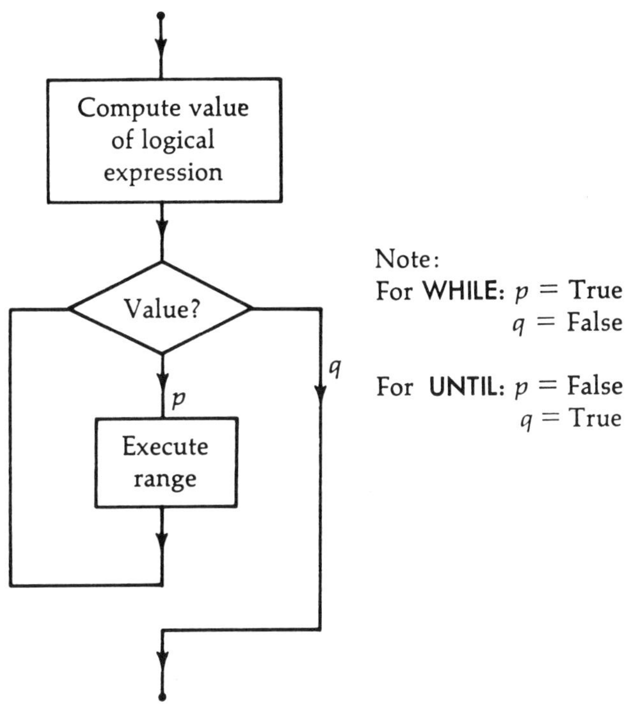

FIGURE 8.4 Generalized flowchart for DO ··· WHILE or UNTIL.

assignment statement (or in any other statement which will modify its value), then the compiler should manipulate the expression so as to maximize the operations which can be included within an initialization phase. Of course the programmer can be encouraged to do this also by carefully writing his program so that the logical expression is minimized.

Consider the statement

do until A+B > C−D

which encompasses a range in which only the variable C is modified. A modification of the logical expression A+B>C−D into the equivalent expression A+B+D > C will permit the removal of the evaluation of the expression A+B+D to outside of the range.

SUMMARY

In an era when the concept of **go to**-free languages is regarded as being high on the priority list for the language designer, it is doubtful whether the level of sophistication expected of the programmer can be attained without much more education than we give him now. If we expect to provide languages by which the nonexpert programmer who is an expert in some other field can easily resolve his problems, then we must provide a means for him to express his concepts in a manner similar to his usual way of expression. APL has gone part way along this route by realizing that in the majority of cases where a programmer used a regular array, he would step in a regular way through that array to perform his task. Thus the *n*-dimensional array became the basic element of data and the operations to step through an array are built into the regular data operations rather than being explicitly described by the programmer. When this is done, the programmer apparently has a **go to**-free program; the implementation (or the translation of the source statement) is by no means **go to**-free. In the meantime, we shall have to compile control statements.

9
Input/Output and FORMAT

The free-form style of input has already been discussed in connection with the extraction of data units from the textural portion of programs. The algorithms for the free-form input of data elements are identical. Free-form output is merely a special form of formatted output where the **FORMAT** is specified by the system (which may be the language itself) rather than by the programmer. That is, the implementation of free-form output (which is truly a misnomer) can be achieved by the generation of an appropriate **FORMAT** statement by the compiler. In this chapter we shall omit specific consideration of free-form input and output.

The relationship between input/output statement lists and their corresponding **FORMAT** statement cannot be expressed in simple static terms. In particular, the control of data conversion either from internal mode to the output mode or from external form to internal mode is sometimes under the direction of the input/output statement, while on other occasions it is the responsibility of the chosen **FORMAT** statement. As a result, the manner in which input/output statements and **FORMAT** statements are compiled is closely related.

However, **FORMAT** statements cannot be compiled as a simple set of links to system routines since such a statement refers both to input and output. For example, a numeric specification (**E**,**F** or **I**) on input describes a transformation from external to internal mode, while on output the reverse is intended. On the premise that such translation routines are not themselves reversible, the FORMAT specifications will have to be interpreted at object time to ascertain the correct routine with which to link. Because of this need to interpret the FORMAT statement at object time, there is a question as to how far it is worth translating the FORMAT statement at compile time.

At best, the compile-time translation of a FORMAT statement can only present the specifications in a form convenient for fast interpretation at object time. Further, if the compiler is to include in the object time routines a routine to translate variable FORMAT, there must be a routine to translate source form FORMAT statements to this interpretive form. Hence, one may argue that all FORMAT statements should be translated and interpreted at object time. However, this has the disadvantage that object time is wasted in favor of saving compile time. Further, special steps need to be taken to insure that source form FORMAT statements are not repeatedly translated when those statements occur in the original source program. On the other hand, variable FORMAT statements must be repeatedly translated since the FORMAT source form character string may have been altered by programming and not only by a direct input statement. This argument assumes that the compiler has recognized that an array name has occurred in an input/output statement and has attached a tag to that array, this tag being set to one value whenever the array data are manipulated and to some other value when these data are translated by the FORMAT routine.

Even with such refinements, the accumulated object time in a series of production runs may be such that an alternative manner of translation and interpretation is necessary. Even though there may be a routine to translate source form FORMAT statements in the object time relocatable routines, the translation of source code statements still may be performed at compile time while variable FORMAT statements are translated at object time. This keeps object time translation time to a minimum, and only those programmers who utilize variable FORMAT will suffer from an increased execution time and a loss of available storage due to the inclusion of the variable FORMAT translation routine. The effect of such a compromise depends on the manner in which the total system is to be used. For example, in a computing center where few programs are generated and there is a substantial number of production runs, the saving of object time at the cost of compile time is important. On the other hand, in an educational or research environment, where the majority of runs are compile-run sequences, it is relatively unimportant as to whether FORMAT translation is performed at compile time or run time provided that the translation itself is programmed as efficiently as possible.

THE INTERACTING LISTS

Fundamentally, the operation of input/output in FORTRAN is performed by the extraction of data from a character string or the insertion of data into a character string under the direction of two lists which are generated from the I/O list and the **FORMAT** statement respectively. The I/O generated list is composed of a set of addresses, each referring to a location, while that generated from the **FORMAT** statement is a set of transformation specifications. In either case, (input or output) the object of attention of the operation is assumed to be a data buffer. Depending on the specified I/O operation either the buffer will be filled prior to the action of I/O statement (if it is an input) or emptied subsequently if the action is an output. Associated with each list is a pointer which, for the purposes of this discussion, will be named:

SP	data string pointer
LP	I/O list pointer
FP	**FORMAT** specification pointer

These pointers will traverse each list under the control of the system input/output routine. These pointers are diagrammatically related to the data elements in Figure 9.1.

The transformed **FORMAT** list is composed of a set of address/field specification pairs where the address refers to the appropriate transformation routine (corresponding to, say, **F**-format, **E**-format, etc.) and where the field specification is a fixed form modification of the user-

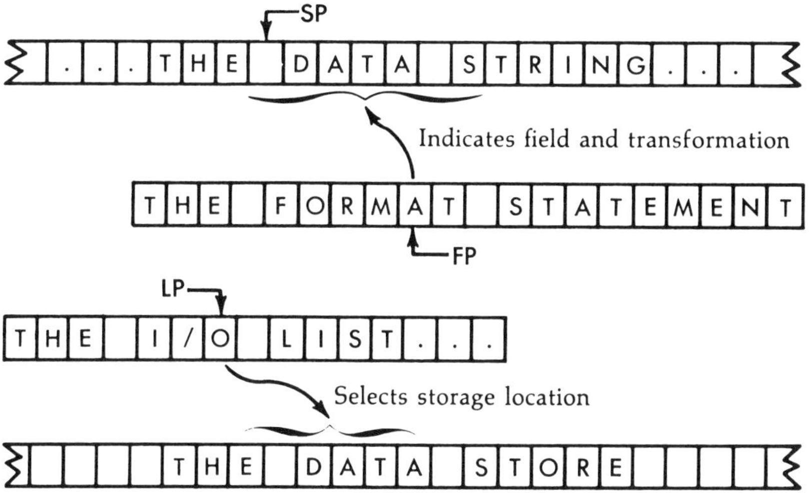

FIGURE 9.1 The Input/Output-related pointers.

defined field width and fractional part size. Owing to the schizophrenic purpose of **FORMAT** statements, the link addresses merely point to another set of tests that divert the flow of control to a pair of routines which are relevant to input and output, respectively. However, since all data are converted in either direction, irrespective of the input or output physical unit, and all manipulation takes place in an internal data buffer area, these **FORMAT** routines are independent of the device used. The routines given in Table 9.1 are necessary.

TABLE 9.1

Name	*Data form*[a]	*Purpose*
ETYPE	**WWDD**	**E**-type specifications where **WW** = w and **DD** = d of **E**$w.d$
FTYPE	**WWDD**	**F**-type specifications where **WW** = w and **DD** = d of **F**$w.d$
ITYPE	**WW00**	**I**-type specifications where **WW** is the field width of the specification.
ATYPE	**WW00**	**A**-type specifications, where **WW** is the w portion of the specification.
HTYPE	**WWXX**···	**H**-type specifications, where **WW** is the number of characters in the string and **XX** ··· is the character string. Note that in fact the actual string may be stored in **BCD** mode, and the number denoted by **WW** may be adjusted to reflect this internal size.
XTYPE	**WW00**	**X**-type specifications, where **WW** is the field width in n**X**.
REPET	**WW00**	Repeated specifications where **WW** = n of the forms n**S**$w.d$ or n**T**w, where **S** is either an **E** or **F** specification and **T** is an **I** or **A**.
NRPAR	—	To denote the right parenthesis of a repeated group of specifications.
NLPAR	**WW00**	A left parenthesis of a repeated group, where **WW** = n of $n(\cdots)$
SLASH	—	The / specification, i.e., end of record.
LTPAR	—	The left parenthesis of an unrepeated group.
RTPAR	—	The right parenthesis of an unrepeated group.

[a] This data form assumes a character orientation of the data words and restricts the field widths to two digits. Neither of these restrictions is necessary in practice.

Each of the **TYPE** routines in the table (**ETYPE**, **FTYPE**, etc.) has a direct influence on the string pointer (**SP**), whereas the other routines either direct the operation I/O unit (to empty or fill the buffer) or control the **FORMAT** pointer (**FP**) to pick up a new piece of data by a new specification.

In particular, **LTPAR** has no direct influence on the I/O action but rather prepares the **RTPAR** routine for possible reflection when the I/O list is longer than the **FORMAT** list. Hence the only action of the **LTPAR** routine is to place the current value of the **FORMAT** pointer (in fact, the address of the word to which the pointer is set) in the **RTPAR** routine. Similarly, the **NLPAR** routine must place the value of the number of repetitions and the return address in the **NRPAR** routine so that the repeated group may be traversed the correct number of times. Since repeated groups may be nested in a **FORMAT** statement, the number of repetitions and the addresses must be placed in a push down list with a last in, first out (LIFO) property. Provision must be made in this routine for ensuring that the list is renewed as each new **FORMAT** statement is used and that any list left over from an unsatisfied **FORMAT** is not carried over to the next statement.

The input/output list is also interpretive but contains facilities for in line object time computations. In particular, a system of tags and addresses is used to form the basis of an interpretive process, so as to facilitate the input and output of whole arrays and groups controlled by implied **DO** loops, the computation of subscripted variable addresses, and the checking of mode as well as to allow the possibility of outputting the result of an expression contained in the output list.
For example, the following items may be compiled:

Item in I/O list	*Tag*	*Address*
Simple integer variables and subscripted integer variables with constant subscripts	**0**	Address of variable
Simple real variables and subscripted real variables with constant subscripts	**1**	Address of variable

On the assumption that the interpreting routine can transfer control to inline instructions and that control can be returned to the interpreter by branching to a point in the interpreter named **RENTR**, variables subscripted by variables or expressions containing variables may be compiled by the inclusion of inline instructions. For example, if a tag of **2** is taken by the interpreter to mean that control is to be transferred to the instruction in the next word and the instruction

```
B       RENTR
```

is to transfer control back to the interpreter, the presence of subscripted variables may be compiled as:

```
2                (tag)
...
...              Compiled instruction to compute
...              address of subscripted variable,
...              provided by the ASCAN routine.
...              Store address in interpretive list.
STA  *+4         Reset list pointer.
ENA  *+3
STO  LP
B    RENTR
1    Address     (tag) Location of absolute address
                 of element to be input or output
                 after the execution of the inline
                 instructions.
```

Entire array references may be entered into the object interpretive list by the use of a special repeating tag. For example, a list containing an A that has been dimensioned as A(3,4) would compile to

```
1  Address(A(1,1))
3  0011
```

where the tag is assumed to be in the operation portion of the word and the address (or constant) in the operand position, and where a tag of 3 indicates that the address in the previous word is to be used as a base and incremented by unity 11 times so as to read in the remainder of the elements in the array. The number following the tag of 3 is one less than the number of elements in the array since the first element has already been referenced. The mode denoted by the first reference must, of course, be maintained throughout this operation. In this type of I/O operation, the order in which the elements are considered depends on the ordering of the elements in the data table. In the ordering proposed in Chapter 4, the elements are referenced in such a manner that the first subscript changes most rapidly and the last (or farthest right) most slowly.

IMPLIED DO IN I/O LISTS

The same technique of leaving the interpretive mode may be utilized for the coding of implied DO loops within the I/O lists. Such a group may be recognized in a left to right scan by encountering an opening parenthesis. However, the compiler must scan the right-hand side of the group to obtain the variable name to be used as the implied DO index (control) variable. As a simple case, consider the I/O list

(I, I=1,N,2)

which compiles to the instructions and list:

```
        2
        ENA   1        I=1
        STO   I
NEXT    ENA   *+3      Reset LP.
        STO   LP
        B     RENTR    Return to interpretive mode.
        0     I        List entry, integer variable I.
        2              Execute inline instruction.
        LDA   I        Increment I.
        INA   2
        STO   I
        SUB   N        Test for completion of loop.
        BZ    NEXT
        BN    NEXT
        ENA   *+3      Reset LP.
        STO   LP
        B     RENTR    Return to interpretive mode.
```

When the element in the group controlled by an implied DO is a subscripted variable dependent on the control variable of the DO, the oscillation between the inline coding and the interpretive mode can be extremely wasteful of execution time unless one recognizes at compile time that such an oscillation will occur and takes appropriate remedial action. For example, one can argue that, in general, elements are placed in an implied DO group since they are dependent on the control variable of the DO. Thus it may be anticipated that after one leaves the interpretive mode to initialize the DO control variable, inline instructions will need to be executed to compute the address(es) of subscripted variable(s). Similarly, if the I/O list contains more than one element in the implied DO group, it is wasteful to return to the interpretive mode to manipulate one variable address without checking whether the next set of instructions to be executed is also inline. To return from the inline mode to interpretive mode requires the execution of three instructions; the reverse motion requires one word of interpretive storage and the execution of innumerable instructions in the interpreter routine. Thus if the number of transfers of control to and from the interpreter can be minimized, the speed of execution may be enhanced. For example, consider the compilation of the I/O list:

(A(I),B(I+3,1),I=1,K,L)

as shown in Table 9.2.

The difficulty of compiling with economization results from the fact that the set of inline instructions must place the computed addresses into the interpretive list and the addresses into which these results are to be placed are not known when the inline coding is being gen-

TABLE 9.2

Compile without economization				*Compile with economization*			
	2				2		
	ENA	1			ENA	1	
	STO	I			STO	I	
NEXT	ENA	*+3		NEXT	...		Compute
	STO	LP			...		address
	B	RENTR			...		of A(I)
	2				...		Compute
	...		Compute		...		address of
	...		address		...		B(I+3,1)
	...		of A(I)		ENA	*+3	
	ENA	*+3			STO	LP	
	STO	LP			B	RENTR	
	B	RENTR			1	A(I)	
	1	A(I)			1	B(I+3,1)	
	2				2		
	...		Compute		LDA	I	Incre-
	...		address of		ADD	L	ment I
	...		B(I+3,1)		...		
	ENA	*+3			...		
	STO	LP					
	B	RENTR					
	1	B(I+3,1)					
	2						
	LDA	I	Incre-				
	ADD	L	ment I				
	...						
	...						

erated; consequently, the object time loader must backfill these addresses. Further, when a group contains both variables dependent on the control index of the implied **DO** and "free" variables, all inline instructions should be compiled together and similarly all interpretive mode data kept in a single list.

With the ability to include inline instructions in an output list, it is not inconceivable to allow expressions in the list so that output data may be computed without storing the result in a storage location. In general, if every item in an output list is considered to be an expression (that is, an *executable*), then without appropriate tests in the I/O generator, the right-hand side scanner of the arithmetic statements may be utilized to generate both required inline instructions and addresses. However, when any single arithmetic operation is to be executed, the arithmetic generator will normally leave the result of the computation in the accumulator. Thus if control is transferred back to the interpreter, this result may be lost. A special set of tags, such as **8** and **9**, would indicate that the next word contains not the address of a variable but the actual value to be output. Only two tags are needed in this instance since no other inline operations can be performed. Thus the inline instructions to compute the value of an expression would place this result in the interpretive list behind the appropriate tag. Such a facility during input is meaningless, since an input list is a list of addresses in which data are to be stored and may be considered as a set of left-hand sides or loadables.

In the interpretive mode, one more code or tag is essential. Tag **2** transfers control from the interpretive mode to inline coding with the expectation that control will be returned; but a code is needed to signify the end of the I/O list and thereby to force an I/O action such as outputting the record created by a **WRITE** statement and reinitializing the interpreter and other associated routines in preparation for the next I/O statement execution.

IOPAK

The I/O list interpreter is merely a portion of the overall supervisor which must control all input/output by manipulating the pointers **LP**, **FP** and **SP**, combining the actions required by the I/O list and the **FORMAT** lists. The general aspects of this supervisor, which we shall name **IOPAK**, are shown in Figure 9.2

The diagram in Figure 9.2 is based on the assumption that an I/O statement is compiled as:

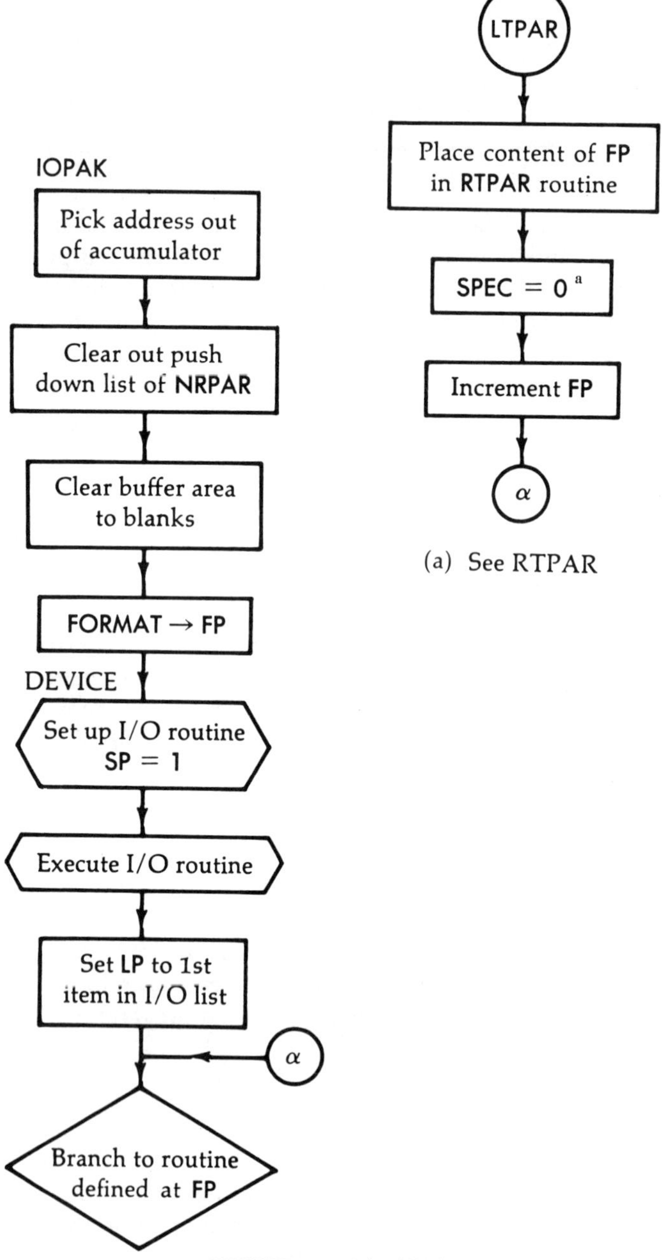

FIGURE 9.2 The IOPAK routine.

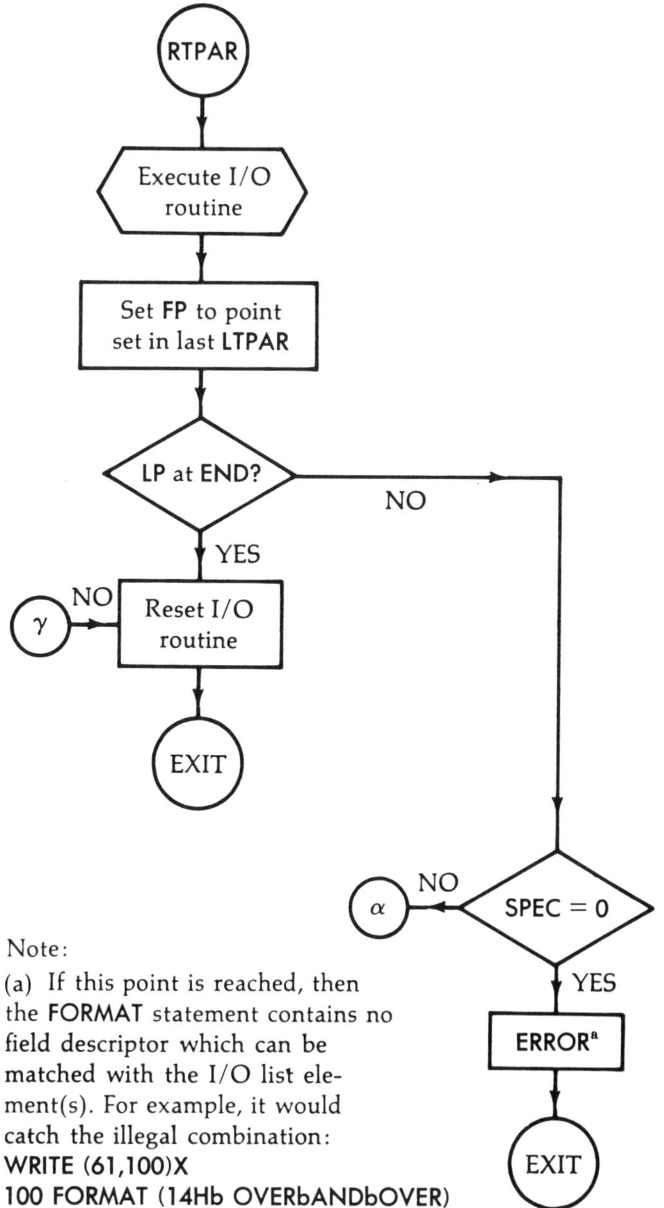

Note:

(a) If this point is reached, then the **FORMAT** statement contains no field descriptor which can be matched with the I/O list element(s). For example, it would catch the illegal combination:

```
WRITE (61,100)X
100 FORMAT (14Hb OVERbANDbOVER)
```

FIGURE 9.2 (Continued)

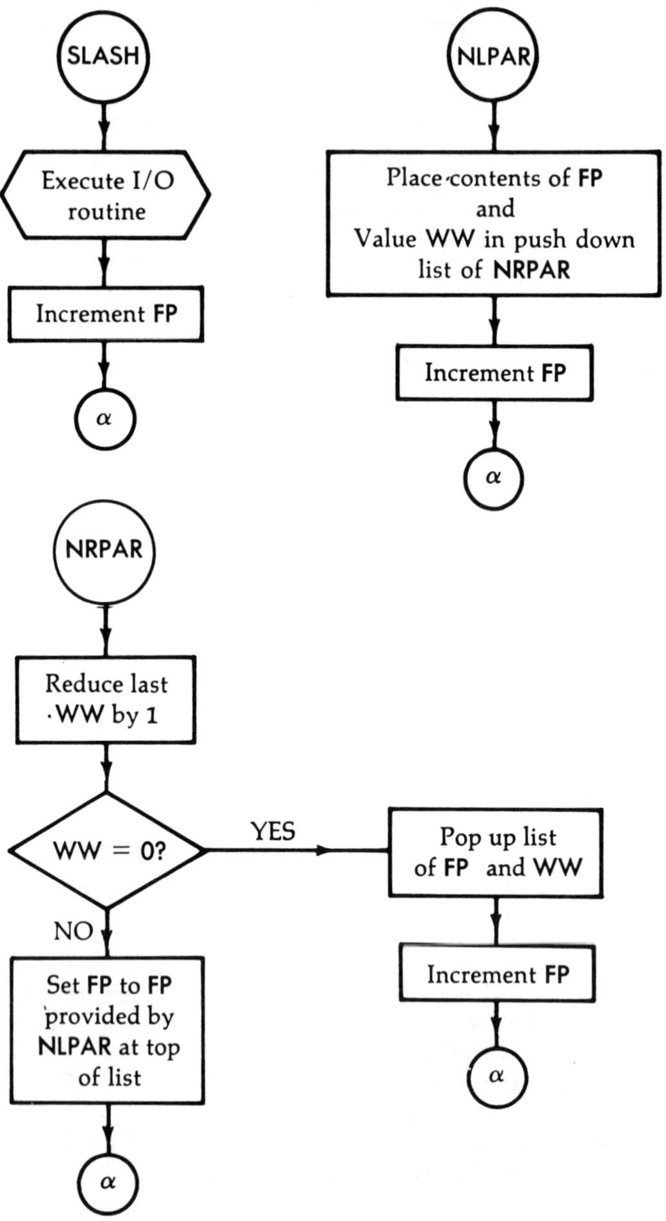

FIGURE 9.2 (Continued)

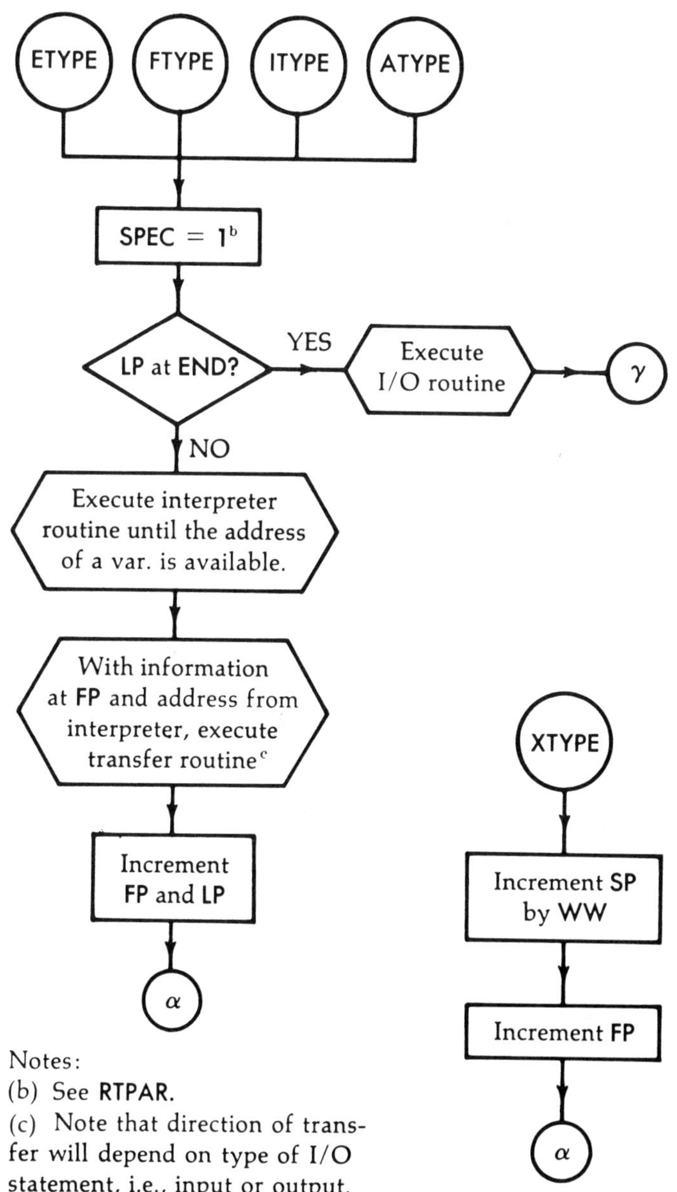

Notes:
(b) See RTPAR.
(c) Note that direction of transfer will depend on type of I/O statement, i.e., input or output.

FIGURE 9.2 (Continued)

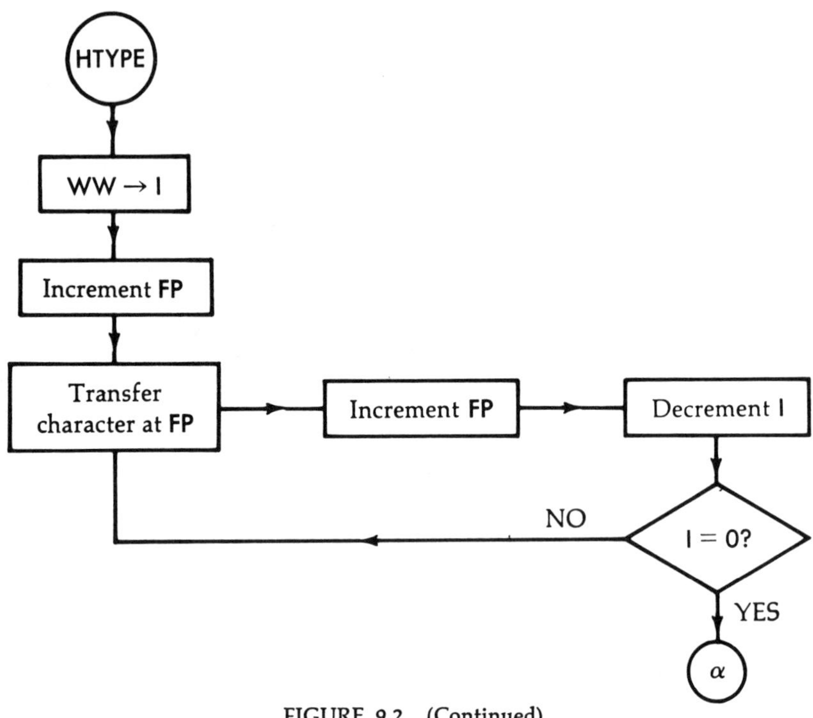

FIGURE 9.2 (Continued)

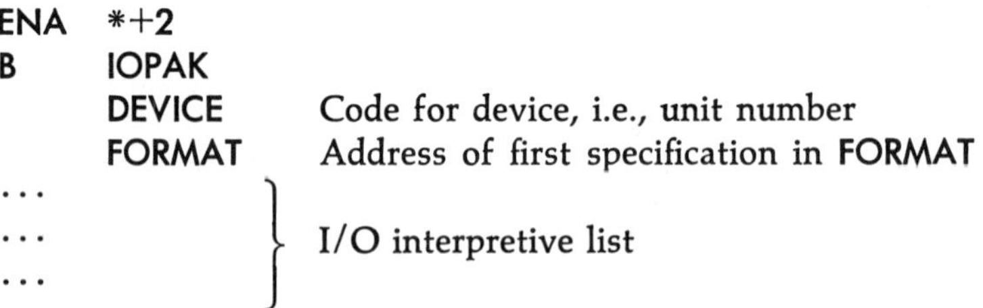

```
ENA   *+2
B     IOPAK
      DEVICE    Code for device, i.e., unit number
      FORMAT    Address of first specification in FORMAT
...           }
...           } I/O interpretive list
...           }
```

Since some devices for input/output are bidirectional, a special tag is included in the device code to provide **IOPAK** with the information on the direction of the transference of data. The instruction to "Execute the I/O routine" appears at several points in the flow chart. Since the device code contains a tag specifying the direction of the action to be taken, some of these execution operations are bypassed. For example, if the operation is one of output, the execution of the I/O routine within the initialization phase is bypassed in favor of an output operation either when **RTPAR** or **SLASH** is reached, or when the output list of variables is exhausted in one of the **TYPE** routines. Similarly, the

I/O routines in the TYPE routines are not executed on input, the input of the data having taken place during the initialization phase.

FORMAT in the above coding is the address of the referenced FORMAT statement, which will be used as the initial value of FP, the FORMAT pointer. The content of the accumulator on entry to IOPAK is the address of the first item in the I/O list which is, in fact, DEVICE.

In Figure 9.2, several other routines are referenced. The I/O list interpreter has already been discussed. The I/O routine is possibly a single instruction into which the pertinent bits can be placed so as to execute the input to an internal buffer or to transfer the contents of the buffer to an output device.

Within the E, F, I and A TYPE routines there is a reference to a transfer routine which is merely a routine that transfers data to or from the internal buffer, from or to the internal data areas, with conversion from or to BCD or ASCII mode, if necessary.

When the I/O statement references a variable FORMAT statement that was read in at object time, reference must be made to the FORMAT translation routine before the IOPAK routine is entered, this FORMAT routine placing the translation into the area where the source form was stored. Thus to prevent the retranslation of this data by a second reference to the same variable FORMAT, a special tag should prefix the translation. Since some compilers allow the manipulation of the data in the variable FORMAT arrays and there is no restriction regarding the timing of this manipulation (that is, manipulation may take place after the use of that FORMAT specification), then the source form of the specification must be inviolate, the translation must be stored in a separate area, and the statement retranslated at each reference. A variable FORMAT input/output statement may be compiled as follows:

```
WRITE(5,A)  ...
            ENA  Address(A(1,1))    Address of array to ACC
            B    VARFM              Branch to variable FORMAT
                                    translation routine
            ENA  *+2
            B    IOPAK
                 DEVICE
                 FORMAT
                 ...
                 I/O list
                 ...
```

UNFORMATTED READ AND WRITE

Where the **READ** or **WRITE** statement does not specify any **FORMAT** statement to be used, but a logical unit is specified, as in the form

READ(57)A

which specifies the use of logical unit **57**, as opposed to

READ 57,A

which specifies the use of the standard system input unit (usually the card reader) in connection with **FORMAT** statement **57**, the mode of transfer is without intermediate conversion. Thus on **READ**, if the external form is **ASCII** the contents of the buffer will be transferred directly to the elements of the input list without conversion. Similarly on a **WRITE** command, the internal mode of representation will be used to fill the buffer and the output onto the external device will operate over that representation. This can lead to some strange results on output when the receiving device attempts to translate the transmitted code into its own code system.

As in the case of free form input and output where the system provides the **FORMAT** statements, so in unformatted I/O, the system provides a **FORMAT** specification (say, called **UNFMT**) which performs no transformations, but merely transfers the data between the store and the buffer. The direction of this transfer obviously will depend on the statement: **READ** or **WRITE**.

ENCODE AND DECODE

Control Data Corporation equipment has for some years been supportive of FORTRAN systems in which the data manipulation instructions **ENCODE** and **DECODE** have been an integral part. Both instructions are comparable to **WRITE** or **READ** instructions in which no peripheral equipment is involved. In particular the **DECODE** instruction has the form:

DECODE (*<length>*, *<format>*, *<input record>*) *<output list>*

where *<length>* is the number of characters in the *<input record>* which are to be converted, *<format>* is the statement identifier of a **FORMAT** statement whose specifications are to control and direct the conversion process, *<input record>* is a specification of the first element of a sequential set of data cells (usually arranged to be a dimensioned array), and where *<output list>* is a list of variables which are to receive the transformed input record data. As may be realized, this statement is comparable with a **READ** statement where the number of characters (specified by *<length>*) in *<input record>* correspond to the characters in a record received from an external device. It is necessary to specify the number of characters in the **DECODE** statement since the *<input record>* is specified in terms of its first element only, not the whole sequential set.

Similarly, the **ENCODE** statement has the syntactic form:

ENCODE(*<length>*, *<format>*, *<output record>*) *<input list>*

where the semantics of the statement specify that the data extracted from the *<input list>* of variables are to be transformed into external code according to the specified **FORMAT** (referenced by *<format>*) and then are to be stored into the sequential storage cells which commence with the variable named in *<output record>*, at the rate of *<length>* characters per word. Overlooking the various actions to be taken when peculiar parameters are given for this statement (such as the value defined in *<length>* is greater than the word size of the machine), the **ENCODE** statement is similar to a **WRITE** statement where the *<output record>* is some internal device (possibly a buffer) instead of a peripheral device.

Recognizing these similarities between **DECODE** and **READ**, and between **ENCODE** and **WRITE**, it seems to be obvious that the facilities provided to implement **READ** and **WRITE** should be utilized to implement **DECODE** and **ENCODE**. Obviously the relationships between the I/O list and the **FORMAT** statement are the same in both sets of statements. In fact the only variations that occur are related to the manner in which data is extracted from the input list in the **DECODE** statement and inserted into words in the **ENCODE** statement. In the case of **READ** and **WRITE** these features are peculiar to the particular peripheral device and are transparent to the higher-level language user.

REREAD AND NOPRINT

Certain in-house FORTRAN implementations have included the specialized instruction **REREAD** which takes advantage of the implementation of both **READ** and **WRITE** which we discussed earlier. That is, if the implementation involves the use of an intermediate buffer which is not destroyed either after or during the process of input or output, then it is possible to perform a "truncated" **READ** which utilizes the contents of the buffer. Careful examination of the process of input or output which was described previously will reveal that the intermediate buffer always contains an external representation of the data being either input or output. In the case of input, the external form which is a direct copy of the representation on the external media (perhaps with minor transformations which are performed by the peripheral equipment itself, such as the conversion from Hollerith code on punch cards to ASCII code) is maintained in the intermediate buffer. Provided that in the process of conversion for internal storage, the contents of the buffer are not modified in situ, then the truncated READ is possible. This is called REREAD. In the case of output, the transformed internal representations are stored in external code (probably ASCII) in the buffer before the WRITE operation is performed. If this data string is not destroyed as part of the WRITE operation, then it is possible to REREAD this data also. Unfortunately, it is not possible to load the buffer without a real input or output operation. Hence we shall propose that there exists, corresponding to the truncated (or no device) READ statement, a truncated PRINT statement, in which the data is fetched from storage, the transformations are performed in accordance with the specified FORMAT statement, and the output string is formed in the intermediate buffer, but the real output operation is never initiated. This statement we shall call NOPRINT.

While actual REREAD statements were implemented in some domestic systems, in fact their implementation can be considerably shortened by specifying that a particular logical unit (say unit 0) is the internal buffer. Thus REREAD is equivalent to a READ on logical unit 0, while NOPRINT can be implemented by the use of WRITE onto logical unit 0.

RELATIONSHIP BETWEEN ENCODE, DECODE, REREAD, AND NOPRINT

By careful examination of the effects of ENCODE and DECODE it may be seen that the same operations can be achieved by the use of REREAD and NOPRINT. In particular a DECODE can be simulated by the use of an unformatted WRITE to unit 0 (the buffer) followed by a formatted READ from the buffer. For example, if the DECODE statement is

```
      DECODE(24,16,A(I))X,Y,Z
   16 FORMAT(I8)
```

where the array A is dimensioned greater than 4 elements and the machine on which this system is implemented contains 6 characters per word, then the equivalent pair of WRITE-READ statements are

```
      WRITE(0)A(1),A(2),A(3),A(4)
      READ(0,16)X,Y,Z
   16 FORMAT(I8)
```

Unfortunately, the implementation of **ENCODE** and **DECODE** are not machine independent since the word size of the machine influences the actions taken. However, by the use of I/O using unit **0** (the internal buffer), the operations of conversion are machine independent.

Whether or not unit **0** is implemented to be the internal buffer for use by the programmer, it is proposed here that the implementation of **ENCODE** and **DECODE** be achieved by the simulations outlined above.

SUMMARY

The complications that arise at object time in executing the interacting I/O statements and their referenced **FORMAT** statements are similar to those connected with compiling the interacting statements **COMMON, DIMENSION** and **EQUIVALENCE** (see Chapter 4). However, the compilation of definition statements at compile time has a unique solution, whereas the object time execution of an input/output statement interacting with a **FORMAT** statement may lead to invalid combinations that must be routed out at object time. For example, it is difficult, without actually executing the statement of output, to ensure that a real variable is output under control of the appropriate specification. Since the specifications do not define the action to be taken in this type of situation, most compiler writers (and hence object code writers) make their own decision as to the appropriate action. In an educational system, this situation may be considered a fatal error, whereas in a commercial environment it may be intentionally decided that the appropriate mode conversion is to be executed when this anomaly is encountered. Thus a piece of data stated on the input medium as an integer may be stored as a real variable value without recourse to storing it as an integer and then including a special statement to change mode.

Similarly, the specification of a too narrow field width on output has no definite solution. One system will refuse to output the data, giving an object time error message, while another will output, without comment, only those low order characters that fit the specification.

The inclusion of expressions as valid elements in an output statement can lead to a considerable saving in execution time in a program outputting a great amount of information that is not required at later stages or that can be computed without logical decision instructions. In fact, with continuation lines it is quite possible for a program to exist that contains only a single instruction, except maybe **STOP** and **END**. For example, a complete table of trigonometric function values may be produced by the statement

```
PRINT,(FLOAT(I),SIN(FLOAT(I)),COS(FLOAT(I)),I=1,180)
```

by making use of a free **FORMAT** output statement and executables.

Problem

9.1 Redesign the flow chart in Figure 9.1 to include free-form input. As the key to this requirement in the compiled instructions, assume that free form is required when the address in the I/O list normally referring to the **FORMAT** statement is zero.

10
Compiling the Subprogram

The subprogramming in algebraic languages serves two main purposes. In the first place, a subprogram conserves both memory space and programmer time when a particular operation or set of operations must be performed repeatedly under different circumstances and with varying sets of data. The programmer may consolidate his coding into a single set of statements and then execute that set by either using a single statement or including a reference to that subprogram in some other statement. Secondly, subprogramming enables the creation of program libraries where the programmer can find programs already coded by others. This provision may be available in one of two forms: Either the executive operating system of the computer may be programmed to fetch the subprogram from auxiliary storage where it is kept in relocatable machine language or compilable code, or the computing center may keep a card library of subprograms in source code available for inclusion by the programmer.

RECOGNIZING THE PROBLEM

To use a subprogram, the programmer must follow one of two courses: He must provide, from a library or by creating it himself, a subprogram in source code which requires compilation, or he must rely on the system to provide a subprogram from its own host library. In either case, the compiler must provide the instructions, within the object code produced from the calling program, to link the calling program to the subprogram, to provide a means of return from the subprogram to the calling program, and to transmit the data to be used to the subprogram. When an algebraic language is to be developed to operate under an already existent host system, the compiler originator may have no choice in the design of the linkage instructions to system library subprograms; for the sake of consistency, he should use the same linkage instructions to link into subprograms that were defined in source code by the programmer.

In general, references to subprograms in FORTRAN source programs may be recognized by the compiler by default. Since a subscripted variable has the same syntactic form as a reference to a function, the symbol table routine must provide to the appropriate generator the information that the reference is being made to an item that has not been defined in a **DIMENSION** statement. By default, this is to be considered a reference to a function subprogram. A reference to a subroutine subprogram is specific in that reference is made through a special calling statement.

In either event, the compiler will, at the recognition of an **END** statement, have in its possession the necessary information to determine which subprograms are required by the program being compiled. However, it cannot tell at that time which of these subprograms are to be obtained from the library and which are to be provided in source code by the programmer. Thus only when the entire job has been processed, can the system decide which subprograms the programmer has assumed are available in the system library. Also when the decision is postponed until this time, the system can be provided with subprograms whose names are the same as those stored in the library; thus if the system removes the names of required subprograms from its list as they are provided, there will be no confusion in the naming. For some peculiar reason, this is a serious shortcoming of many systems.

When the programmer requests the use of a library subprogram, the task of the compiler is influenced not only by the form of the standard linkage, but also by the manner in which the subprogram is loaded into memory and the tasks which are fulfilled by the loader. In particular, since previously compiled subprograms are usually stored in machine language form, they must be programmed (or compiled) so as to be relocatable in memory. To insist that any particular subprogram be placed in memory at the same set of addresses each time it is loaded will so restrict the use of available memory that inefficient systems will result. For example, assume that a system library contains 50 subprograms, each consisting of about 200 words. If it were possible for a single program to call upon any one or all of the subprograms and if it could be shown that in any one program the use of one subprogram would not destroy the usefulness of any other subprogram, then 10,000 word positions would have to be permanently reserved for their possible storage. On the other hand, if the subprograms were to be stored in the same locations each time they were used, this would alleviate some of the problems of linking to them from the calling program.

The problems of creating relocatable machine codes will not be considered here since the implementation of this option is machine dependent. The loader of relocatable programs is required to provide data which will be resident during the execution of the object program and which may not be considered a part of the function of the loader. As a general rule, the linkage instructions in the calling program must refer to the entry point to the subprogram in order to execute that subprogram. At the time of compiling a subprogram reference, the final storage location of that subprogram may not be known. This is not, in fact, a disadvantage when it is realized that references may be made to subprograms by the use of a parameter in a subprogram, without the compiler being aware of the request. Thus at compile time, an instruction may be generated which references an address in the object time data table indirectly and into which address will be placed the actual entry address to the subprogram.

When, as part of the job, the subprogram being referenced is provided in source language, the compiler will arrange to store the object time address in this location. When the subprogram is to be provided by the system, the loader must undertake this task. Similarly, in a multiprogramming environment where subprograms are shared by several programs, a common transfer vector can be used by the host system to direct linkages between the calling program and the referenced subprogram. In this situation, a resident vector (or directory) keeps track of the current location of a subprogram and the existence of the subprogram in accessible memory.

PROVISION OF DATA TO THE SUBPROGRAM

Now that a means of transferring control from the calling program to the subprogram has been established, it is necessary to provide a means for transferring data. In particular, since the relationships between the names of arguments in a reference to a subprogram and the formal parameters are not indicated in the defining statement, the references to parameters in the subprogram are not linked directly to the object time data table entries of the arguments. These links must be forged at object time.

Pass by value

In the section dealing with the compilation of code relevant to a function reference (Chapter 7), a skeletal code sequence was chosen which organized the transference of data between the calling program and the function (subprogram) through the use of the addresses of the arguments to be utilized. However, after close examination of the requirements for the transfer of data between the calling program and the function subprogram, it is obvious that the same linkage could be achieved using the values of the arguments rather than the addresses of the arguments. That is, since one of the properties of a function is that the generated value is passed back to the calling program separate from any identifier in the environment, then the need for argument addresses is obviated, if values are provided instead. Thus the skeletal form of a function subprogram linkage could be

```
MPT  function
DC   arg1
DC   arg2
...
...
DC   ≠
```

where **arg**$_i$ are the actual argument values instead of the addresses of the storage location of those arguments. This technique of linkage (call by value), ensures that the nonreturn property of a function subprogram is observed. In a subprogram with style of linkage, all parameters have only a local scope and thus the assignment of a value to the parameter does not reflect back to any identifier in the calling program, since the linkage does not provide a path back to the source of the data values.

Pass by location

The linkage of a program to a **SUBROUTINE** subprogram in FORTRAN necessitates the provision of a path in reverse from the subprogram back to the calling program since data values are passed back through the parameters. That is, in a ALGOL-style procedure or FORTRAN subroutine, changes in the values assigned to parameters are expected to be reflected back in the values of the actual arguments. Thus the method of passing addresses satisfies this need. This method is known as "call by location," or "call by address."

This technique also provides an ability for "short-circuiting" return values when this could create undesirable side effects. For example, when an identifier (or array element) is used as the source of data for an argument of a subroutine, the address of the identifier can be used by the subroutine both as a source and as a sink, thus changing the value of the identifier as the value of the corresponding parameter is altered. However, if the argument is a constant, it would be unfortunate if the value of that constant were changed at the same instant that the parameter to which it is assigned is also changed. Thus the placement of a copy of the value of the constant into a temporary storage location and the passage of the address of that location to the subroutine will permit the contents of that temporary location to be altered without actually changing the value of the constant. Some FORTRAN compilers (particularly those provided by a manufacturer) do not take this possibility into account. For example, the following program and subroutine, with the values of 2 and 3 assigned to I and K respectively, will produce the effect that all references to the value 1 after reference to the subprogram will act as the value 2! That is, the output to the program will be

1 = 2

if the nondestructive return to a constant has not been implemented.

```
      PROGRAM TEST
      I=2
      K=3
      CALL IT(1,I,K)
      J=1
      GO TO (1,2),J
    1 PRINT 100
      STOP
    2 PRINT 101
      STOP
  100 FORMAT(* 1 = 1 *)
  101 FORMAT(* 1 = 2 *)
      END
      SUBROUTINE IT(L,M,N)
      IF(M.GT.N) GO TO 99
      L = M
   99 RETURN
      END
```

It is obvious that where the argument of the invocation of a subprogram (which is to be passed by location) is an expression which requires evaluation, the return of a value from the subprogram to that argument has no semantic meaning, and in any case, since the value of the expression must be placed into a temporary storage location, the effects of any changes of the corresponding parameter are not reflected back in the calling program. This is not the case in the situation where the argument is an array element, and where the subscript is an expression which must be computed at run time. In this case, the necessary computations are to determine the address of the array element; that address corresponds to an actual element of the data set of the program being executed and thus this address is to be used both as a source of data as well as a recipient of values. Where the argument is a constant, the compiler should regard the argument as being a degenerate expression which requires evaluation (actually is "evaluated" by a simple fetch operation) whose evaluated result is to be placed in a temporary storage location. Thus it will be impossible for the invoked subprogram to return a value to the location of the constant and thus effectively alter the value of the constant.

The concepts of pass by value and pass by location can be visualized in terms of source text manipulations which occur at run time. In both cases, the values of the arguments are computed in advance of the execution of the subprogram. Where the argument is to be passed by value (or in the case of ALGOL-style procedures, is to be *received* by value) the operation of parameter passing can be simulated by inserting into the header of the subprogram a statement of the form

<parameter> ::= *<argument>*

By this means the argument is evaluated and its value passed to the parameter. Thenceforth, the parameter is the sole reference to the argument and since the parameter is local in scope to the subprogram no side effects are possible.

In the case of pass by location it is necessary to associate the location transmitted with each and every reference to the corresponding parameter. This can be accomplished by substituting for each occurrence of the parameter in the body of the subprogram, a reference to the location of the argument. For example, let us define a set of special identifiers of the form $\mathsf{L}(\mathsf{arg}_i)$ which are associated with the location of argument arg_i. Then the substitution of $\mathsf{L}(\mathsf{arg}_i)$ for each occurrence of the appropriate parameter simulates the pass by location process.

In both of these substitutions it is important to be aware of the scope of the identifiers being referenced. In particular consider the following ALGOL-style program segment:

```
begin real b; b := 2;
   begin real procedure P1(x); [value x;]
         P1 := x + b;
      begin real a,b,c;
         a := 2; b := 1;
         c := P1(a + b);
      end;
   end;
end;
```

This example has been contrived to exemplify the scope of the identifiers named **b**. In particular there can be some confusion as to which particular version of **b** is being referenced in the procedure **P1**, particularly when called (invoked) with the argument **a+b**. Let us here consider the case where the parameter of the procedure is to be passed by value. The confusion arises when the actual operation of executing the procedure is examined. One school of thought is that the meaning of the procedure reference can be determined by substituting the body of the procedure into the invoking statement. That is, the program is equivalent to:

```
begin real b; b := 2;
   begin real procedure P1(x); value x;
         P1 := x + b;
      begin real a,b,c;
         a := 2; b := 1;
         c := (a+b) + b;
      end;
   end;
end;
```

where the parenthesized group (**a+b**) is the substitution for the parameter **x**. An alternative definitional form is to consider that a call is equivalent to a jump out of the current environment into that of the procedure at the place where the procedure is defined, the substitution of the argument for the parameter and then a return as diagrammed as follows:

```
begin real b; b := 2;
   begin real P1;
         P1 := (a+b) + b;
      begin real a,b,c;
         a := 2; b := 1;
         c :=         ;
      end;
   end;
end;
```

In these two examples it can be seen that there is an ambiguity as to the particular identifier **b** which is being referenced and hence the value to be used in the evaluation of the procedure. In the first case it would appear that the value assigned to the identifier **c** in the inner block will be **4**, whilst in the second case the value will be undefined! This is due to the apparent unknown identifier **a**. However, if there existed an outer block in which **a** was defined to have the value **2**, then it would appear that **c** would eventually be assigned the value **6**. In fact, neither of these cases is correct.

To explain this, we must consider the two separate identifiers named **b**. Where a procedure utilizes an identifier which is not specified in its header statements, then that identifier is in the environment of the encompassing block irrespective of the apparent location of the execution of the procedure. Thus in any event, the **b** in the statement **P1 := x + b;** has the value **2** associated with it. Secondly, in a pass by value, the value of the argument is evaluated in advance of the argument/parameter passing. Thus the value of the phrase **a+b** is **3** since it is computed in the environment of the innermost block. Thus it would appear that the best model for parameter passing by value is the second above; that is where the control is transferred from the calling point to the location of the definition of the procedure. However, in the case of pass by name (as we shall see shortly) the former is a more accurate model. In the case of pass by location, the value of the argument is computed in advance as in the case of pass by value, and thus the second model is still applicable.

Pass by name

The third classical method of passage of parameter values is pass by name. In this style of passage, the expression which forms the argument is not evaluated until it is referenced within the referenced subprogram. In fact, the argument expression is evaluated on each and *every* reference to the corresponding parameter. Thus if some elements of the argument change in value during the execution of the subprogram, then successive evaluations of the argument expression do not result in the same value. As a simple example consider the program segment:

```
begin procedure P3(x,y); begin
   z := x;   x := y;   y := z;   end;
   real i; real array a[81];
      i := 2;   a[i] := 81;
         P3(i,a[i]);
end;
```

ALGOL defines that where a parameter is not explicitly declared to be passed an argument by value (by the statement **value** x) then the method is pass by name. Thus in the above segment of program, the parameters x and y are to receive their values by name. In this example, there only exists a single environment; hence we shall be unhampered by the problems of scope of identifiers as occurred previously. In the case of pass by name, we replace each reference to a parameter by its corresponding argument expression, causing the argument to be evaluated on each reference. That is, the equivalent program is (in the mode of substituting the procedure into the place of its invocation):

```
begin real i; real array a[81];
   i := 2; a[i] := 81;
   z := i; i := a[i]; a[i] := z;
end;
```

Now close examination of the procedure shows that it is reminiscent of the classical exchange algorithm; thus one would expect the result to be an interchange of values between i and a[i]. At the instant when the procedure is invoked, the value of i is 2, and hence we could expect an interchange of values between i and a[2]. However, this does not take place. In fact, the sequence of statements

```
z := i; i := a[i]; a[i] := z;
```

result in the assignment of the value 81 to i and the assignment of the value 2 to a[81]! It was expected on what was thought to be close examination that the value 2 would have been assigned to a[2]. However, even closer examination shows that the value of i changes in the process of executing the procedure which effects the evaluation of the location of a[i]. If this same procedure had been evaluated with the process of pass by location, the locations of i and a[i] would have been computed in advance and this shift of subscript value would have not affected the result.

The general case of passing by any one of the three methods (pass by value, by address, or by name) is exemplified by a language of the form suggested by Ledgard[1] in his mini-language number 5. For our purposes we have made slight modification to that language in order to expose more clearly the parameter/argument transfer features. We shall define a program to be composed of two parts; a set of procedure definitions and a sequence of executable commands. Since the procedures of this language directly affect the storage of the machine and do not by themselves have values as in the case of functions, references to procedures are themselves executable commands, as is the **CALL** <*subroutine*> statement in FORTRAN. Thus the statement of the syntactic form

<*procedure name*> (<*argument list*>)

references the named procedure and passes the arguments listed within the parentheses. The only other statement form which we permit in the executable sequence is the assignment statement of the form <*identifier*> ::= <*expression*> where the right hand side is a simple arithmetic expression including the dyadic operators +,−,* and /. Identifiers are the upper case characters (**A**,**B**, . . . , **Z**). Included in the operands of expressions are both identifiers and integer constants (**0**,**1**,**2**, . . .). Procedure names have the following general form: **P**<*integer*>.

Procedure definitions are composed of three elements:

1. A header statement specifying the name of the procedure and the parameters used with the syntactic form

proc <*procedure name*> (<*parameter list*>)

where a parameter is a lower case alphabetical character (**a**,**b**, . . . , **z**)

2. A set of declarations of the passing process to be followed with respect to each parameter, where each declaration is of the syntactic form

<*pass form*><*parameter list*>
and where <*pass form*> ::= **value**|**address**|**name**

3. An assignment command sequence terminated by the statement

1. H. F. Ledgard, "Ten Mini-Languages," *Computing Surveys*, vol. 3, no. 3 (September 1971).

end in which each assignment command is of the form

<p-identifier> ::= *<p-expression>*

where *<p-identifier>* is either an identifier (as in the executable part of the program) or a parameter and where *<p-expression>* is an arithmetic expression containing the dyadic operators +,−,*, and /, and operands which may be identifiers, constants, or parameters.

The penultimate statement in a procedure is of the form

return *<p-expression>*

which is taken to mean that the value of the *<p-expression>* is to be returned to the calling program. The final statement in a procedure is an **end** statement.

The complete syntax of this language is as follows:

<program> ::= *<procedure definition set>* *<executable statement sequence>*

<procedure definition set> ::= *<procedure definition>* {*<procedure definition>*}$_0^\infty$

<procedure definition> ::= *<header statement>* *<pass form sequence>* *<p-statement sequence>* **end**

<header statement> ::= **proc** *<procedure name>* (*<parameter list>*)

<procedure name> ::= P*<integer>*

<parameter list> ::= *<parameter>*{,*<parameter>*}$_0^\infty$

<parameter> ::= a|b|c|· · ·|x|y|z

<integer> ::= {1|2|3| · · · |8|9|0}$_1^2$

<pass form sequence> ::= *<pass form declaration>* {*<pass form declaration>*}$_0^\infty$

<pass form declaration> ::= *<pass form><parameter list>*

<pass form> ::= **value**|**address**|**name**

<p-statement sequence> ::= *<p-statement>* {*<p-statement>*}$_0^\infty$ **return** *<p-expression>*

<p-statement> ::= *<p-assignment>*|*<p-procedure call>*

<p-procedure call> ::= *<procedure name>*(*<p-argument list>*)

<p-argument list> ::= *<p-argument>*{,*<argument>*}$_0^\infty$

<p-argument> ::= *<p-expression>*

<p-expression> ::= *<p-multiply factor>*| *<p-expression>*{+|−}$_1^1$*<p-multiply factor>*

<p-multiply factor> ::= *<p-term>*|
<p-multiply factor>$\{*|/\}_1^1$*<p-term>*
<p-term> ::= *<parameter>*|*<constant>*|(*<p-expression>*)
<identifier> ::= A|B|C|···|X|Y|Z
<constant> ::= $\{1|2|3|\cdots|8|9|0\}_1^\infty$
<p-assignment> ::= {*<parameter>*|*<identifier>*$\}_1^1$:=
<p-expression>
<executable statement sequence> ::= *<executable statement>*
{*<executable statement>*$\}_0^\infty$
<executable statement> ::= *<assignment statement>*
<assignment statement> ::= *<identifier>* := *<expression>*
<expression> ::= *<multiply factor>*|
<expression>$\{+|-\}_1^1$*<multiply factor>*
<multiply factor> ::= *<term>*|*<multiply factor>*$\{*|/\}_1^1$*<term>*
<term> ::= *<identifier>*|*<constant>*|(*<expression>*)|
<procedure call>
<procedure call> ::= *<procedure name>*(*<expression list>*)
<expression list> ::= *<expression>*{,*<expression>*$\}_0^\infty$

Weil[2] developed a short ALGOL program which exemplified the differences between the two techniques of parameter passing which are employed in that language; that is, pass by value and pass by name. Using the same basic elements as that example, consider the following program segment which is written in the language expressed above:

```
proc  P1(a)
      value a
      a := a + 1
      return a
end
proc  P2(a)
      address a
      a := a + 1
      return a
end
proc  P3(a)
      name a
      a := a + 1
      return a
end
```

2. R. L. Weil, Jr., "Testing the Understanding of the Difference Between Call by Name and Call by Value in ALGOL 60," *Comm. ACM*, vol. 8, no. 6 (June 1965).

```
proc  P4(b)
      value b
      return b + b
end
proc  P5(b)
      address b
      return b + b
end
proc  P6(b)
      name b
      return b + b
end
```

Using these procedures we can now examine the inter-related effects of various statements. In particular the above procedures have been designed to show both the effect of passing values to and from the procedure through the argument and parameter lists, and the effect of returning a value through a commonly known mailbox, the object of the statement **return**. In each of the following cases we shall consider that the following of assignment statement has been executed:

$$X := 1$$

Let us firstly consider the assignment statement

$$Y := P4(P1(X))$$

The procedure **P4** is defined as having its single argument passed by value, hence the value of its argument can be evaluated in advance. Similarly **P1** is a call by value procedure. Thus after the execution of the two procedures the value assigned to **Y** is **4** and the value associated with **X** is unaltered. That is, **Y** is assigned the value **4** through the use of the **return** statements in each procedure, but **X** is unaffected since its value was passed to the procedure by value, thus providing no route back for the value assigned to its corresponding parameter. On the other hand, let us consider the case

$$Y := P4(P2(X))$$

In this case, the procedure **P2** is called by address and hence a bridge is built between the argument **X** and the parameter **a** (in **P2**) which is bidirectional. Both procedures referenced here are such that their arguments are to be evaluated in advance of the parameter passing. Thus the value of **X** is passed to **P2** by the use of the address L_X. Thus following the execution of the procedure **P2**, the value associated with the location L_X is **2**, and the value of the argument of the procedure

P4 is also 2. Thus following the execution of the procedure P4, the value to be assigned to Y is 4 and the value associated with X is still unaltered.

In the case of the statement

$$Y := P4(P3(X))$$

the procedure P3 is called by name, but since P4 is called by value, the single value obtained from the execution of P3 is used as the argument. Hence, the resulting effects on X and Y are identical with those for Y := P4(P3(X)).

However, in the case of

$$Y := P6(P2(X))$$

where the outer procedure is called by name and the inner by address the timing of the evaluation of the argument values is significant. In particular, since P6 is called by name, each and every reference to the parameter b in procedure P6 requires the evaluation of the procedure P1. Now although P2 is called by address it has the effect of modifying the value of argument. Thus the procedure P6, being evaluated under these circumstances is equivalent to the procedure body

return P2(X) + P2(X)

Initially X is associated with the value 1 and thus after the execution of the procedure P2 for the first time, the valued returned to the calling program is 2 and the value of X is modified to 2. On the second reference to P2, the computed value to be returned is 3 and the value associated with X is also 3. Thus executing procedure P6 results in the assignment of the value 5 to Y, the identifier X having been modified to be associated to the value 3 in the process. Conversely, in the case of Y := P6(P1(X)), the value associated with X is unmodified and finally, Y = 4 and X = 1.

The remainder of the cases which permute the six procedures are left to the reader for examination.

The important difference between the process of parameter/argument association for the pass by address and pass by name modes is related with the binding time of the values. In the case of pass by address (and pass by value) the value of the argument is computed in advance of the passage of the argument. Thus only one value or location is associated with the parameter. In the case of pass by name, the value of the argument is to be computed on each and every reference; thus the time of computing the value of the argument is following passage. To accomplish this, it is necessary for the compiler to provide a new procedure (generated internally) which is to be referenced by the actually called procedure, which will compute the value of the argument. These internally generated procedures are called "thunks" by Ingerman.[3]

In a system where it is possible for arguments to be passed in any one of the three methods, it is not possible for the compiler to ascertain in advance the method of passage since this information is contained in the referenced procedure, not in the calling program. Thus it is necessary for the compiler to generate code for each argument and then to provide the location of that code to the referenced procedure. Where the procedure is called by value or address, the procedure can invoke the appropriate thunk at the time of invocation of the procedure. It is then the procedure's responsibility to pass the information to the parameter. In the case of call by name, the location of the thunk is to be passed to the parameter and code appropriate to the linkage to the thunk is to be compiled in place of each parameter reference.

AN ARGUMENT TRANSFER MODEL

Let us assume that the transfer facilities between a procedure reference and the compiled procedure body is accomplished with the aid of a procedure directory as shown in Figure 10.1.

In this language the mode of transfer of arguments from the reference to the procedure is defined not in connection with the reference but instead within the procedure. Thus the compilation of the reference cannot be completed to the extent that the argument list is converted into the precise form required by the procedure but instead the argument list must be of such a form as to permit the passing of the arguments by any one of the three methods. Provided that arguments are restricted to identifiers, the three modes of argument passing can be seen to be related to each other as the nodes of the reference graph for each identifier, as shown in Figure 10.2.

It may be noted in this graph that the arrows representing the stages of reference are unidirectional—given the node at the tail of the arrow it is possible to derive the element at the head but not vice versa. Thus to achieve the greatest generality it is necessary to pass to the procedure the head of the reference graph, that is the identifier. On the other hand if either the address (location l_{id}) or the value (v_{id}) is passed

3. P. F. Ingerman, "Thunks," *Comm. ACM*, vol. 4, no. 1 (January 1961).

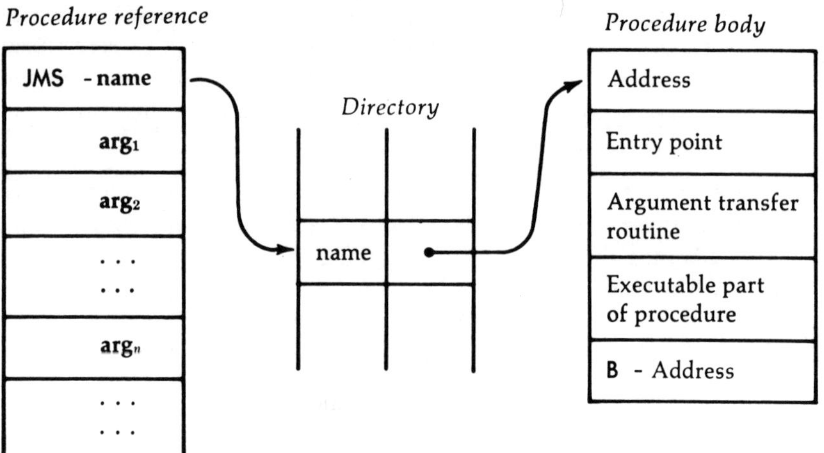

FIGURE 10.1 Procedure transfer model.

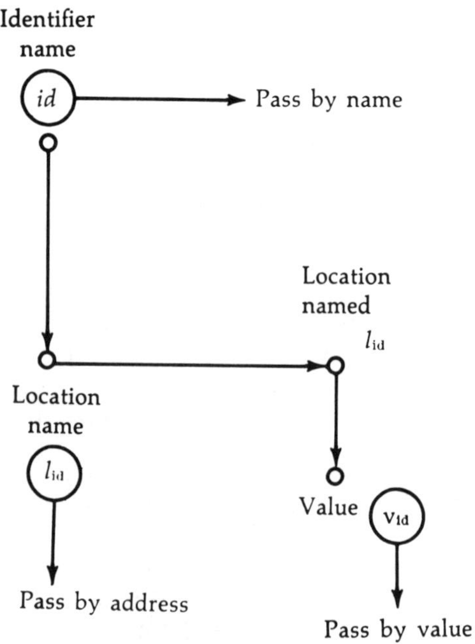

FIGURE 10.2 Identifier reference graph.

then it is not possible to ascertain the name of the identifier within the procedure. Similarly, if only the value is passed across the interface then it is not possible to derive either the location from which the value was obtained or the identifier with which that value was associated. Hence in the absence of information regarding the mode of passing arguments to a procedure it is necessary to be ready with the most general item of data relating to the argument, that is the identifier name. Given this item of information together with access to the symbol table, it will be possible for the procedure to obtain the required argument feature. Hence although the declarative statements of the procedure define the mode of argument passing they must be expected to compile into sequences of executable code which accomplish the task of collecting the arguments from the referencing program.

In the case where the argument is an identifier of a single data element, such as a simple variable or an array element, the thunk will consist of a simple routine which merely provides the address of that element. That is, provided that in the case of an array element, the subscripts are constants. Where the subscripts are expressions (including the degenerate expression which is composed of a single identifier), it is necessary to compile a thunk which evaluates the subscripts and computes the array element address at each reference, in the same way as an expression must be evaluated repeatedly.

NOMINATIVE ARGUMENT PASSING MODE

The problem of argument passing is complicated by the fact that it is the procedure which defines the mode in which arguments are to be received. Thus to maintain sufficient generality it is necessary to compile thunks for all arguments in the absence of the necessary information. Thus the invocation, or initialization routine associated with the referenced procedure must perform the task of retrieving the arguments in the correct (or appropriate) mode. A converse arrangement is worthy of consideration; that is, the case in which the mode of passage is prescribed in the calling reference. This would permit the compiler to generate thunks only for those arguments which are to be passed by name. If the calling sequence (JMS plus argument list) contains the addresses of the arguments which are to be passed by value or address the procedure need not differentiate between these parameter references if the protective measure of transferring the values of arguments (to be passed by value) to temporary storage locations is followed. In this situation the temporary storage location forms a "dead end" through which the original argument cannot be referenced, thereby simulating the pass by value mode in pass by address methodology.

In the case of pass by name, the address in the calling sequence is the address of the thunk which is to be referenced by the procedure. It is necessary to distinguish this address of a location of a thunk to which control is to be transferred as contrasted with an address which is to be used as the source or sink of data in the case of pass by value or address. In our previous examples of the sequence of code for linking between a calling program and the procedure, we have symbolized the argument list as a sequence of addresses which follow the actually linking command. In fact, these addresses will probably only occupy the lower portion of the words, the upper part (the operation code location) being irrelevant. However, that is not to indicate that the upper part not be used. In the case of I/O statements (Chapter 9), the translation of the specifications for the source or destination of data elements is coded as an address preceded by a interpretive code. The two cases of parameter/argument association (pass by address and pass by value being considered to be synonomous) are distinguished only by the fact that in one case the address in the linkage list is the actual address of the argument (pass by address) whilst in the other case the address is the entry point to the thunk. If it is prescribed that the procedure is passed an argument address through the accumulator, then the passage of an argument by address can be accomplished by the instruction **ENA arg** and the thunk can be entered by **JMS arg**. Unfortunately, if these two instructions occur in the linkage list, they cannot be executed in situ since they are not succeeded by an instruction which will transfer control to the point in the procedure where they are referenced. Furthermore, it is not possible for the procedure to simply perform a **JMS** to the locations of these instructions since the return address must be stored somewhere. One solution would be to make each argument entry in the linkage list into a three-word sequence—a dummy word to receive the return address of a **JMS**, a word to contain either the instruction **ENA arg** or **JMS arg**, and a word to contain the branch back instruction, in the form **B −(*−2)**. One of these words can be saved if the target machine utilizes (makes available) the instructions **MPT** and **BB**. In this case the return address is maintained in an internal register. However, since it is almost certain that the procedure itself would have been entered through the **MPT** command, the return address register must be implemented as a stack in order to facilitate the compound calls.

A further alternative which was made available on some machines and which would be useful here, is the instruction **execute** (**EXT**). This command takes the form **EXT** a, where a is the address of an instruction which is to be performed. The operation of this **EXT** instruction is to fetch the referenced instruction into the instruction register of the target machine and to execute it as if it had been located at the location of the **EXT** command. Only one instruction can be executed in this manner and no change is made to the program counter,[4] so that the succeeding instruction which is executed is that which succeeds the **EXT** command. The compilation of the parameter reference within the procedure will result in the generation of the instruction **EXT** p_i where p_i is the location of the address of the referenced parameter. If the code succeeding this reference proceeds on the assumption that the address of the argument is to be found in the accumulator, then there is no difference in the coding within the procedure which is dependent on the method of argument passage.

PASS BY STRING

In the considerations for the passage of parameter associations it turns out that the environment of the argument is the environment of the calling program rather than the environment of the called procedure. This result is directly attributable to the environment of the routine (thunk in the case of call by name) which determines the address of the argument. However, there is another style of parameter passing which is not used in higher level languages, but which is common is assembly level systems; that is, pass by string, or macro-expansion. In this case, as outlined below, the environment of the argument is the environment of the activated procedure rather than the activating program.

In our mini-language outlined previously, let us now add the pass form **string** with the semantic specification that the actual symbolic string which composes the argument be passed into the procedure. As a simple example of the difference that this can make, consider the following vignette of program:

```
proc P7(x)
   <pass form> x
   return 7 − x
end
```

In this definition the syntactic component *<pass form>* has not yet been expanded. Consider the call upon this procedure with the statement

$$C := P7(3 + 4)$$

4. Unless of course, if the referenced instruction changes the contents of the program counter.

In the case of pass by value (and equally for pass by address and name) the result returned by the procedure would be **0** since the value of **x** is computed as a single entity, that is, **x** is assigned the result of evaluating the expression **3 + 4**. However, when **x** is passed a value as a string, the return statement becomes

return 7 − 3 + 4

and thus the value returned to the calling program is **8** instead of **0**. Similarly, variations in the scope of identifiers can be explored using this mode of parameter passing. In the case of assembly languages, a macroexpansion statement is regarded as a global procedure having the scope of the point of call rather than the scope of the point of definition.

SUMMARY

We have purposely separated the problems of parameter passing and the argument referencing processes from the problems of storage allocation which were considered in detail in Chapter 5. Whilst it is obvious that storage management can affect the means by which argument/parameter associations are implemented, the converse is not necessarily true. In fact, it is the author's opinion that the whole question of argument/parameter associations needs to be reviewed, particularly with respect to the implicit features which tend to cause untold grief to programmers. This problem is partially tied up with the problems of identifier passage and inheritance in block-structured programs. In both cases, it would appear that the most widely accepted (and implemented) schemes for passage of elements between subprograms is the "afterthought" system wherein the method of passage is prescribed after the inner subprogram has been reached. As proposed here, it is feasible to specify the method of argument passing in advance of the procedure activation and moreover not to maintain any consistency with respect to pass mode over many activations. That is, simply because in one activation an argument is passed by one technique, it is not necessary that all subsequent associations be accomplished in the same method. Similarly in the case of block structured languages, it would appear to be more beneficial to specify which identifiers are to be non-local in the header to the block rather than to assume that all identifiers are inherited, unless otherwise specified (by naming as being local). Similarly, our suggestion that passage by **string** should be considered as one form of argument/parameter association is worthy of further investigation.

APPENDIX A

A Multipass Compiler of Note

The compiler outlined here[1] was originally produced for an IBM 1401 processor with a small memory system. It was not possible for the whole compiler to reside in memory at one time and thus a multi-pass system was necessary. Add to this the empirical fact that the memory space required to contain the generated code for a FORTRAN program is approximately equal to that required to contain the original program text, a scheme was developed whereby the compiler was passed against the text instead of the usual converse process. The result was an object program already in memory ready to be executed. Although the IBM 1401 processor is not the most modern machine available today, and has been widely replaced by other systems, the compiler is still of sufficient interest to be outlined here. In particular, this outline gives an excellent overview of the various segments of a compiler which are required, irrespective of the manner in which the compiler execution is implemented.

Phase 01—System Monitor

Note: This phase is resident in the computer memory throughout the compilation. When any other phase has completed its task, control is transferred back to the monitor.

1. L. H. Haines, "Serial Compilation and the 1401 FORTRAN Compiler," *IBM Systems Journal*, Vol. 4, No. 1, 1965, Form No. 321-0002. Reprinted and edited by permission from *IBM Systems Journal* © 1965, by International Business Machines Corporation.

1. Brings in next phase from the current input unit.

2. Ensures that between phases, no extraneous material is left which would jeopardize the execution of the incoming phase.

Phase 02—Loader

1. Stores the information on the control card that precedes each source deck.

2. Checks the storage information on the control card against the available memory unless the program is not to be compiled for execution on this machine.

3. Reads in the source program and stores it in memory, appending to each statement a three-character position for a sequence number and a one-character position for a statement type code.

4. Deblanks the statements except in the Hollerith fields of FORMAT statements.

5. Collects continued statements and checks for an overabundance of the same.

6. Checks for special input statement characters and converts any, if found, to special internal codes.

7. Places special delimiters around each statement. (Because of deblanking, the statements are not of equal length.)

8. Generates a STOP statement after the last statement.

Phase 03—Scanner

1. Determines the statement type of each statement and inserts the appropriate code in the appendage to the statement.

2. Numbers each statement in sequence.

Phase 04—Sort I

Tests available memory to determine whether each statement can be expanded by three characters. If this is not possible, the compilation is terminated after a message is output, indicating that the object program is too large.

Phase 05—Sort II

By expanding each statement by three characters, statements of the same type are linked so that each statement has the address of the next statement of the same type appended to it.

Phase 06—Sort III

The source program is sorted by statement type and shifted to low storage.

Phase 07—Insert Group Mark

The delimiter that separates the statement from its appendage is replaced by a group mark.

Phase 08—Squoze

1. Keywords are eliminated from the source statements, and the statements are squeezed to expand the available storage.
2. Statements with invalid keywords are eliminated from the program and appropriate error messages printed.

Phase 09—Dimension I

1. A table containing the names of variables mentioned in the chain of DIMENSION statements is constructed in high memory.
2. Each table element contains: (a) the array name, (b) the number of dimensions, (c) the size of each dimension, and (d) a space for control characters and data to be generated in the EQUIVALENCE phases and the second DIMENSION phase.

Phase 10—Equivalence I

1. Checks all arrays mentioned in EQUIVALENCE statements to ensure that they have occurred in DIMENSION declarations.
2. Adds simple variables that occur in EQUIVALENCE statements to the table of arrays generated in phase 09. These variables are inserted into the table as if they were single element arrays.

Phase 11—Equivalence II

Computes the offsets of equivalenced arrays and notes the relationships between arrays (that is, implicit equivalencing as a result of the mentioning of a single array in more than one EQUIVALENCE group).

Phase 12—Dimension Phase II

Arrays are assigned object time addresses.

Phase 13—Variables I

1. The source statements are scanned for variable names.
2. Simple variables are tagged for processing in phase 16.
3. Subscripted variables with constant subscripts are replaced by object time addresses.
4. Subscripted variables with variable subscripts are replaced by the computation required at object time to compute the location of that element.
5. Array names appearing in lists are replaced by two memory addresses denoting the limits of the array when no subscripts are appended to the name.
6. Array names appearing without subscripts in other places are replaced by the address of the first element of the array.

Phase 14—Variables II

The entire source program is moved to high memory, leaving room for subsequent phases. The remaining storage is then cleared for tables including that generated in phase 12.

Phase 15—Variables III

This is not a self-sufficient phase, but is resident during phases 16 and 17. Phase 15 is a housekeeping routine.

Phase 16—Variables IV

1. The compiler scans input statements and the left-hand side of assignment statements for simple variables. Each unique variable is assigned an object time address.
2. All variables in statements are checked against the object time address table, and when a match is found, the object time address is substituted for the variable name. When a match is not found, it is assumed that the variable is undefined.

Phase 17—Variables V

A check is made for unused variables.

Phase 18—Constants I

Constants in the source program are extracted and converted to internal mode with truncation if necessary.

Phase 19—Constants II

This phase is the same as phase 14. The table of simple variables is destroyed.

Phase 20—Constants III

The constants are assigned object time addresses at the low end of memory. The constants are then placed in these locations and are replaced in the source program by the addresses.

Phase 21—Subscripts

Subscripts that require object time computation (that is, consist of expressions) are reduced to a set of parameters.

Phase 22—Statement Numbers I

All statement numbers appearing in the source program are converted to a unique three-character code.

Phase 23—Format I[2]

All input/output statements are checked against the FORMAT statements to ensure that all the FORMAT statements are necessary. Unreferenced FORMAT statements are discarded.

Phase 24—Format II[2]

The object time FORMAT strings are developed and stored in the low end of memory.

Phase 25—Lists I

Lists are compared to eliminate duplicates and thus to optimize object time storage.

Phase 26—Lists II

The object time lists of addresses and instructions (to compute array element locations) are developed and stored at the low end of memory.

2. The authors of this system named phases 23 and 24, Tamrof I and II.

Phase 27—Lists III

Each input/output statement is reduced to the address of the first item in the list string (if present), the address of the FORMAT string, and the logical unit number.

Phase 28—Statement Numbers II

This phase is the same as phase 14.

Phase 29—Statement Numbers III

The three character codes of statement numbers appearing within statements are stored in a table.

Phase 30—Statement Numbers IV

The statement numbers appearing as identifiers in statements are checked against the table of statement numbers generated in phase 29. When a match is found, the sequence number generated in phase 03 is placed in the table. Undefined and multiply defined statement numbers are also checked.

Phase 31—Statement Numbers V

Unreferenced statement numbers are noted.

Phase 32—Input/Output I

The linkage to the object time FORMAT routine is inserted in each input/output statement prior to the data generated in phase 27.

Phase 33—Arithmetic I

This phase is a resident housekeeping phase for phases 34–38:

1. The unary minus and exponential operators are converted to unique one-character symbols. The unary plus is discarded.
2. Error checking takes place.

Phase 34—Arithmetic II

1. All arithmetic and arithmetic IF statements are coded by a forcing table technique (see Chapter 7).
2. Error checking continues.

Phase 35—Arithmetic III

Initialization for phase 36 occurs.

Phase 36—Arithmetic IV

The data generated in phase 35 are scanned to optimize the number of temporary accumulators needed for each statement.

Phase 37—Arithmetic V

1. IF statement tests and exits are coded.
2. Involution routine linkages are coded.

Phase 38—Arithmetic VI

The optimization of temporary accumulators started in phase 36 is completed, and object time storage locations are assigned.

Phase 39—Input/Output II

Instructions for executing tape-manipulation commands are created, that is, ENDFILE, REWIND and BACKSPACE.

Phase 40—Computed GO TO

Computed GO TO statements with two to ten exits are coded by the use of in-line instructions. For statements with more than ten alternate exits, linkage to a system subroutine is generated.

Phase 41—GO TO

Unconditional GO TO statements in the soure program are replaced by in-line branch statements.

Phase 42—STOP/PAUSE

The object time instructions to halt (for STOP) or halt and continue (for PAUSE) are generated together with the instructions necessary to display the indication number.

Phase 43—SENSE LIGHT

In-line instructions are generated to execute the sense light operations.

Phase 44—Hardware IF

The instructions to test and branch on IF(SENSE SWITCH i) or IF(SENSE LIGHT i) are generated in line.

Phase 45—CONTINUE

This phase merely collects data for later phases. It does not generate any instructions.

Phase 46—DO

1. The DO statements are replaced by: (a) an unconditional branch and (b) a set of parameters describing the elements of the DO statement.
2. An unconditional branch is prepared which will be inserted after the last statement within the range of the DO.

Phase 47—Resort I

Initializations for phase 48 are executed.

Phase 48—Resort II

A special table (the resort table) is filled with the current location of each statement in memory.

Phase 49—Resort III

The source statements are sorted back into their original order, that is, the order before the execution of phase 06. The statement number table is updated to show the current address of each statement.

Phase 50—Resort IV

The statements are relocated to occupy the places in memory that they occupy at execution time. The statement number table is adjusted to show these addresses.

Phase 51—Replace I

1. Object time instructions that contain references to statement numbers (which presently appear as code characters rather than as actual addresses) are corrected to reflect the object time addresses of the referenced statements.
2. Subscript strings are cleaned up.

Phase 52—Function/Subroutine Loader

1. The relocatable functions and subroutines called in the source program are loaded into memory.
2. A table of the starting addresses of these routines is prepared.

Phase 53—Relocatables

This is not truly a phase of the compiler since it takes no part in the translation of the source program. This phase (maybe better called a package) consists of the routines that are loaded by phase 52.

Phase 54—FORMAT routine loader

This routine loads the object time FORMAT routine.

Phase 55—Replace II

The instructions that were generated in phase 34 and that reference system routines are corrected to reflect the object time location of these routines after being loaded by phase 52.

Phase 56—Snapshot

If requested on the control card (see phase 02) a snapshot of the generated object program is printed provided that no source program errors have been recognized that would create a "no go" situation.

Phase 57—Condensed Deck I

If requested, and provided an "OK" program has been produced, a condensed object program will be punched. This phase punches only the clear storage and bootstrap cards.

Phase 58—Condensed Deck II

This phase duplicates phase 59 into the object deck.

Phase 59—Fixed Routines

This package, which is duplicated into the object deck by phase 58, consists of: (a) the arithmetic routines, (b) initialization routines that set up the index registers and sense lights, and (c) the snapshot routine for use in debugging at object time.

Phase 60—Condensed Deck III

The generated object time instructions and data are punched together with the FORMAT routine, which was loaded at phase 54. Only the actual used storage is punched.

Phase 61—Geaux I

This phase prints the end-of-compilation messages.

Phase 62—Geaux II

The arithmetic routine is read into storage, and communication between this package and the relocatable routines is established. Note that the arithmetic routines were not loaded at phase 58 since there was insufficient space to contain both phase 01 (the monitor) and phase 58 while the arithmetic routine was loaded. This phase destroys the monitor.

Phase 63—Arithmetic Package

This package consists of the fixed arithmetic routines which are to be loaded by phase 62. In fact, this package is a duplicate of phase 59.

After the monitor is destroyed in phase 62, the control is transferred to the existing program which is now ready for execution. However, even though this is a load and go compiler, an object deck has been produced for subsequent executions.

APPENDIX B

The Semantics of the Instructional Target Language

Each statement in this hypothetical target language has the syntactic form:

<label> <opcode> <indirect bit> <address>, <comments>

where any one of the constituents may be omitted at the option of the user. In the absense of a specific instance of one of these elements, the contextural content of the statement is maintained by requiring a fixed format be used; that is, a format which uses four fields containing the *<label>*, the *<opcode>*, the addressing information and the *<comments>* respectively. There are two exceptions to the above syntactic form; the statements which constitute the declarations of addresses or constants (DA and DC) which are to be inserted into the store of the target machine. In these two cases addressing information is restricted to be either an address without index modifications in the case of DA (define address), and the address field contains the representation of the constant to be assembled in the case of DC (define constant). In general addresses can be represented either as numeric constant (integer mode) or as a symbolic name, provided that in the complete program (not shown anywhere in this whole text!) that name appears in the label position of one unique statement. Addresses also are used in immediate commands (**ENA, INA, ENR, INR**) as values, the value being the address location associated with the symbolic name. To facilitate relative addressing, addresses may be expressed as arithmetic expressions, the operations being normally restricted to addition (+), subtraction (−) and multiplication (*). However, the use of unary minus (−) is restricted to the denotation of indirect addressing. The computation of the effective address signified by the address field of each instruction takes place in two stages. At assembly time, the value of address expressions is computed; at run time the effects of index modification and indirect addressing are added. Although the symbol for unary minus is used as the indirect addressing bit, its domain is the whole address expression. Thus −A+3 is parsed to the form −(A+3) since A+3 represents the address and the unary minus symbol represents the indirect addressing to be applied at run time. Similarly, the index modification is applied to an address prior to the indirection being applied. For example, if the word contains the indirect address 13753 and is influenced by the register 3, which contains the value 00217, then the address is to be extracted from the word at location 14070. If this word contains the address 00279, then this is the address that is to be used in conjunction with the OPCODE in the original instruction. That is, if the instruction

LDA − 13753,3

were to be executed under the above conditions, it would act effectively as

LDA 00279

The define address statement can develop an address in a word which contains both indirect addressing and index modification. Thus an indirect reference can be cascaded through many levels until an address is located which contains no indirect addressing bit. For the purposes of addressing relative to the current instruction the * symbol is taken to imply "the address of this instruction." It is contexturally separable syntactically from the symbol for multiplication. In many instances in the text the address *−* is used to indicate an address field which is to be provided at run time. Obviously the result of *−* is the address 000; the symbolism is merely to assist the reader. Similarly, −0 or −*−* should result in an address of 000; however, the indirect addressing bit is maintained in the resulting address field of the assembled instruction.

The actual internal structure of the target machine is purposely left vague so as not to restrict the imagination of the user. For example, the number of index registers is unbounded and the use of base registers (signified by BR_i) is unrestricted. The target machine is assumed to be one in which there exists a single accumulator symbolized herein by ACC. In the description associated with the instructions here, the two registers PC and RAR are assumed to exist; these are the program counter (**PC**) and the return address register (**RAR**). The latter is used only in connection with the instructions **MPT** (mark place and transfer) and **BB** (branch back).

Many other features of actual machines are omitted in order to maintain the clarity of the generated code. For example, no consideration is given to the need for a double length register for use in connection with the multiply and divide operations. However a simple macroexpansion of the code given here would provide these essential features.

THE ASSEMBLY CODE STATEMENTS

In the following description of the statements in this hypothetical target language, the labels associated with each statement are omitted in general. This in no way affects the operation of the instructions generated from the assembly statements, except in the cross referencing of control statements and their referenced instructions, or between addresses and their point of definition. For the purposes of definition we shall use the following nomenclature:

C(a)	The contents of address a.
ea	The effective address.
IR_i	The index register *i*.
ACC	The accumulator.
PC	The program counter.
RAR	The return address register.

The development of an effective address, given the data in the address field of an instruction, takes place in two stages initially. The address field of an instruction contains three elements; the address, an index modifier and an indirect addressing bit. The operation of determining the effective address (ea in the descriptions) can be expressed by the following algorithm:

1. Add to the address specified in the field the contents of the referenced index register. If no index register is specified then the address is unmodified.

2. If the indirect addressing bit is set (signified by a unary minus sign) fetch the contents of the location whose address was determined in step 1. Then return to step 1.

In the absence of indirect addressing the address computed in step 1 is the effective address.

In those instructions in which the index reference is used to specify actions on that register, such as in the case of load register (**LDR**) the address is *not* modified by the index register contents, but instead the destination of the contents of the effective address (which may be modified by indirect addressing) is the register specified. Similarly, in the case of instructions which contain values in place of addresses, such as in the increment accumulator (**INA**), the contents of the index register are added to the specified value but no indirect addressing is performed. Instead, the indirect addressing bit is carried into the accumulator; arithmetic operations over this value will be consistent with the interpretation of the indirect addressing bit as a minus sign.

Instructions which affect the accumulator.

Instruction format:

<Opcode>	*<Address field>*	*Meaning*
LDA	(−)a,i	C(ea) → ACC
STO	(−)a,i	C(ACC) → ea
ADD	(−)a,i	C(ACC) + C(ea) → ACC
SUB	(−)a,i	C(ACC) − C(ea) → ACC
MUL	(−)a,i	C(ACC) × C(ea) → ACC
DIV	(−)a,i	C(ACC) / C(ea) → ACC
RDIV	(−)a,i	C(ea) / (ACC) → ACC
EXP	(−)a,i	$C(ACC)^{C(ea)} \rightarrow ACC$
REXP	(−)a,i	$C(ea)^{C(ACC)} \rightarrow ACC$
RVS	not used	−C(ACC) → ACC

The following instructions utilize the address field as a source of data:

ENA	(−)a,i	$(-)(a + C(IR_i)) \rightarrow ACC$
INA	(−)a,i	$C(ACC) + (-)(a + C(IR_i)) \rightarrow ACC$

The following instruction is designed especially for address modification since it stores the address part of the accumulator into the address field of a word (presumably an instruction mask) without affecting the other parts of the destination. Thus the destination can be set in advance to contain the opcode, the indirect addressing bit and the index register reference.

STA	(−)a,i	C(ACC) → address part of (ea)

Transfer of control instructions.

In the following descriptions, the program counter of the target machine is signified by **PC**.

B	(−)a,i	ea → PC
BZ	(−)a,i	if C(ACC) = 0 then ea → PC else null
BP	(−)a,i	if C(ACC) > 0 then ea → PC else null
BN	(−)a,i	if C(ACC) < 0 then ea → PC else null
BNZ	(−)a,i	if C(ACC) ≠ 0 then ea → PC else null

Subprogram Linkages.

Within this text three styles of program linkage are used. These are not synonymous. The first style used existing instructions and presumed that the subprogram would be responsible for the return through the storage of the return address which is passed to it in the accumulator. The pair of instructions were

```
ENA     *+2
B       (−)a,i
```

Two "built in" instructions were also provided.

JMS	(−)a,i	C(PC)+1 → ea, ea + 1 → PC

The return from this linkage is assumed to be where entry is the effective address of the JMS instruction.

MPT	(−)a,i	C(PC) +1 → RAR, ea → PC
BB	not used	C(RAR) → PC

This latter pair of instructions utilize the special return address register (RAR). As suggested in Chapter 10, this register should actually be a stack so as to permit the successive linkages to nested subprograms. Failing that, it would be necessary to use the JMS instruction and to program the returning sequence into each subprogram. One last instruction provided the facility to execute a one instruction subprogram. The semantic model used here is not sufficient, without extensive additions, to explain this instruction. Suffice it here to regard the execute instruction as being composed of two parts:

1. Fetch the instruction from ea and place it in the instruction register.

2. Initiate the usual instruction interpretation cycle from the point at which the instruction is in the instruction register.

In no way does this instruction affect the contents of the program counter unless the referenced instruction is a control instruction. If the referenced instruction is either a JMS or a MPT, the return address is the address of the instruction following the EXT.

EXT	(−)a,i	execute the instruction stored at ea.

Declarative Statements

There exist two explicit declarative statements.

DA	(−)a,i	This statement develops a word which contains the address, with modifiers, which is defined in the address field. The opcode part of the word is undefined.
DC	v	This statement develops a word which contains the internal representation of the value v.

In a number of cases, the code generators for arithmetic expressions are shown to develop instructions of the form (say) LDA C(2.) It is assumed that this symbolic instruction would be expanded by the assembler to include a declarative

C(2.) DC 2.

Instructions which affect index registers

In chapter 5 we discussed the use of base registers and used the notation BR_i to indicate such a register. For our purposes here, we shall not distinguish between base registers and index registers, though we shall assume that index registers and base registers are disjoint.

ENR	(−)v,i	$(-)v \rightarrow IR_i$
LDR	(−)a,i	ea[1] $\rightarrow IR_i$
INR	(−)v,i	$C(IR_i) + (-)v \rightarrow IR_i$

In the text here, there is never any mention of any tests over index registers, except with respect to the historical reference to the IBM 704 and the semantics of FORTRAN DO statements. It should be anticipated however, that in an actual machine such tests would be available.

1. In this case, ea is not computed with any index modification. In certain instances in the text, this instruction is used to transfer data from the accumulator to an index register, symbolized by LDR ACC,i. If ACC has a distinct address then this will not cause any special problems. However, if the accumulator cannot be addressed in this fashion, the assembler should probably expand this instruction to the pair of instructions

```
STA    *+1
ENR    *-*,i
```

Index